Pete
12.

THE EMIL AND KATHLEEN SICK LECTURE-BOOK SERIES
IN WESTERN HISTORY AND BIOGRAPHY

THE EMIL AND KATHLEEN SICK LECTURE-BOOK SERIES
IN WESTERN HISTORY AND BIOGRAPHY

Under the provisions of a Fund established by the children of Mr. and Mrs. Emil Sick, whose deep interest in the history and culture of the American West was inspired by their own experience in the region, distinguished scholars are brought to the University of Washington to deliver public lectures based on original research in the fields of Western history and biography. The terms of the gift also provide for the publication by the University of Washington Press of the books resulting from the research upon which the lectures are based. This is the fifteenth book in the series.

The Great Columbia Plain: A Historical Geography, 1805–1910 by Donald W. Meinig

Mills and Markets: A History of the Pacific Coast Lumber Industry to 1900 by Thomas R. Cox

Radical Heritage: Labor, Socialism, and Reform in Washington and British Columbia, 1885–1917 by Carlos A. Schwantes

The Battle for Butte: Mining and Politics on the Northern Frontier, 1864–1906 by Michael P. Malone

The Forging of a Black Community: Seattle's Central District from 1870 through the Civil Rights Era by Quintard Taylor

Warren G. Magnuson and the Shaping of Twentieth-Century America by Shelby Scates

The Atomic West, edited by Bruce Hevly and John M. Findlay

Power and Place in the North American West, edited by Richard White and John M. Findlay

Henry M. Jackson: A Life in Politics by Robert G. Kaufman

Parallel Destinies: Canadian-American Relations West of the Rockies, edited by John M. Findlay and Ken S. Coates

Nikkei in the Pacific Northwest: Japanese Americans and Japanese Canadians in the Twentieth Century, edited by Louis Fiset and Gail M. Nomura

Bringing Indians to the Book by Albert Furtwangler

Death of Celilo Falls by Katrine Barber

The Power of Promises: Perspectives on Indian Treaties of the Pacific Northwest, edited by Alexandra Harmon

Warship under Sail: The USS Decatur *in the Pacific West* by Lorraine McConaghy

WARSHIP UNDER SAIL

THE USS *DECATUR* IN THE PACIFIC WEST

Lorraine McConaghy

CENTER FOR THE STUDY OF THE PACIFIC NORTHWEST

in association with

UNIVERSITY OF WASHINGTON PRESS
Seattle & London

Publication of Warship under Sail *is supported by a grant from 4Culture.*

Center for the Study of the Pacific Northwest
P.O. Box 353587, Seattle, WA 98195 U.S.A.

University of Washington Press
P.O. Box 50096, Seattle, WA 98145 U.S.A.
www.washington.edu/uwpress

Library of Congress Cataloging-in-Publication Data
Warship under sail : the USS Decatur in the Pacific West /
   Lorraine McConaghy.
p. cm. — (The Emil and Kathleen Sick lecture-book series
   in Western history and biography)
Includes bibliographical references and index.
ISBN 978-295-98955-6 (hbk. : alk. paper)
1. Decatur (Sloop of war) 2. Northwest, Pacific—History,
Naval—19th centure. 3. Pacific Area—History, Naval—19th century.
4. Pacific Coast (Latin America)—History, Naval—19th century.
5. United States, Navy—History—19th century. 6. United States—
Territorial expansion. 7. Seafaring life—Northwest, Pacific—19th
century. 8. Seafaring life—Pacific Area—History—19th century.
9. Seafaring life—Pacific Coast (Latin America)—History—19th
century. I. Center for the Study of the Pacific Northwest. II. Title.
VA65.D38M38 2009   359.3'22—dc22   2009018659

Contents

Preface

In Seattle's founding story, the U.S. sloop of war *Decatur* swept out of nowhere into Elliott Bay, its reverberating carronades shaking the very mountains, saving the settlement from annihilation during an Indian attack on January 26, 1856. Reminiscence lionized the ship's officers, who became heroes in a saga in which civilization confronted savagery at the hard edge of the frontier, representatives of a distant federal government whose power enforced its treaties and defended its citizens however far from home they might stray. As the *Decatur's* story was retold by settler descendants, the tale featured a handful of stock characters: the stalwart pioneer, his pious wife and their plucky child, the fierce hostile Indian, the weak friendly Indian, and the gallant naval officer. Then, as the grandchildren of the founders died, as memory faded and attitudes changed, the saga was satirized with heavy irony as the "Battle of Seattle," and then essentially forgotten.

This project began with mistrust of both the saga and the satire and with simple curiosity spurred by two of the earliest drawings of Seattle, sketched by a young officer on the *Decatur*. What was life in the settlement like? On the ship? Where had the ship come from and where did it go? Why did some Indian people attack the town? Why did others not? And what was the larger mission of the *Decatur*? Answers to these initial questions suggested a much more complicated story than the saga or the satire and opened the door to further avenues of inquiry. The narrative of the *Decatur's* tour of duty in the

Pacific Squadron slowly emerged: the social history of a warship under sail and a collective biography of its officers, sailors, marines, and passengers who participated in beach encounters with men and women of the antebellum Pacific West.

Historians have richly addressed the history of the eastern Pacific Basin—the sea itself, Washington Territory, Oregon, California, the Hawaiian Islands, Mexico, Nicaragua, Costa Rica, Panama, Peru, and Chile—but few have examined the shaping role of the U.S. Navy in the Pacific West. Michael Tate has pointed out historians' "almost total neglect . . . of the frontier army as an element in the westering story," and with the exception of the Wilkes expedition, the navy in the West has received even less attention. The foremost monograph on the Pacific Squadron remains Robert E. Johnson's *Thence round Cape Horn*, now more than forty years old. The *Decatur's* Pacific cruise received brief consideration in Johnson's work and that of Robert E. May, Arrell Morgan Gibson, and James Valle as, respectively, a member of the squadron, a filibuster rescue ship, a warship at Seattle, and the site of one of the rare mutinies of the 1850s. Though the *Decatur* made only a small contribution to Western conquest, communication, and commerce, the ship's story is a significant one, at first sustaining and then challenging prevailing expansionist initiatives. The *Decatur's* final, troubled commission paralleled the unraveling of the nation and the navy and the failure of maritime nationalism as a remedy for disunion.[1]

The principal sources for the *Decatur's* Pacific Squadron cruise are found in the Old Navy and U.S. State Department records held by the National Archives and Records Administration (NARA). This material includes a wealth of bureaucratic paperwork: logbooks, medical logs, and records of courts-martial that document daily naval life, as well as correspondence among the secretaries of the navy, squadron commodores, and numerous sea officers and site commandants, and among Secretary of State Lewis Cass, Special Agent William Carey Jones, and other U.S. ministers and consuls. There is an additional scatter of *Decatur* material: one medical journal, one punishment return, a few hull surveys, and so forth. Few *Decatur* officers have been the subject of biography: Henry Thatcher, Guert Gansevoort, Levi Cooper Lane, and Felix Senac are the exceptions. But most sent correspondence home, and some has survived. Gansevoort's family presented his letter books to the Navy Department Library, and they are now held at NARA. Two other officers prepared reminiscences; one was published widely and the second never was, but some of the latter's manuscripts and drawings are held at NARA and at Yale University Library. One complete journal kept by a *Decatur* officer and the journal of an officer on a ship that accompanied the *Decatur* have survived. My narrative history is primarily based on such firsthand accounts and records. However, when the *Decatur* sailed in the Pacific Squadron, the United States was a seafaring nation and American readers devoured naval and maritime fiction, reminiscence, and nonfiction by Cooper, Melville, Nordhoff, and Dana. In the 1850s, the ship was considered newsworthy, reported by newspapers as varied as the *San Francisco Daily Evening Bulletin* and the *New York Times* and mentioned in articles in a number of popular periodicals. These articles, novels, and personal accounts have proven invaluable for understanding the Old Navy, the sailing life, the Pacific West, and the military and diplomatic activities in which the squadron was engaged.

This work has been constrained in two ways. In 2006, Alison Games identified the disciplinary divisions that fragment the unity of the Atlantic Ocean as an organizing principle of study and called for a "vantage that is not rooted in any single place." Although a warship's deck offers that vantage, the opportunity has inherent drawbacks. The *Decatur* sailed from sea to sea and to many ports and harbors and, in doing so, ventured into many fields of history. I have tried to establish a special place for my study by viewing the Pacific West from the bay and the beach, but exasperated specialists in a dozen fields will look in vain for my mastery of the appropriate historiography. I do hope that my work will interest scholars who will bring a more sophisticated voice than my own to future interpretations of Old Navy resources, which are unparalleled in their richness. That very richness raises a second constraint to this work as biography. More than three hundred men served on board the *Decatur* from 1854 to 1859, and most did not readily yield to my amateur genealogical research. The dozens of seamen named Drew, Brown, and Smith were obscure before and after the voyage, though they emerged in vivid color from ship's records. However, they will not remain long in obscurity. As I write, new resources are becoming available on a monthly basis that will transform historical research into the lives of ordinary people of slippery identity and will soon render this book and much other scholarship incomplete.[2]

I always hoped that this book would interest a wide variety of readers and I have avoided scholarly jargon to that end. Additionally, the ship's logbook includes dozens of phrases that were jargon of another sort, and I have omitted references that I did not understand as a casual reader of naval fiction and nonfiction. I have tried to tell an engaging story, but readers who expect a nostalgic portrayal of the Old Navy will be disappointed. Though I never intended to write a celebratory book about the *Decatur*, I did not know at the outset of this research how unhappy this antebellum commission would prove to be. Some circumstances were typical of any Pacific Squadron ship at the time but others were not. I think that the *Decatur* became exceptionally troubled because of the vessel's small size and poor state of repair, because two commanding officers were suspended from duty, because the ship was at anchor off Seattle and Panama for extended periods of time, and because so many men fell sick in Central America. Certainly, at sea or under threat, the *Decatur* was always at its best. And, of course, if roughly half the ship's crew smuggled liquor, brawled, insulted their officers, and mounted two mutinies, the other half were sober, steady men who did their jobs—they sailed the ship with exquisite skill, worked in their gun crew, and drilled with small arms. However, a great many more ship-level studies need to be completed to get behind service-level generalizations about the antebellum navy, some of which are too rosy to describe the *Decatur*'s experience.

Over the years, I have incurred many debts that I hope to one day repay. I am very grateful for the Vice Admiral Edwin B. Hooper Research Grant, administered by the Naval Historical Center, which supported my work at NARA in Washington, D.C., and College Park, Maryland—a magnificent gift. I sincerely thank Leonard Garfield, executive director of Seattle's Museum of History & Industry, and my museum colleagues there for long forbearance over the years of weekend and evening writing represented by this book. I also thank King County 4Culture for a grant that aided production of the book. My deep gratitude, too, goes to my editors at the University of Washington Press, Julidta Tarver and Pamela Bruton; to John Findlay, who listened and helped when no one else could; and to Redmond Barnett, at the Washington State Historical Society, who made the exhibition of Surgeon John Y. Taylor's drawings a reality. As a public historian, I am indebted for collegial feedback about this project from participants at conferences of the Western History Association, the Organization of American Historians, as well as the National Council on Public History, and from readers of my articles in *Sea Chest* and *Pacific Northwest Quarterly*. I am especially grateful to archivists Charles Johnson, Sally Kuisel, Candace Lein-Hayes, and Rebecca Livingston at NARA; to John Kelly, Johnnie Ridgeway, and other friends at the Puget Sound Maritime Historical Society; to my military history colleagues Michael Crawford, Bill Galvani, Janne Lahti, Harold Langley, Ed Marolda, James Valle, and Robert Wooster; to *Pacific Northwest Quarterly* editors Michael Allen and Kim McKaig; to archivists and librarians Nicole Bouché, Glenn Helm, Greg Lange, Gary

Lundell, Carolyn Marr, Marge McNinch, Carla Rickerson, Gary Zimmerman, and many more who opened their collections to me. I would like to convey my warmest thanks to friends and colleagues Sherry Boswell, Brian Casserly, Benjamin Filene, Kyra Kester, Greg Lange, Karen Luetjen, Gary Luke, Cathy Lykes, Trish Nicola, Linda Palmer, Alan Stein, Coll Thrush, Mike Vouri, to my sons, Brian and Jeff, and to my daughter-in-law, Shirin. Above all, I would like to thank my husband, Rob McConaghy, who has helped me in every possible way.

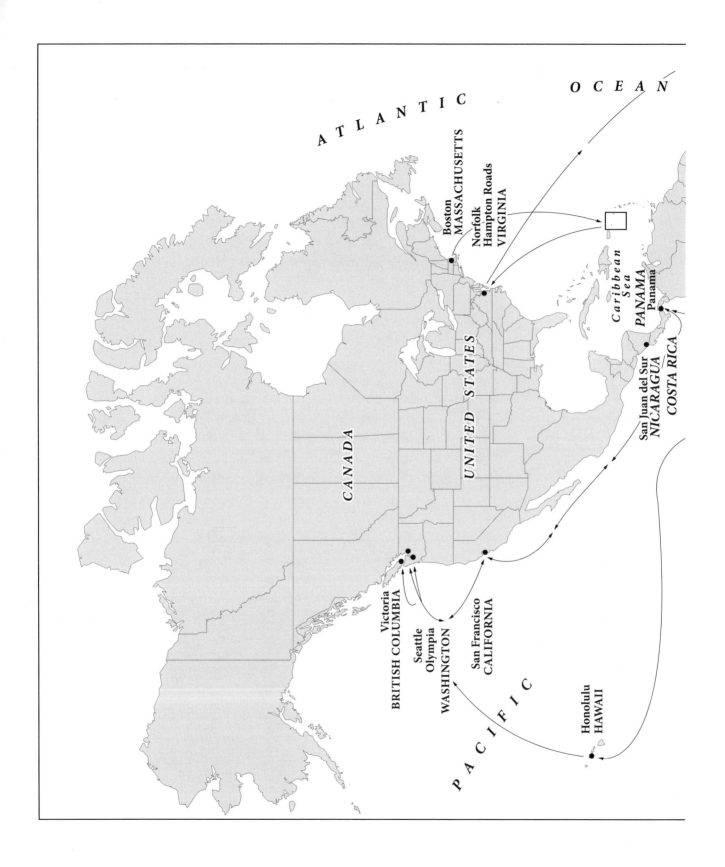

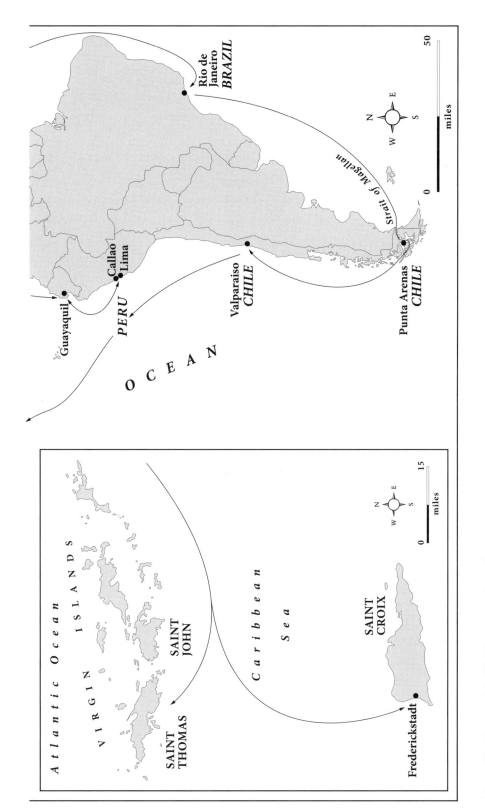

Map 1. The Voyages of the USS Decatur, 1854–1859

WARSHIP UNDER SAIL

Introduction

On May 1, 1857, seaman John Drinkhouse stared anxiously across the bay off San Juan del Sur, on the west coast of Nicaragua, at the U.S. Navy officers gathered on the quarterdeck of the *St. Mary's*. Two years earlier, he had shipped on the navy warship *Decatur* in San Francisco, sailed to Puget Sound to fight Indians, and then returned with the ship to California. There, Drinkhouse deserted the *Decatur* to join William Walker's invasion of Nicaragua—his "filibuster," as such private military expeditions were called at the time—in pursuit of fame and fortune in Walker's tiny filibuster navy: fame as a sailor of American manifest destiny and the reward of a fortune in Nicaragua. But the filibuster failed and Charles Davis, commander of the *St. Mary's*, had arranged Walker's surrender. Defeated and sick, Drinkhouse appealed to Davis for help, but the officer scorned the deserter and left him to share the common fate of Walker's private army.

St. Mary's Lieutenant David McCorkle was ordered to lead the long retreat of barefoot filibuster fighters south from Nicaragua, during which they suffered terribly from fever, infected wounds, and dysentery. Drinkhouse and the other survivors traveled across the Isthmus of Panama and eventually into a blaze of publicity in New York; the sailor returned home to Pennsylvania an invalid after his western adventures and soon died. Negotiation of the filibuster surrender brought antebellum fame to Captain Davis: reviled in the South and honored in the North. McCorkle anguished over the filibuster retreat, the hardest duty of his career. When the Civil War began, Davis remained loyal to the Union and McCorkle joined the Confederacy. Afterward, Davis served out his navy career and ended his days back East, but McCorkle became an expatriate officer in the Peruvian navy, a Pacific man. These three lives had intersected one sunny day in 1857 off the Pacific coast of Nicaragua, at a crossroads of western stories.

During the 1850s, Davis, McCorkle, and Drinkhouse joined thousands of navy men sailing the borderland of Pacific West Americanization, following their ambition and convictions, their duty and fantasies. The long beach frontier between land and sea ringed islands and edged continents, easily crossing boundaries of every kind and extending far beyond the shores of newly gained U.S. territory in Washington, Oregon, and California. Men sailed along this shore in the context of American maritime nationalism, furthering national advantage while pursuing personal advantage, using service in the U.S. Navy as a public means to private ends in the West. Distant from the old center of power back East, the Pacific had grown increasingly central to American strategies for the future as the balance of interest tipped westward, and rabid Young America expansionists in the Democratic Party hoped that gaining new overseas colonies might heal the nation's domestic discontents, that turning national energy outward would somehow resolve or disguise deepening conflict at home. These impulses to empire failed—increasingly influenced and then consumed by sectionalism—but they governed the commission of the *Decatur* in the Pacific Squadron, which lasted from 1854 to 1859.

Historians have set a shifting American frontier into the larger unity of the Pacific Ocean to chart a waterworld framed by changing imperial perspectives, the place that John Eperjesi has called the American Pacific. The ocean itself becomes the locus for stories that encircle and permeate the great sea, stories integrated by the movement of sailing ships and steamships among the "intermediate environments" of beaches, ports, and harbors. The aggressive expansionists of the Young America movement were convinced that antebellum organization of the American West led out into the vast Pacific itself, to seaborne imperialism: annexation of the Sandwich Islands, occupation of Panama, seizure of "guano islands," conquest of Old Mexico and Vancouver Island, and more. When America seemed destined to master and regenerate the Pacific, "opening" Japan and "filibustering" Nicaragua were spoken of in the same breath as completing a transcontinental railroad to California. When the *Decatur*'s cruise began, in 1854, Pacific expansionism had gained momentum. From Washington Territory to Panama, so much that was new in the maritime West was American, including the busy coastal steamship lines, the Mare Island Navy Yard and the port city of San Francisco, the little sawmill town of Seattle on Elliott Bay, the transit route across Nicaragua, and the railroad across the Isthmus of Panama. Newly decentralized, the United States reframed nationhood and manhood, as adventurers were drawn to the western sea by stirring calls to arms, the promise of free land, or the hope of striking it rich. The antebellum Pacific surge combined two broad American impulses: the development of a maritime empire to further territorial and commercial expansion, and the exercise of an individualized, striving, modern masculinity eager for personal success. The *Decatur*'s sailors, marines, deserters, and officers played their parts in these powerful initiatives into the West.[1]

Presidents Franklin Pierce and James Buchanan, Secretaries of State William Marcy and Lewis Cass, and Secretaries of the Navy James Dobbin and Isaac Toucey were protagonists in the *Decatur*'s antebellum narrative. One of only five ships in the Pacific Squadron, the *Decatur* was their imperial agent for acts of peace and war, one node on a floating, shifting, thinly distributed net of federal sea power in the Pacific, showing the flag and ready to clear for action with cutlasses and muskets, the howitzer and the carronades. A visible surrogate for the United States, the warship became the focus for colonial hopes and fears: protecting commerce, fighting Indians, suppressing vigilantes, transporting secret agents, thwarting and abetting filibusters, enforcing treaties, and fostering settlement. The *Decatur* served to broaden the West's economic base at shipyards, coaling stations, chandleries, and victuallers (as well as brothels and taverns) in ports from Valparaiso to San Francisco and at remote colonial outposts like Seattle. Representing the armed force of American foreign policy at sea and on the beach, the *Decatur* contributed a modest measure of firepower, money, and muscle to the far-flung federal presence in the 1850s Pacific West and Young America's imperialist agenda.

Looking back, not only Young America but the antebellum nation as a whole is obscured from view by the Civil War's great storm, which, once it had passed, became the nation's defining nineteenth-century experience. Suddenly, everything beforehand seemed to lead to the war and everything afterward seemed to rush away from it; 1850s technology, politics, medicine, foreign policy—everything that will concern us in this book—became quaint overnight. The navy itself was so dramatically transformed that it is difficult to see *behind* the war, to the tiny antebellum service of three dozen wooden ships and a few hundred commissioned officers, when sailing ships outnumbered steamers. The Old Navy was steeped in tradition: the ship's routine, the names of sails, the rigging, the lore and customs—all looked to the past. Innovators struggled to modernize the navy, pushing new approaches to gunnery, navigation, and propulsion and reforms to the discipline of naval officers and enlisted men, while the old guard held tight to the traditions inherited from the British navy, refined during the Revolution and vindicated in the War of 1812. When the *Decatur* began the 1854 cruise, grog was still served twice each day, and many *Decatur* men bore the scars of flogging, abolished only four years earlier. A sailor's work on board a warship had changed little in centuries. Reminiscing in 1907, Alfred Thayer Mahan observed that a sixteenth-century captain would have felt more at home on an antebellum sailing ship than the captain of that antebellum ship would have felt on an ironclad steam frigate of the Civil War. The men on the *Decatur* had more in common with Ferdinand Magellan's crew on the *Victoria* in 1520 than with David Farragut's crew on the *Hartford* in 1864. But by the time the Civil War was over, the Old Navy—the *Decatur*'s navy—had utterly passed away, documented by engravings and remembered with nostalgia.[2]

Nevertheless, the Old Navy underwent considerable change in the 1850s, and the *Decatur*'s cruise offers a case study in these institutional fault lines and transitions. Three of the ship's four commanding officers recommended that a war steamer replace the sloop of war in the Pacific. The *Decatur*'s younger officers had trained at the new Naval Academy and were formed by the imperialist war against Mexico; the older officers were self-made men, formed by the War of 1812 with Great Britain. The 1855 Efficiency Board affected the career of every *Decatur* commissioned officer, through either discipline or promotion. The ship's enlisted men experienced the innovation of the honorable discharge and the introduction of summary courts-martial. And as the warship sailed in the Pacific Squadron, the Old Navy was slowly torn apart by the same conflicts about slavery, expansionism, and secession as the nation as a whole. Navy secretaries Dobbin and Toucey and squadron commodores William Mervine and John Long took partisan positions in that increasingly polarized debate and dispatched squadron commanders on missions that translated distant policy into deck-level practice. The officers on the *Decatur* held political convictions of their own, disciplined by duty, and their antebellum experiences and wartime choices suggest the personal dimensions of the navy's role in Pacific maritime imperialism, from Puget Sound to Honolulu, San Francisco, Nicaragua, and Panama.

Few *Decatur* officers anticipated professional advancement in their Pacific Squadron assignment, and some resisted the posting, preferring an Atlantic-side station. Washington, D.C., was the hub of the orderly world of these career navy men, all white, all born in the United States, all respectable gentlemen. They deplored the raw disorder of Pacific beach boomtowns and the venality, cowardice, and brutality of many Americans from Seattle to Valparaiso. However, as it turned out, the West offered them unforeseen opportunities. Scientifically inclined officers charted islands and shoals and collected samples of coal and timber for future naval installations. In San Francisco, *Decatur* officers ordered the great guns loaded and aimed toward shore, to prevent capture of the federal treasury. Indian rebellion on Puget Sound provided the chance for career distinction in a real shooting war. Off Panama, the officers drilled squads of sailors with the new minié rifles, preparing for marine-style shore actions to protect the isthmus railroad from revolutionary Panamanians. In Nicaragua and Costa Rica, the *Decatur* rescued filibuster invalids and then staked out the Gulf of Fonseca to prevent the landing of filibuster steamers. The ship's commanders negotiated with commandants, governors, and presidents. The *Decatur* officers found opportunities in the Pacific West to achieve honor, gain military experience, pursue diplomatic initiatives, and also fulfill their expectations of an exotic and primitive world.

Familiar with naval fiction and travel memoirs, the ship's officers played out Pacific fantasies in the Strait of Magellan, Hawaii, and Puget Sound. Most *Decatur* officers enjoyed the manly fun of roughing it in the West and participated in expeditions to hunt, fish, and explore. A naval officer published a utopian adventure story about the *Decatur*'s Strait of Magellan experience, and the ship's commander wrote up his trip to San José, the capital of Costa Rica, as though he were drafting a travel article about a remote, mysterious destination. During the siege of Seattle, officers abandoned their uniforms to dress up like "brigands," donning the dashing costumes of Western adventurers such as Nicaragua filibusters or California prospectors. The ship's assistant surgeon was an eager amateur ethnographer, collecting bones and feathers and sketching Pacific people and landscapes. Native people were intrinsic to officers' perspectives of Pacific exoticism, and the ship's officers regarded most indigenous men and women as specimens, curiosities, or "savages." However, officers acknowledged a spectrum of Native identity, from friend to foe and from westernized to uncivilized, and Native men were invited to board the *Decatur* in visits that ranged from the formal welcome of a Hawaiian prince to the humiliation of the Tierra del Fuegian "John Decatur" and the intimidation of Chief Seattle. Further, the officers admired Indian enemies more than they did Indian allies, and distant Indians more than nearby ones; they made fun of the Duwamish Suquardle and the Snoqualmie Patkanim but wrote with respect about the remote "Patagonians," the elusive Nisqually Leschi, and the fierce Northern Indians from Alaska. During their stay at Seattle, when military success against some Indians depended on the cooperation of others, *Decatur* officers contracted only out of necessity with Native people as fighting men, carpenters, guides, and spies, reluctant to engage with them on equal terms.

The *Decatur* officers saw western people and prospects in the context of their duty and career and their political and cultural convictions. With two exceptions, they remained eastern men who returned "home" after the Pacific assignment, followed their careers in Union or Confederate service, and lived out their days in the Atlantic states. Although both officers and enlisted men engaged with the West in their own self-interest, the personal advantage pursued by most sailors differed dramatically from that of their officers. While the officers' engagements were powerful ones of science, war, and diplomacy, the sailors' smaller-scale engagements were far more numerous, more intimate, and, in many ways, more successful. The *Decatur's* commissioned and warrant officers numbered fewer than two dozen, while more than three hundred marines and seamen served on the ship, hailing from all over the world. Throughout the Pacific commission, sailors behaved consistently at widely distant places on the beach: chasing opportunities and bringing cash, disease, and violence to each sailor town. Unlike their officers, most sailor encounters were with Native and postcolonial people as equals, whether enemies, allies, lovers, or shipmates, eye-to-eye at water level, in bed or across a faro table. It is likely that the undermanned warship enlisted Kanaka seamen at Honolulu, and that some of the men who joined in Valparaiso, Panama, and San Francisco were of mingled European, African, and Native descent. In Seattle, dozens of Native men worked side by side with *Decatur* sailors, and enlisted men created an underworld of vice with Native people and West Coast drifters back in the woods, as much like the beach sailor towns at Realejo, Honolulu, and Panama as possible. Sailors shared forecastle songs and stories that celebrated the charms of mestizo women in Chile and mulatto women in San Francisco and the kick of *aguardiente* in Nicaragua. They sang about deserting the ship and they sang about the gold that lay along the banks of California's Sacramento River. Agents of their own advantage, sailors made plans to pursue the opportunities of the Pacific West: high times, land, trade, and gold.[3]

California gold seemed there for the taking. Popular pamphlets promised a life of "leisurely gold-gleaning" that was "wholly new, adventurous, golden— a fine contrast to the commonplace work of older American communities." After 1848, hopeful gold seekers boomed California's non-Indian population from 14,000 to nearly 225,000 in less than five years, all intent on making a killing. For either the homesteader or the speculator, however, Western land held a different appeal. The 1850 Oregon Donation Land Claim Law offered

320 acres to each adult, white, male citizen and 640 acres to a married couple; five years later, filibuster William Walker promised 250 acres to each fighting man and 350 acres to each family immigrating to Nicaragua. The sea presented its own opportunities: hundreds of merchant ships traced pathways through the Pacific, carrying gold, mail, and merchandise, mining the waters and shores of their whales, guano, and lumber; coastwise steamers and sailing ships linked the ports along the beach, paying seamen double the navy wages. The *Decatur*'s enlisted opportunists could choose gold, land, the sea, or a freebooting crusade. They did not need an editor to tell them to go West; they were as likely to "see the elephant" in Nicaragua as California, and they joined a restless roughneck population pulsing up and down the long, sandy border between land and sea, at home on a whaling ship or a warship, in a filibuster or a boomtown, in a civilian militia or a San Francisco mob. These "tramps of the sea" casually crossed boundaries of language, race, and nation in the continuous West to sell their muscle and their skills, hopping a ship to chase the main chance. Unlike their officers, many sailors who sailed on the *Decatur* never returned "home" but found a hospitable new place among the West's "roving characters . . . a reckless, rollicking set, wedded to the Pacific [who] never dream of doubling Cape Horn again." Some left their words in court-martial records, but most have only left the evidence of their behavior—their high rate of desertion and offense, their high incidence of venereal infection, and their decision to remain in the West. Many deserted the ship, some were dishonorably discharged, and others served out their time and stayed on the Pacific, taking advantage of the chance to make a fresh start among adventuring strangers of uncertain identity.[4]

In the Old Navy and in the Pacific West, individual identity was slippery, as enlisted men shipped with phony "purser's names" and changed their names and stories from port to port, ship to ship, and opportunity to opportunity. For instance, a Seattle settler was nicknamed "Tom Pepper," which was sea-going slang for a preposterous liar. William Walker's army included "Private Dewitt from Germany" and "Leon McKeevey of France," among many other dubious characters. One of the men killed at Seattle was identified after his death as Pocock, Wilson, and White by three different acquaintances. California newspapers reported stories involving "the man known as 'Sam'" or "the pock-marked man known as Liverpool Jack," among dozens of such references. In Costa Rica, the man "known here as Tom Edwards" was a rogue who had been run out of San Francisco by the Vigilance Committee; he had had another name in California. On board the *Decatur*, there were a dozen men named "John Smith" or "William Brown," hailing from Denmark, London,

FIG. 1 In 1854, this "shaggy-haired and bronzed-faced" miner awaits the steamer in San Francisco to head south and cross the transit at Panama or Nicaragua. According to Frank Soulé, the "b'hoy" wears his usual woolen shirt and battered hat but is packing a bag of gold dust and a weapon on his hip. Deserter, prospector, settler, or filibuster, he is a Pacific West adventurer. Frank Soulé, Annals of San Francisco. Courtesy University of Washington Libraries.

Matagorda, Italy, Boston, and Florida. *Decatur* officers spotted deserters serving on other ships; officers on other ships discovered deserters serving on the *Decatur.* The navy was desperate for any man willing to sail and fight the ships of war, as were the other crusaders and boomers of the Pacific West. Everywhere you looked along the beaches in the 1850s—Realejo, Seattle, or on shipboard—there were shiftless, ingratiating, opportunistic characters from "back home." Men took aliases and invented alibis simply by declaring them to strangers, echoing the California Gold Rush ditty "Oh, what was your name in the States? Was it Thompson, or Johnson, or Bates? Did you murder your wife and run for your life? What was your name in the States?" The *Decatur* men who slipped over the side to swim to shore or never returned from liberty were running away from the past and running toward the possibilities of the Pacific beaches, with a kaleidoscope of motives and identities. They were, of course, as likely to fail as to succeed. However, their self-interested opportunism defied the ship's mission, undermined settler narratives of heroism, sacrifice, and manifest destiny, and compromised projection of American naval power in the West, particularly in Seattle, San Francisco, and Panama.[5]

FIG. 2 *The American Hotel beckoned to homesick U.S. travelers at the halfway point of the Nicaragua Transit road between Lake Nicaragua and San Juan del Sur on the Pacific. Opportunists awaited the unwary here, as well as in every Pacific West boomtown.* Frank Leslie's Illustrated Newspaper. *Courtesy University of Washington Libraries.*

Ordered to the Pacific in 1854, the *Decatur* sailed from Boston to Norfolk, Virginia, and then to Valparaiso, Honolulu, and Puget Sound, and on to San Francisco, Panama, Nicaragua, and Costa Rica. After providing an introductory political and institutional framework, I will focus on four episodes that set the *Decatur* in the context of place and people, foreign policy, domestic politics, and institutional change and that allow us to explore that larger world through the lens of this American ship. First, the *Decatur* sailed from the old Atlantic to the new Pacific through the Strait of Magellan, an adventurous passage born of the captain's pride and the officers' fantasies, Young American exuberance passing into the West. Second, the *Decatur* was a principal player in a Seattle war story of treaties and settlement in an American colony on a Pacific beach. This founding story became the subject of contested memory and meaning that ignored the primitive sailor town established in the woods behind the settlement. Third, after a brief stay in San Francisco, the *Decatur* joined other squadron ships to provide support for American maritime expansionism when a Western story became a Southern one, carrying some of William Walker's wounded filibusters to safety and conveying U.S. State Department agent William Carey Jones on his mission to Central America. Fourth, the *Decatur* anchored off Panama for nearly a year as a stationary battery and hospital ship. During that stifling, monotonous duty, illness and offense skyrocketed on board, and some officers joined many enlisted men in the ship's descent into disorder. In 1859, the *Decatur* was itself mistaken for a filibuster ship, initiating the final grim burlesque of Young America's hopes, as Nicaraguan troops protected their country against feared invasion by slavery expansionists, burning the Pacific-side bridges to close the transit once and for all. These four stories offer naval perspectives on antebellum nationhood and manhood, viewed from the deck of a warship under sail. The *Decatur*'s imperial mission integrated and organized the dispersed Pacific West, and the behavior of the ship's sailors identified, shaped, and unified the distant opportunities of its continuous beaches.

~

In 1839, the *Decatur* was brand new, one of a class of experimental sloops of war that were designed by Philadelphia Navy Yard constructor John Lenthall and that included the *Yorktown, Dale, Preble,* and *Marion.* All five represented the navy's best efforts to build fast, economical, and lethal cruising warships intended for duty on distant stations. At the Brooklyn Navy Yard, Lenthall's design was adapted by yard constructor Samuel Hartt. The *Decatur* was built of oak and southern pine and was 117 feet in length and 32 feet at the beam; the maximum draft was 15 feet 6 inches, displacing 566 tons; and the ship held a complement of nearly 150 men. The ship was well armed, boasting sixteen thirty-two-pound carronades, and its design was reminiscent of the *Wasp,* which had been victorious against the Royal Navy's *Frolic* in the War of 1812, Stephen Decatur's war.[6]

When his namesake ship was launched, Stephen Decatur, one of the young nation's naval heroes, had been dead for almost twenty years. He had distinguished himself during the Barbary Wars and the War of 1812, leading his men to extravagant feats of bravery. Decatur shared in the development of a distinctly American navy, one that incorporated the traditions of the Royal Navy but had a style all its own. His unforgettable toast expressed unquestioning loyalty to the new Republic. Raising his glass of port, Decatur cried, "Our country! In her intercourse with foreign nations, may she always be in the right; but our country, right or wrong!" And his officers drained their glasses, inspired and ready to risk their lives to fulfill their duty, for honor and perhaps glory. Praised in the 1850s for his "headlong daring, his chivalrous

exploits, [and] the blaze of splendor he always drew after him," Stephen Decatur died in a duel to settle a debt of honor; his dramatic death only added to
the luster of his name. The new *Decatur* basked in that glow.[7]

On April 9, 1839, the sloop of war was launched at Brooklyn "in fine style"
before a large throng of spectators: "a multitude of small boats, people hanging in the shrouds of the neighboring vessels." The crew of the navy frigate
Hudson manned the yards to give three cheers, while a shoreside band played
"Hail, Columbia." At launch, the *Decatur* "broke all her fastenings and dashed
out into the water, so strong was the first impulse of existence." "She would,"
predicted a local reporter, "be a fast sailing ship, a favorite with seamen. . . .
Prosperity to the good ship *Decatur,* wherever destiny may lead her!"[8]

The *Decatur* sailed from New York to Rio de Janeiro, assigned to duty in
the Brazil Squadron. On Saturday morning, July 11, 1840, the weather was
bright, fine, and clear as the breeze whipped up Gloria Hill off the bay, tossing the long grasses here and there. Two dozen young men stood along the
bluff, grouped by their uniforms: midshipmen from England, Brazil, France,
and the United States. Each man held a spyglass, directed down toward the
harbor, intently following the movements of one ship, the *Decatur.*

The *Decatur* was David Farragut's first command, and his choreography
drove these young men to climb the hill almost daily, to watch and to marvel.
The warship sped across the bay at breathtaking speed under full sail, then
turned on a dime and began to tack into the wind, the ship's "smart, well-
trained crew" racing to adjust the canvas. The *Decatur* fired the port guns at
a floating target and then came around, to offer the starboard battery. The
young officers admired Farragut's drills, which were "simply perfect in execution and celerity," and surely, one later recalled, "A more tidy and taut beauty
floated upon no sea" than the elegant little *Decatur.*[9]

In his journal, Farragut proudly noted that the *Decatur* outsailed every ship
in the squadron, and he was bitterly disappointed when the secretary of the
navy laughed off his "pretensions for retaining command" and called him
home. Leaving the harbor at Rio, Farragut daintily threaded the warship
through a labyrinth of hazards—a sloop of war to starboard, then a large
merchantman and a Brazilian frigate to port. The tide was at flood and the
wind to the south, but he managed to beat out of the harbor, "just clearing
the stern of the frigate." Farragut dutifully sailed the *Decatur* back to the Norfolk Navy Yard, to be turned over to another commander. The ship was sent
off to duty in the Africa Squadron, then to the Mexican War, again to the
Africa Squadron, to the Home Squadron, to the Caribbean and West Indies,

and finally to the North Atlantic in the summer of 1853, to patrol the fishing grounds. Then the *Decatur* headed to Charlestown Navy Yard in Boston to be overhauled for distant service in the Pacific Squadron.[10]

~

Afloat, from shore and in memory, the *Decatur* always looked beautiful, a graceful sailing ship under towering white canvas, busy with sailors racing to their tasks at the pipe of the boatswain's whistle. The ship's paint was gleaming and the brass brightly polished as the *Decatur* flew before the wind or rocked at anchor. The ship's commander was carefully uniformed and impeccably correct: firing national salutes, hoisting the colors, and offering hospitality to visiting dignitaries. From shore, the *Decatur* embodied James Fenimore Cooper's golden romances—a magnificent stage for the storied brotherhood that faced the sea's mysteries, its thousand perils and adventures. But by the end of its Pacific Squadron commission in 1859, the *Decatur* was a small, wooden sloop of war in a navy transitioning to iron and steam. The ship, once cutting-edge, was no longer considered worth repairing.

The *Decatur*'s assignment concluded with a long stint at anchor in the Bay of Panama (the least desirable duty in the squadron), and then it was sent to Mare Island to be decommissioned. The *Decatur* returned to official life during the Civil War, when it was stationed in San Francisco Bay to guard against Confederate naval attack. The ship's officers and enlisted men made their choices when the navy and the nation came apart. One of the *Decatur*'s captains, two lieutenants, two surgeons, and one purser joined the Confederate States Navy; the other *Decatur* officers remained in the U.S. Navy. And some of the ship's company lived on into a distant imperial future in which a few of Young America's expansionist impulses in the Pacific West were realized. This book is the story of the *Decatur*'s antebellum commission that led to those choices and outcomes.

1

Young America on the Pacific

"The Sailor of Manifest Destiny Views"

Young America enlists in the officers' corps and fights the battles of his
private interests on the fields of Mexico, and incidentally attends to his
country's wrongs. . . . Young America . . . sighed that there were no more
Mexicos to conquer on this (North American) continent. . . . We next see
him on his way to California [and] in Panama he fell in with the outpost
of the advanced guard of the army of occupation—the sailor of manifest
destiny views, who was waiting for his country to overtake him.
—*Young America on the Pacific* (San Francisco), March 1854

East by sunrise, West by sunset, North by the Arctic Expedition, and
South as far as we darn please.—*Philadelphia Public Ledger*, July 8, 1853

While the *Decatur* was being overhauled in Boston, the Pacific coast
was newly secured, culminating a "precise and calculated" program of westward territorial expansion: Oregon Territory was
organized in 1848 and California admitted to the union as a state in 1850;
three years later, Washington Territory was separated from Oregon. The
United States gained control of the three great western harbors at San Diego,
San Francisco, and Puget Sound, spaced along 1,300 miles of coastline, and
the way was cleared for transcontinental access from cities back East and for
trade with Asia. But though the coast had been achieved, western boundaries
seemed fluid to many. Middle-aged Americans had experienced a dynamic
nation that expanded aggressively in their lifetimes as the United States

purchased the huge Louisiana territory and moved northward and westward to the Pacific Northwest and southward and westward through Texas,
New Mexico, and California in the Mexican War, a war of blatant imperialist expansion. Appetite, as Albert Weinberg observed, grew with the eating.
The nation's destiny seemed manifest to continue its imperialist momentum
of Americanization, pursuing an ordained mission. By sea, Young America
expansionists embraced the Pacific Ocean as a newly framed field of possibilities: the "empire of the seas."[1]

The growing U.S. presence in the Pacific West gave new direction to the
navy, which was tasked with advancing a variety of American interests and protecting settlement, commerce, communication, and transportation. Washington, Oregon, and California were, in a sense, overseas colonies, weeks distant
from the eastern states and essentially accessible only by water. Additionally,
the Pacific had become a vast field of American commerce: whaling, gold,
lumber, silks, porcelain, tea, sandalwood, guano, and "cargoes and markets of
opportunity." Though waterways were traced across the great ocean by American sailing ships and steamers, it was to its island and continental beaches that
the Young America initiative turned for "expansion of the American republic
southward and westward, and the grasping of the magnificent purse of the
commerce of the Pacific." But the Old Navy could not penetrate and master
the Pacific West with its small squadron of antiquated ships, and expansionism reinvigorated the navy under President Franklin Pierce and Secretary of
the Navy James Dobbin. With Pierce's election, Young America entered the
White House, and the American empire would advance by sea as well as by
land to accomplish its mission of manifest destiny.[2]

On December 5, 1853, President Pierce delivered his first annual address to
Congress. He noted the acquisition of "vast" territory in the wake of the Mexican War and proudly described a new nation along "the Atlantic and Pacific
shores," one day to be linked by a railroad to the Pacific Ocean. While loudly
deploring filibustering expeditions, Pierce also pointed out that every expansion was once questioned, but with time, each was judged to be a benefit to the
United States and "with it, of the human race, in freedom, in prosperity and in
happiness." Pierce expressed delight at Commodore Matthew Perry's "opening" of Japan and America's growing Pacific trade with Central and South
America and with China. He prophesied that "laboring masses from eastern
Asia" would throng to western America, and that men and women living "in
other parts of our hemisphere" would "seek the privilege of being admitted
within [our] safe and happy bosom." In fact, growth would yield "incredible
results"—Pierce imagined that the national population would more than tri-

ple to a hundred million in the lifetimes of many Americans. This outcome would require a strong federal government, potentially troubled by the grave dangers of sectional controversy. Pierce strongly asserted the rights reserved to the states to conduct "the ordinary business of life" unmolested by abolitionist "casuists" and hoped that recent compromise would settle the matter. Also, he was "fully satisfied that the Navy of the United States is not in a condition of strength and efficiency commensurate with the magnitude of our commercial and other interests": a modernized navy was vital to fulfillment of the national destiny. Pierce recommended favorable attention by Congress to the proposals in Secretary Dobbin's report.[3]

Dobbin unveiled the "most ambitious program of naval construction and personnel reform" in the history of the Navy, arguing that "maintenance of our proper and elevated rank among the great powers of the world; just protection of our wide-spread and growing commerce; the defence of our thousands of miles of coast along the Atlantic and Pacific oceans, the lakes and the Gulf of Mexico; the recent marked improvements in the art of naval architecture adopted by other nations—are all united in demonstrating . . . the necessity of an increase of the Navy." Like Pierce, Dobbin marveled at the Pacific coast from "Mexico to the far northwest [where] a new empire has, as by magic, sprung into existence," and "San Francisco promises, at no distant day, to become another New York." The secretary continued, with emphasis: "I take it to be a fair proposition that our Navy should, *at least, be large enough to command our own seas and coasts*" and informed Congress that in the event of war, only forty warships could put to sea within three months. Concerned by the West's strategic isolation, Dobbin called for the assignment of a new steam frigate to the Pacific and for construction of a West Coast navy yard to build and maintain such ships. He then reviewed the recent duty of the Pacific Squadron, reminding Congress that, at the time of his remarks, the squadron consisted of only two ships: a sailing frigate and a sloop of war, supported by a stationary receiving ship at San Francisco and a storeship at Valparaiso. The sloop of war *St. Mary's* was en route to the Pacific, and though he did not say so, the *Decatur* had also been ordered to join the squadron.[4]

Pierce's and Dobbin's remarks were reprinted in newspapers throughout the United States. At midcentury, American readers eagerly read literature with naval and maritime themes, and the weight of their interest gradually shifted from the Royal Navy to the U.S. Navy, from the Atlantic Ocean stories of James Fenimore Cooper to the Pacific Ocean stories of Richard Henry Dana, Charles Nordhoff, and Herman Melville, from romance to realism. Cooper encouraged a salty, brawny maritime nationalism of warships and

merchant ships, expressed in his many sea novels and his recent history of the U.S. Navy. John Schroeder has argued that aggressive U.S. expansionism paralleled development of a mercantile empire marked by extraordinary growth of American seaborne trade, doubling between 1844 and 1853. An 1852 observer proudly noted that the U.S. merchant fleet had already grown to half that of Great Britain, and "England is in the decline of advancing age [while] the United States is in the first flush of youth." The dramatic expansion of America's merchant marine peaked during the *Decatur* cruise: *Young America* was launched in 1853, one of two dozen extreme clipper ships built in that year. The antebellum decade represented the high-water mark for American war, commerce, and diplomacy in wooden ships under sail and for American cultural identification with the sea and seafaring men.[5]

The Pacific Squadron's cruising ground ranged from Cape Horn to the North Pole and westward from the new American coastline to longitude 180°. A number of antebellum initiatives—Wilkes's Exploring Expedition (1838–42), Perry's opening of Japan (1853–54), and Ringgold's North Pacific Expedition (1853–55)—marked the accelerating pace of American interests in the Pacific and underscored the navy's crucial role there. The secretary of the navy's instructions to successive squadron commodores during the *Deca-*

tur's commission set out their general responsibilities. The commodore was to order the five ships under his command to make a continual round of visits to the settlements along the coast from Puget Sound to Valparaiso, protecting American citizens wherever they might be found in the continuous West. He was to display the flag along the coasts of Mexico and Central and South America and keep one vessel continually cruising among the Pacific islands. The squadron was to chart unknown islands, reefs, and shoals and gather samples of any commodity that might have commercial value. Commanders were also to comb the Pacific for strategic sites to supply their ships and to collect samples of wood useful for warship construction at future naval shipyards. Oriented to the sea rather than to the land, navy men developed a "Pacific consciousness" that perceived the ocean as a highway to expansion rather than a barrier, and many antebellum navy officers became "irrepressible advocates" for a growing naval presence in the Pacific, to extend Young America's territorial and maritime empire.[6]

Ralph Waldo Emerson's lecture "The Young American" was a paean to the "sublime and friendly Destiny" of the nation without a past that only looks to the future. "The beautiful continent is ours," he wrote, "state on state and territory on territory, to the waves of the Pacific sea," and his phrase "Young America" conveyed that hopeful poetic metaphor. But the movement within the Democratic Party termed "Young America" celebrated national values through an aggressive program of territorial expansion and development. During a college commencement speech, slavery expansionist Edwin de Leon described the "manly vigor" of Young America, as the youthful nation stood before the world in the "full flush of exulting manhood." Yonatan Eyal has identified this "generational self-consciousness" as the "crucial unifier" of Young America, with its demonization of timid Whigs as "old fogies." The Young America political movement emerged simultaneously with a new understanding of American manhood: both rejected tradition and age and praised youth and audacity, individualism and achievement. This assertive spirit underlay the annexation of Texas, the conquest of Mexico, and the "winning" of California and the Northwest as "stepping stones to the Pacific." The new state of California was claimed by the Democratic press as "the latest representative of Young America" and the portal to further empire, in which American "fleets [would] establish themselves on the Pacific," gaining access to "the wealth and commerce and populations of Australia, Oceanica, the fabled Ind and the unknown China." Bold Young Americans were out ahead of their country, accomplishing the national "manifest destiny." They fought "the battles of [their] private interests . . . and incidentally [attended to their] country's wrongs," as stated in the chapter-opening epigraph.[7]

The phrase "manifest destiny" was coined by journalist John O'Sullivan in an 1845 article concerning the Oregon country: it was manifestly clear that America's destiny was to "overspread and to possess the whole of the continent which Providence has given us for the development of the great experiment of liberty." Manifest destiny justified expansion as divinely ordained and identified an Anglo-Saxon mission to liberate and "regenerate" former European colonies, disguising conquest as redemption. In 1853, the Young America senator Stephen Douglas derisively recalled the debate of fifty years earlier about whether it was wise to acquire territory west of the Mississippi River; since then, expansion had rolled over that barrier, passed the Rocky Mountains, and was "only arrested by the waters of the Pacific." The nation's destiny was manifest to turn elsewhere, Douglas continued, to make conquest southward and westward. Pierce agreed. In his inaugural address, the president anticipated the "acquisition of certain possessions not within our jurisdiction," and journalist James DeBow exulted: "The North Americans will spread out far beyond their present bounds. They will encroach again and again on their neighbors. New territories will be planted, declare their independence and be annexed. We have New Mexico and California! We will have Old Mexico and Cuba!"[8]

The Mexican War's "easy and cheap" success had made "heroes by the dozen" and created a generation of trained fighters accustomed to fulfilling American destiny by gaining new territory and subduing its inhabitants under force of arms. Many antebellum navy men fondly recalled the heroics of the Mexican War, including those of *Decatur* captains Isaac Sears Sterrett and Guert Gansevoort, who had commanded vessels in the Gulf of Mexico. On the Pacific, formal American occupation of California began with the 1846 seizure of Monterey by Commodore John Sloat and the raising of the U.S. flag on shore by William Mervine, commodore during the *Decatur*'s commission. During its two-year duration, the Mexican War revolutionized the navy's responsibilities and perspective. The postwar challenge was to defend a new "nation with two sea frontiers, 2500 miles apart by land, and more than 14,000 miles apart by sea." Many eager expansionists remained in uniform, and civilian veterans formed a pool of recruits for a filibuster: a private military expedition to conquer territory outside the borders of the United States. Unsanctioned by the government, the filibuster was not always unwelcome to some of the government's officials and agents. According to Young America advocates, annexation of Mexico and Cuba was inevitable; however, aggressive expansionists looked further south, to the conquest of Panama and Nicaragua and control and development of their transits.[9]

To depict the Young America movement journalists often employed virile, martial images: a smiling young man with a confident grip on the hilt of his sword, striding forward and easily tossing his exhausted enemy to one side. However, the expansionist impulse was directed not only toward armed conquest: Young America might just as well have been depicted with surveying tools or blueprints in his hands instead of a weapon. In 1853, a columnist urged Young America to turn his energies to civil engineering: construction of railroads and canals between the oceans, including the Central American transits, the pathways through which "the electric vigor of our national muscle can be discharged into the far Pacific," enabling the "fulfillment of 'manifest destiny.'" Young Americans were enthusiastic inventors and entrepreneurs, heralding improvements to transportation and communication such as mail steamers, telegraph lines, railroads, and canals in the West.[10]

As California's annual gold exports soared, swift, safe passage between the Pacific and Atlantic oceans became of vital importance. The United States had concluded an 1846 treaty with New Grenada, as Colombia was then called, to secure the transit right-of-way across the Isthmus of Panama, and a group of American businessmen soon contracted to build a railroad there. Two American steamer routes met the railroad at either end: the first between New York and Colón—soon renamed Aspinwall—on the Atlantic, and the second between Panama and San Francisco, on the Pacific. Compared with sailing around the Horn, the Panama transit cut travel time from California to New York by more than half, but it was rivaled by Nicaragua's transit, which trimmed a further seven hundred miles off the trip. In 1850, American secretary of state John Clayton and British envoy Henry Lytton Bulwer hammered out an agreement that any future transit at either Panama or Nicaragua would remain unfortified, and that neither nation would ever colonize any part of Central America. The Clayton-Bulwer Treaty was met with dismay by those Americans who hoped for annexation or colonization of the transits and who distrusted the British.[11]

American financier Cornelius Vanderbilt controlled the Nicaragua transit route, and he grew irritated with British influence on the Nicaraguans at Greytown, on the Atlantic. Vanderbilt decided to relocate company warehouses to a nearby island, but local authorities resisted this move and razed some of the new buildings. Navy commander George Hollins landed marines from the sloop of war *Cyane* on Nicaraguan soil to defend Vanderbilt's property. The Greytowners backed down but Americans, outraged by their resistance, even more stridently advocated the occupation of Nicaragua, or at least the transit route, to protect American investment and ensure safe passage. In 1854, U.S. minister to Nicaragua Solon Borland called for abrogation of the Clayton-Bulwer Treaty and for American annexation of Nicaragua. Instead, Secretary of State William Marcy firmly rebuked Borland and the indignant diplomat resigned. Before returning home, Borland was attacked by a crowd of infuriated Nicaraguans and cut by a thrown bottle. Once stateside, he insisted on redress, and Secretary of the Navy Dobbin sent Commander Hollins back to Nicaragua. On July 14, 1854, Hollins turned the *Cyane*'s battery on Greytown for more than two hours, following up with a shore party that burned whatever buildings were left standing. Hollins gained notoriety for "leveling Greytown," and Central Americans did not soon forget the navy's gunboat diplomacy, even under sail. Hollins acted out a Young America fantasy, dismissing the Clayton-Bulwer Treaty, avenging Borland, and thumbing his nose at old fogies like Marcy. Borland had urged annexation of Nicaragua as "a bright star in the flag"—William Walker's filibuster seemed to fulfill Borland's suggestion.[12]

In May 1855, Walker first landed at Realejo, leading sixty filibuster soldiers from San Francisco, and he would soon become the "general" of an army of more than two thousand fighters in a private war to conquer Nicaragua. At first, many expansionists saw the filibuster as a legitimate option, the first step to "pave the way for large scale American settlement and eventual annexation of these areas to the United States." The *United States Democratic Review* defended filibustering, pointing out that two-thirds of the United States had been acquired by a spectrum of "Americanization" including revolution, purchase, conquest, colonization, and filibuster, or private war. The article flatly stated that "every sensible man . . . has expressed a strong desire for the Americanization of Central America [and its] possession . . . [This] is no less desirable than was the acquisition of Texas or Kansas, or even of California." And Young America Democrats harbored the "dreamy hope," as Yonatan Eyal described it, that domestic unity could be restored by aggressive expansion. For a time, the Nicaragua filibuster was part of that hope, and Walker was celebrated as Young America's agent, the messianic pioneer of the "Isthmian and Caribbean frontier," destined to fulfill Borland's imperial aspirations. Walker was the man of action, waiting for his country to overtake him.[13]

The aims of Young America appealed to many "sailors of manifest destiny views" in the U.S. Navy. Many young officers supported Secretary Dobbin's program, hoping for advancement in the modernizing navy of an imperial America. The airy rhetoric of manifest destiny became deck-level reality off

FIG. 4 *In 1856, the popular tabloid* Frank Leslie's Illustrated News *devoted numerous feature articles to Walker's filibuster of Nicaragua. Here, in April, an officer inspects a squad of filibuster soldiers at Virgin Bay in Nicaragua, "about to depart for the scene of war." These men included "sailors of manifest destiny views" drawn from ports throughout the Pacific West. April 19, 1856. Courtesy University of Washington Libraries.*

Western beaches as the navy was involved with expansionist initiatives at every stage. Though obligated by the 1818 Neutrality Act to prevent "unlawful expeditions," naval officers did not always vigorously do so nor were they always expected to by their superiors. An officer on board the *Decatur* maintained that Walker's Nicaragua filibuster "had the sanction of [the presidential] administration, and the aid of the Navy, as far as it was possible to go without arousing international suspicions." Though it is unclear which Pacific Squadron officers were Young America adherents, an 1852 article in *Democrat's Review* urged all Young Americans in the navy, wherever they might be stationed, to brush aside "the web of Fogyism from the stars and stripes." Squadron commodore William Mervine was a self-proclaimed Fogy, and he complained that "the spirit and progress of Young America is rapidly digging the grave of our Navy," lamenting the widespread appeal of that cultural and political message to his officers. Squadron naval officers' "expansionist fantasies" had been fueled by their professional training, their personal ambitions,

FIG. 5 The "Young America Polka" was dedicated to Commander Duncan Ingraham of the U.S. Navy, who freed Hungarian revolutionary Martin Koszta from captivity on the Austrian vessel Hussar at Smyrna in 1853. Secretary Dobbin singled out Ingraham for approval in his first Report to Congress, and the navy officer was the darling of Young America, like naval commander George Hollins, who "leveled Greytown." Ingraham later resigned his commission to join the Confederate States Navy, as did Hollins. In this engraving, a young sailor nails the U.S. flag to the masthead, indicating that the ship will never strike its colors and never give up the fight. Courtesy Library of Congress.

their developing "Pacific consciousness," and the prevailing maritime nationalism of literature about the sea.[14]

In fact, aggressive expansionism and assertive manhood found their most natural expression at sea, in the American navy. John Paul Jones's biography was adapted as usable history by expansionists—the fable of the archetypal naval hero who combined skill, patriotism, and daring as he "fought for and established the navy of American freedom." Jones claimed to have been first to unfurl the colonial standard on board an American naval vessel, first to raise the new Stars and Stripes, and first to receive a national salute from another vessel; it was he who declared, "I have not yet begun to fight!" on the battered *Bonhomme Richard*. James Fenimore Cooper's widely read 1846 biography of Jones sketched a dashing man—"our hero"—a natural leader, a successful lover, a bit of a rogue, unexcelled in "spirit, enterprise and seamanship," sailing for the new American navy but also in more ambiguous naval ventures, not unlike filibusters. Repeatedly thwarted by the schemes of jealous American Fogies, Jones was a dashing "sailor of fortune," forever young.

He was a naval hero in whom expansionists could believe, combining the manly and political attributes of the Young American. His midcentury biographers meaningfully pointed out that Jones had always intended "a voyage of commercial enterprise" into the Pacific: to Japan, the Pacific Northwest, the Sandwich Islands, and, as Cooper put it, "the ends of the earth," the real world of the Pacific Squadron.[15]

Drawn by the cultural appeal of Young America, many naval officers adopted the movement's political agenda as well. Although historian Peter Karsten and others have argued that naval officers loved authoritarianism and traditionalism and were fundamentally apolitical, historians exploring the nineteenth-century U.S. Army have found ample evidence that military men were "by no means indifferent to the political world." Durwood Ball estimated that three-quarters of army officers were expansionist Democrats by 1860. William Skelton argued that, while a minority of army officers actively supported civilian filibusters, the vast majority advocated more legitimate American territorial aggression in "the expansionist . . . surge of spirit of Manifest Destiny." Robert May found widespread sympathy among army officers for filibusters and pointed out that West Point had become a "breeding ground" for expansionist "apostles." It is instructive to apply what is known and suspected of the private political convictions of U.S. Army officers to U.S. Navy officers.[16]

In the mid-1850s, some navy men were public advocates for maritime imperialism in the Pacific. Naval officers who openly supported crusades of "manifest destiny [that] point to a very proximate occupation of the whole of this vast Continent by our people" were ordered to silence those opinions and were forbidden "to speak politics in a foreign port." But on his return home, Commander Charles Wilkes fervently promoted the commercial potential of San Francisco Bay and Puget Sound and advocated West Coast expansionism. Likewise, after his voyage to Japan, Commodore Matthew Perry urged U.S. initiation of a "European style empire in the Pacific," including colonization of the islands and intervention in Asian politics. Some former military men who achieved prominent office became advocates for expansion, and some expansionist elected officials became deeply interested in military matters. To name just three, Robert Stockton, a navy veteran of the Mexican War and the conquest of California, resigned to run successfully for the Senate as a Young America Democrat. Likewise, Illinois Young America senator Sidney Breese was an army veteran and a scion of the Breese military family, which included numerous naval officers. Florida senator Stephen Mallory was a Young America Democrat who headed the U.S. Senate Naval Affairs

Committee throughout the *Decatur*'s cruise. Antebellum naval officers from Samuel Francis Du Pont to the *Decatur*'s Isaac Sterrett, Francis Dallas, Guert Gansevoort, and others cultivated the influence of these and other political figures. In fact, naval appointments ranging from midshipman to secretary of the navy were the result of political patronage: "A cruise of a few months in Washington," went the old saw, "told more in an officer's favor than a three-years cruise at sea."[17]

Antebellum military officers were men of their time, in agreement or disagreement with the prevailing expansionist ideology of the Pierce and Buchanan administrations. Likewise, sectionalism compelled their loyalty. Ball has argued that the resignation of one-third of the army's officers at the outset of the Civil War suggests the strength of their Southern sectional conviction beforehand. In the navy, one in four commissioned and warrant officers followed their states out of the Union into the Confederate States Navy, and it is reasonable to suppose that, like army officers, naval officers held their pro-Southern convictions prior to the war. Thwarted in the states and territories of the American West, slavery expansionists grew convinced that Walker's filibuster would lead to annexation of Nicaragua as American slave territory or a slave-owning republic independent of the United States. In either case, the private war in Nicaragua became a sectional crusade rather than a national one, a Southern venture rather than a western one. May has argued that army officers' support for filibusters was influenced by the growing "sectionalist imperative," and it is likely that antebellum sectional affiliations of navy officers had the same effect on their support for the Nicaragua filibuster or, at the very least, for aggressive expansionism in the West.[18]

Navy men took sides in the controversies that stirred the nation at large and often were more loyal to their home state than to their nation. At the outset of the Civil War, mistakenly anticipating Maryland's secession, George Hollins—who had "leveled Greytown"—resigned his commission to join the Confederate States Navy. So did Josiah Tatnall, captain of the Pacific Squadron flagship *Independence*, *Saratoga* commander Frederick Chatard, who allowed Walker's second filibuster to land, and *St. Mary's* Lieutenant David McCorkle, who led the dreadful parade of defeated filibusters from Nicaragua. Indeed, so did some of the *Decatur*'s officers. Officers' decisions to stay loyal or to resign are matters of record; it is more difficult to track the choices of sailors and marines. However, it is reasonable to suppose that many enlisted men acted on their convictions; in fact, it seems unreasonable to assume that they had no convictions. The *Decatur* seaman from Virginia who yelled, "Damn the

Yankees! I'll toe the line with any man!" likely headed south, as the men from Massachusetts who took up his dare likely headed north. Former Decaturs found themselves enemies in battle when their ship, the navy, and the nation broke in two.

But when Pierce addressed Congress in 1853 and the *Decatur* was preparing for distant duty, many Americans said with Mahan, "American fight American? Never! Separation there might be . . . but brother shed the blood of brother? No!" Young America's optimism was at a high-water mark in the Pacific West. The Young America Engine Company had organized in San Francisco, and the new clipper ship *Young America* sailed from San Francisco to Honolulu and then to New York in less than four months. In California's mining district, the newspaper *Young America* first went to press in September 1853, and a score of hopeful mining enterprises were named "Young America." The numerous "manifest destiny projects of Young America" in Pacific filibusters had driven the price of muskets in San Francisco from $1.50 to nearly $4.00. An editorialist for San Francisco's *Bulletin* took "Young America" as his pen name. The California steamer *Young America* was launched for coastwise service, the Young America Guards were organized as a city militia, and San Francisco racing fans bet on a fast trotter named "Young America." In 1854, the confident editor of *Young America on the Pacific* published his first issue, eager to join a crusade to fulfill manifest destiny in Panama. Western optimists named their businesses and hobbies in honor of Young America, clothing their personal ambitions in the national interest of expansion. The navy men on the *Decatur* also sailed to the Pacific in pursuit of personal and professional goals, in the service of national policy.[19]

2

The *Decatur* in the Old Navy

"To Command Our Own Seas and Coasts"

Thirty years of Fogy night-mare rule have ruined [the navy's] esprit
de corps, blighted its energies, stifled progress, suppressed every
stimulus . . . destroyed all hope of advancement to talent, energy, or
character, and done their best to bring every body and every thing
connected with the Navy to the dreary level of Fogy dullness, sloth
and mediocrity.—*Democrat's Review,* July 1852

The antebellum navy would have been inhospitable to the dashing
John Paul Jones, celebrated by Young America. The Old Navy was a
hierarchical and bureaucratic system: plodding, clumsy, and unfair,
wrapped up in red tape. However, during the 1850s, the service faced a set
of profound institutional challenges and each can be explored on board the
Decatur. These dramatic transitions, utterly eclipsed by the Civil War, were
crucial in their time and shaped the lives of the men who served on American
warships. Struggling to shake off the paralysis born of tightfisted funding,
poor discipline, and slavish respect for tradition, the navy was fortunate in
the tenure of Secretary of the Navy James Dobbin, who remained in his position for four years—previously, there had been five secretaries in only seven
years. An eager expansionist and intent on making strategic choices for the
future, Dobbin carried the work forward of building a better educated, better
equipped, better disciplined, and more effective navy. Supported by Presi-

dent Pierce, Dobbin was able to accomplish most of the revolutionary naval reforms recommended in his December 1853 report to Congress.[1]

In the 1850s, the *Decatur* was fast becoming obsolete as the romance of sail was overtaken by the science of steam. Traditionalists insisted that sail would always be best for long voyages, citing the dangerous unreliability of steam engines and boilers, steamers' dependence on coaling stations, and the high cost of coal as a fuel. Many older officers also mourned the passing of sail as the death of the seagoing culture and the end to seamanship and tradition. The ship's namesake, Stephen Decatur, had gloomily remarked of an early experiment in steam navigation that "it is the end of our business; hereafter, any man who can boil a tea-kettle will be as good as the rest of us." Popular literature celebrated the rich legacy of the old sailing navy, and the *Decatur*'s officers respected the "marling-spike seaman" who could rig a ship from scratch and handle it on every sea.[2]

However, once Commodore Perry steamed to Japan, it was just a matter of time before sail would pass away altogether. Dobbin's 1853 annual report identified steam as "unquestionably the great agent to be used on the ocean . . . for purposes of war as of commerce" and called for the construction of six first-class steam frigates. Sailing warships were ill-equipped to sail against wind, current, and tide in the huge Pacific Squadron cruising ground, to show the flag, demonstrate the power of the great guns, and meet demands for timely communication. Squadron commodore Bladen Dulany recommended that two war steamers patrol the western coasts of North and South America and rendezvous regularly at Panama. Despite his Old Fogy status, Dulany's successor William Mervine also called for assignment of a steam frigate to the Pacific and additionally requested two smaller steamers. Between 1843 and 1860, the number of steam warships in the U.S. Navy increased from six to thirty-eight, and thirty were built during the *Decatur*'s Pacific cruise, including the steam frigate *Merrimac,* which replaced the venerable sailing frigate *Independence* as the squadron's flagship in 1857.[3]

Despite his determination to innovate propulsion, Secretary Dobbin argued in 1853 that the navy's greatest problem was not its technology but its denial of advancement to Young America. "Gallant, chivalrous men of the Navy feel subdued, dispirited, discouraged; their ardor is chilled; the fire of their young ambition and pride is well nigh extinguished," Dobbin reported with emphasis, because "neither merit nor sea-service nor gallantry nor capacity, but *mere seniority of commission regulates promotion and pay.*" In 1853, superannuated officers managed the navy's five bureaus, each bureau chief ensconced in a comfortable niche in a "smug Navy oligarchy," "maggots in the kernel of [naval] strength" who were thoroughly inadequate to the challenges of a modernizing service. The Democratic press attacked the U.S. Navy as "the worst administered navy in [the world]" and demanded aggressive personnel reforms to accomplish the expansionist agenda. If it were not for incompetence in the diplomatic corps and the navy, argued one writer, the United States could "make itself the arbiter of the world." While young officers yearned for innovation and command, seniority entrenched their elders in a sleepy, impregnable bureaucracy. "To get rid of their ideas," wrote a Young America journalist decisively, "it is necessary to get rid of them."[4]

But such radical reform proved to be no easy task. In December 1853, when Dobbin's dramatic annual report was published, the navy lacked any retirement system and the Old Fogies continued to set the traditional style of the service. The Old Navy was a small, inbred service of enemies and allies, friends and relatives, and patrons and protégés. Senior officers secured midshipman appointments for youngsters and advanced their own careers by leveraging their obligations and influence, protecting their alliances, nursing old grudges, and modeling the behavior they wished to see emulated. For instance, naval officers cultivated an exaggerated sense of reputation, too easily insulted, and encouraged this stiff-necked touchiness as a proud navy tradition. In 1820, Stephen Decatur had dueled with another naval officer and died for his honor; in the midcentury navy, dueling was forbidden and the defense of manly honor became a matter of litigation. The explosion of courts-martial and courts of inquiry at the return of the Wilkes Exploring Expedition eclipsed its achievements, with mutual accusations among officers that became front-page news. Rather than exceptional, such surrogate duels were embarrassingly characteristic of the Old Navy. Moreover, for a time, the subculture of dueling lingered, tolerated by some senior officers as part of the naval tradition—one of the *Decatur*'s lieutenants participated in the last duel fought between Annapolis midshipmen at Bladensburg, the site of Decatur's own duel. On board the *Decatur*, an outraged officer forced a wardroom quarrel into a court of inquiry although he would have preferred to defend his reputation in a traditional duel. Forbidden that alternative, he litigated his honor.[5]

Such intransigence impeded the good discipline of the Old Navy and discouraged cooperation among commanders. During the *Decatur*'s cruise, squadron ships were usually widely scattered on single-ship cruises across the Pacific and rarely engaged in joint missions. However, when a situation required collaboration, Old Navy commanders were often unable to work together. For instance, in the Strait of Magellan, the commanding officers of the *Decatur* and the steamer *Massachusetts* were on such bad terms that the steamer cut the towline between the two vessels without warning, abandoning the sloop of war to its fate in a storm. Likewise, the captains of the *Decatur* and *Active* carried on a bitter feud off Seattle, disputing which was in command of the other. Only the arrival of a commander senior to both put an end to their quarrel. William Mervine, the prickly, suspicious squadron commodore during much of the *Decatur*'s cruise, accused many of his commanders of disrespect and insubordination, of offending his dignity and resisting his authority, and of seeking to pursue independent commands. The correspondence of the Pacific Squadron testifies abundantly to the acrimonious atmosphere among Mervine's officers and between him and his officers. Though Mervine was scolded by two secretaries of the navy for his steady stream of complaints, feuds, and reprimands, he persisted in them, and his behavior in the squadron exemplifies a wider navy problem.[6]

Antebellum senior officers like Mervine had apprenticed as boys under captains legendary in the history of the new Republic. These veterans of the War of 1812 encouraged a heroic mythology of that war and enshrined those traditions. Alfred Mahan recalled with wry amusement a distinguished senior officer of the 1850s who could remember "nothing later than 1813." Young America journalists ridiculed these Whigs as "old fogies," but older officers remained in the service not only because there was no dignified way to leave but also because they wanted to protect the navy as they knew it. They thought the young officers were too involved in public life; they did not just "do their duty" but had political opinions, and unpalatable ones at that. And they not only did not value naval traditions, thought their elders, but they were not particularly good seamen: Mervine, venerating the skills of a sailing navy that was fast passing away, expressed withering contempt for a young lieutenant who did not know how to tack a sloop of war into the wind. The Young America press attacked such "incurable old fogies," who were blocking the advancement of the men of the "highly educated young Navy," who "craved distinction." These ambitious officers were veterans of the Mexican War of 1848—an expansionist "romp" that encouraged a newer kind of naval heroism than the War of 1812 had—and they had all trained together at the new Naval Academy.[7]

Secretary of the Navy George Bancroft established the U.S. Naval Academy at Annapolis in 1845, to better prepare young officers for command. A historian of the academy has identified the school's founding as one of the turning points that marked the "passing of the Old Navy." Modeled on the U.S. Military Academy at West Point, the naval college provided a common experience for all midshipmen, and the school's curriculum established a solid foundation in mathematics and navigation, steam engineering, gunnery, history, geography, law, and modern languages, particularly French and Spanish. Naval officers trained as skillful navigators, fighting commanders, confident naval diplomats, and gentlemen who could display a "cultivated mind and polished manners." In 1854, the first class graduated from Annapolis who had completed four years of study there as well as two sea cruises, for a total of seven years of shared training. The academy produced a generational revolution: these young officers knew their gunnery and steam engineering, their Marryat, Cooper, and Dana; many were expansionists, and they all opened each issue of the *Navy Register*, eager for promotion.[8]

Twenty copies of the annual *Navy Register* were sent out to the *Decatur* to be distributed to the officers on board. This publication listed the General Orders chronologically as they accreted like barnacles, governing the navy's way of life down to the smallest minutiae. The *Register* also set out the seniority lists for each officer grade, and the ship's aging midshipmen and graying lieutenants scoured each new issue to see who had been court-martialed or had died. The number of naval officers in each grade was set by Congress, and the old officers—the "drones"—could not retire and did not resign, and their seniority left hundreds of resentful young men languishing for promotion. By 1853, not one of the navy's captains had been born in the nineteenth century, and many other senior officers were otherwise incompetent—alcoholic, insane, or ailing. At midcentury, aged and inept command in the navy had become the butt of popular jokes: the "tottering footsteps" of the navy's "decrepit old men" were satirized as those more appropriate to a funeral procession than the "firm tramp of a man to battle." Herman Melville publicly scorned these "national pensioners in disguise, who live on the Navy without serving it," clogging the seniority list and blocking advancement to those below.[9]

In 1853, commissioned officers in the navy held the rank of captain, commander, lieutenant, passed midshipman, or midshipman—the title "commodore" was a courtesy to the captain of a squadron. Of the sixty-seven captains on the active list, forty were on leave of absence, and the youngest man was fifty-six years of age. Of ninety-seven commanders, three-quarters were older than fifty, including the *Decatur*'s commander Isaac Sears Sterrett. If the situation continued as it was, a lieutenant could expect to be promoted to commander at fifty-three and to captain at seventy-four, and a new midshipman would serve fifteen years before he could hope to become a lieutenant. So, asked Secretary Dobbin rhetorically, why—"in a country like ours . . . presenting so many paths . . . to fame and fortune"—would an intelligent, ambitious young man join the navy at all and why would an intelligent, ambitious officer stay? He proposed retirement for the aged, furlough or discharge for the incompetent, and a new system of promotion based on merit, not seniority. Dobbin was not the first to make such recommendations but he was the first to accomplish them, and on his watch, the Efficiency Board of 1855 was established to evaluate the commissioned officers of the U.S. Navy in "the most radical personnel reform since the Navy's founding."[10]

With Dobbin's full support, Commander Samuel Francis Du Pont drafted legislation designed to open the floodgates of renewal: "An Act to Promote the Efficiency of the Navy." The act defined inefficient officers as those "incapable of performing promptly and efficiently all their duties both ashore and afloat." Dobbin elaborated: "The law requires capacity, but it stops not there, but it must be a capacity to perform 'all duty,' ashore and afloat. But it stops not here, for it is not content with a mere capacity to perform duty, but demands that it shall be done, not merely 'promptly,' but 'efficiently.' . . . Efficiency—efficiency—that is what is required. Inefficiency—inefficiency—that is what is to be withdrawn."[11]

Authorized by Congress, the Efficiency Board was composed of five captains, five commanders, and five lieutenants, and to avoid the appearance of improperly advancing personal interests, no officer was to vote on the case of anyone senior to himself. The act established two reserved lists, on which inefficient officers of every grade could be placed and earn only furlough pay or leave-of-absence pay. A third category was created for those officers who were to be dropped entirely from the navy rolls. Known popularly as the "Plucking Board," the panel deliberated in secret, reviewing the "mental, physical and moral state" of about 250 officers, including Captain Isaac Sterrett of the *Decatur*. Eventually, 201 men were removed from the active list, nearly one-third of the navy's commissioned officer corps. A wave of promotions followed as men moved up the seniority list—a whole class of young men became lieutenants and commanders overnight on September 15, 1855, as a result of the board's actions. Young America had flexed its muscles. The board's decisions became public when the *Decatur* was under the command of Commodore Mervine, who lamented that the board had advanced "a large number of young officers . . . so inflated with their own importance and attainments as to foster a belief that they are the soul of the Navy [and who have] banded together to break down the little remnant left of the old fogy discipline which carried the Navy so gloriously through the War of 1812."[12]

Mervine was not the only one to criticize the Plucking Board's decisions. Reform had been sorely needed to remove aged and incompetent officers and to reward young officers of merit, but the board's secrecy and haste encouraged a backlash against its closed-door proceedings. Those aggrieved claimed personal grudges, sectional interest, and the eagerness for promotion of pushy youngsters, and many officers disciplined by the Plucking Board submitted protests to their home state senators, their influential patrons, and the press. The board's decisions affected officers on board the *Decatur*, and their experiences, explored in later chapters, will allow us to examine the personal and ship-level consequences of board actions. Plucked officers, long trained to identify their personal honor with their public reputation, were humiliated as failures and tarnished by insinuations of inefficiency due to age, laziness, or drunkenness.[13]

Hard drinking was the besetting disciplinary problem at every rank in the Old Navy—men drank in camaraderie but also drank alone to escape the monotony, regimentation, and lack of privacy of shipboard life. Mahan recalled the commonplace remark of the 1850s: "[He is a] first-rate officer, when he is not drinking," and during the Pacific Squadron cruise, the *Decatur* lost two captains, one lieutenant, one boatswain, and two gunners to charges of habitual drunkenness. During the same period, sailors and marines on the *Decatur* received more than 2,500 punishments for drinking. There was a tremendous differential between the punishments for enlisted men and officers for the same infraction: a seaman was punished each time he was caught drunk on duty, whereas the only punishment for an officer was court-martial—but only if his condition could be proved to be chronic and incapacitating. In 1856, during the *Decatur*'s cruise, a group of sailors wrote a letter to the editor of a popular magazine for seafaring men pointing out the severe punishments readily handed out to drunken sailors, "but let an officer come on board dead drunk—which has often been the case this cruise—and nothing is said to him." In the Old Navy, officers sometimes covered up one another's drinking problems, throwing the cloak of brotherhood around an alcoholic. On board the *Decatur*, the ship's officers signed an 1856 petition calling for the reinstatement of their commander, who had been removed for public drunkenness; two years later, the *Decatur*'s commanding officer averted his eyes from his lieutenant's drinking and sacrificed two enlisted men to his whitewash.[14]

As we will see in subsequent chapters, from minor offenses to the gravest crimes, nearly every infraction on board the *Decatur* was committed by drunken men. However, liquor also offered a temporary means of escape and was consciously employed as a means of socialization and discipline, a "controlling inducement" that fostered enlisted men's addiction to alcohol. In fact, the grog ration was often the best way to maintain order: an extra tot was the only reward that officers could give to enlisted men. In the 1850s navy, grog meant the daily ration of one gill of whiskey—half a cup—diluted with water and served at breakfast and supper. On board the *Decatur*, the officer of the watch gave the order to "splice the main brace" twice a week on average. This was navy jargon for authorizing an extra round of drinks after particularly rough duty, a time-honored ritual that encouraged good order. An officer reported that "it is of great consequence that the men should have some little comfort to look forward to daily; it produces cheerfulness and good feeling and I think it conduces to good conduct, [and] this effect is produced at grog-time." However, when many of the enlisted men on board the *Decatur* were able to drink freely, they drank to oblivion, the typical "drunken sailor" regarded by his officers with amused distaste. Such drunkenness often excused breaks in self-discipline: lapses that allowed sailors to let off a little steam. In such instances, navy regulations warned officers to be careful "not to afford [intoxicated persons] opportunity to be guilty of mutinous or seditious conduct" by ensuring that they were arrested by "persons of their own grade," and drunken Decaturs were usually arrested by warrant or petty officers. During the cruise, there were dozens of examples of disrespectful or seditious speech by seamen on the *Decatur*, their tongues always loosened by alcohol. *Decatur* drunks who railed at "this damn ship and everybody in it" were confined in double-irons for a day or two and then docked some pay. They had lost their discipline but they had been "in liquor," which freed them of most responsibility.[15]

When the *Decatur* was at sea or in a tight spot, infractions of every sort declined dramatically. But at peace or in port, offenses skyrocketed. Many of the "best men" on the *Decatur* spent their liberty in drunken sprees, involving men and women who lived on Pacific West beaches in robberies, rapes, and fistfights. In every port, the log recorded punishments for bruised, hungover Decaturs, often returned to the ship by local police. A core group of forty men committed the majority of offenses, usually insolence, skulking, or disobedience, and almost always when they had been drinking. However, while anchored off Seattle, more than half the crew offended, and the *Decatur* suffered an even more criminal period off Panama. At times, the ship teetered on the edge of anarchy when boredom, repression, and incurable illness pushed drunken men to grudge fights among themselves or to making common cause against the officers. Then, all it took was a flashpoint to ignite mutiny, when desperate sailors would cooperate to protect one another, rush the officers, overpower the marines, and seize the ship. Two mutinies took place during the *Decatur*'s five-year cruise and both were fueled by liquor smuggled on board.[16]

An old seaman informed his lieutenant, "A man don't get drunk on his allowance but on that which is smuggled off from the shore," and officers made every effort to discover the ingenious ways sailors invented for sneaking liquor on board ship or breaking into the spirit room. Many stateside temperance advocates agitated for an absolute end to grog, arguing that the smuggling of liquor, theft from officers' liquor supplies, and the drunken mayhem of liberty were the inevitable consequences of allowing whiskey on board at all. These reformers and a few naval officers pointed to alcohol as the cause for the typical sailor's rootless, reckless way of life. One reformer noted that shipboard grog encouraged that "intemperance [which] is the bane of the sailor [because grog is] an habitual stimulus provocative of excess when temptation and opportunity present, to the injury and degradation of the seaman." The tradition of grog did not end until 1862, in the wartime U.S. Navy.[17]

Antebellum reformers had better success in their crusade to put an end to flogging. Until 1850, enlisted men in the navy were disciplined for most offenses by public whipping with a cat-o'-nine-tails—a heavy leather handle that separated into nine knotted whips. For instance, the *Decatur*'s resident old salt, seaman Samuel Silk, had gone before a general court-martial in 1840, charged with offenses on the *Ohio*. At Port Mahon, Silk had walked aft to ask for an interview with the *Ohio*'s captain and then requested liberty for the crew in a manner that the captain deemed insolent. In fact, he told Silk that he was the last man on board who should speak for his shipmates, having returned to the ship with a broken jaw from a drunken brawl the last time he had been permitted shore leave. Found guilty of disrespect, Silk was downgraded to ordinary seaman and sentenced to eighty-four lashes on his bare back with the cat, later reduced to sixty. In 1854, on the *Decatur*, Silk bore the scars from this punishment.[18]

Flogging was challenged by humanitarian reformers as un-American, brutal, and inhumane, suggesting Southern mistreatment of African slaves. In 1850, Congress outlawed flogging on ships in the navy, to the dissatisfaction of many officers. Isaac Sterrett responded to a questionnaire on the subject circulated by the secretary of the navy:

Corporal punishment cannot be dispensed with consistently without prejudice to the naval service. My reasons for the above opinion are founded from experience, gained as the first lieutenant of a frigate and sloop-of-war, during which time I tried, without success, various modes of punishment rather than report for punishment at the gang way with cats. . . . I have had frequent consultation with old and intelligent seamen on the subject of abolishing corporal punishment in the Navy, and they have expressed themselves opposed to it because in their opinion there would be a regular system of skulking and thieving kept up and none but the good men would suffer.

Most officers and some sailors agreed with Sterrett. After flogging was banned, minor offenses were punished by "confinement," ironing a man at wrists and ankles for a varying number of hours and days. By October 1855, a *Decatur* sailor could be disciplined in three ways for escalating offenses: given a subjudicial punishment or tried before a summary court-martial or general court-martial. Subjudicial offenses, such as skulking, lying, disobedience, drinking, fighting, and other minor infractions, had traditionally been punished by fewer than a dozen lashes, assigned by the captain or the first lieutenant without trial; after 1850, such offenses were punished by confinement. The summary court-martial was one of Dobbin's innovations: a "minor court" of the ship's own officers to try a range of "judicial" offenses including seditious speech, disrespect, theft, smuggling, drunkenness on duty, or attempted desertion. Summary court-martial punishments included dishonorable discharge, as well as extended periods of confinement, denial of grog and tobacco, and loss of pay. The general court-martial required the presence of officers from other ships and was convened to try grave crimes: cowardice in battle, mutiny, murder, assault with a deadly weapon, or assault on an officer. Convicted by a general court-martial, a man could be sentenced to a shoreside prison, discharged dishonorably, or executed.[19]

During the *Decatur*'s Pacific Squadron cruise, the ship's officers struggled to enforce the discipline necessary to living in close quarters and the instant obedience necessary to working together, to sail and fight the ship in an emergency. The *Decatur* was launched in 1839, built for the flogging era when punishment was harsh and swift: the ship had no brig, and during the Pacific Squadron cruise, confined men lay in a row under the forecastle or stood chained to stanchions on deck. And it seemed to many officers and sailors that confinement offered the ship's ne'er-do-wells the leisure to sober up in irons while the ship's steady men did the hard shipboard work. Often, the worst-behaving seamen on the *Decatur* had served in the English navy and were accustomed to a flogging discipline. In the American navy, they did as they pleased, and if they were punished with dishonorable discharge, they simply moved on to another ship. According to an advocate for American-born sailors, by changing his name and deserting one ship for another, a foreign seaman "may nowadays be disgraced and sent on shore and the next hour, almost, go to a rendezvous and ship again; for, with the mere general description that is had of him, it is next to an impossibility to detect such rascals."[20]

Secretaries of the navy, politicians, and journalists expressed concern at the number of foreign-born sailors in the navy; half the men in the *Decatur*'s 1854 crew were born in Europe. In 1850, the protagonist of Herman Melville's *White-Jacket* deplored the lack of patriotism among his shipmates because so many of them were "foreigners"; others complained about these "stupid turf-lumps from the muddy bogs of Ireland, and smoke-dried, beer-soaked villains swept like vermin from the rottenness of Germany." A writer in the *Monthly Nautical Magazine* agreed: "Why is it that our ships are manned with foreigners and the refuse of creation? . . . The objection is not so much to foreigners as foreigners, but to those who are worthless as seaman, who cannot speak the language and who, in their moral natures, are little better than the beasts that perish. . . . The English [sailors] as a class are among the worst, for they are sulky, dogged and—what one would scarcely expect in John Bull—treacherous."[21]

Just as it seemed a reasonable proposition that the U.S. Navy should be adequate to command the nation's seas and coasts, it also seemed reasonable that young American men would be eager to man the navy's ships. However, Dobbin's 1853 report pointed out the difficulties of enlisting and retaining American-born sailors. "Hundreds of merchant vessels," he complained, "are darting forth from our busy marts readily filled with cheerful seamen . . . while our ships-of-war are lingering in port until the recruiting officers, by hard effort, can manage by the aid of the . . . landlord of the sailor-tavern and a small bounty, to procure tardy enlistments." The same manly self-interest that drove ambitious naval officers to leave the service encouraged American sailors to seek the highest wages for their skills. When the *Decatur*'s Boston crew signed on in January 1854, seamen, the most experienced men on board a man-of-war, earned only $12 a month and could have nearly doubled that wage on any Atlantic seaboard merchant ship; the wage disparity was far greater on the Pacific coast. In his 1853 report, Secretary Dobbin recommended a 30 percent increase in pay for each rating, to offer navy men "at least as much as their skill, experience and character will command in the merchant service."[22]

American sailors were also discouraged from joining the navy by a lack of security. In 1853, men signed up at a receiving ship for a three-year cruise on a particular navy ship—for instance, the *Decatur*—and they were identified with that ship rather than with the service. Dobbin called for a series of reforms that pointed the way toward a lifelong career path in the navy for American seamen, recognizing sailors as "permanently a part of the Navy and attached to the service." By the innovation of an honorable discharge, awarded at the end of a man's enlistment or a ship's commission, a sailor's skill and good character were recognized, and this certificate also served to document his experience and identify him by name, place of birth, and physical description—height, color of eyes and hair, and complexion. Dobbin also successfully recommended reenlistment bonuses and furloughs between ship assignments for sailors, as well as an apprentice system to recruit and train sea-struck American boys. Two years later, Dobbin was pleased to report to Congress that the "toil-worn tar" cherished his honorable discharge, a sheet of parchment "worthy to be preserved in the modest archives of his family," and that it appeared to be effective, as well as the other reforms, since enlistments nationwide had tripled in the six months following the adoption of the program. In the Pacific West, the *Decatur* and the other ships of the Pacific Squadron did not fare as well.[23]

The *Decatur* sailed to join the U.S. Navy's Pacific Squadron as the balance of American expansion tilted toward the maritime West. Determined by stateside politics and schemes, the ship's mission advanced the daring initiatives of a seafaring nation, furthering global American strategies of mercantile and territorial expansion. The men and boys on board the warship faced daily, deck-level challenges that mirrored Secretary Dobbin's own systemic concerns with navy institutions, technology, and discipline. The *Decatur* sailed through the final decade of America's Old Navy, when naval reforms responded to the expansionist agenda to send to sea the best-equipped, most modern, and best-staffed warships possible.

3

Boston

Getting Under Way

The Navy is the asylum for the perverse, the home of the unfortunate. Here the sons of adversity meet the children of calamity, and here the children of calamity meet the offspring of sin. Bankrupt brokers, bootblacks, blacklegs, and blacksmiths here assemble together; and castaway tinkers, watch-makers, quill-drivers, cobblers, doctors, farmers, and lawyers compare past experiences and talk of old times.
—HERMAN MELVILLE, *White-Jacket*

America is just the country for alibis—everybody is everywhere and nobody anywhere. The whole nation is in motion, and there is every imaginable opportunity for alibis.—JAMES FENIMORE COOPER, *Afloat and Ashore*

On January 10, 1854, a bitterly cold day in Boston Harbor, Acting Master Thomas Stowell Phelps opened a new Logbook for the *Decatur*. Phelps was thirty-two years old and still a passed midshipman; as master, he was responsible for stowing the ship's stores in the hold so that the weight was distributed for maximum speed. But the *Decatur* was being frantically loaded for sea: water and whiskey, blankets and pea jackets, barrels of salt beef and pork, and nine cords of firewood. Phelps could hardly keep up with the stream of supplies, let alone stow them properly. Dockyard crews swarmed over the ship finishing what absolutely had to be done to put to sea in the emergency. Phelps began the new log by listing the officers attached to the ship: the commander and lieutenants, the passed midshipmen and midshipmen, the surgeons, the purser, and the other warrant officers—the boatswain, gunner, carpenter, and sailmaker.[1]

A week earlier, the *Decatur* had been tied up at a wharf at Boston's Charlestown Navy Yard, and its decks were knee-deep in drifted snow. The sloop of war had arrived in mid-September 1853 to undergo a complete overhaul for assignment to the Pacific Squadron. Yard crews had installed a new rudder and new pumps, repaired the capstan, and replaced the planking at the head. They sent up a new mizzen topmast and main and fore topgallant masts and replaced all the rigging and many of the sails. They rebuilt the furniture in the wardroom and the captain's cabin as well as the berth deck hammock rails. When Christmas rolled around, there was still plenty to do: the berth deck and the wardroom and cabin were unpainted, and shipyard gangs were in the midst of caulking the deck and hull.[2]

As the *Decatur* hastily readied for sea, Commander Isaac Sears Sterrett stood on the quarterdeck. Back in December, he had received orders to take command of the ship and to join the Pacific Squadron "as soon as the ship is in all respects ready for sea." But an emergency intervened. An urgent telegram arrived at Sterrett's Boston hotel on January 9, ordering the ship to set out in search of the disabled steamship *San Francisco,* which had been transporting eight companies of the U.S. Army's Third Regiment to California to bring order to that raw society. The steamer left New York on December 22, 1853, with nearly eight hundred passengers and crew and carrying so much coal that half the soldiers were forced to camp out on deck. On Christmas Day, the ship was laboring in a gale when its engines failed; the steamer was reported disabled and adrift. The *Decatur* was to join a number of ships sweeping the North Atlantic for the *San Francisco,* hoping to rescue survivors.[3]

Commander Sterrett was fifty-three years old, descendant of an old Maryland family of shipbuilders and military men. The Sterrett shipyard in Baltimore had built the venerable *Constellation,* launched in 1797. His uncle Andrew Sterrett was a naval hero who had earned renown fighting the Tripolitan pirates but who resigned his commission in a huff when Stephen Decatur was placed senior to him on the Navy list. Isaac Sterrett was named a midshipman in 1819 and grew up in the Old Navy's "narrow quarters, hard fare and continuous hustling." Not promoted to commander until 1850, Sterrett had spent twenty years of his life at sea: in the Coast Survey, in the Mediterranean Squadron and the Pacific Squadron, and in command of the *Reefer* during the Mexican War. Sterrett had most recently commanded the Philadelphia Naval Asylum—the retirement home for enlisted Navy men—until his orders arrived to join the *Decatur.*[4]

Once on board, Commander Sterrett became Captain Sterrett. His orders, signed by Secretary Dobbin, set out his authority and responsibilities. Assisted by his officers, Sterrett was responsible for everything on board from the health of the crew to the condition of the sails. He was to give all orders respecting the safety of the ship, at port and at sea, in and out of battle. He was to maintain good discipline but not apply any eccentric or cruel punishments. He was to remind the crew to obey the laws of the places they visited on liberty "to avoid as far as possible giving the least ground of complaint." Sterrett was instructed to set Sunday aside as a day of rest and to read the divine service "in a solemn, orderly and reverent manner."[5]

Sterrett was responsible for the accuracy of the Logbook, maintained in turn by each officer of the watch. The log was to carefully note the weather, ship's position, and shipboard activities, as well as unusual events such as exchanging national salutes, going into action, or running aground. If the ship were wrecked, the captain was required to save the muster roll, the pay and receipt books, and the Logbook. If unlucky in battle, he was to destroy signals and secret orders that might prove useful in enemy hands. In fact, he was to keep those classified papers weighted, ready to be thrown overboard at a moment's notice.

The captain was also responsible for all financial and personnel matters on board ship and was authorized to instruct his purser to draw drafts either on the Department of the Navy or on Baring Brothers of London to meet necessary expenses of the ship. Dobbin called Sterrett's attention to the stacks of blank forms he had received; on one—the muster list—he was to ensure that the names and ranks of everyone on board were noted, as well as the terms of service of all enlisted men, and promptly send it back to the Department of the Navy. The captain was to deal with the men on board impartially, playing no favorites, and was directed to pay particular attention to the studies and moral development of the midshipmen. Sterrett was also required to encourage his officers in the active duties of their profession, affording them "occupation and excitement by exercises of the guns, clearing the ship for action, exemplifying the arrangements necessary in alarms of fire" and "all the maneuvers necessary to an efficient man of war."

The lieutenants and midshipmen of the *Decatur* were from families who had been able to exert the influence necessary to secure appointments for their sons. When the *Decatur* left Boston, Van Rensselaer Morgan was first lieutenant and executive officer, seconded by Lieutenant Aaron K. Hughes. Morgan was the commander's right hand, expected to act as the general manager of the ship. The first lieutenant, remembered one ship's boy, was "a terror to all

CAPTAIN.   MASTER.   CHIEF ENGINEER.

SERVICE DRESS OF THE UNITED STATES NAVY.

what we have is efficient, and should be strengthened by immediate and timely additions. We have not such a fear of the cry of "a standing army" as some profess, and we would like to have our army rendered more powerful by being increased at least one half more. War and trouble are often prevented by the existence of ample means to prosecute such affairs, if need be, to the extremest point. A foreign power, for instance, would hesitate to declare war, if their enemy was known to possess a large and efficient navy; whereas, if he was weak in this point, they would be less apt to hesitate at the outset. It may be amusing to some of our readers to have us give place in this connection to a sailor's description of a naval fight; for the regular routine of duty is as much set down and followed by rule, as that of the nicest mechanical operation. Assuming the advantage of the weather-gage, let us prepare for action. Topsails, top-gallant-sails, jib and spanker, with the courses hauled up, ready to be set again, are good sails

COMMANDER.   MIDSHIPMAN.   PASSED MIDSHIPMAN.

SERVICE DRESS OF THE UNITED STATES NAVY.

FIG. 6 This engraving from Gleason's Pictorial Drawing Room Companion shows U.S. navy officers in 1850s service dress—essentially, their shipboard working clothes. From Commander Sterrett to Passed Midshipman Phelps, this is the way the Decatur *officers were dressed on board ship. Courtesy Brown University Libraries.*

evil-doers and slovenly, idle fellows"; by another young man, as "omnipresent." It was vital that the first lieutenant command respect: "Good sailors like a strict and just officer," it was said. "Then they well know that everything will go on with system and regularity on board of such a ship." Morgan depended on the support of his fellow officers but the *Decatur* departed in such haste that only two lieutenants had joined the ship.[6]

Thomas Stowell Phelps, Francis Gregory Dallas, and George U. Morris were the *Decatur*'s "passed" midshipmen; that is, they had successfully sat for their examinations and were qualified to be promoted to lieutenant whenever a vacancy might open on the seniority list. They had entered the navy in 1840 and 1841 and were considered oldsters—"41'ers." They had learned their trade in the rigging and on the quarterdeck and had survived the gunroom's horseplay and practical jokes. Appointed before the opening of the Naval Academy, they had returned to Annapolis after years at sea to complete their required education. The 41'ers were men of the world, notorious for their high spirits. "Frank" Dallas, for instance, had fought a duel and been dismissed from the service; the *Decatur* was his first U.S. Navy ship after years of exile in the Germanic Confederation navy. Hughes, Phelps, Dallas, and Morris had attended the academy, and Sterrett and Morgan had not—they represented different generations in the service.[7]

The *Decatur*'s surgeon, assistant surgeon, and purser were warrant officers, as opposed to commissioned officers like the commander, lieutenants,
and midshipmen. They had not entered the navy as boys but chose to do so
as grown men, seasoned professionals in their fields. To gain their warrant,
each man was required to gather letters of recommendation and to pass written and oral examinations. Warrant officers were not trained in command,
but during the 1850s, surgeons and pursers fought to gain "equivalent rank"
with line officers and to receive the perquisites that would reflect their professional standing and years of experience at sea. Richard Jeffery was the *Decatur*
surgeon; John Y. Taylor, the assistant surgeon; and John J. Jones, the purser.
Jones was the ship's accountant, responsible for every aspect of ship finances,
and the medical officers supervised the health of the crew.[8]

As part of their medical duties, Surgeons Jeffery and Taylor were required
to inspect the ship's food and water, prepare reports for Captain Sterrett on
their quality, and "condemn" any food that was spoiled. They were to super-
vise the preparation of meals and certify that the cook worked with care and
cleanliness. At sea, ship's fare for enlisted men was made entirely from salted,
dried, or pickled foods, stewed in water that often had an "off" taste and
odor. Bureau rules allowed the crew fresh meat and vegetables four days each
week while in port but then required their return to seagoing rations, not
only for reasons of economy but to discourage overindulgence, which was
thought to endanger good health. In all climates, the men were to be allot-
ted a daily allowance of one gallon of water and were not permitted to drink
ship's water until "the mud and other impurities it might contain shall have
had time to settle." "Cleanliness, dryness and pure air" were held to be necessary to good shipboard health, and navy regulations required the washing of
clothes and bedding at least once every two weeks. The medical officers maintained the daily log of men admitted to sick bay, and they also kept journals
that described these cases in greater detail. Responsible for diagnosis and
treatment of a wide variety of illnesses and injuries at sea, the surgeons likely
brought their own medical books. However, each sloop of war's sick bay was
furnished with Wood and Bache's *Dispensatory,* the U.S. *Pharmacopoeia and
Formulary,* and the navy's formal list of diagnostic nomenclature.[9]

The apothecary was allocated according to the size of the ship, from schooner to frigate, but there were few anesthetics or antiseptics and, of course,
no antibiotics whatsoever. Naval medicine was bounded by the limitations of
antebellum medicine in general and the *Decatur* chest was carefully packed
with useless medications: ammonia, silver nitrate, mercury, sulfur, camphor,
zinc, antimony, olive oil, and myrrh. Quinine, digitalis, ipecac, and iodine

were useful; morphine, opium, and brandy were effective anesthetics and certainly helped to ease suffering. The surgical kit included amputation instruments, lancets, scalpels, trocars, and a hone to sharpen them all, as well as forceps, catheters, tourniquets, syringes, and a stomach pump. For bandages, the navy packed splints, muslin, flannel, and lint, and the ship carried ten trusses to ease the hernias so common on board ship. Sick men on the *Decatur* slept on mattresses and pillows, covered with clean sheets and blankets. The sick bay's "cellar" stocked ale, brandy, port, and sherry. Easy access to narcotics and alcohol tempted surgeons and their stewards, and medical officers were urged to choose men to assist them who were of "a respectable class [having] some knowledge of pharmacy and of industrious and temperate habits."[10]

The surgeons and the purser were the social equivalent of the line officers, and they shared the wardroom and its table. On board the *Decatur*—a small ship—there were four other warrant officers, who messed together separately from the wardroom; they had hard hands and a trade and were said to have "come in at the hawse holes" rather than up the gangplank. On a lower social plane, they were the ship's essential craftsmen. On the *Decatur*, the warrant officers included Boatswain Henry Bright, Gunner Thomas Venable, Sailmaker Augustus Warren, and Carpenter James Miller. Each had passed an examination in his trade and successfully served a year at sea in an acting capacity. Boatswain Bright was the sloop of war's chief sailor—the foreman, in a sense, of the crew; just as the first lieutenant was the captain's right-hand man, so the boatswain was the first lieutenant's. Gunner Venable was responsible for all military stores and took charge of the powder magazine at quarters and during action, and Sailmaker Warren was to keep the sails in good order. Carpenter Miller's responsibility was the upkeep of the ship's entire wooden frame: decks, masts, spars, booms, and hull. Each warrant officer was supported by a set of mates, petty officers whose work he directed.[11]

Petty officers were selected by Captain Sterrett and First Lieutenant Morgan in consultation with the warrant officers from the most experienced and trustworthy seamen. On board the *Decatur*, petty officers included the master at arms, armorer, coxswain, boatswain's mate, quartermasters, quarter gunners, wardroom steward, and captains of the forecastle, maintop, mizzentop, and afterguard.[12]

At first light, January 10, 1854, the receiving ship *Ohio* sent fifty seaman, twenty-nine ordinary seamen, fourteen landsmen, and five boys out to the *Decatur*; then, twenty-five marines came aboard, including officers and a drummer and a fifer. Phelps mustered the men in and entered their names into the ship's Logbook, as their officers eyed them speculatively. The *Decatur* was crewing up with men who had enlisted at the Boston rendezvous. Their officers referred to them as "the hands," "the people," and "the Decaturs." An experienced man-of-war seaman, a Jack Tar, was usually built small and wiry; Jack on land walked with the rolling gait he had acquired at sea. His white duck trousers were tight on his hips and hung loose at the legs, belling at the ankles; he tied a black neckerchief around his neck above his short blue jacket and wore his hat at a jaunty angle. In the 1850s, he likely had been tattooed with an anchor, star, or shield, perhaps a woman's name. His officers held Jack to be rough and skeptical, sensual and profane, superstitious, contemptuous of danger and risk, and eager to indulge his "everlasting adolescence." While reformers insisted that American sailors were responsible men who could look "beyond a grog-shop and a brothel," the old saying "The gallows and the sea refuse nothing" had staying power in the Old Navy, hungry for recruits.[13]

The Boston rendezvous lodged new recruits on the receiving ship until assignment to a warship. Each man had passed a physical examination, though its rigor depended on how well recruiting had been going. The recruit had to demonstrate that his hearing, vision, and speech were "good" and then strip naked for the surgeon, who directed him to "move about, exercise [his] limbs," to demonstrate "free use of them." He was to be rejected if he had tumors and rashes or admitted to epileptic convulsions, and the surgeons were to determine "as far as practicable" whether he had ever received a head wound, "which may produce occasional insanity," and reject such a man. Finally, the recruit was vaccinated against smallpox if his face did not exhibit the telltale scarring.[14]

Once men had passed the physical exam, the receiving ship officers had their work cut out for them to guard against enlistment of "improper, unsound or incompetent persons." They were to take care not to enlist any man "known to have been convicted of a felony" or any man who was drunk at the time of his enlistment. A few applicants were certainly hungover. Men who had never traveled farther from their homes than Grandpa's cornfield mustered Dutch courage to join a warship that would take them around the world to fight unknown enemies and to try their luck with the opportunities of the Pacific West. The Boston receiving ship contingent included one group of family members who surely pooled their last few dollars the night before, daring one another to enlist and toasting their exciting future at sea into the wee hours.[15]

Next, the receiving ship recruits were classified by rank. In 1854, ordinary seamen were required to have spent at least two years at sea, and seamen not only had to have four years' sea experience but also had to have passed an examination of their skills and knowledge. "A man's skill," wrote Richard Henry Dana, "is the chief test of his seamanship," and seagoing skill commanded respect. Robert Shorter, Sam Silk, and John Drew were seamen, able to "hand, reef and steer" and to cut, set up, and mend the ship's intricate sails and rigging, while ordinary seamen, like Robert Biddle and Ebenezer Cumberland, were still gaining proficiency in these shipboard tasks. Seamen earned better wages than ordinary seamen, and ordinary seamen earned more than landsmen, who were the unskilled laborers of the crew. Landsmen like Abijah Burbank and Thomas Johnson merely had to be strong enough to do hard work under direction. On board the *Decatur*, men were reclassified frequently, advanced as their experience grew and downgraded as punishment. However, Dobbin's initiatives to increase sailors' wages had not yet taken effect when the *Decatur* was crewing up at Boston, and sailors of every rank earned far less in the Old Navy than they would have on merchant ships.[16]

Enlisted men signed on for a three-year stint and were assigned to a particular warship. "Jack," an advocate protested, "wants to feel that he is looked upon as something more than a mere machine"—to feel that he was not just an interchangeable "hand." But in 1854, a sailor did not join the navy; rather, he joined the *Decatur*. The new recruit listened to the officer read the shipping articles; then, he signed his name if he could, or if he was illiterate, he made his mark and an officer printed his name for him. The sailor was given a small advance in pay so that he could outfit himself. He was to bring two blankets and a set of clothing, including one hat and one blue jacket, a black silk handkerchief, five pairs of blue trousers, five pairs of white linen trousers, five white shirts, and five blue flannel shirts, one pair of shoes, and five pairs of socks. These were to be "equal in quality to and of like fashion with that used in the Navy" and were stocked by shops within easy walking distance of the receiving ship.[17]

The navy faced a perpetual shortage of men, and every rendezvous rule was written to be bent, qualified with "if" and "unless." The *Decatur*'s crew offers good evidence for this. Although the recruiting articles specifically prohibited the enlistment of free blacks except with the approval of the commander of the station they were destined for, the *Decatur* shipped black seamen, such as Robert Shorter, without the permission of the commodore of the Pacific Squadron. Peter Karsten has noted that the navy at midcentury was making efforts to hold black enlistment to 5 percent of its total force. The *Decatur*'s surviving records do not provide the race of all hands, but three African Americans are documented to have been on board, and it is likely that there were seven or eight. Recruiting officers were also directed to turn away boys who were younger than fourteen and shorter than 4 feet 8 inches; in fact, every recruit under twenty-one years of age needed the consent of his parent or guardian, "if such may be found." Yet the rendezvous officer had only the recruit's word for his age or the location of his guardian. Likewise, no landsman older than twenty-five was to enlist unless he was skilled at a trade useful on board ship, and no landsman older than thirty-five was to be enlisted at all; yet one finds half a dozen landsmen on board the *Decatur* who were older than thirty-five. And, of course, unless an officer recognized a recruit, it was very easy for men to assume a new identity at the receiving ship.[18]

Dobbin's innovative honorable discharge had not yet taken effect, and many Decaturs gave false names or were given "purser's names"—on the *Decatur*, John Smith, seaman, hailed from France; Charles Mason, seaman, from Prussia; and Charles Brown, ordinary seaman, from the Netherlands. Men provided their names, ages, and places of birth and answered the officers' questions as best they could or as best they could pretend. It was nearly impossible to be certain where and when a man had been born, or whether he was a deserter or running from the police. If a sturdy boy was required to have the permission of his guardian but claimed that he was an orphan, he was unlikely to be rejected. And if a man claimed his name was William Smith and that he was twenty-four years old and born in Boston and had served on the frigate *Independence*, it was difficult to prove otherwise. Many seamen who joined the *Decatur* were dodgy characters of uncertain identity who had assumed an alias; as James Fenimore Cooper remarked in this chapter's epigraph, they were men of alibis.

However, the *Decatur* officers prided themselves on their ability to handle all kinds of men. There were plenty of two-fisted wise guys on every ship: insolent, quarrelsome, and dissolute. In the 1850 brochure "Naval Discipline and Corporal Punishment," a navy lieutenant described the average crew, from an officer's perspective:

> There are, of course, many very good men. . . . Then there is a middle class, who require close watching and punishing occasionally. . . . Then there is a third class: a set of lazy vagabonds, who would not be able to get a living anywhere but in a man-of-war; these are very frequently found to be refugees from justice. . . . without that stern justice and perfect command which the naval code requires, an American man-of-war would become a rabble, dangerous only to their friends and harmless to the enemy.

Phelps wryly described the crew of the *Preble*—a sister sloop of war to the *Decatur*—as including "a good proportion of ex-galley slaves, convicts, murderers, deserters from the British army, slavers and pirates . . . determined upon making matters lively aboard ship and deserting whenever they could." In 1854, the *Decatur* officers were confident they could apply "stern justice and perfect command" to shape their rabble into a crew.[19]

The *Decatur* muster roll and log give only the most minimal description of the enlisted men. The medical log and courts-martial records offer more information about sailors and marines who were seen by the surgeons or provided testimony during the cruise. Court-martial testimony clarified Robert Shorter's ethnicity, for instance: he was an African American seaman who was called as a witness in a summary court-martial. However, these records also clearly demonstrate the crew's uncertain identities. For instance, seaman John Peckham claimed on the Boston receiving ship and to the *Decatur* surgeons that he was born in New York, but he was actually born in England—the truth emerged at his court-martial. And veteran seaman Sam Silk also claimed to have been born in New York City, though he was born in Ireland. Of the *Decatur* seamen who acknowledged foreign birth, their homes ranged around the North Atlantic: England, Finland, Sweden, Denmark, Scotland, Ireland, and Canada; American-born seamen hailed from Louisiana, Maryland, Virginia, New York, and Massachusetts.[20]

Based on available evidence, the more unskilled the position on board the *Decatur* in January 1854, the more likely it was to be filled by an American-born sailor; and the more skilled the position, the more likely it was to be filled by a foreign-born sailor. Half the *Decatur*'s crew were foreign-born, but six of the *Decatur*'s seven most skilled seamen's jobs—the petty officer positions—were filled by foreign-born seamen. The captain of the foretop was from Finland, the captain of the maintop and the captain of the mizzentop were from Scotland, the captain of the forecastle was from England, the captain of the afterguard was from Denmark, and the captain of the hold was from Ireland. The ship's coxswain, however, was born in Baltimore. The ship's marine privates were almost entirely German or Irish by birth; their officers were American-born. The contingent of twenty-five marines included a drummer, a boy of fifteen from Washington, D.C. Of the rest, one each claimed to be born in North Carolina, New York, and Connecticut; seven were from Ireland and three from Germany. Of the ten marines whose place of birth is unknown, the surnames Friedburgh and Barkenfeldt suggest German origin, and the surname Reilly suggests an Irish one.

By the time Captain Sterrett took command of these men, the *Decatur* was no longer the sleek greyhound that Farragut had put through its paces at Rio. By 1850s standards, the ship was designed broad in the beam and built heavily, to take the recoil of the carronades on the main deck. As the *Decatur* put to sea, one officer considered the ship "short and stumpy," clumsy sailing against wind and tide. Now classified as a third-class sloop, the *Decatur* was an aging warship and the victim of shoreside chicanery. Overhauled at a cost of $12,400, the *Decatur* was cynically pronounced "in good condition for three years" although dry rot of spars, planking, and deck bracing was clearly visible to the trained eye. Rather than sailing "in good condition," decay continued to spread throughout the ship, weakening every structural member.[21]

Towed by a small steamer, the ship slipped from the buoy and headed out, anchoring in Nantucket Roads. During the afternoon watch, Passed Midshipman Francis Dallas noted that the crew was busy preparing for sea and being assigned their stations for working and fighting the ship, their messes for eating, and their spaces to sling their hammocks on the berth deck. They were sizing each other up, sizing up the officers, and sizing up the ship.[22]

The *Decatur* sailed at dawn on January 13, 1854, to join the search for the *San Francisco*, out into a winter storm. As the ship pitched and rolled in the wild ocean, sheets of icy rain swept through the rigging, turning to sleet, then snow. The raw crew worked the ship under shouted orders, making and unmaking sail and tending to the rigging. The men's sweat soaked their clothes from the inside, the sleet from the outside. The deck was icy, and the ship's movements were dramatic and unpredictable. The new hands were seasick, bruised, and scared, and they did not know one end of a rope from another. Every tool became a weapon, and every loose line, whipped by the wind, became a lash. The sea was limitless and gray, great waves crashed over the deck, and the air was white with driving snow. During the first dogwatch at sea, from four to six in the evening, the men in the crew who were not too seasick to eat had dinner and grog. Captain Sterrett ordered an extra tot for the crew, to "splice the main brace," as it was put. Then, they went back to work.

After four days weathering the storm, keeping a sharp lookout, and finding no survivors or wreckage, the *Decatur* encountered the mail steamer *Alabama* and sent a boat to gather any news of the lost ship. The *Alabama*'s crew had spotted some floating planks and barrels and part of a lifeboat. The *Alabama* and the *Decatur* never found any survivors from the *San Francisco*, and the warship soon learned that the search had been called off. The *Decatur*'s errand of mercy turned into a shakedown cruise, and Sterrett and Morgan completed their selection of petty officers, confirming some acting positions and filling others. Under the boatswain, the captains of the tops, the boatswain's mate, and the quartermasters were the *Decatur*'s best seamen. One quartermaster stood behind the helmsman and conned the ship, directing its steering; the other quartermasters acted as lookouts. The boatswain's mate helped the boatswain in his duties and, like him, wore a whistle to relay quarterdeck orders. As the crew practiced the everyday exercises of manning the boats, heaving the lead, knotting and splicing lines, rowing, mending sail, and loosing and reefing sail, they sorted themselves out from the least skillful landsman to the most skillful seaman. The ship's elite were the topmen, who handled the topsails and royals of the fore-, main-, and mizzenmasts, "in readiness to jump aloft and make or take in sail" under all conditions, one hundred feet above the deck. In nineteenth-century naval fiction, these aristocrats of merit were nature's gentlemen: capable, noble, and intelligent. The forecastle men were responsible for the anchors and the bowsprit, and the afterguard tended the

FIG. 8 *The* Decatur *mounted only eight carronades a side, but this view of a larger U.S.*
warship under sail gives a sense of the sloop of war's guns and open deck, with its masts,
rigging, capstan, and wheel. Harper's Monthly *July 1871. Courtesy University of*
Washington Libraries Special Collections, UW 27975z.

mainsail and spanker sail and the lines at the ship's stern. The waisters were burly landsmen who pushed the capstan—"the rag-tag and bob-tail of the crew." Sorted by various stations and duties, the Decaturs practiced maneuvers described in the log as "bringing ship to anchor," "setting the flying jib," or "boxhauling the ship." The new men learned the way of life at sea, and in time, they came to "know the ropes."[23]

The Decaturs were trained not only to sail the ship but also to fight enemies on sea and shore. Each massive carronade was tended by a gun crew, which included a gun captain, rammers, spongers, men to haul the tackles, and a powder boy. The great guns were exercised sometimes with powder and sometimes in "a sham-fight with an imaginary foe." The gun carriages were run out by the side-tackle men, who helped the gun captain to raise or lower the gun's angle with handspikes, to get a better aim at the target. The powder boy carried a lidded leather bucket filled with cartridges from the gunner down in the powder magazine up to the gun. Stationed at their guns, the crew was said to be "at quarters," and mustering to quarters took place twice a day on the *Decatur*. The men also drilled with small arms from muskets to cutlasses at target practice and in mock battles with one another.[24]

While practicing the skills of sailing and fighting, the ship's company also learned shipboard discipline, enforced by the marines. In battle, the marines were placed as sharpshooters in the fighting tops and formed landing parties for beach actions, but they also acted as the ship's everyday police force. Melville wrote, "What standing armies are to nations, what turnkeys are to jails, these marines are to the seamen in all large men-of-war," and, he continued, hostility between the groups was cultivated by the officers in a divide-and-conquer strategy. Another sailor wrote that the seamen "cordially hate" the marines, toasting "A messmate before a shipmate, a shipmate before a stranger, a stranger before a dog, but a dog before a soldier." *Decatur* master-at-arms Ephraim Davis, a petty officer, assisted the marines in their disciplinary capacity and was responsible for those in confinement. By profession an informer, the master-at-arms was, according to Melville, the one "whom all sailors hate" and should be careful on dark nights, to beware a murderous, falling marlinespike.[25]

In principle, the sloop of war was a dynamic structure, powered by the wind and enlivened by disciplined human action. Like the hull, masts, sails, and rigging, the officers and crew were a set of disparate forces held in tension; on command, they had to work together as an intricate mechanism to respond reflexively to orders shouted in a battle or a tempest. The *Decatur*'s officers represented the navy's authority as navigators, strategists, disciplinarians, and taskmasters and gave the orders that were passed down the ship's line of command to coordinate each crew member's every action at work and at war. Everyone had a job, and every man and every thing had its place in this organization, held in delicate balance by discipline.

On Sunday, January 22, 1854, the crew was mustered, and Purser John Jones read aloud the rules of discipline—the Articles of War. Most had been written in 1800 and were based on the Royal Navy's own rules, and they remained the laws that governed this wooden world and its men:

> Every officer or other person belonging to the Navy who shall not do his utmost to take or destroy any vessel which it is his duty to encounter . . . shall on conviction thereof by a general court-martial suffer death. . . .
>
> If any officer or other person belonging to the Navy, shall disobey the lawful orders of his superior officer, or strike him . . . he shall on conviction thereof before a general court-martial suffer death, cashiering, or such other punishment as the said court shall adjudge. . . .
>
> If any person in the Navy shall make . . . any mutinous assembly, or shall utter any mutinous or seditious words . . . he shall on conviction thereof suffer death or such other punishment as a general court-martial shall adjudge. . . .
>
> If any person in the Navy shall in time of peace desert . . . he shall on conviction thereof suffer such punishment as a general court-martial shall adjudge.
>
> If any person in the Navy shall through intention, negligence, or any other fault, suffer any vessel of the Navy to be stranded, or run upon rocks or shoals . . . he shall on conviction thereof by a general court-martial suffer death, or such other punishment as the said court shall adjudge. . . .
>
> If any person in the Navy shall quarrel with any other person in the Navy, or use provoking or threatening language or gesture, he may at the discretion of the captain be punished . . . or brought before a court-martial.[26]

At sea, the Decaturs crowded into a small ship, living on rations, disciplined in every act, governed by an inflexible routine, working in a rigid hierarchy, and trained to follow orders with unquestioning obedience. The nineteenth-century wooden warship, observed James Valle, was "crowded almost beyond endurance," and each man found a small measure of privacy only in his own hammock, creating to his best ability his way of getting along. Back at the receiving ship, the promise of regular grog, a full belly, and reliable pay convinced many a jobless recruit to go to work on the *Decatur*. But for some men, it turned out to be "low pay, bad food, dangerous work, sexual frustration, primitive health facilities and savage discipline." There was no escape at sea—desertion was impossible and acts of desperation were crimes. Some men thrived in the seagoing life: they enjoyed their skilled work, the hearty camaraderie, and the strange and wonderful sights by day and night. They found congenial messmates, bowed to shipboard discipline, and shrugged their shoulders at their officers' caprice. Maybe they welcomed their meager pay, doing the sum over and over again of what they would be due when their hitch was up. Maybe they liked working the great guns, practicing loading, aiming, and firing, getting better and faster. Maybe they enjoyed the "three squares" because they had eaten far less on shore. Maybe they dried out on board, held to two drinks a day. Maybe they saw a real doctor for the first time in their lives. Men learned their duty, made their enemies and friends, and made their plans: perhaps to desert at San Francisco, perhaps to save money and go back to Boston. Some men made their peace with life on board the *Decatur*. Some did not.[27]

The officers came to know one another, too, and learned how to live together, under every circumstance. The captain had his own quarters on the *Decatur*; the officers each had a tiny sleeping space to call their own and shared the common wardroom, eating meals prepared by the wardroom cook from their own stores. Some of the *Decatur* officers were congenial: Master Phelps, Surgeon Jeffery, Assistant Surgeon Taylor, and Purser Jones seem to have gotten along particularly well. Every ship carried a well-thumbed library, but the officers also shared their personal books with one another. Though gambling was strictly forbidden on the ship, officers played friendly games of cards while discussing general topics or chatting about their families. Each officer was "to be regarded as a gentleman" and to behave toward his fellow officers "as well-bred gentlemen in society": no one was to discuss religion, women, or politics in the wardroom. Custom and discipline were as essential to officers as to enlisted men. Especially as sectional differences intensified back home, Surgeon Jeffery from Virginia and Master Phelps from Maine would have been foolish to discuss the Kansas-Nebraska Act. Lifting their glasses to the memory of Stephen Decatur, to their country right or wrong, the *Decatur*'s officers drank a toast together each evening. But the wardroom was a very small world to share with one's officer messmates, year in and year out, as "my country right or wrong" became an increasingly ambiguous and troubling phrase.[28]

While the men learned their jobs and learned to live together, the *Decatur* sailed south, for warmer weather and smoother sailing—"to thaw out," as Surgeon Taylor put it. Everyone looked forward to visiting his first foreign port.[29]

4

Episode 1. Through the Strait of Magellan

"Off to Californio!"

From Liverpool to Frisco a-rovin' I went,
For to stay in that country it was my intent.

Blow, boys, blow,
For California, O!
We're bound for Sacramento
To dig the yellow gold.

Oh the times are hard and the wages low
Oh leave her, bullies, leave her
I guess it's time for us to go
It's time for us to leave her.

On January 28, 1854, the *Decatur*'s lookout sighted Tortola, in the Virgin Islands, and the ship anchored that afternoon off Saint Thomas. After learning of a local outbreak of cholera, the *Decatur* filled away for Santa Cruz (today known as Saint Croix). Here, at Frederickstad, the Decaturs went on their first liberty, and the officer of the watch logged the ship's first liberty disciplinary action when landsman William Coleman and seamen Robert Knox, Daniel McKinnon, and George Williams took "French leave," failing to return on time after running into town from the market boat. Recaptured, they were brought back to the *Decatur*. On board, seamen Charles Mitchell and Patrick Welch got drunk on smuggled liquor.

Those men and a few others were punished in Santa Cruz, but when the *Decatur* sailed, six other men sat glumly in irons under the forecastle, bound for a general court-martial to be convened at Norfolk.[1]

Everything began late on the night of January 30, 1854, with the disciplining of John Barlow, one of the five ship's boys. The boys were to be instructed in making sail, sewing canvas, exercise at the great guns, making musket cartridges, reading and arithmetic, and the basic use of nautical instruments. Attention was to be paid to their moral training and self-discipline, to encourage young American seamen to remain in the navy. Boys under twenty-one were forbidden liquor in the navy, but that had proven impossible at Santa Cruz.[2]

The ship was at anchor on a soft, warm night. Johnny Barlow was drunk and noisy and refused to obey Lieutenant Morgan's order to quiet down. Instead, Barlow addressed "contemptuous, disrespectful and obscene language" to Morgan. Nearly everyone on board was drunk on liquor smuggled from shore or stolen from the ship's spirit room. Morgan was ill with chronic bronchitis and too sick to be on watch; perhaps he was unable to sleep because of the noisy carousing. Morgan irritably ordered Gunner Venable to chain Barlow in double-irons until he sobered up. As Barlow was being confined, he yelled out, "I am one of the boys; come along, the rest of you!" Barlow was one of the ship's boys and also "one of the boys" in another sense, in that he was part of an extended family on board the ship. His appeal to "Come along" to his relatives and friends from home was the first step to mutiny. Venable ordered marine private John Downey to help him subdue and confine Barlow, not realizing that Downey was himself "in liquor." Instead, Downey tried to free the boy, struggling with Venable. Lieutenant Morgan then ordered Downey to be confined, too. The marine resisted violently, yelling, "I'll be damned if there are men enough on board this ship to put me in irons!" Downey fought hard, kicking Master-at-Arms Ephraim Davis in the testicles. Other witnesses testified that Davis himself was drunk. It took eight men to wrestle Downey down and lock him in irons.

When Downey was finally confined in irons on the wardroom hatch, he yelled, "Now is your time; go it!" A group of angry, drunken seamen had gathered near the mast; they seemed filled with menace to Lieutenant Morgan, who ordered them to move along, to go forward. Morgan feared that the "gang who was following [Downey] up to the mast" would band together, free Downey and Barlow, and take the ship. The lieutenant ordered Downey gagged, to shut him up. Ordinary seaman Samuel Kays yelled at Morgan, "If it were not for the marines, you would not have it all your own way; there are men in the ship who have not spoken out, but they will yet!" In the commotion, other officers on board rushed from below to the deck.

Robert Biddle was one of the "gang" who tried to free young Barlow, exclaiming, "Barlow is a cousin of mine! I'll be damned if I will see him treated like a dog!" At the mast, the mutineers brawled with loyal sailors and marines, as the officers hung back. Kays punched ordinary seaman Dennis McCarty for "siding with the officers." Biddle struck Master-at-Arms Davis in the face and knocked him down. Lieutenant Morgan contemptuously told Biddle that he was a "mutinous scoundrel" and threatened to run him through with his cutlass. Biddle replied loudly—addressing the crew at large—"I for one am ready to step out," declaring himself, Morgan stated, "boldly as a mutineer." Marine sergeant Charles Corbin agreed, later testifying that Biddle's "manner was mutinous" and that the crowd of sailors gathered around the mast intended mutiny. Morgan ordered the marine guard to wade in and capture Biddle and double-iron him, lashing him down to the deck, but marine private Samuel Taylor refused the lieutenant's order to move against Biddle, the second marine to join the mutiny.

The drunken men were shouting and fighting; the ship was spinning out of control. Seaman John Drew said something to Morgan on the lines of "God damn you, you sickly son of a bitch! You're not man enough to do more than order your marines to chain a boy!" At that, Morgan commanded Sergeant Corbin to have the loyal members of the marine guard fall back and form up on the quarterdeck, face forward, and load their muskets with live cartridges, each man having five rounds. Under threat of death, order was restored to the *Decatur*.[3]

Two weeks later, the crew subdued and apprehensive, the *Decatur* entered Hampton Roads and received a local pilot to take the ship in to moorings at Gosport Navy Yard, off Norfolk, Virginia. The general courts-martial began on the following day, on board the flagship. A boatload of witnesses left the *Decatur*, including Lieutenant Morgan, Master Phelps, Assistant Surgeon Taylor, Gunner Thomas Venable, Carpenter James Miller, Sailmaker Augustus Warren, marine sergeant Charles Corbin, marine private George Hitchins, and five seamen and marines: Ephraim Davis, Peter Ritchie, Archibald Sprague, Charles Powell, and Dennis McCarty. A captain, two commanders, and four lieutenants presided over the general court-martial trial of the six accused men. The *Decatur*'s purser, John Jones, acted as judge advocate.[4]

The court asked Lieutenant Morgan whether there appeared to be any organization among the ship's crew to resist the proper authorities of the ship. Morgan replied that "four or five men acted in concert to resist being put in irons . . . three of them seemed to act together and make common cause." When asked whether Biddle and the others were drunk, that is, whether this was anything more than just "a drunken row," Morgan maintained that they were *not* drunk and that they had "set at defiance the legal authorities of the ship." What happened at Santa Cruz was a mutiny, Morgan claimed, thwarted only by the threat of death.

The deliberations were swift and the sentences heavy, read aloud throughout the fleet as a warning. Ship's boy John Barlow pled guilty to charges of treating his superior with contempt by addressing Morgan with disrespectful and obscene language. He was sentenced to irons on board the receiving ship off Norfolk for six months, to work as a sweeper with ball and chain, to forfeit his grog and tobacco, and to half pay.

John Drew, seaman, was also charged with treating his superior with contempt, specifically, addressing contemptuous and profane language to Morgan. He pled guilty and threw himself on the mercy of the court, explaining that he had only been a short time in the U.S. Navy and that he was drunk at the time and regretted what he had done. The court sentenced him to confinement in the cells of the Navy Yard at Norfolk until the *Decatur* sailed. Once back on board, Drew was to be deprived of grog and tobacco for six months after the ship sailed.

John Downey, marine private, was charged with mutinous conduct and thus was on trial for his life. He pled not guilty. The Articles of War, which had been read aloud on board ship, defined a mutineer as one who "shall make . . . any mutinous assembly, or shall utter any mutinous or seditious words, or shall conceal or connive at any seditious or mutinous practices." Downey was found guilty and sentenced to nighttime solitary confinement in the Navy Yard prison and to work during the days wearing a ball and chain. He was to receive no pay, grog, or tobacco and to be "disgracefully discharged" at the end of his term of service.

Samuel Taylor, the other marine private, pled guilty to disobedience of orders. He was punished by a reprimand from Captain Sterrett before the entire crew and then was transferred to the Navy Yard prison for six months of daily drills and no pay.

Richard Biddle, ordinary seaman, was also charged with mutinous conduct and contemptuous and profane language, and he pled not guilty. Of all the men accused, he was the only one to hire an attorney to represent him. The court found Biddle guilty and deliberated whether or not he should be executed. Their vote split five to two against execution, and Biddle was instead dismissed from the navy and sentenced to ten years at hard labor in the District of Columbia penitentiary. Biddle could not write his name; he made his "X" mark on court documents.

Samuel Kays, ordinary seaman, was tried for mutinous conduct and contemptuous and profane language, the same charge as Biddle. Kays pled guilty and asked for leniency, saying: "I have only been in the service five months and have never been on a man-of-war before. I did not really understand the importance of my conduct. I was under the influence of liquor at the time and I remember nothing but a mischievous disposition to join in the row, as a good frolic. I did not know what mutiny was. I had never heard the articles of war except when they were read by Purser Jones on board the *Decatur* the Sunday before, and I was so far forward that I heard very little of them." Kays was sentenced to five years hard labor in the penitentiary, a sentence later reduced by presidential order to one year. Less than a month after the *Decatur*'s recommissioning, six drunken enlisted men and marines had made common cause against the officers. As Paul Gilje points out, sailors depended on one another for their very lives in the everyday work of the ship and developed a common identity. In port, freed from responsibility, liquor encouraged them to throw off the seaborne roles set by naval discipline and defy order and authority. On March 3, 1854, the sentences, signed by Secretary of the Navy Dobbin, were read aloud to the *Decatur*'s crew and solemnly entered into the Logbook.[5]

The officers were brisk and matter-of-fact about the courts-martial as the ship was prepared for distant duty in the Pacific Squadron. A new executive officer, wealthy South Carolinian Edward Middleton, reluctantly joined the ship to replace the ailing Lieutenant Morgan, who remained on board. Off Norfolk, the Decaturs ran in the guns and scrubbed the ship, while gangs of caulkers, riggers, plumbers, and painters from the Navy Yard completed the work left unfinished at Boston. The hold was stocked with everything needed to cruise to the new station. The hands loaded brooms and saucepans, lanterns and candles, soap and shoe polish. They loaded eighteen looking glasses, fifty tin pans, and five hundred pounds of soap. They loaded a new chronometer and spyglasses, a barometer, and two hydrometers. And they loaded barrels of salt beef and pork, flour and rice, sugar and raisins, mustard and pepper, pickles and tea, boxes of butter and cheese, bushels of dried beans and ship's biscuit, and gallons of molasses, vinegar, and whiskey. And the ship was stocked with weapons, balls, and powder.[6]

The men, too, were being prepared for distant duty—they had been through a short cruise, in storm and out, and through a crisis. If they had not known what it meant to be under orders as sailors in the U.S. Navy, they knew now. Off Norfolk, Sterrett continued to prepare them for situations they might meet in the Pacific. The divisions were exercised at the great guns, running them out and often firing them at targets afloat in the bay. The sailors practiced with small arms and with cutlasses. They were inspected at quarters at least once a day. The *Decatur* was ready for duty, but the ship did not receive orders to sail south, and the monotonous weeks wore on.

To drunken men in a Boston tavern, the navy had seemed like an adventure and the Pacific West a tantalizing destination; the next day, on the receiving ship, it was too late to turn back. But the long stay in Norfolk gave the Decaturs time to think things over as they looked at the same shore, day after day. Some men successfully deserted in Norfolk, too angry or discouraged to continue a three-year enlistment. They took the risks of desertion: being captured, tried, convicted, and given a heavy sentence. Among many examples, on March 14, Abijah Burbank deserted from the dinghy at Norfolk; on April 29, John Short deserted from the gig; on May 10, John Lewis deserted from the dinghy. Desperate seamen came up with ingenious schemes to abandon the *Decatur*. John Wilson tried to disappear into Norfolk while on liberty but he was captured and punished with confinement. Back on board, Wilson pled illness, and Surgeon Jeffery compassionately requested his release from irons and ordered his transfer to the Navy Hospital at Norfolk on May 1. Within the week, news came back to the ship that Wilson had deserted from his hospital bed, escaping through the window. He was never recaptured.[7]

William Fletcher was so desperate to leave that he tried swimming to shore from the ship. The *Decatur* sent a small boat to haul him out of the water and bring him back on board. A week later, Fletcher was in confinement late one night when he asked to be unchained so he could go to the head. He eluded the marine sentry, who was asleep on duty, and hid on the ship. Perhaps he meant to try to swim ashore again. The entire crew was called to quarters and ordered to search the ship. Fletcher's hiding place was eventually found, and he was once again confined in double-irons, as was the unfortunate marine who had dozed off and allowed him to escape. On April 16, the *Decatur* anchored farther out to make desertion more difficult. Civilian authorities became involved when Captain Sterrett publicized cash rewards for local policemen who apprehended "the men found on shore without leave." Among others, Benjamin Lewis was brought back to the *Decatur* by two Norfolk policemen, who claimed the reward.[8]

The officers were eager to put to sea and remove the men from shoreside temptations. The three-month delay was never satisfactorily explained, and Passed Midshipman "Frank" Dallas complained in his journal of this "long and most extraordinary" confinement under "sailing orders," unable to take shore leave. Finally, in late May, Sterrett was directed to prepare for sea, and the *Decatur* observed a ritual of departure, auctioning the belongings of deserters to their shipmates. Two days later, the commodore of the Home Squadron, Charles Morris, came aboard for a final inspection of the ship, officers, and crew and to observe their precision and speed at their drills.[9]

Even after several last-minute additions to the crew from the receiving ship, the *Decatur* was shy of its full complement. Sterrett requested the return of landsman William Coleman and seamen Robert Knox, Daniel McKinnon, and George Williams from confinement on the flagship. They had all tried to desert, either at Santa Cruz or at Norfolk. And mutineer John Drew was brought back on board, too. Certainly, Sterrett would have preferred not to bring these troublemakers and malcontents on board, but he needed them. However, the captain made every effort to replace his gunner. Gunner Venable had resigned while the ship was at Norfolk, and his replacement, Robert Stocking, had been "repeatedly drunk on duty" and was actually under medical treatment on the *Decatur* for the "consequence of his intemperance" when Sterrett wrote to Secretary Dobbin, appealing for a replacement. Likely, Stocking was suffering from delirium tremens, withdrawing from a heavy debauch, but no gunner was to be had. Stocking—and his problem and his bad example—remained on board.[10]

Commander David Farragut visited the ship and dined in the *Decatur's* wardroom. As he rose after dinner, he said, "Gentlemen, you have here the finest little ship in the Navy." Once Farragut was on his way to shore, one of the *Decatur* officers remarked, "I suppose you all know the secret of Farragut's partiality for this boat. The *Decatur* was the first command he ever had." Someone else recalled the sloop of war's halcyon days, in the early 1840s, at Rio. Farragut's visit represented a benediction and a promise. He, too, would soon be on his way to the Pacific West, as commandant of the new navy yard at Mare Island, in San Francisco.[11]

Finally, the men hoisted in the small boats, crossed the topgallant yards, and made final preparations for sea. On June 16, 1854, at dawn, the pilot came aboard and the crew heaved up the anchor and got under way. With a last hurrah for port, Edward Norris and Thomas Cooper had gotten drunk on smuggled liquor and were confined in irons when the *Decatur* headed out. Once out of the harbor, the *Decatur* made full sail on the open sea, heading south. The following day, the lookout spied the wreck of a merchant vessel, stern out of the water—the *Cicero*, out of Beauport—and the crew wore the *Decatur*. For two hours, the gun crews practiced firing at the wreck. It was exhilarating. At sea, finally bound for the Pacific, headed south to catch the trade winds, the *Decatur* left behind the dull routine, make-work, and binge-ing of port. Master Phelps plotted the ship's course using Lieutenant Matthew Maury's charts in *Explanations and Sailing Directions to Accompany the Wind and Current.*[12]

Outward bound, the *Decatur* entered the routine of everyday life at sea. The warship's day began at dawn with "holystoning" (sanding), then sluic-ing and drying the deck. The two ship's watches stood alternating four-hour stints round the clock, except for the two two-hour dog watches in the eve-ning that staggered the duty. Each watch set lookouts, checked over the ship stem to stern, conducted meteorological measurements, and logged the *Deca-tur*'s speed. The flag was hoisted every morning and lowered every evening. Throughout the day and night, the bell was struck for each half hour in the four-hour watch (i.e., from one to eight bells). The men sailed the ship, per-formed the round of chores that kept the paint and rigging looking "ship-shape," and practiced exercises of seamanship or mock combat. They could be called to quarters at any time to deal with an emergency, but that ritual usually began and ended the workday. In the early-evening dog watches, discipline relaxed. Then the men could "skylark" on deck or in the rigging, arm-wrestling or racing each other up to the fighting tops. Some men reread letters from home; others carved ivory and wood or stared off to the horizon, dreaming. Sometimes, there was music and dancing; an officer remembered a song from this period:

> And thus in a snug man-of-war, did I say,
> With a cook to attend me and make me sea-pie;
> With my half pint of whiskey to drink every day,
> How sweet could I live, and how calm could I die.

Each evening, the ship's drummer beat the tattoo, which meant lights out for the enlisted men. The officers could keep the wardroom lamps lit until ten at night, reading and talking together.[13]

Sailing southward, this routine was broken by meals, high points of the day. In 1843, the navy ration had been established for "the people," and those rations were still in force. Daily, the menu included two servings of grog for those enlisted men over twenty-one who did not turn the liquor back and keep the money. One day, the ration for each man could be a pound of salt pork, served with half a pint of stewed dried peas or beans. Another day, the ration was a pound of salt beef and half a pound of flour, the flour made into a glutinous pudding sweetened with molasses and studded with dried fruit.

FIG. 9 *In a daily ritual, an officer looks on as sailors holystone and swab the deck of a U.S. Navy man-of-war in this 1858 engraving, from Charles J. Peterson's* The American Navy. *This ritual opened each naval day. Peterson borrowed this image from J. G. Heck, whose* Pictorial Archive *was published in 1851. Courtesy University of Washington Libraries.*

Or the menu might be a pound of salt beef and half a pound of rice and two ounces each of butter and cheese, together with fourteen ounces of ship's biscuit. Each day, every man was to receive a quarter pound of raisins or dried apples; he was entitled to two ounces of sugar and an ounce of coffee or cocoa or a quarter ounce of tea. And each week, he was due half a pound of pickles, sauerkraut, or cranberries, half a pint of molasses, and half a pint of vinegar. It took a gifted cook to turn these staples into tasty meals, and the cooking duties passed around each mess; most suppers at sea were likely more filling than appetizing.[14]

Life on the *Decatur* cycled through the ship's routine and the rhythm of the rations. The warship was beautiful, as men looked up at the towering pyramid of white canvas or out along the shining deck. Sailing through clear, warm weather, the *Decatur* sped south at eight knots on some days and whispered along at three knots on others. The sea, remembered one naval officer, was the "great physician," curing the diseases and cares of land, as time seemed to slow and then to stop. The voyage became hypnotic, almost timeless. Men were humbled by the arch of pure blue over their heads and the spread of blue sea to every horizon, entranced by the hiss of water cleaving back from the bow and the endless wake to the past.[15]

The amateur naturalists on board the *Decatur*—Phelps, Jeffery, and Tay-

lor—delighted in their observations of the sea. They were familiar with Charles Darwin's *Journal of Researches into the Geology and Natural History of the Various Countries Visited by the H.M.S. Beagle,* published in 1839. Just as Darwin carried Humboldt, so did these naval officers carry Darwin. On this cruise south, Taylor shared Darwin's enthusiasm for flying fish and noted in his journal that they really *did* seem to fly, not just skim from wave crest to crest. "They lead," he wrote, "a precarious existence, pursued by larger fish in the water and pounced upon by fish-eating birds in the air," concluding in the spirit of the age, "thus the order of nature appears to be, that all living creatures shall prey upon each other."[16]

When the *Decatur* entered the Gulf Stream's "mighty river" in the ocean, Phelps brought gulfweed on board to examine under the ship's microscope. Phelps, Taylor, and Jeffery eagerly netted dozens of sea creatures to study, with help from the crew. An unnamed sailor reached overboard to grab a Portuguese man-of-war and "received a shock which completely paralyzed both hand and arm, producing intense pain . . . nearly a week elapsed before the limb recovered." One imagines some members of the crew good-naturedly sharing the officers' interest and others hanging back, silent—baffled or annoyed by these bizarre hobbies.[17]

On July 4, the ship beat to quarters at noon and fired a salute to mark the anniversary of the signing of the Declaration of Independence. That afternoon, wrote Taylor, the Decaturs celebrated with "several occurrences, not mentioned in the log." "Such refreshments," he continued, "as could be produced were sampled early and often, as long as they held out," by the officers.

Exocœtus volitans.

The enlisted men celebrated by splicing the main brace. On the following day, Taylor, likely nursing an aching head, wrote with regret, "Merriment can be often excused, excess never."[18]

Then, topman Israel Purdy made an error in judgment that entered the Logbook—in hauling down the head yard, the fore royal yard was broken in two because Purdy kept the lee brace fast, not releasing the tackle that held the yard in place. The crew brought down the broken yard and the tangle of rigging and canvas. But a few days later, the main topgallant yard cracked, and this time, no one could be blamed. Seven months out of Charlestown Navy Yard, Carpenter Miller jotted the ominous note in the Logbook that the *Decatur*'s upper yards were shot through with dry rot and were too weak to withstand much strain.[19]

The *Decatur* entered the doldrums, becoming enchanted: "a painted ship upon a painted sea." Slowly making for the equator, the *Decatur* ghosted south in very light winds, the tedium relieved by a series of spectacular sunsets. Phelps and Dallas noted in the Logbook the daily appearance of stormy petrels and whales, their boyish delight apparent. At night, the moon rose

FIG. 11 *In an uncharacteristic flight of fancy, Surgeon John Y. Taylor depicts the* Decatur *under full sail sharing the scene with a flying fish in the Atlantic, both headed south to Rio. Courtesy NARA.*

over the dark water, edging the swells with white light, and the very sea shivered with pale green and silver phosphorescence. Day after day, the *Decatur* was utterly alone and nearly still; even for experienced sailors, the solitude was profound. For new men, the vast ocean was like nothing they could have ever imagined. Then a "monstrous shark" began to circle the ship, a long, dark, sinuous threat. The old hands grumbled, sharing the superstition that when "a shark follows a vessel at sea, it is a harbinger of death on board," and the new seamen grew fearful.[20]

Then, Phelps, charged with management of ship's stores, made what Taylor called "a hideous discovery": two tanks of drinking water had been filled with salt water straight out of Boston Harbor. On anxious inspection, many wooden barrels of drinking water loaded at Norfolk were found to be contaminated with salt or vinegar. The barrels had either once been filled with brine and carelessly reused, or the barrels had actually been filled with salt water to save time and effort. Or perhaps the water had been stored under barrels of salt meat which leaked into the drinking water. This was serious business. The crew consumed nearly two hundred gallons of water each day; by August, the *Decatur* was down to less than two weeks of water. Becalmed or blown off course, the ship could easily run out. The orders went out instantly to reduce the water ration and to put up sailcloth to funnel rainwater into barrels during any squalls.[21]

On August 3, 1854, Taylor faced his first crossing of the equator into the Southern Hemisphere, a rite of passage marked with traditional ceremonies, and like other greenhorns on board, he expected the typical rough hazing: "This night," he wrote, "we cross the line, and if Neptune comes on board, woe is me." Would he be shaved with a rusty iron hoop? Have a tub of salt water thrown over his head, in a harsh baptism? Two officers who had already crossed the line planned the prankish ceremony, aided by the experienced seamen, and a delegate visited Captain Sterrett's cabin. But, asked whether "the captain would be pleased to receive a visit from His Majesty [Neptune] on board the good ship *Decatur* tonight," Sterrett declined with a salty response that would have made "Neptune's ears tingle, if he ever heard it." The *Decatur* had recently experienced a mutiny; perhaps Sterrett did not want to permit a rowdy ceremony of manhood that was "a grotesque satire on institutions and roles of power." There was no equatorial initiation on the *Decatur*, but once across the line, the ship's crew shared a new identity that bound them together. They were "shellbacks" and "sons of Neptune," initiates who had crossed the equator and learned the way of life on board the warship.[22]

In August, the weather turned rainy, and the quarters below became hot and humid. The ship encountered dozens of sperm whales, and former whalers in the crew managed to harpoon a porpoise so that the crew could have a "fish" feed. The officers were amused by sailors who stoutly insisted they would rather eat salt meat than fresh fish, a choice as typical of Jack Tar as his tattoos. The following day, the *Decatur* met a fishing fleet of flimsy, agile catamarans far from shore. The ship's old salt, Irish seaman Sam Silk, remarked to Dr. Taylor, "Them catamarans, sir, can sail right in the wind's eye." The officers were able to buy a dolphin from the fishermen, to dissect and then to eat. When the weather cleared, the crew aired their hammocks and bedding and washed their clothing. At night, the stars wheeled in the sky and meteors traced arcs beneath the Southern Cross, as familiar constellations passed away to be replaced by new fields of light. Taylor noted that Humboldt had written that nothing had ever so thoroughly disoriented him as looking up to see unfamiliar constellations in the nighttime sky.[23]

In the late afternoon on August 26, a "brilliant and beautiful Brazilian butterfly" flew along the deck but could not be captured. The following day, the *Decatur* anchored off Rio de Janeiro, joining men-of-war from all nations. The *Decatur* conducted the rituals of greeting and honor expected of a sloop of war of the U.S. Navy on arrival in a foreign port. The frigate *Savannah*, flagship of the Brazil Squadron, was in the bay, and the *Decatur* saluted Commodore William Salter with thirteen guns. Then the *Decatur* hoisted the Brazilian flag at the fore and fired twenty-one guns, returned gun for gun from the fort. The French rear admiral visited the *Decatur* from his ship *Andromeda*, and so did the English commodore from the *Madagascar*. Both were honored with salutes, a tour of the ship, and dinner on board.[24]

Finally, Commodore Salter came aboard the *Decatur*, received with all due ceremony. Salter climbed on board to an honor guard of eight side boys (crewmen standing at the gangway) and was welcomed by all the ship's officers in full-dress uniform. The marine guard paraded and presented arms, the drummer gave two ruffles, and the commodore inspected the ship. Salter then went below to dine with the *Decatur*'s officers on the best food and drink they could offer.[25]

Meanwhile, the *Decatur*'s crew prepared for liberty in Rio de Janeiro. The storeship sent aboard dozens of shaving brushes and shoe brushes, as well as one hundred pairs of new blue trousers. The Decaturs went watch by watch on shore to Rio, one of the best liberty ports in the world. Afterward, the usual round of punishments began: marine corporal Coon was confined in double-irons for unspecified "disgraceful conduct," and dozens of sailors and marines were punished for drunkenness, disobedience, and "French leave" (failing to return from liberty on time). Having been confined to the ship for the past two months, the Decaturs went on a spree. Sterrett was forced to sweep the port for laggards and bail one of them out of jail. He wrote an apologetic note to Secretary Dobbin acknowledging the delay in leaving harbor, pleading the "unexpected embarrassment, arising from the imprisonment of one of my men." The *Decatur* stayed in port at Rio de Janeiro for nearly a month. The ship's crew pumped out the salt water from the tanks and filled them with fresh. Lieutenant Morgan was invalided out from the ship and sent aboard the *Savannah*. At Rio, the *Decatur* added six new seamen and loaded beans, molasses, pork, pickles, whiskey, and cheese from the storeship.[26]

The U.S. *Massachusetts* arrived on September 9, also bound for duty in the Pacific Squadron. Sterrett and the war steamer's commander, Lieutenant Richard Meade, decided to cruise together and make a joint attempt to pass from the Atlantic to the Pacific through the Strait of Magellan. The *Decatur* was towed out of the harbor by the *Massachusetts* on September 21, 1854; once at sea, the steamer cast off the hawsers, put out the fires, hauled up the propeller, and lofted its sails. Both ships sailed southward together. But the following afternoon, they were separated in a sudden violent storm, and the *Decatur*'s lookouts could not spot the *Massachusetts* in the morning. The *Decatur* sailed on alone.[27]

During a break in the weather, the officers announced promotions among the crew: landsmen to ordinary seamen, ordinary seamen to seamen, and seamen to vacant petty officer positions. Francis Purcell was promoted to captain of the forecastle; John Gray to captain of the foretop. Lewis Wart and John Davis, who had joined as landsmen, were rated as seamen, and David Johnson was promoted from ordinary seaman to seaman. Each man earned a raise in pay, noted by the purser. Everyone's safety depended on the seamen's skill as the *Decatur* plowed south through storm after storm, pitching so violently that both ship's thermometers were broken. But the ship sometimes flew with the wind—on October 2, the *Decatur* raced south, making an exciting ten knots hour after hour.[28]

Three weeks out of Rio de Janeiro, the weather cleared and the lookouts sighted Cape Virgin, Patagonia, far to the southwest. Hoping to meet up with the *Massachusetts* and to let any nearby ship know of their presence, the *Decatur* fired the guns, burned blue lights, and sent up a rocket. But the steamer was nowhere to be seen. Sterrett had to decide whether to wait for the steamer, return to Rio, round Cape Horn, or go ahead and thread the strait without the *Massachusetts*. He made up his mind to go it alone.[29]

Sterrett's orders were clear: to join the Pacific Squadron "with all practi-

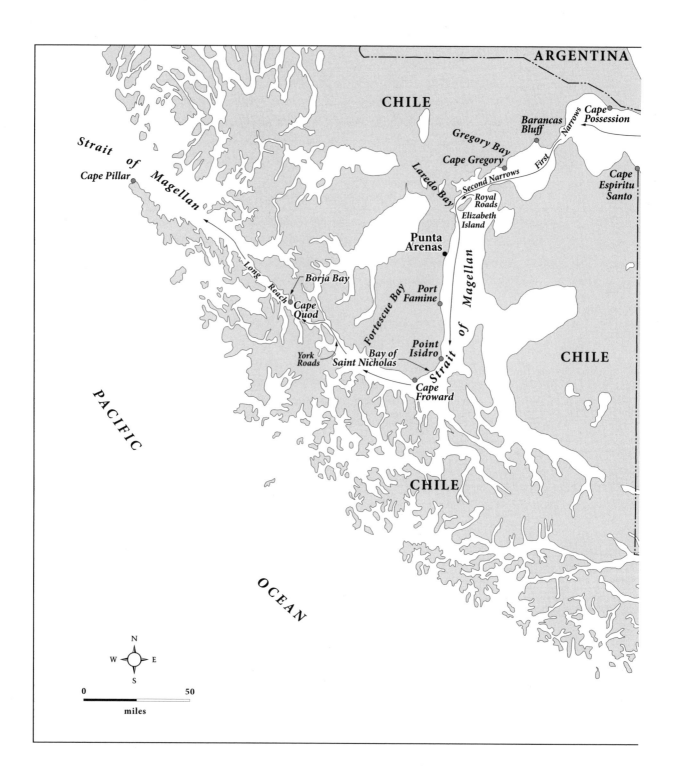

ARGENTINA

CHILE

Barancas Bluff

Cape Possession

Gregory Bay

Cape Gregory

Strait

of

Cape Pillar

Magellan

First *Narrows*

Second Narrows

Royal Roads

Elizabeth Island

Cape Espiritu Santo

Laredo Bay

Punta Arenas

Long Reach

Borja Bay

Cape Quod

Port Famine

Fortescue Bay

Strait of Magellan

York Roads

Bay of Saint Nicholas

Point Isidro

Cape Froward

Strait of Magellan

CHILE

PACIFIC

OCEAN

CHILE

N
W · E
S

0   50

miles

ATLANTIC

Cape Virgin

Strait of Magellan

OCEAN

ARGENTINA

Map 2. The Strait of Magellan

cable dispatch . . . , touching at Rio de Janeiro for supplies, taking care that no more time is lost for this purpose than is absolutely necessary." Though Sterrett later justified his course to the squadron commodore as a carefully considered choice that went unpredictably awry, Phelps only halfheartedly defended his captain's decision. According to Phelps, Sterrett's orders stipulated that he should "afford exercise and excitement to those under him," a tongue-in-cheek misreading of those original orders, which expected the "exercise" to involve no more than practice at the normal work and drills on board a man-of-war.[30]

Isaac Sears Sterrett was a peppery, old-school naval officer whose pride and confidence were well known in the service. When Sterrett commanded the *Reefer* during the Mexican War, a midshipman from a large line-of-battle warship was rowed over in the ship's launch, which was nearly as long as Sterrett's little gunboat. The midshipman casually stepped over the freeboard onto the schooner and was rebuked by Sterrett, "in no very gentle tone," and reminded that there was a *gangway* to this vessel, sir! He expected his ship to be respected, whatever its size. And Sterrett had brought along his son as his clerk on the *Decatur*, and doubtless the teenager and the ship's venturesome officers enjoyed the audacious notion of following Magellan's storied path to the Pacific. The *Decatur* would have been the first ship of its class in the U.S. Navy to successfully sail the strait from east to west, a great distinction.[31]

It is possible, too, that one of the officers shared around his copy of Benjamin Bourne's brand-new novel, *The Captive in Patagonia, or Life among the Giants,* a rousing adventure tale of a young man (supposedly Bourne himself) with "gold fever" who was sailing on a schooner from New Bedford to California through the strait but was captured by Patagonian Indians. While Bourne's Patagonia was colder and grimmer than Melville's Nukuheva, the captive also found Native women who loved trinkets, whose men misused them, and who "would be very comely, if only cleanly, and content to leave nature less strenuously adorned" with paint. After an improbable stint as an American Scheherazade, Bourne escaped to sail through the Strait of Magellan and return to his pursuit of "high golden hopes" in the Pacific West. Whether or not the *Decatur*'s officers were boyishly intrigued by this tantalizing tale, the sloop of war sailed south, alone.[32]

Within sight of Cape Virgin, a gale blew up, increasing "to a furious storm, without a cloud in the sky." The wind, Surgeon Taylor noted, was described by the officer of the deck as Force 11. Force 12 was hurricane strength, and there was no Force 13. Then clouds raced into the sky, and rain, hail, and snow drove horizontally across the deck with blinding force, as men cupped their mouths and noses to breathe. Towering waves followed one another so rapidly that the *Decatur* could not recover from one before a second and third were upon the ship. Under close-reefed topsail, the *Decatur* was borne over to a "terribly dangerous degree," once completely on the beam-ends and in danger of capsizing. Then, the storm passed as quickly as it had arrived, and the ship continued to sail along the shore, followed by half a dozen albatross. The sky was leaden; the air very cold. Relieved and exhilarated by their baptism of fire, the officers confidently proclaimed the *Decatur* "an admirable sea boat."[33]

The ship rounded Cape Virgin on October 13 and entered the eastern entrance of the Strait of Magellan, a narrow, curving channel more than three hundred miles in length that funneled wind and weather eastward. Everyone hung over the rail, "greedily viewing" the scenery of this desolate land, so strange to men familiar with the verdant coasts of Ireland and Virginia. This shore looked stripped and dead; there seemed to be no vegetation on the gray rocky ground sweeping up to hills which rolled away to craggy mountains, black in the distance. Throughout the day, the officers exclaimed over huge columns of fog that rose from the highlands forming Cape Espiritu Santo, named by Magellan for this phenomenon. The *Decatur* passed Cape Possession and anchored to await the flood tide, which reached twenty-seven feet in the First Narrows—the strait's tides and currents were ferocious. Later, sailing with the tide and a light breeze, the sloop of war passed ranks of solemn, observant penguins and anchored two miles off Barancas Bluff; over the next few days, it traveled on to Cape Gregory and then into and through the Second Narrows. The *Decatur*'s adventure in the Strait of Magellan seemed to be going rather well, and the officers congratulated one another.[34]

Through the spyglass, they spotted the remains of Royal Navy captain Philip Parker King's observatory on the highest point of Cape Gregory. In 1826, King commanded an expedition to explore the coast in the ship *Adventure,* and those explorations were continued in 1831 by Captain FitzRoy in the *Beagle,* accompanied by Charles Darwin. Here the Decaturs first glimpsed guanacos—"an elegant animal in a state of nature," as Darwin described these wild llamas. A *Decatur* party went ashore and Taylor noted numerous guanaco skeletons, their skulls crushed and the brains extracted. He also observed horse dung and the molelike rodent that Darwin—and Taylor—called tuco-tuco (*Ctenomys magellanicus*), which sounded like it was grunting "tuco-tuco" while digging its underground burrows.[35]

After a month in the ship, the Decaturs enjoyed stretching their legs on

Off "Cape Fairweather", coast of Patagonia. Oct: 11ᵗʰ 1854.

FIG. 12 *On October 11, 1854, the* Decatur *encountered a fierce storm off Patagonia's Cape Fairweather, north of Cape Virgin. The Philadelphia doctor, on his first cruise, captures the huge seas and flying wrack of the storm, as the ship struggles under stormsails to keep from foundering. Courtesy Beinecke Rare Book and Manuscript Library, Yale University.*

shore. Taylor and a companion had strayed far afield when they heard the recall gun fired from the ship. They ran for the beach and found the whole party waiting for them, "thoroughly fatigued by the exertions of the day, after a month's confinement on board ship." The wind and waves were rising, and Taylor had to be carried "ignominiously" through the rough water to the cutter by the boat's crew. The doctor wrote that his muscles ached for three days but that he was the "proud, envied and only possessor of a guanaco skull, complete and perfect in every respect." Also here at Cape Gregory, the Decaturs caught several albatross; Taylor remembered a "magnificent specimen with breast white as the driven snow, resting complacently on the waves very near the ship." Brought on board for study, the birds were avoided by seasoned sailors as harbingers of bad luck; they snapped "their great bills viciously at all who came near."[36]

On October 15, the *Decatur* was slammed by another furious gale, "almost a hurricane," but the sky was again perfectly clear and the sun brightly shining. This surreal weather was typical of the strait but seemed unnatural to men born and bred in the Northern Hemisphere. Taylor reassured himself that this very same sort of storm hammered the *Beagle* in Gregory Bay, as described by Captain King in his 1839 narrative. Two days later, as soon as the weather moderated, a "well-armed hunting excursion" was rowed from the *Decatur* to the Patagonia side of the strait. The party brought an empty barrel to set up on the beach for the ship's gun crews to use for target practice. The plan was that once the shore party saw the American flag hoisted at the fore, they were to expect a bombardment and be well away from the landing site. But Taylor, who was in the landing party, joked that they were nearly killed, having to race away down the beach from the premature shot howling through the air. Once out of range, they turned to beachcombing, and the "rage for collecting" swept the officers. Some of them then climbed up the bank to "see what was to be seen." Hiking a mile inland, Taylor found that Patagonia was "not quite so barren as a distant view would seem to indicate." It was October—the Patagonia springtime. Low, springy green plants covered the earth, and Taylor observed a beautiful, fragrant flower growing on the sunny side of a steep bank.[37]

The *Decatur* officers hunted to "gratify the sportsman's thirst for blood and feathers" and occasionally bagged game good for the pot. Seals and otters inhabited every cove along the strait, and there were tens of thousands of seabirds of every sort. Dallas shot snipe, plover, and wild ducks, but there were rhea ostriches, guanacos, tuco-tucos, and large rabbits, at all of which the *Decatur* hunters fired in vain. At the first sound of their guns, a noisy

Cascade at Borja Bay.

②

bird—"the first class nuisance called the teru tero (*vanellis cayanus*)"—inevitably flew up, screaming shrilly to alert the game and swooping down to harry the hunters. Darwin had disliked this bird, which disturbed his observations, as much as the *Decatur* officers disliked it for disturbing their hunting. On one such foray, Taylor's companion—likely Purser Jones—gathered a beautiful light blue egg of the South American ostrich, *Rhea americana,* to take home as a souvenir. "Here," he exclaimed, "this is just what I want!" and put it in the pocket of his overcoat. The egg, having been "exposed for an indefinite period to the sun and rain of Patagonia," soon burst, unleashing a terrible stink in a coat that had to be worn day in and day out.[38]

The *Decatur* very slowly tacked southward and westward. The ship entered Royal Roads, settling down to a few days of snow squalls, and then moved to a more sheltered moorage northeast of Elizabeth Island. As soon as the weather moderated, the hunters and collectors headed for shore, spotting the steamer duck, which Phelps described as a "diminutive penguin" that struck the amateur biologists as swimming just like "a miniature side-wheel steamer divested of her smokestack" and that impressed the sailors with "marvelous" speed—as much as fifteen knots. Though they were difficult to catch and kill, two steamer ducks were bagged and prepared for the wardroom dinner, but their flesh proved too rank to eat.[39]

The Decaturs were not alone in this place; they had seen evidence of human beings on shore. Though wild, the Strait of Magellan was no wilderness. The officers noted distant fires on shore by night and found animal skeletons marked by human tools. Inland, they had strayed upon plains of grass where fires had been set and later quenched, apparently with intent. Finally, on October 19, the Decaturs met the people living in the eastern strait. A group went ashore and built a large fire on the beach for warmth. One who went exploring alone looked up to lock eyes with a half circle of silent Patagonians on horseback. The officer backed away and ran to the beach. Phelps noted that the area "was said to be inhabited by the most ferocious tribe in southern South America, in whose veins mingled the blood of both the Patagonian and Fuegian races." The *Decatur* officers were eager for further encounters out of scientific interest and sheer curiosity, but they wanted to be in a position of power.[40]

The anchorage northeast of Elizabeth Island proved excellent. The island itself was nine miles long, with freshwater springs. Mussels grew in huge black masses in every cove and were pronounced by "the gourmet of our mess" to be equal in flavor to those back home. The island moorage had sheltered other crews. Exploring, one of the *Decatur* officers found a board inscribed in

Chilian colony at Punta Arenas, Straits of Magellan.

FIG. 14 *Taylor has drawn the* Decatur *at anchor in the bay off Punta Arenas, the Chilean penal colony; the gig heads to shore to visit the gloomy little settlement. From the John Y. Taylor Sketch Books, Western Americana Collection, Beinecke Rare Book and Manuscript Library, Yale University.*

heavy pencil, "From San Francisco, Bound to Rio, Jno. Baker Master, 152 days passage, *B.B. Swasey*, 1851." Baker had been headed east, the easier direction, and his three-year-old marker on the stony shore was a reminder of the loneliness of the *Decatur*'s pursuit.[41]

Painfully working their way onward, always sailing into the wind and making about three miles each day, the *Decatur* entered Laredo Bay on October 24, 1854. The northern shore here was heavily wooded, undergrown by low holly with bright yellow flowers. But west of this oasis, the scenery on both sides of the strait "began to assume the characteristics of Tierra del Fuego"—rugged tablelands, then up past bold cliffs to distant snow-covered mountains; some glaciers came right down to the water, beautifully blue in their shadowed folds. Wooding and watering parties on shore picked up lignite, which the Decaturs called "Patagonia coal" and which made a smoky, hot fire. A flash of insight struck Surgeon Taylor that one day "a line of steamboats" would pass steadily through the Strait of Magellan as though it were a manmade canal, carrying freight between the great oceans. And since sailing vessels would always find the east-to-west navigation "uncertain and tedious and unprofitable," the American steamers of the future would burn Patagonia coal. Taylor was impressed by the strait but he was not overawed by it, and he suggested its integration into the growing maritime empire of the Pacific West, the world of Young America.[42]

The *Decatur* sailed into the harbor of Punta Arenas, Chile, on October 27, 1854. The "Chilean Settlement," as the Logbook described it, seemed at the windswept end of the world. The town numbered about eighty residents—the governor, the commandant and his wife, soldiers, artisans, the priest, and a small population. The settlement included a stockade, chapel, storehouse, smithy, carpenter's shop, and several primitive dwellings. The *Decatur* officers found the inhabitants to be "wretchedly poor." Punta Arenas residents raised goats and pigs but their vegetable gardens did not thrive in the inhospitable soil and climate. The town was supplied once a year from Valparaiso; when the *Decatur* was there, the colonists were anxiously awaiting the supply ship, long overdue. Desperate settlement residents bartered any souvenir the Decaturs might want for tobacco, sugar, or shoes, turning down their money as useless.[43]

The *Decatur* remained at Punta Arenas for three days. The settlement was dark, cold, and mysterious; Taylor was at first told that a few residents had been convicted of crimes in Chile, but he soon learned that "the actual truth is that this is just a plain penal establishment." The commandant, Captain José Gabriel Salas, had been at Punta Arenas for five years and was married with two small children—Senora Salas confided in Taylor that her life there was "very, very sad." The settlement governor, Jorge Schysthe, was Danish by birth, and the *Decatur*'s officers found him a pleasant gentleman, "cut off from civilization by thousands of miles of howling wilderness and stormy ocean" in an unexplained exile.[44]

Taylor joined the settlement doctor on his rounds, saddened by the settlement's misery; the inhabitants "seemed," he wrote, "destitute of all ambition and all hope." In one hut, a crippled man stretched on the ground beside a fire over which a pot of gruel simmered, while two emaciated children and two ragged women sat nearby. "Yet even here was the abode of gentle hearts," wrote Taylor, as the family made the doctor a small present when he left. But why, he wondered, did they not help themselves? Why did they not take a good axe and build log cabins like "the pioneer settlers of the western frontier?" American westward expansion offered a model, the Philadelphia doctor thought, to regenerate the world.[45]

The most desirable trade articles brought down to the Chilean settlement from the Patagonian interior were guanaco robes. The Patagonians hunted the guanaco with stone bolas: two or three heavy stone balls joined by strong leather thongs. In San Francisco, guanaco robes sold for fifty dollars each, wrote Taylor, but "the most fastidious member of our mess" disdained them, choosing instead a dramatic black and white cloak made from skunk skins, paid for with a "lavish expenditure of tobacco." The robe was the only one of its kind in the settlement, a magnificent thing. And it smelled fine in the chill outside air. But once it had warmed up for a few hours, "you could tell what it was made of without seeing it," reminisced Taylor, chuckling. The beautiful cloak was banished from the wardroom.[46]

Governor Schysthe boarded the ship, honored by the Chilean flag at the fore and a thirteen-gun salute. Invited to dine with the officers, the governor soon became ill with seasickness as the *Decatur* pitched in the chop. Then a gale arose during the afternoon that made it impossible for him to return to shore, and the poor man was forced to stay on board all day, sick as a dog. In the evening, the gig that took him to shore was swamped in the rough surf off Punta Arenas, and some oarsmen nearly drowned.[47]

Schysthe requested from Captain Sterrett "a large supply" of food, as well as seventy fathoms of heavy rope, tacks and screws, and seventeen pounds of cast steel. And the governor also asked Sterrett for "that uncertain and dangerous weapon, a Jenk's carbine," with plenty of ammunition. Perhaps he feared for his life. The governor's predecessor had been killed in a raid by Tierra del Fuegian Indians, or so it was said; but just before the ship left, someone, likely the settlement doctor, confided to Surgeon Taylor that the previous governor had actually been murdered in a convict uprising. No Patagonian utopia, Punta Arenas seemed full of lies.[48]

The Decaturs weighed anchor and sailed away on October 31, beating for two anxious days against head winds that drove snow into their faces. The ship was unable to find a nighttime anchorage and struggled around the clock, as watches of exhausted men succeeded one another. Finally, off Port Famine, the *Decatur* found snug harbor: driftwood, drinking water, and some game. They stayed for three days. Port Famine bore a terrifying name and it was a gruesome spot, marked by the blackened ribs of an ancient ship. The hopeful Spanish had created the settlement of Port San Filipe here, where nearly four hundred colonists starved to death in the 1580s. Seven years later, Captain Thomas Cavendish carried away one survivor, and Captain Andrew Mericke rescued the last in 1588, who died en route to Europe. In the ceaseless wind, the officers visited a small cemetery; the graves had been torn apart and human bones littered the ground. A second group of ruins at Port Famine was of an abandoned Chilean penal colony. And it was here that the officers and crew of the *Beagle* quarreled with Fuegian natives, who found the food, clothing, and instruments of the expedition irresistible. Darwin related a story of the encounter—the *Beagle*'s great guns fired inland to frighten the Fuegians away from the shore encampment. Watching through his glass, Darwin described the natives, more than a mile distant, throwing stones at the ship in response, "as a bold defiance" to the cannon in a kind of mimicry. But no matter how hard they threw, their stones did not reach the British ship.[49]

In this desolate place, John Jeunesse, who had shipped at Rio on August 29, deserted from a watering party on November 2. His shipmates told the officers, "He strayed away and did not come back." Jeunesse left behind his water bucket and disappeared, wearing the clothes on his back. The men believed that he was heading back to the Chilean settlement, a place that the officers found unbearably dreary, almost beyond words. Whatever Jeunesse experienced in the Chilean settlement at Punta Arenas, he preferred it to life on board the *Decatur*. The ship did not sail back to track him down—Sterrett let him go.[50]

And then reminisced Phelps with relish, the *Decatur*'s struggle to survive *really* began. After Port Famine, the ship fought southward through "thick weather, heavy rains and fierce squalls," slowly clawing past Point Isidro and into the Bay of Saint Nicholas, seven miles east of Cape Froward. The cape loomed up ahead, drifting in and out of cloud and squall, a grand, high, abrupt promontory forming the southernmost tip of the continent, the dividing point between Atlantic and Pacific. The extreme variability of the weather struck Phelps. Within the space of two hours, one could be driven by howling winds through a violent sea, struggling to keep the ship afloat and stay alive, and then turn into another channel and "find oneself becalmed." Once past Cape Froward, the *Decatur* slowly tacked northwestward between squalls. During breaks in the weather, the scenery was austere: "sharp snow-capped peaks rising many thousands of feet above sea-level," as Phelps put it, "standing in bold relief against a leaden sky." On clear, calm afternoons, the officers continued their shooting, sightseeing, and botanizing jaunts, while the men wooded and watered the ship. On November 7, Surgeon Taylor and Purser Jones went ashore for an hour's quiet hunting and encountered a large puma. Jones raced out of the brush and down to the beach to leap into the cutter, leaving behind his overcoat, likely the one the ostrich egg had burst in. Taylor kidded Jones about his misadventures: the purser was "an enthusiastic and singularly unsuccessful sportsman."[51]

Beating in for an anchorage in Fortescue Bay, the *Decatur* was blown out into the strait by a "furious williwaw." The ship spent a terrifying night battling wind and current in "inky blackness," wearing every few minutes to avoid the rocky shores. The wind howled through the rigging, blocks slammed into the masts, and the whole vessel groaned with strain. Men hauled themselves hand over hand on the manropes, along the wet and slippery decks. The risk was absolute: if the *Decatur* ran aground, the ship would be beaten to death, the crew tossed into the wild sea and smashed on the rocks. Those who made it to shore would be shipwrecked, living on mussels, crabs, and steamer ducks, terrified of the Fuegian Indians. Thirty years later, Phelps wrote feelingly of this night, running blind, battered by the wind and rain, in which "many years of anxiety [were] crowded into a few hours time."[52]

On November 10, 1854, the *Decatur* anchored in Fortescue Bay. In the log, Phelps judged the best anchorage to be "on the northwest side, within about two or three cables length from the shore, in seven or eight fathoms of water." The site was sheltered from the prevailing winds, and offered abundant drinking water and firewood, as well as mats of "fine, large, delicious mussels." Spider crabs "of unsurpassed delicacy" were hiding in the kelp, measuring more than three feet across, each one yielding, according to Phelps, the meat of about four dozen Chesapeake Bay crabs. The *Decatur* would become familiar with the advantages of Fortescue Bay, retreating five times to its safety, beaten back by weather and wind.[53]

In November, the Fuegians had begun to follow the *Decatur* in their canoes, at a distance. But in Fortescue Bay, men rowing one of the ship's cutters first

Beating round Cape Froward.

FIG. 15 *Taylor's drawing of the* Decatur *in the Strait of Magellan, beating against contrary winds around Cape Froward, the southernmost tip of South America. This "turn" in the strait was abrupt and dramatic. Courtesy NARA.*

encountered "some natives of the Tierra del Fuego side" paddling their canoe. As the two small boats approached one another, Taylor described the Fuegian family: one man, two women, two children, and three dogs. The women carried their infants suspended in a pouch from their shoulders, leaving their hands free to tend the precious fire kept burning on every canoe the Decaturs saw in the strait. The American sailors admired these canoes built of bark and splints, with sharp prow and stern, constructed with skill and ingenuity. After this first face-to-face encounter at water level, the Fuegians and Decaturs became interested in one another. There was time to meet and stare, to barter and try to communicate. The *Decatur* officers followed their authorities in their observations of these Native people. Robert FitzRoy, captain of Darwin's ship, had considered the Fuegians "satires upon mankind" and characterized them as "ill-looking" with "villainous expressions" and referred to "she-Fuegians, by courtesy called women." Following Darwin's verdict that the Fuegians were "stunted, miserable wretches" who he could scarcely make himself believe were "fellow creatures," Phelps agreed that the Fuegians were a "diminutive, miserable race, occupying the lowest scale of humanity," and Taylor wrote that he, like Darwin, was embarrassed to be "constrained to acknowledge, sadly, that they [were] human beings."[54]

To the American ear, the Fuegians did not really have a language. Again echoing Darwin, the Decaturs were struck by what they considered the Fuegian powers of mimicry; soon they were hearing the words "ship," "captain," "tabac," and the names of some *Decatur* sailors. The Decaturs, in turn, learned that a Fuegian canoe was a "chirouk," an arrow a "kip," and a "picalilly" was a child as well as a dog. They never heard the word that Darwin had written as "yammerschooner" and that he had heard so often and reported as meaning "give me." Bourne's adventurous captive had noted that the Patagonians referred to their bitter enemies, the Fuegians, as "Yamaschoners."[55]

The Patagonians rode horses; the Fuegians rode canoes. Taylor believed that the Fuegians were cannibals who ate their Patagonian enemies as well as missionaries and stranded sailors. The Fuegians lived in the strait, he wrote, for the simple reason that they could not get away. Taylor saw these people shaped by a "constant struggle for subsistence and existence; cold and hunger and the hostility of their neighbors [who are] their ever-present and implacable adversaries." Taylor may have been referring to Darwin's tentative notions of natural selection in the *Beagle* journal that would inform the revolutionary *Origin of Species,* published in 1859. The American officers were at times unsure how to understand their encounters with the Fuegians: they described them with pity and contempt but occasionally with grudging admiration for their ability to survive in this harsh and unforgiving place. One day, Taylor was out exploring alone and ran across some Fuegians spearing fish at the mouth of a small stream. A duck flew in and the surgeon shot it down "to the unbounded admiration of the natives," who claimed the bird: "the meat for themselves, the bones for their dogs and the feathers for the picalillies." But Taylor wanted to keep his bird. The arrival of a boat's crew saved the day for Taylor when one of the sailors knocked down a Fuegian man and recovered the duck. "The stricken savage," wrote Taylor, "with blood in his eye, sullenly retired into the bushes to nurse his impotent rage." On reflection, Taylor was ashamed of himself and the Decaturs. He wrote that the Fuegians depended on the mussels, the fish, and the ducks for their very lives, and "we never molested them again in their claim."[56]

These encounters were interesting diversions for the Decaturs, inching through this endless passage. But initial friendliness faded to suspicion as the natives "became a little too familiar" and begged constantly and stole occasionally. The Fuegians seemed to have no compunction about theft but Taylor was not inclined to call for a preacher. Indeed, he did not think missionaries should come here at all. He considered it the "acme of impertinent interference" to "go among a people with a religion of their own, which has satisfied them and answered all their purposes, generation after generation, to try to convert them to some other creed for which they care not at all." However, the Fuegians showed signs that missionaries may have visited them. On one occasion, a canoe came alongside the *Decatur* bearing two Fuegian women: one was sobbing as if her heart would break, and the other said, "Picalilly, picalilly," pointing to the sky. The Decaturs were mystified, but after a number of repetitions, "an irreverent and unsympathetic Jack" explained to his shipmates, "She means that the picalilly has gone up the spout," meaning that the woman's child had died and its spirit had ascended heavenward. Taylor dismissed her behavior as a begging device and recounted the incident in his journal principally because he was amused by the old salt's caustic interpretation.[57]

The officers continued their anthropological observations. Fuegian men stood about five feet tall; they wore their black hair long and straight and painted their faces with a reddish pigment. The Fuegians dressed in pelts with the fur side against their skin and lived in wicker huts covered with animal hides. To the *Decatur* officers, the Fuegians seemed to have "no general or tribal government" but were organized instead by families, one family per canoe. The women handled the "menial labor," and the men, the hunting. The Fuegians, the officers observed, prized their hunting dogs above all else.

"John Decatur".

And although the Fuegians—"these Indians"—were peaceable toward the Decaturs, violence always lay at the edge of their encounters.[58]

The only Fuegian invited on board the *Decatur* was the head of a family, apparently a man of consequence. Out on the open deck, he "drank several pots of tea with great gusto and devoured salt beef voraciously." The ship's crew dressed him in "full tog": in an officer's old coat with brass buttons, pants too long, the first shoes he had ever worn, rings on his fingers, gloves on his hands, and a high plug hat—"the *tout ensemble,*" wrote Taylor, "was irresistibly comical." They dubbed him John Decatur, and he clapped his hands for joy, continued Taylor, and laughed aloud. The old man's teeth chattered with cold or excitement, but after he had sniffed the whiskey offered to him, he refused it, "the first and only instance on record where a savage man has

FIG. 16 Here, Taylor sketched the only surviving shipboard drawing of the Decatur, *as sailors and officers gather to mock "John Decatur," dressed in motley. The Indian's family looks on from the gangway, and the Fuegian canoes are in the middle distance, each with its precious cargo of fire. Note the carefully coiled rope and the carronade to either side of the gangway. Courtesy NARA*

ever been known to decline a drink of 'firewater,'" according to Taylor. Then someone fetched a mirror and showed him to himself, and he laughed louder than ever. A man who had seen his face reflected in still pools along the shore, as part of the world, now saw himself reflected from a looking glass, framed and isolated. To the Americans, he "saw himself" for the first time; they had provided the context for his self-knowledge as the butt of their joke.[59]

Every encounter between these strangers was characterized by misunderstanding: the Decaturs continued to struggle against wind and tide that the Fuegians thoroughly understood. Yet the officers and crew mocked their visitor, tricking John Decatur out in motley, a fool who was barely human. Perhaps the cruel joke was Taylor's idea; Darwin described a similar situation on board the *Beagle* in which a Fuegian admired his new haircut and European clothing in a looking glass. Taylor's drawing of this encounter is the only representation we have of life on board the *Decatur*, and it depicts a rare shared experience between officers and men. They stand at midships, laughing, the officers to one side and the hands to the other, briefly united in derisive amusement at John Decatur. Soon, the Fuegian native left the ship, still wearing his seaman's clothing, and the officers "shipped their quarterdeck faces again."[60]

Nearly every day, the *Decatur* ventured out to tack westward, struggling to make York Roads, but time and again, the ship retreated to the safety of Fortescue Bay. It was not always possible to get back. Caught out late at night on November 26, Captain Sterrett, "under the influence of a presentiment and much to the surprise of all," ordered the sails to be struck. At once, the *Decatur* was staggered by a sudden, hard squall, as though the ship had been punched by a huge fist, "one of the most terrific squalls I have ever experienced," wrote Phelps. The solid mass of rain that fell was "stunning and bewildering": the ship trembled under its weight and water jetted out of the scuppers. Then wind screamed through the rigging, threatening to snap the yards from their masts, and the *Decatur* "rushed madly" back up the strait. The officer of the watch called all hands, rousing up the sleeping watch to come on deck and fight to keep the ship running before the wind in the pitch dark. Under fore storm staysail, with close-reefed main topsail and double-reefed main foresail, the *Decatur* sped through a blur of rain and sleet "while the officer at the conn prayed for a glimpse of the land or daylight." When morning finally dawned, the *Decatur* had been driven thirty-seven miles in less than three hours, back in the direction from which the ship had come, losing many days of patient westering.[61]

Sterrett later wrote that the real trouble began here, when "heavy westerly gales" drove him back time and again to Fortescue Bay, where he "expected daily to see the *Massachusetts*." Sometimes, the *Decatur*'s lookouts spotted lights to the east and sent up rockets to alert the much-anticipated steamer, but the *Massachusetts* did not appear. As the weather grew even colder, the men were permitted to wear whatever they could "scrape together" to try to keep warm: comforters, oil-skin suits, buffalo robes, seaboots, whatever they could find. At Cape Quod off Borja Bay, the *Decatur* was surprised by another williwaw: a "sudden squall . . . which roared down without warning from the mountain gorges with great force, as from the mouth of a funnel." Though Sterrett did not admit it, perhaps at this point his goal of beating the strait changed into a more sinister compulsion. After all, he could have followed the path of least resistance at any point and sailed with the wind back to the Atlantic and the comparative safety of a passage around Cape Horn, in company with most other Pacific-bound sailing ships.[62]

The Cape Quod squall marked the beginning of two weeks of heavy weather that continued well into December. Always barreling down the narrow strait from the west, these snow and sleet storms brought screaming winds that sliced through clothing and numbed feet and hands; the medical log became crowded with treatment of wounds, fractures, and bruises. The usually stoic Logbook routinely attached adjectives like "furious" and "heavy" to brief descriptions of bad weather.[63]

As the weeks went by, rations ran low. On December 2, the daily bread allowance was reduced to twelve ounces per man; on December 13, it was cut to seven ounces. When Sterrett assembled the crew "and informed them of the necessity of reducing the ration," he said that he was determined to take the *Decatur* through the strait, that he would continue, "with their concurrence," to attack the passage until there were only twenty-one days of reduced rations left. Then, Sterrett said, "[I] will run [back to] Montevideo, fill the ship with provisions and return to continue the fight until the Pacific [is] reached." Recalling the event, Phelps wrote that every man responded enthusiastically, "preferring to be subjected to any number of hardships and deprivations rather than suffer defeat." Consistently, Phelps maintained that the *Decatur* crew was determined and cheerful; likewise, Taylor called them "true-blue American sailors, who never shirked duty of any kind." This may have been true of some but it was surely not true of all. In our understanding of this ordeal, we are limited by our sources—the ship's master and assistant surgeon—whose memoirs were written to celebrate the Old Navy of iron men in wooden ships. The ship's boatswain remembered, years later, that he often could not sleep for hunger in the strait; he was certainly not alone.[64]

On the day the rations were cut, as on many others in the strait, the officer of the watch permitted the crew to "splice the main brace" in the evening; an extra tot of grog was the only comfort that could be offered to hungry men who were wet and cold, exhausted in body and mind. There was no way to get warm or to change into dry clothing; off duty, the men fell into their hammocks and slept until their watch was called. Then they got up, wolfed down some salt pork and stewed peas, and went on deck again. Taylor wrote that the miserable grind began to tell on them: "overwork, too much salted meat, insufficiency of fresh food and loss of sleep and anxiety when the ship was under weigh all night." After only six weeks of seagoing rations, several of the *Decatur*'s sailors and marines began to suffer night blindness, and many showed other classic symptoms of scurvy: pallor, bleeding gums, and old wounds reopening. On a calm day, Surgeon Jeffery went ashore at Fortescue Bay to gather sacks of wild celery and earnestly lectured the men that eating these vegetables would cure their scurvy, but "the very fact of the doctor's interest" put the sailors off, wrote Phelps. The men, agreed Taylor, did not like innovations in their diet, but once the celery was stewed and called "greens," they came to enjoy the novel dish and their physical symptoms began to improve.[65]

The *Decatur* attempted to gain Long Reach with no luck; the ship was driven back to Borja Bay. Even on reduced rations, the *Decatur* had less than two weeks' provisions, and Sterrett showed no signs of heading back to Montevideo. The worse symptoms of scurvy were gone but "it had left in its wake debility, and mental as well as physical depression." The crew was roused to one more attempt on Long Reach, which was "a flat failure, punctuated with the bitterest disappointment." Finally, on December 18, the *Massachusetts* chugged into Borja Bay. The *Decatur* immediately sent over a boat for bread, flour, beans, whiskey, and an explanation: why had the steamer abandoned them? The *Decatur* officers learned that the *Massachusetts* had been dismasted in the September storm and steamed back to Rio. After repairs, the steamer had just caught up with them.[66]

Surgeon Taylor was simply glad to be alive, happy beyond words to see the *Massachusetts*. The *Decatur* was no longer alone, fighting a desperate, quixotic battle. The worst had to be over, and everyone was relieved and overjoyed. If there was ever a night to celebrate, this was it, and the main brace was doubtless spliced again and again. Taylor wrote, "to say it was a festive evening . . . would not convey an adequate idea of the transactions." The next day, officers from both ships conferred. Convinced that no sailing ship could have survived the September storm, some *Massachusetts* officers had given up the

Decatur for lost. Back in Rio, they incautiously shared their fears with a correspondent for the *New York Herald,* and the news was published back home that the *Decatur* "suddenly disappeared in a furious squall, and it was believed that she had gone down, carrying all on board with her to the bottom." Some men had no one at home to worry about them or their folks did not read the newspaper, but many others realized that their families and friends believed them dead. Phelps worried about his wife, thinking herself a widow with a young child, heartsick because of an "article written with little judgment, productive of infinite and useless distress." The Decaturs had to live with these worries until they reached a port and could send letters home.[67]

The following day, the *Decatur*'s crew worked to cut and load seventy cords of wood to fuel the steam boilers on the *Massachusetts.* Sterrett was convinced that the weather was about to worsen and he tried to persuade Meade to wait a day or two but the steamer's commander insisted on setting out. On December 20, 1854, the *Massachusetts* sent a hawser astern to tow the *Decatur* through Long Reach, but a "furious squall" blew up, confirming Sterrett's uncanny weather sense. The steamer cast off the *Decatur* and headed back up the strait, leaving the sloop of war behind in a screaming gale. Abruptly released from tow, the *Decatur* carried no sail and was out of control. The ship was driven so near the rocks that, as Taylor remembered it, Phelps swore he could have tossed a ship's biscuit and scored a bull's-eye on the biggest rock. As soon as a scrap of sail was lofted, the *Decatur* tore before the wind, forced to abandon a cutter of men who were struggling to save the hawser. Once again, the crew was fighting to preserve the ship in a ferocious tempest. After dark, seaman Robert Hamilton was at work on the yardarm trying to furl the frozen fore

FIG. 17 Here topmen furl sail on a square-rigged man-of-war. Decatur *seaman Robert Hamilton lost his footing and fell to his death from the yardarm, while furling the frozen sail in a fierce wind in the Strait of Magellan. J. G. Heck published this engraving in his* Pictorial Archive *in 1851. Courtesy University of Washington Libraries.*

topsail when he lost his footing and fell to his death on the ship's forecastle. The *Decatur* made it back to Fortescue Bay, once again. One sailor had died, a dozen men were adrift in the cutter and surely lost, the steamer was nowhere to be seen, and they were back where they had started from so many times. This was the worst, remembered Taylor, of the *Decatur*'s many bad days in the Strait of Magellan.[68]

Taking advantage of a break in the weather, Hamilton's body was rowed ashore for burial, with the flag on board the *Decatur* at half-mast. Captain Sterrett read the burial service over Hamilton's lonely grave—"the last sad rites," as Phelps put it, for "a deceased and lamented shipmate" buried at the world's end with a simple inscription on a wooden marker. For days afterward, the men were subdued; they had made it through so much, and Hamilton lost his life after the *Massachusetts* finally caught up with them.[69]

On December 23, the *Decatur* rode at anchor in Fortescue Bay, the same harbor the ship first entered on November 10. The *Massachusetts* steamed into the bay, and against all odds the *Decatur* cutter's crew was on board, alive and well. On Christmas Day, the *Decatur* was towed twenty miles by the steamer, all the way to Borja Bay. The tow continued on December 26, until a sudden squall blew up. Meade infuriated Sterrett and his lieutenants by once again casting off the hawsers without warning, and "with every sail snug in the gaskets." Without sails, the *Decatur* was helpless. Working for their lives in a fierce wind, the *Decatur* sailors were in familiar territory. "In less time than it takes to narrate it," wrote Phelps, "the men were on the yards, topsails sheeted home and mast-headed, jibs hoisted, fore tack boarded and the ship . . . wearing sharply around, barely clearing the danger close aboard under her lee."[70]

The *Massachusetts* returned on the morning of December 27 and sent over bread and whiskey and a hundred pairs of heavy woolen socks. For the next three days, wooding parties cut more fuel for the *Massachusetts* boilers to power one more westward push. On December 31, the *Decatur* passed hawsers to the *Massachusetts* and the sloop of war was towed past Cape Quod, into Long Reach, then past Cape Notch, to anchor in Playa Parda Bay. Taylor remembered the bay with delight and relief—"more like a mountain lake than a salt water bay [where] a magnificent cascade tumbles with a roaring noise from the rocks [and] scarcely a breath of wind penetrates though a tempest may be raging outside." Under tow on January 1 and 2, 1855, Phelps noted that Meade "frequently threatened to cast the *Decatur* adrift" when they encountered strong seas. There was no love lost between the men on the two ships, and the *Decatur* unsuccessfully tried to go it alone on January 3. The *Massachusetts* took the *Decatur* in tow one more time, and the ships separated for good that evening, well past Cape Pillar. The *Decatur*'s passage through the Strait of Magellan had begun on October 13, 1854, and ended on January 5, 1855—an unenviable record of eighty-three days. As Phelps reminisced, the *Decatur* engaged in "one of the most persistent, determined, desperate struggles ever entered into by a ship against the elements."[71]

Sitting with the Logbook, his journal, and his charts in 1883, Phelps figured that the ship's keel had crossed every square foot of the strait at least once. He claimed that, even if the *Massachusetts* had not arrived, the *Decatur* could have sailed through to the Pacific, a claim that no one could disprove though it seems highly unlikely. Phelps wrote that there was no better way to develop "thorough old-time sailors" than to send them through the strait, east to west, "a few times." If that experience did not turn them into seamen, "they may," concluded Phelps, "be safely abandoned as hopeless." All but one of the *Decatur*'s seamen had survived the Strait of Magellan. These "thorough old-time sailors" shared a life-changing experience, man and boy, officer and landsman. The strait made seamen of them all. Crossing the equator was marked by the theater of initiation, but no ceremony marked this passage between two worlds: to leave the Atlantic, die in the strait, and be reborn as new men in the Pacific.[72]

The *Decatur* had come to new life after a long voyage at the edge of death, at almost daily risk of foundering with all hands. Isaac Sterrett disregarded his orders to join the Pacific Squadron as soon as possible and took a U.S. Navy man-of-war on a personal quest to captain the first ship of its class to sail westward through the fabled strait named for Ferdinand Magellan. Accompanied by his son and a group of eager young officers, Sterrett decided on a mid-nineteenth-century passage of exploration to one of the least-frequented places on the planet. Obsessed by sailing through, Sterrett endangered his ship and his crew: the men developed scurvy, their rations were cut, one man fell to his death, the ship was wrenched and beaten, and Sterrett vowed to restock the *Decatur* and try again and again until he made it through.

On January 5, the *Decatur* was once again at sea, in the Pacific Ocean, making for Valparaiso, Chile's major port. Using the ship's most powerful glass, the officers could see condors circling high over the distant mountains—this, wrote Taylor in delight, was his first view of the largest bird of flight on earth. The *Decatur*'s amateur naturalists continued their observations, shaded their sketches from the strait, and wrote up their "discoveries." Worldly men at home on any sea, the *Decatur* officers were venturesome and far better traveled than most Americans, yet they remained provincial men at heart. For the officers, the contemporary United States was their frame of reference, and their ship was a projection of American values and the American way of life, wherever it might sail. Each prepared his collection of specimens to be sent stateside for display in glass and mahogany cases.[73]

Surgeon Jeffery had gathered a number of "rare objects of interest to various scientific institutions at home," including a dozen huge spider crabs from Fortescue Bay, which he had spread out flat, lashed to boards, and set to dry in the sun. The surgeon was very protective of these specimens, which had come safely through every storm; now that the ship was sailing north along the coast of South America, Jeffery "growled fearfully," wrote Phelps, at anyone who moved too carelessly near the shells. After two weeks of wind and sun, the surgeon declared the crabs ready for crating, to ship home from Valparaiso. At that very moment, a sudden heavy roll sent the boom sweeping amidships, and its slackened sail caught the boards and over they went, "crab side downward," covering the deck with thousands of tiny fragments of shell. Jeffery was a thorough Virginia gentleman, but his language on that occasion, chuckled Phelps, "beggars description."[74]

On January 17, 1855, the *Decatur* finally entered Valparaiso Harbor, catching up with the *Massachusetts*, already at anchor. It had taken the *Decatur* seven months to complete a journey that should have taken, at most, four months. Bladen Dulany, commodore of the Pacific Squadron, was in port on the flagship *St. Lawrence*, and he demanded an explanation of Captain Sterrett for the tardy arrival of the *Decatur*, long given up as lost. Sterrett replied that he was a seaman of experience who had doubled Cape Horn "several times" and was worried about the *Decatur*'s ability to sail into the head winds that were typical there. Sterrett claimed that, while in Rio, he had frequently heard that the Cape Horn passage was especially difficult that year. He told Dulany that he had consulted "men of sagacity and professional knowledge" about his own plan of passing through the Strait of Magellan and concluded that the strait would be a faster and safer route. He added that he would not have attempted the strait, even with these considerations, had not Lieutenant Meade of the *Massachusetts* also decided to take that route, "as both safety and expedition [were] assured by being in his company."[75]

Taylor recounted the dialogue between Sterrett and Dulany:

Where have you been all this time?

I have been in the Strait of Magellan, Commodore, for nearly three months.

By what authority did you do this instead of coming by the usual way around Cape Horn?

My orders were to join the Pacific Squadron, without designating the route.

On the same principle, you might have come by way of the North Pole, instead
    of the Strait of Magellan. Do you know that your ship has been reported lost?
    I suppose after your hardships and privations in the Strait, you will expect to
    remain for a long time in port to rest and recuperate.
On the contrary, Commodore, I am ready to go to sea at any moment.
Very well, sir, get up your anchor tomorrow morning and go to the Sandwich
    Islands.
Aye, Aye, sir.

Sterrett had not sailed to the Pacific by way of the North Pole but his tardy arrival deprived the Pacific Squadron of a much-needed man-of-war. Secretary Dobbin had ordered Commodore Dulany to prevent "unlawful expeditions"—filibusters—throughout the squadron's cruising ground. Specifically, Dobbin asked Dulany to send a squadron vessel to the Sandwich (Hawaiian) Islands "at the earliest day practicable," to discourage a filibuster threat. Dulany dispatched the *Decatur* to Oahu, ordering Sterrett to sail as soon as possible.[76]

At Valparaiso, the *Decatur*'s men had their first opportunity to send messages home, to reassure friends and family that they had not perished at sea. As late as March 7, 1855, the *New York Times* reported glumly, "The friends of the officers of the *Decatur* have given up all hopes of her safety." Dulany promised to send mail home by the fastest means, and in late March, stateside newspapers finally published the happy news of the *Decatur*'s survival. One of the *Massachusetts* surgeons was soon in print with an account of the steamer's passage through "wild and peculiar regions," describing the Fuegians as "short, stupid, half naked and . . . anything but human beings" and Borja Bay as "the most disagreeable place I was ever in." Accounts in the *New York Times, New York Herald, Ballou's Pictorial Drawing-Room Companion,* and elsewhere described how the *Decatur* had suffered in "gales of wind, with torrents of rain, hail and snow."[77]

The *New Orleans Picayune* published a fanciful April Fools' Day tale of mock heroics that satirized the *Decatur*'s lengthy passage, during which it came upon "fairy islands never before visited." A fictitious *Decatur* officer— "Oliver Hazzard Green"—claimed to have discovered a five-thousand-year-old civilization during the ship's passage through the strait. After climbing a Tierra del Fuego mountain, "Green," accompanied by Surgeon "Bainbridge," stumbled upon a verdant plateau. There, the men spent two weeks with "the noblest race [Green] ever saw," of tall athletic men and short plump women who all spoke Latin, worshiped the sun, were vegetarians, and supported a sizable priestly class. Their report was said to be accompanied by two artifacts: an image made of gold and iron and a piece of painted porcelain. Both, claimed the *Picayune,* were on public view in New Orleans, before heading to the World's Fair at Paris. The article was widely reprinted. The secretary of the navy and the commodore of the Pacific Squadron were likely unamused to see the errant warship a figure of fun in stateside newspapers.[78]

Ambitious Tom Phelps made the most of the passage. He submitted to Sterrett a report entitled "The Navigation of the Strait of Magellan," which his commanding officer considered "important to commerce, or at least interesting in a hydrographical point of view." A kindly and interested commander, Sterrett forwarded Phelps's report on to the secretary of the navy, who in turn forwarded it to the Naval Observatory for review. On January 1, 1855, Phelps received the appointment of acting lieutenant from Captain Sterrett, and Francis Dallas became acting master in Phelps's stead; these promotions were later confirmed by the secretary of the navy.[79]

At Valparaiso, the *Decatur* hastily readied for sea, sending cutters over to the storeship for shoes, pea jackets, and more woolen socks, kettles and pots, pickles and onions, barrels of tobacco, and gallons of whiskey. The watches were sent on liberty and the local police brought back seven hungover Decaturs from "the calabosa," as the Logbook put it: Jackson Abbott, Charles Brownell, William Coleman, Joseph Bass, James Thomas, Franklin Gray, and Charles Wilson. There is no indication in the Logbook that they were punished at all on board the *Decatur*; perhaps Sterrett authorized an act of grace.[80]

Commodore Dulany directed the *Decatur* to rendezvous in Honolulu with the sloop of war *St. Mary's.* In the event of the ship's absence, Sterrett was to inform the secretary of the navy of his arrival and await orders. On January 24, 1855, the *Decatur* headed out. On mustering the ship, the officers found that eight men had not returned from liberty at all and had successfully deserted in Valparaiso. These five seamen, two ordinary seamen, and one landsman had had enough of the *Decatur* and remained in Chile.[81]

The sail to Honolulu turned out to be a beautiful cruise. Sterrett did not hurry the battered ship, and the *Decatur* made about one hundred miles each day. Taylor remembered the passage from Valparaiso to Honolulu as a long series of halcyon days and nights, fanning along at five knots in a balmy breeze. "We are better thus," he reflected, "away from Navy Yards and squadrons and flagships." Taylor claimed that the crew did not touch a sail for forty days but just took it easy in the sunshine and let the wind do the work. The *Decatur* crossed the equator again heading north; this time, there was no fuss about greenhorns. On March 8, the *Decatur* sailed in sight of the island of

"Diamond Head," from the harbor of Honolulu.

Oahu, and a pilot came on board to guide the ship in to the bay of Honolulu. The *St. Mary's* was not in port, and Sterrett promptly informed Secretary Dobbin of his arrival, as he had been ordered.[82]

The Decaturs basked in the balmy warmth of the Kingdom of Hawaii, also known as the Sandwich Islands. The islands were the hub of American commerce in the Pacific, the principal stop for whalers and other commercial vessels to crew up, refit, restock, and go ashore. The capital, Honolulu, was the only Hawaiian port whose harbor offered safe anchorage in all winds; more than two hundred American whaling vessels visited Honolulu in 1854, carrying oil, bone, and ambergris valued at $15 million. According to an 1855 article, more than ten thousand American merchant sailors stopped in the islands each year. The *Decatur* crew spent four months anchored off Honolulu,

FIG. 18 After the relaxed passage from Valparaiso, Taylor sketched this view of Honolulu in February or March 1855. This voyage was almost certainly Taylor's first visit to the Pacific Ocean. From the John Y. Taylor Sketch Books, Western Americana Collection, Beinecke Rare Book and Manuscript Library, Yale University.

showing the flag, protecting American commerce, and joining the merchant seamen and whalers in seeing the onshore sights.[83]

They toured a bustling town on a magnificent harbor. Honolulu's beach was crowded with wharves and warehouses, taverns and brothels, and the harbor bristled with the masts of warships and merchant ships. Along the waterfront, the fort and customs house were built of pastel coral and glowed behind the sandy beach. Inland, the 1855 visitor strolled through the outdoor market, which featured coconuts, papayas, parrots, and "curios" of every sort. Further on, Main Street was the little city's major thoroughfare, running the length of the town parallel to the beach, from the Pearl River to the coconut groves of Waikiki. Most of Honolulu's principal public buildings were located on Main Street, including the courthouse, Government House, and the royal palace and walled gardens, all built of dressed coral blocks. Off Main Street, along narrow lanes patterned with bright sunlight and deep shadow, the city's elegant shops offered the latest hats from Paris and the newest books from London. Nuuanu Street intersected Main Street and ran inland from the sea up the Nuuanu Valley and out to the elite residential neighborhoods. Surgeon Taylor sketched the picturesque sights in Honolulu and the dramatic scenery nearby, carrying his pad and pencils wherever he went.[84]

At first glance, pleased American visitors described Honolulu as familiar: "a large, thriving and handsome *American* town, with wealthy merchants, spacious streets, creditable hotels [and] pleasant society." Looking harder, they saw a port town undergoing dramatic, almost violent change, focused in the crosshairs of the Pacific West. The islands were "precisely in the track of the coming trade," an ideal spot for a coaling station. Seamen from all over the world brawled and drank and whored in Honolulu's beachfront sailor town. The sea brought traders, sailors, whalers, botanists, missionaries, and entrepreneurs, and indigenous Hawaiians suffered under their collective cultural and biological assault. Only six years earlier, the squadron flagship *Independence* had called at Honolulu and a mild outbreak of measles among the crew spread to the Hawaiian people with devastating effect. The ensuing epidemic killed 10 percent of the Native population.[85]

Young America expansionists had their eyes on the Sandwich Islands. Less than two weeks' sail from San Francisco, Hawaii was a likely target of a California filibuster, and advocates of American annexation claimed that retention of native sovereignty "invite[d] [such] filibusters" to the Hawaiian Islands. Californian Samuel Brannan had mounted a serious filibuster against the islands in late 1851, and alarms persisted throughout the 1850s. In May 1853, a drunken escapade by "fast young men" who had taken a steamer from San

Francisco inspired new fears of conquest. While the *Decatur* was at Honolulu, a stateside journalist published "dire rumors" of another filibuster expedition from San Francisco to Hawaii. Well into 1855, the Pacific Squadron commodore was concerned by rumored "attacks by lawless adventurers" against Hawaii. Under general orders to prevent filibuster landings, the presence of the *Decatur* discouraged piratical schemes to seize the islands.[86]

Nevertheless, the *Decatur*'s stay at Honolulu was a prolonged vacation after the rigors of the strait, an idyllic time as the watches revolved around the clock and there was little to note in the Logbook except pleasant weather and the usual shoreside punishments. The crew enjoyed fresh beef, vegetables, and fruit and received frequent liberty. On shore in Honolulu, many Decaturs celebrated the usual spree. Charles Brownell and a dozen of his shipmates were still drunk and noisy when they returned to the ship and ended up double-ironed for a few days. Liquor was smuggled aboard in a variety of inventive ways, and Bernard Dougherty and many others who had not set foot on shore were nevertheless confined for drunkenness. William Fredericks and Charles Wilson managed to get fall-down drunk ashore while on duty in a boat crew, waiting for shipmates on liberty to return to the ship. The Honolulu police brought ordinary seaman Thomas Cooper on board, arrested by civil authorities for assault after drawing a knife on Warrant Officer James Miller, ship's carpenter. The shore offered a release from shipboard vigilance and discipline, and the crew settled old scores.[87]

Quite a few Decaturs successfully deserted at Honolulu. The Sandwich Islands were a sailor's dream of tropical paradise: a warm and scented shore, lush with fruit and flowers. Many Hawaiian women were beautiful and some seemed welcoming. There was plenty of work for a sailor on a merchant ship or whaler, and there were other opportunities as well. Some Decaturs ended their voyage in the Sandwich Islands because they had achieved the goal of their enlistment: to reach the opportunities of the Pacific West. The *Decatur* shipped new crewmen to replace the deserters, and Kanakas—Native Hawaiians—may have been among them. The *Decatur* brought on board Thomas Gorman, John Mason, John Barber, William Carr, John Williams, William Jones, and half a dozen more. Two newcomers, Abraham Reed and Franklin Sanford, seemed particularly furtive. They were soon spotted on the *Decatur*'s deck by the sharp-eyed master of the whaling ship they had just deserted. Sterrett reluctantly yielded, sending these two prime seamen back to their fate, doubtless to plan another escape.[88]

The *Decatur* crew scrubbed paint, scraped and repainted the yards, booms, waterways, and gun carriages, and repaired and tarred the rigging. Once the

Ruins of the "country-seat" of Kamehameha I.
Cocoa-grove, Watiti, Oahu, S.I.

FIG. 19 *Taylor took his sketchbook far afield on Oahu. Here, he drew the ruins of the country residence of King Kamehameha, who had died in 1819. From the John Y. Taylor Sketch Books, Western Americana Collection, Beinecke Rare Book and Manuscript Library, Yale University.*

FIG. 20 *An 1853 article in* Putnam's Magazine *depicts Hawaiian women dancing the hula, to a "low, wild chant." The movements of this dance were suggestive of sexual abandon to contemporary American eyes and promised a Pacific West paradise to* Decatur *deserters. Courtesy University of Washington Libraries, Special Collections,* UW27980z.

ship was ready for company, a number of official visits passed between the *Decatur* and other ships in harbor, requiring Sterrett's careful attention to protocol. The French sloop of war *Eurydice* and the Royal Navy sloop of war *Dido* both anchored off Honolulu, as did six other European men-of-war over a two-month period, each giving and receiving the appropriate salutes. Civilian dignitaries visited the *Decatur,* including the French commissioner, the American consul Darius Ogden, the English consul general, and the governor of Oahu. On March 28, the Hawaiian prince Lot visited the ship; the Hawaiian flag was hoisted at the fore and the prince was honored with a salute of nineteen guns. Though the logbook did no more than note these "visits," it is likely that the officers dressed in their best uniforms, wined and dined their guests, and regaled them with the Strait of Magellan adventure.[89]

In late May, Consul Ogden asked Sterrett to search for the celebrated packet ship *New World*. Throughout its stay, the *Decatur* had been called on to assist a number of American merchant or whaling ships in distress. One or two such vessels passed through Honolulu Harbor each day, pausing at this Pacific intersection. For instance, the *Decatur* officers visited the American whaler *Huleina,* which was homeward bound for New England from the Sea of Okhotsk with three hundred barrels of whale oil. The American lumber brig *Rolian* was headed from Puget Sound to Canton, representative of the new trade between the American West and Asia. The French ship *Montauk* anchored nearby, bound from New Zealand for Puget Sound with fifty barrels of whale oil. But the *New World* was in a class by itself, one of the most famous ships in the U.S. merchant fleet. On June 1, 1855, the *Decatur* crew hoisted in the shore boats and lofted sail. Off Kauai the following day, Lieutenant Drake took the gig ashore and learned that the damaged *New World* was safe at Waimea. At sea, the *Decatur* exercised the divisions at the great guns and then returned to Honolulu to continue the long wait for orders.[90]

As the months passed, the *St. Mary's* did not arrive. Bladen Dulany had been succeeded by William Mervine, and the new squadron commodore ordered the steamer *Massachusetts* to cruise the coasts of Washington, Oregon, and California to "afford aid and protection to the increasing emigration from the Atlantic states." Mervine gave a packet of orders to the *St. Mary's* to pass along to Sterrett at Honolulu, directing the *Decatur* to relieve the *Massachusetts*. But in response to an urgent plea from John Wheeler, U.S. ambassador to Nicaragua, Mare Island Navy Yard commandant David Farragut redirected the *St. Mary's* to San Juan del Sur on the Pacific side of the Nicaragua transit. In May 1855, William Walker was preparing to sail from San Francisco to filibuster Nicaragua, and he made no secret of his plans. Farragut was unable to consult with Mervine and shouldered the responsibility of redirecting a squadron ship. So, unwilling to proceed without orders, Sterrett and the *Decatur* stayed put at Honolulu.[91]

Mervine commanded the Pacific Squadron from his flagship, the venerable *Independence*. The squadron included the sloops of war *John Adams, Decatur,* and *St. Mary's* and the steamer *Massachusetts*. In the enormous eastern Pacific, Mervine was responsible for the advancement of American interests and commerce and the protection of American citizens. Popular opinion called loudly for a larger naval squadron to protect the "nation fast rising" on the shores of the Pacific West.[92]

William Mervine was not a patient man and he had not received a forward of Sterrett's note to the secretary of the navy informing Dobbin of the *Decatur's* arrival in Honolulu. In July, writing to Dobbin, Mervine was convinced that the *Decatur's* captain was lazing about in sunny Honolulu and deliberately avoiding receipt of his orders when "[his] services are much needed in several places." In fact, Mervine had been sending orders for the *Decatur* all over the Pacific—via the Royal Navy ship *Rattlesnake*, via the *St. Mary's*, and to David Farragut at Mare Island—with no result. To Mervine's fevered imagination, Sterrett was behaving as though he were in independent command. Reading the newspapers, Mervine found an item detailing the *Decatur* officers' social activities in Honolulu Bay, and he wrote angrily to Sterrett:

You have been absent from the flagship since January 24, a period of nearly five months, during which not a line has been received by me from you, although you were directed by my predecessor to advise the Honorable Secretary of the Navy of your arrival at Honolulu, S.I., and to forward duplicates of your correspondence with him to [me]. I have therefore been left to seek out your whereabouts in the newspaper, in the last notice of which located you at Honolulu on April 14, but what particular reasons required your continuance there . . . I am at a loss to conjecture.

Mervine went on to reiterate the *Decatur*'s orders to cruise the coast of California and Oregon and "to the Straits of Fuca, and along its shores, for the same object: many of the emigrants to that Coast have been murdered and other outrages committed." A "vessel of war," Mervine concluded, "will restrain the savages from further commission of such acts." He closed by noting that he had sent a letter bag for the *Decatur* to Mare Island, California—such a bag would include letters from home, newspapers and magazines, books and charts, and correspondence from the Navy Department and naval bureaus.[93]

Returning to Honolulu from Kauai, Sterrett learned "from private sources" that the *St. Mary's* had sailed from California for Nicaragua and probably would not call at Honolulu for months. On June 22, the *Kaluna* arrived at Honolulu from Puget Sound, and after talking with the schooner's captain, Sterrett put to sea, bound straight for "the coast of Oregon," even though he had not yet received Mervine's orders. Sterrett read the Articles of War to the crew, and the *Decatur* did not celebrate the July 4 holiday. On July 18, land was in sight, and the *Decatur* soon anchored in San Juan Bay, off Vancouver Island. Here, Sterrett heard reports that thousands of Northern "British-Russian Indians" planned to attack the Vancouver Island and Puget Sound settlements. Two days later, the *Decatur* met the U.S. revenue cutter *Jefferson Davis*, headed to San Francisco, and then the lumber bark *Brontes*, bound from Seattle for Honolulu; both ships bore the same information: Washington Territory was soon to be attacked by Northern Indians. Sterrett sailed south, into Puget Sound.[94]

The *Decatur*'s arrival was cause for celebration as the ship ventured to Port Townsend and met the U.S. surveying steamer *Active*, commanded by James Alden. On July 23, the warship anchored off Whidbey Island and exercised the great guns at a target on the beach: "put 23 shots into a log 22 feet long out of 41 discharged," enthused Dallas to his journal, "Capital firing." At Port Townsend, the *Decatur* shipped a landsman, George Neal, who turned out to be a deserter run from the sloop of war *St. Mary's*. Then, Thomas Cooper, John Maher, Charles Wilson, and Harley Burr abandoned the *Decatur*'s cutter to sample the delights of the tiny port town and then to successfully desert into Washington Territory.[95]

Meanwhile, Sterrett consulted with Alden and gathered local information. Noting the *Decatur*'s arrival, the *Puget Sound Courier* reported the warship's mission to sail "in quest of the northern tribes of Indians, who have been so daring of late." The *Courier* made no reference to any threat from territorial Native people. After distributing nearly all the food, ammunition, and arms on board the *Decatur* at Port Townsend, Sterrett raced south to Mare Island in San Francisco to stock up on supplies for American colonists on Puget Sound. The *Decatur* finally reached "Californio," anchoring at Mare Island on August 7, 1855.[96]

In 1855, Mare Island Navy Yard was brand new, located on an island off Vallejo in San Pablo Bay. When the *Decatur* arrived, Commandant David Farragut and his wife and son were living in an old house left behind by an island settler evicted by the navy. Officers' Row, the machine shop, and the warehouses were still under construction, but Dobbin enthusiastically predicted that one day the yard would "assume its position among the most useful and complete yards in the country," building and maintaining a growing fleet of navy ships in the Pacific. In the meantime, during its first years of operation, the shipyard repaired more merchant ships than naval vessels. When the *Decatur* arrived, the Mare Island yard was equipped with a wharf, a crane, a blacksmith shop, and a barely operational floating dry dock that had been transported in modular elements around the Horn.[97]

Sterrett intended to load food, arms, and ammunition in great haste but ended up spending a full three weeks at Mare Island. Farragut, who had pirouetted the *Decatur* in Rio's harbor, was surely delighted to visit his old ship and his old friend Sterrett. But the ship had not had been docked since the stormy journey through the strait and needed work inside and out. Meanwhile, the Decaturs stowed whiskey, apples, flour, salt meat, and lots of bread in the hold. Heading for war in the damp cold of Puget Sound, the ship loaded flannel drawers and undershirts, woolen overshirts and socks, and heavy pea jackets—and as many weapons and as much ammunition as Farragut could spare. The *Decatur* also crewed up for Puget Sound.[98]

It proved extremely difficult to keep men on board in "Californio." Since the gold strikes became widely known, navy ships commonly lost 10 percent of their crew at San Francisco in just a few days. During the *Decatur*'s brief stay, Isaac Williamson, Edward Norris, Franklin Gray, Charles Mason, and a dozen

other men made unsuccessful efforts to desert—they were tracked down, arrested, and brought back to the ship. But John Barber, George Williams, and William Brown deserted and got away clean, into the golden opportunities of the Pacific West.[99]

As Commodore Mervine saw things, this "serious evil" of desertion was based on the foolish delusion that it was easy to strike it rich in 1855 California. "Many a poor fellow, alas!" wrote one naval officer, "has changed a comfortable ship and Uncle Sam's 'good old salt horse,' 'duff,' and 'rice pudding' for a cold and comfortless cabin amid the damp and noisome swamps of the Sacramento, Yuba and San Joaquin." Officers were frustrated with short-sighted seamen—"proverbially a discontented set of beings"—who were lured from their duty by the siren song of gold for the taking. But naval deserters chased their ambitions, slipping into a welcoming network of California taverns, hotel rooms, and wagons, abetted by "the assistance receive[d] from persons on shore." In fact, it became a crime for anyone to entice or conceal a navy deserter, and those convicted were liable to a fine of $300 or a prison term of one year. But many sailors had signed on in Boston or Norfolk to work

FIG. 21 *Frank Soulé's* Annals of San Francisco *was published in 1855, the year the* Decatur *first visited Mare Island Navy Yard. The book's frontispiece proudly shows off San Francisco's Montgomery Street—the Wall Street of the Pacific West. The open door to fame and fortune was just beyond the hill. Courtesy University of Washington Libraries, Special Collections,* UW 27547z.

their way West: getting to San Francisco was their goal and naval desertions were reported daily in local newspapers.[100]

Some men who had served their time left the ship eagerly in San Francisco. Others, like Samuel Silk, Robert Shorter, Benjamin Lewis, and Charles Cloyd, played it safe and took advantage of Dobbin's benefits. Shorter was a seaman, and Cloyd and Silk were quartermasters. It is tempting to speculate that the name "Benjamin Lewis" in the Logbook was an error for petty officer Henry Lewis, captain of the foretop. The surgeon's records indicate that Lewis was thirty-one, born in Buffalo, New York; Cloyd was twenty-eight, born in New York City. Shorter was African American, also born in New York and about forty-three years old. Silk was born in Ireland, about fifty years old, and the ship's resident character, often quoted in officer memoirs. This quartet of skilled, tough, experienced man-of-war sailors stuck with the ship; they applied for the reenlistment bonus though they had to postpone their furlough because of the ship's urgent duty.[101]

Sterrett struggled to recruit sailors in San Francisco for a warship bound for combat in a miserable outpost. California dreams aside, he hunted skilled men in a highly competitive market and, despite Dobbin's reforms, could still offer only comparatively low pay. In 1855, a sailor in the navy earned far less than his equivalent on board a naval steam vessel or a merchant ship. Even after cross-the-board raises, seamen's wages were $18 a month, ordinary seamen's were $14, and landsmen's were $12. A coal heaver on the *Massachusetts* earned $15 per month—25 percent more than a landsman for the equivalent skill level. The *Decatur* petty officers earned a little more than seamen: the sailmaker's mate was paid $20 and the boatswain's, gunner's, and carpenter's mates each earned $25. The captains of the tops earned $20 each month, as did the captain of the afterguard and the ship's master-at-arms. But in California, a *Decatur* seaman could nearly double his wages by signing on to a merchant ship or joining a filibuster.[102]

Frustrated, Sterrett reported that his departure for Puget Sound was delayed by expired terms of service, desertions, and the difficulty of recruitment. Eventually, he sailed without a full complement, knowing that the longer he stayed in port, the more men would desert. But he did insist on the resignation of boatswain Henry Bright as a "drunken and insubordinate person" who was a bad influence on board. In the week before leaving, the *Decatur* shipped twelve new men—seamen, ordinary seamen, and landsmen. Future deserter and filibuster John C. Drinkhouse joined the ship on September 7, 1855, the ship's last day at San Francisco, at a time when Sterrett and Middleton were scraping the bottom of the barrel for sailors.[103]

In San Francisco, Mervine's angry note finally caught up with Sterrett and the laconic captain replied at, for him, great length. Sterrett wrote that he was distressed to read an "implied censure" in Mervine's note and expressed "the greatest surprise" at the commodore's displeasure. He had, Sterrett wrote, promptly reported his arrival in Honolulu to the secretary of the navy on March 8, just as he had been commanded by Dulany; thereafter, he awaited the *St. Mary's* arrival. He had merely followed his orders: to remain at Honolulu until told to do otherwise. Sterrett continued that as soon as he had learned indirectly of Mervine's orders, he sailed for Washington Territory. At anchor off Vancouver Island, "an English trader [who had] arrived from the North" informed him that the Northern Indians were preparing a war of extermination against settlers on Puget Sound. The trader reported seeing two hundred war canoes filled with two thousand warriors whose behavior had been "menacing" toward the governor of Vancouver Island, where they had committed "serious depredations." The trader's dire predictions were seconded by Isaac Ebey, U.S. customs agent at Port Townsend, and other knowledgeable settlers. Sterrett concluded his letter and dropped it in the squadron letter bag, expecting it to chase Mervine around the Pacific.[104]

The *Decatur* set sail for Puget Sound on September 7, 1855, under charge of a local pilot and ran aground within minutes on the Vallejo Flats in the harbor. Careened at low tide, much of the ship's lower starboard-side copper was discovered to be "eaten through and the wood beneath . . . pierced with worm holes." Once afloat, Sterrett jotted a note to Farragut detailing the accident and requested a quick hull inspection. However, the dry-dock company refused to allow the *Decatur* into the dock unless the ship was stripped of all armament and stores to lighten it.[105]

Farragut and Sterrett were impatient to get the *Decatur* to Washington Territory, and so the *Decatur* weighed anchor uninspected and sailed north. Three days out of San Francisco, the ship unexpectedly fell in with the *Independence,* and the commodore signaled the captain to come aboard. Mervine was frustrated with dilatory commanders, missed opportunities, and protracted delays as documents slowly passed hand to hand throughout the squadron. Sterrett was rowed over to the flagship for an interview with the testy commodore. He repeated that he had remained in Honolulu because he had no orders to do otherwise, and he was presently headed to Puget Sound because Washington Territory was threatened by Northern Indians from Alaska who had assembled a formidable force. When Mervine summarized the conversation for Secretary Dobbin, he also noted threatened "attacks of the Indians inhabiting Oregon," which Sterrett must have told him about, face-to-face.

Mervine sent Sterrett hastening north, with orders to defend American settlement and commerce and to keep him fully informed.[106]

The *Decatur* sailed north for three weeks, beating against head winds to "the point of greatest danger . . . hoping to prevent much mischief if not more deplorable results," in Sterrett's words. The crew was busily occupied with gunnery practice, with both small arms and the great guns. For the first time, the *Decatur* began practicing boarding exercises, defending the ship against enemies attempting to climb aboard and swarm the decks, kill the officers and crew, and take the ship. The *Decatur* was preparing for war with Indian people in the Pacific Northwest.[107]

As Sterrett headed to Puget Sound, he was doubtless thinking about the latest news from back East, fresh from the mailbag. Like all navy officers, he wondered what the outcome would be of Dobbin's Efficiency Board, whether he had been evaluated and, God help him, found inefficient. The board met from June 20 through July 27, 1855, while Sterrett was en route to and from Puget Sound, and assessed about 250 officers, each board member submitting a list of those whom he considered questionable. They discussed each suspect officer, supported by service files supplied by the Department of the Navy. Then they voted. The board spent about half an hour per case and, at the conclusion of their work, forwarded recommendations to the secretary of the navy, who reviewed them and sent them to the president for approval. Once confirmed, the Plucking Board's decisions were final. The board met in private but its chairman, Commander Samuel Francis Du Pont, kept a journal of the deliberations, a page or so per case. The journal is a treasure trove of naval gossip of the 1850s.[108]

Board member Andrew Foote had included Isaac Sears Sterrett on his list of suspect commanders as "a drinking man" who "drank too much at the [Philadelphia Naval] Asylum and was held in low estimate by the pensioners," and added that Sterrett was also heavily in debt. Foote claimed that Sterrett had been arrested at Boston before sailing in the *Decatur* and again while the ship was in port at Norfolk, both times for debt. Samuel Barron told the group that he knew Sterrett owed "a large sum" to a purser with whom he had served. Barron went on to say that, although Sterrett was his old messmate and friend, "he was compelled to admit he drank too much." In general, the officers were critical of how long it had taken Sterrett to get the *Decatur* through the Strait of Magellan, but they marveled that he had tried to do it at all—"all admit him to be a good seaman." At first, the board voted nine to one to keep Sterrett on the active list, but the case was reopened because "several members [were] not satisfied." Du Pont's recent biographer, Kevin Weddle, notes that such reopened cases were "very unusual" and indicate that discussions were contentious and decisions controversial. After a discussion that Du Pont did not detail, the board's vote was reversed, with nine members voting for furlough and only one opposed. Whatever they may have been, the arguments of the dissatisfied members of the Plucking Board were persuasive. Isaac Sterrett was removed from the active list.[109]

Within a week, the lists of those newly demoted and those newly promoted were published in East Coast newspapers. The *New York Times* ran the names on September 18, 1855, as front-page news; Sterrett was one of twelve commanders listed as retired on furlough pay, $900, half the salary of those commanders retired on leave-of-absence pay. The *Times* reported that Sterrett had not been at sea since 1847; in fact, he was sailing to Washington Territory at that very moment, readying his ship for battle and out of reach of the news.[110]

Dobbin sent a dispatch to Mervine on September 29, 1855, that included notes to three lieutenants and one commander whose careers were impacted by the board's decisions: the commander was Isaac Sterrett and one of the lieutenants was Guert Gansevoort, stationed on the flagship *Independence*. Sterrett had been placed on the reserved list, Dobbin informed the commodore, and Mervine should send him home. Gansevoort was to take command of the *Decatur* due to "the promotions arising from the execution of the Act." All new vacancies in the Pacific Squadron would be filled by the officers next in rank as they moved up. A wave of promotions followed as a result: "jackass" lieutenants and commanders, as they were termed.[111]

One pamphleteer objected that some of the commanders plucked as inefficient were "at this moment plowing the deep in the efficient performances of those very duties which the board have declared them incompetent to perform," a remark that certainly applied to Isaac Sterrett. But as the *Decatur* sailed away from California and north to Puget Sound in September 1855, Sterrett did not know whether or not he had been plucked.[112]

5

Episode 2. Seattle

"Down Came the Indians, Like so Many Demons"

The name of Seattle, borrowed from the chief of the Duwam'sh Indians
inhabiting the shores of the bay, was selected by the colonists for the little
town. . . . The advent of the whites was a pleasant episode in the lives of
these savage people; their arms opened to receive them as superior beings,
and the lands they possessed were freely offered. . . . [But by the fall of
1855], excepting a few of the Duwam'sh race residing in and around
Seattle, the entire body of Indians in the Territory were united against
the colonists. . . . Down came the Indians, like so many demons [and] at
this moment, the fate of Seattle hung by a thread. . . in a few moments
the battle [would] have been won, the people given up to indiscriminate
slaughter and the village in flames; but . . . the town remained in our
possession and the Indian cause was forever lost.
—THOMAS STOWELL PHELPS, "Reminiscences of Seattle" (1881)

In 1853, Young America Democrat Isaac Ingalls Stevens was appointed
Washington Territory's first governor by President Franklin Pierce. At
the time, American settlers were scattered throughout the territory, but
no treaties had been signed with tribes. Stevens organized a hasty series of
treaty councils; some Native leaders refused to sign the treaties and others
complied with great reluctance. Indian resistance increased as Native people
experienced the dramatic changes to their world: restriction to small reservations inadequate to sustain their way of life, provocation from some settlers,
and failure by the federal government to fulfill their side of the bargain. Set-

tlers reported growing Indian unrest, and the legislature petitioned Secretary of the Navy Dobbin, among others, to come to the territory's defense. Colonists on this distant periphery had demanded an imperial response: Dobbin ordered Commodore Mervine to send a man-of-war to Puget Sound, and that ship turned out to be the *Decatur*.[1]

Sterrett remained in command, taking the ship north to Puget Sound to enforce treaties and protect settlement in the territory that styled itself the "north-western outpost of American power." The *Decatur* entered Seattle's harbor, Elliott Bay, on October 4, 1855, on a fair breeze, and fired off the carronades to announce its presence, "waking thunderous reverberations far and wide." The *Decatur* let down the anchors off the tiny mill town, which had been built on land ceded to the United States by four principal chiefs, including Chief Seattle, who made his mark on the Point Elliott Treaty at Mukilteo on January 22, 1855, nine months before the *Decatur*'s arrival.[2]

The town was built on the beach, almost pressed into the bay by the woods that ran along the shore. The settlement's southern buildings straggled down a small peninsula separated from the mainland by a salt marsh that nearly filled at high tide, threatening to turn the peninsula into an island. To the north, the land rose up to a bluff, and directly east of the town dock, Phelps noted "a broad Indian trail leading to Lake Duwam'sh"—modern Lake Washington—and on to the passes through the Cascade Mountains. Seattle's scatter of buildings included a church, a few houses, a sawmill, a general store, a blacksmith shop, a hotel, and a boardinghouse. When the *Decatur* anchored, locals were trying to build a blockhouse at the north end of town for protection against Indian attack.[3]

Four years earlier, a group of emigrants led by Illinoisan Arthur Denny had settled on Alki Point, west across the harbor. When the Alki party arrived, a second group of Americans had begun to farm nearby, along the Duwamish River. Most of the Denny party soon moved to the sheltered side of Elliott Bay to stake their claims, naming the little settlement "Seattle" to honor the Duwamish chief. After March 1853, Henry Yesler's steam-powered sawmill ran twenty-four hours a day, shipping rough lumber to ports throughout the Pacific, including Honolulu, Canton, and Melbourne as well as San Francisco and Portland. It seemed that everyone in Seattle worked for the mill, and more than half of its workers were Native people who lived next to Yesler's cookhouse in the camp of mill foreman Suquardle, or "Curley," as Americans called him. The little village of Seattle was brand new, given one of many names in a geography whose layers had been overwritten by newcomers. The Strait of San Juan de Fuca was named by the Spanish, Mount Rainier by the

English, and Washington Territory by the Americans. The settlers anglicized the area's deep Native geography: Duwamish Lake and River, Alki Point, Snoqualmie Pass, Mukilteo, and Nisqually.[4]

In Washington Territory, there were about five thousand colonists and about twenty thousand Indians; in Seattle and throughout King County, there were about as many settlers as men in the *Decatur*'s crew. Perhaps 1,500 Indian people lived nearby, as well as a few dozen employees of the Hudson's Bay Company, including French Canadian and Kanaka (Hawaiian) laborers. American feeling ran high against the English; some colonists were convinced that the company fostered ill-feeling against Americans among local Indian and mixed-world people and encouraged canoe raids on Puget Sound by "Northern Indians," as they were called, from villages up the Inside Passage. Hudson's Bay Company men had traditionally taken Native wives "in the custom of the country," which had generated a complex society of shared descent. Some American settlers arrived with extended families but many lonely men carried on the tradition of "country wives." Sawmill owner Yesler, an Ohio migrant, lived in a "country marriage" with Susan Curley, Suquardle's daughter, and she was pregnant. The *Decatur* had sailed into a complicated colonial world, but by framing this complex world in simple clichés, its officers convinced themselves that they had quickly grasped the situation; as Phelps put it, "The *Decatur* was only a few hours in port [at Seattle] before we had a fair understanding of existing affairs."[5]

The *Decatur*'s stay in Seattle was reduced to misleading simplicities in the reminiscences of both settlers and officers. Phelps essentially created the Battle of Seattle when he published his 1881 memoir, excerpted at the head of this chapter. He remembered a distant American colony inhabited by a handful of respectable settlers and a large number of disreputable drifters who disregarded treaty rights promised to Native people and cheated, bullied, and debauched them. Settler offenses against Indians ranged from rape and robbery to murder and provoked Native vengeance. Nevertheless, Phelps was convinced that the American imperial embrace brought civilization to a benighted people in need of paternal care. As the officer saw things, brutal colonists had outraged territorial Indians, who sought revenge and had become worthy adversaries. Navy officers despised many settlers, but they were ready to fight in defense of the idea of American settlement on Puget Sound and the imperial future of Young America in the Pacific West.

Seattle's founders and their children remembered the siege and battle with purpose by constructing a legend that vindicated American settlement in Washington Territory as manifestly destined. Their war story demonstrated

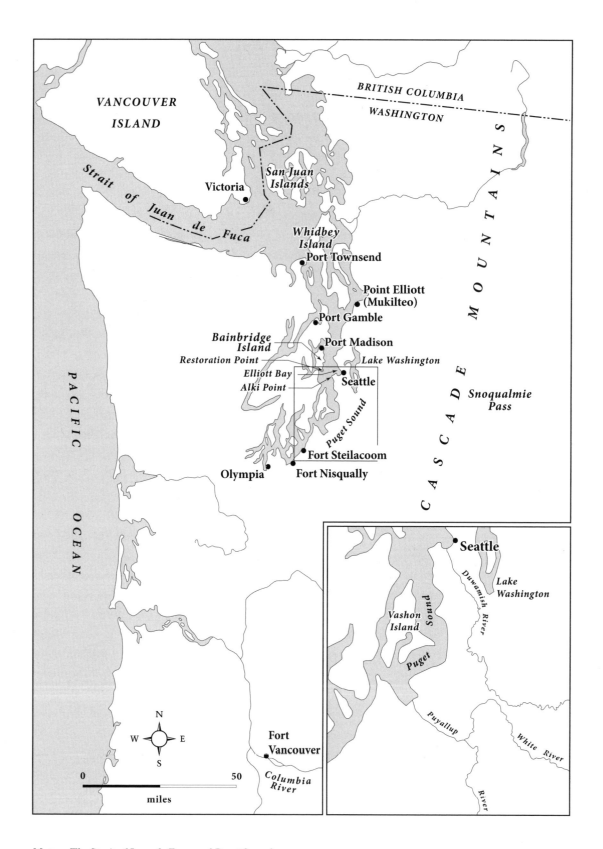

VANCOUVER
ISLAND

BRITISH COLUMBIA
WASHINGTON

Strait of Juan de Fuca

San Juan
Islands

Victoria

Whidbey
Island

Port Townsend

Point Elliott
(Mukilteo)

Port Gamble

Bainbridge
Island

Port Madison

Restoration Point

Lake Washington

Elliott Bay

Seattle

Alki Point

Puget Sound

Snoqualmie
Pass

PACIFIC

OCEAN

Fort Steilacoom

Olympia

Fort Nisqually

CASCADE MOUNTAINS

N
W   E
S

Fort
Vancouver

Columbia
River

0   50

miles

Seattle

Lake
Washington

Duwamish River

Vashon
Island

Puget Sound

Puyallup

White River

River

Map 3. The Strait of Juan de Fuca and Puget Sound

divine will behind military agency: the *Decatur* arrived in answer to prayer to "spread her protective wings over Seattle" like a sheltering angel and to protect innocent settlers in this place ordained for American settlement. In an oil painting by Emily Denny, settlers race to Seattle's blockhouse as though to church, the women clasping babies in their arms and clutching their children's hands. The painting tells stories of family and piety; there is no sense of the federal will represented by the *Decatur* or the expansionist mission of which Washington Territory was a part. In fact, Denny painted no Indian people or Decaturs at all; only the settlers are fully realized. In her painting, the *Decatur* lies at anchor, black and impersonal, a gun on the water pointed inland at an unseen menace that compelled these vulnerable people to seek shelter on the hilltop. In settler reminiscence, the *Decatur* saved Seattle, as an act of providence.[6]

However, the ship's stay in Seattle is well documented day by day in the Old Navy records and reveals stories ignored by the usable histories of both settlers and officers. The hard-edged frontier between Indian and colonist and between Indian and navy man utterly disappears, to be replaced by a shifting, permeable border crossed by commerce, religion, war, and sexuality. The *Decatur* not only brought federal protection to this Pacific West colony but also brought cash, vice, and violence as both officers and enlisted men reshaped the settlement to meet their needs. The majority of the crew offended at Seattle and claimed an outlaw space in the woods, a common ground developed by disobedient sailors with dissolute or opportunistic settlers and where their relationships were mediated by liquor. More than half of the Decaturs were punished for more than three hundred offenses during their eight-month stay at Seattle, some men as many as five times. To Phelps and respectable settlers, the woods were "thronged with Indians" in a world at war, but to many sailors, the forest proved more hospitable than the ship.[7]

When the *Decatur* arrived, Sterrett found Seattle's citizens "almost destitute of arms and entirely without organization" to defend themselves. The nearest U.S. Army post was Fort Steilacoom, near Nisqually, about seventy miles to the south, where two companies of the Third Artillery were stationed under the command of Captain Erasmus Keyes. Sterrett and his officers, consulting with Keyes, decided that Seattle was the most vulnerable of the Puget Sound towns to Indian attack and that the sloop of war should be stationed there, and Sterrett wrote to Mervine that the *Decatur* had anchored off Seattle "in such a position as to command the town" with the great guns. Working hard throughout October 1855, the ship's carpenters completed the town's blockhouse, which was dubbed Fort Decatur. The building was forty feet square

and two-storied, with a number of small rooms upstairs, each with a stove. Someone from the *Decatur* had noticed two old nine-pound cannon on the beach, brought to Seattle as ballast in the hold of lumber schooners. The ship's carpenters built carriages for these guns and remounted them, placing them in defense of the blockhouse.[8]

Throughout the late summer and early fall of 1855, local newspapers reported on Governor Stevens's mulish treaty diplomacy and published increasingly alarming rumors about territorial Indians who had joined together to resist the treaties under arms, intending to drive Americans from the land. Less than a week after the *Decatur*'s arrival, Acting Governor Charles Mason sent an urgent plea up to Seattle requesting that the ship supply the territorial militia with all the arms and ammunition that could be spared. That afternoon, Sterrett ordered Lieutenant Drake to load the second cutter

FIG. 22 *Emily Denny painted her* Battle of Seattle *in about 1880, based on the experiences of family and friends, as well as her own memories from childhood. In this painting, she is the toddler in the arms of her mother, Louisa Boren Denny, bottom right. Her father, David Denny, runs toward them, bayoneted rifle in hand. Courtesy Museum of History & Industry (1955.9216).*

Blockhouse at Seattle W.T. 1855.

with dozens of muskets and carbines, fifty pistols, one carbine ball mold, fifty cutlasses, and thousands of cartridges and percussion caps and sail the arms to the southern Puget Sound. Sterrett similarly supplied customs inspector Isaac Ebey, on Whidbey Island, and also armed Captain C. C. Hewitt's company of Seattle-area volunteers.[9]

The *Puget Sound Courier* commented gratefully:

> It is peculiarly fortunate for us at this time of trouble, that this vessel is in our waters. . . . We have but a few United States troops now in this portion of the territory and our citizens are in a measure unprotected from the Indians that surround us—in fact, in our very midst. We have heard of Capt. Sterritt often; he is one of the most able and distinguished officers of our gallant Navy. His conduct as an officer is equaled by his corteous demeanor as a gentleman.[10]

Sterrett cooperated with territorial authorities and calmed local anxieties, but writing to Mervine on October 15, he was skeptical about an uprising of territorial Indians:

The settlers here were apprehensive of an attack by the Indians. . . . Most of the people residing in the County have repaired to Town for mutual protection. The presence of this ship has quieted their alarm, which seems to have been in a great measure groundless, and most of them have returned to their farms. . . . This place being the most accessible to an attack, I shall remain here for the present.[11]

Sterrett remained unconvinced of the local threat. According to Arthur Denny, once the militia was armed, Acting Governor Mason encouraged the *Decatur* to head off to other squadron duties because the ship's presence in Puget Sound inspired unnecessary panic among the settlers, discouraging settlement. Mason warned Sterrett that he had "been victimized by a set of land sharks" in Seattle, who exaggerated this "false alarm" to keep the ship in harbor and local residents feeding at the federal trough. Indignant, Sterrett "in a very heated manner" told Denny of Mason's accusations and that he intended to get the ship under way at once. Denny recalled that he was barely able to persuade the captain to wait just a few more days.[12]

Then, on October 28, 1855, nine American settlers were killed by Indian raiders at farms along the White River, a few miles southeast of Seattle, convincing Sterrett that the dangers were very real. The next day, Lieutenant Hughes took marines up the Duwamish River to scout for Indians, and that night, for the first time, men from the *Decatur* garrisoned Seattle's shoreline. Three children orphaned by the murders were brought to the *Decatur* by a friendly Indian, whose canoe approached the ship under the attentive surveillance of an officer's telescope. Then, at sundown, twenty-one canoes came down the river heading across the bay to the reservation at Port Madison—Indians who knew what was coming and wanted to be well out of any fighting.[13]

As Sterrett described the attack to Mervine, a group of Klickitat, Nisqually, and Puyallup Indians had "committed a number of murders on the White, Green and Puyallup Rivers, many of which were within a few miles of this place." Sterrett distributed a few more rifles from the *Decatur*'s dwindling supply to Hewitt's Volunteers, and the company marched "to the scene of these outrages but could effect nothing but bury the bodies of the unfortunate victims." Dozens of angry, frightened settlers streamed in from the countryside to Seattle, and their fears were not directed at distant Indians, such as the Yakama and Klickitat of eastern Washington Territory or the Northern Indians, but at local Indians.[14]

On October 31, 1855, Sterrett invited Chief Seattle aboard the *Decatur*, accompanied by his council. Tall and powerful, Seattle was an eloquent, persuasive leader. At the Point Elliott Treaty negotiations, he had both encour-

A map showing the location
of the hostile tribes of Indians
west of the Cascade Range W.T.
1855

Whidby Island

Puget Sound

Lake Washington

Snoqualmie or Snohomish River

Pas Casins Tribe

Seattle

Alki

Duwamish River

Thedew or Cedar R.

Green River

Hamilton killed
by the Indians
Oct 27 1855

Brannan L Slaugter
killed Dec 4 1855

Slaugter
Battle

White River

Puyallup River

Falls

Snowqualmi Pass

Cascade Range

Natches Pass

aged his people to accept the treaty's terms and reproached Governor Stevens's representatives with reminders of the responsibility that comes with power. The *Decatur*'s captain honored Chief Seattle by inviting him to see a demonstration of the great guns. Three days after the White River murders, Seattle's shipboard visit was intended to strengthen the ties between the colonists and the Duwamish, but it was also designed to intimidate the Indians and forestall thoughts of defection to the insurgents.[15]

While the ship remained at anchor in Elliott Bay, colonists, Indians, and Decaturs met in daily encounters. Ship work parties rowed ashore to chop firewood and gather water and to drill on the beach. The purser bought all the eggs, milk, and vegetables that farmers could spare, and the officers distributed weapons and ammunition and rations of salt meat and ship's biscuit. Soon, a number of local settlers were on the navy payroll, and about a dozen Native men and women were employed in various capacities by ship officers. Nightly, marines and sailors patrolled Seattle. As locals caught on to the *Decatur*'s routine, it became easy for men to buy a bottle on shore, and the Logbook noted almost daily offenses. Only three days after the ship's arrival, the first of many Decaturs to desert their duty and get drunk in the woods east of town did so. Seaman William Jones and ordinary seaman George Sargent were confined in double-irons for taking the dinghy to shore and staying out all night. The next day, John Mason and William Robinson ran from the second cutter while it was on the beach. Then, David McKinnon, Franklin Gray, and John Mason deserted from the first cutter—they had all "run" from the *Decatur* before. Though the officers used the word "desertion," these men intended to have their spree, straggle back to the ship, take their punishment, and return to work.[16]

However, on October 24, 1855, Captain Sterrett convened the first summary courts-martial in the vessel's history. The Plucking Board was intended to discipline the officer corps; the summary court-martial was Dobbin's innovation to meet the disciplinary crisis among enlisted men that had been created by abolition of flogging. The *Decatur* hoisted the U.S. flag at the fore and fired a gun to initiate the military trial of John Dennison. He was eighteen years old, born in Virginia, a landsman on his first cruise in a man-of-war, and he stood accused of getting drunk on duty and insulting his superior officer. Witnesses testified that Dennison had been a member of a crew working on shore, cutting firewood, when he slipped away into the woods. He eventually rejoined the party, "very much intoxicated." According to Carpenter Miller, Dennison "had a bottle of liquor under his shirt on the left side. I asked what he was going to do with [it]." Laughing, Dennison said, 'What bottle of liquor?'" Miller told Dennison that he intended to report him for deserting the wooding party and Dennison retorted, "You are a damned liar." Dennison said that he did not care if he was put in double-irons: confinement would give him a break for a few days. The court found the sailor guilty of treating his superior with contempt and ordered him confined in irons for a month, deprived of grog, tobacco, and pay.[17]

The next summary court-martial was that of John Peckham and tried a far more serious offense. English-born Peckham was a veteran seaman, charged with uttering mutinous words. On October 19, while eating supper, Peckham stood up and boldly "declared himself an Englishman, and damned the Yankee flag." Francis Purcell, himself born in England, testified that Peckham— "under the influence of liquor"—yelled, "Damn the Yankees, I say!" Jackson Abbott, a Pennsylvanian, and Charles Brownell, a Marylander, both testified that they'd heard Peckham damn the flag. Brownell, "excited by liquor and temper," started a fistfight with Peckham to defend the national honor. After brief deliberation, the court decided that Peckham should be dishonorably discharged from the U.S. Navy in Seattle.[18]

In January 1856, William Robinson, ordinary seaman, was also tried before a *Decatur* summary court-martial and dishonorably discharged in Seattle, convicted of disobedience of orders and contempt of his superior officer. Robinson ignored an order of Gunner Robert Stocking and sneered at him, "We are getting damned smart, one of us, you're taking a damned sight too much on yourself." Stocking was a notorious drunk and Captain Sterrett had tried to replace him in the past. But naval discipline acknowledged the rank, not the man. Robinson's disrespect for a superior, even for a drunken warrant officer, likely convinced the officers that it was time to get rid of him.[19]

Within three months, the *Decatur* had discharged two incorrigible sailors into the tiny settlement of Seattle, where a handful of army deserters had also gathered. Peckham and Robinson joined the "floating population" of roughnecks, gamblers, and opportunists who drifted up and down the beaches of the Pacific West, joining filibuster armies in Nicaragua, gold rushes in the Queen Charlotte Islands, or mobs in San Francisco. As long as they hung around Seattle, they linked members of the *Decatur*'s crew with the thriving community of vice on shore. They encouraged disobedience among former shipmates; they welcomed at least eight *Decatur* deserters and helped them to escape. Peckham and Robinson became liaisons between the ship and the outlaws out in the brush, east of this little port town in a territory at war.[20]

After the White River murders, Sterrett changed his mind about the "groundless" fears of local settlers and informed Mervine and Dobbin that several tribes located in the vicinity of the White River have commenced open hostility, and inimical feeling is rapidly spreading among the Indians this side of the Mountains. . . . The settlers in the Territory are short of arms and ammunition: I have been obliged to forward nearly all the small arms belonging to the ship to Olympia . . . and to arm the citizens of this place [Seattle] who were entirely destitute of the means of defense.

A week later, Sterrett wrote that the "various tribes of Indians are gradually uniting" and that all the territorial tribes were hostile with the exception of a few on Puget Sound. Sterrett also pointed out that many farmers had abandoned their crops when they came into Seattle for protection and that there would be "great suffering" if the settlers were not supplied with food from San Francisco. He requested that enough bread, sugar, beans, candles, beef, and pork be sent to sustain the crew and the settlers for a siege of four to six months.[21]

The *Decatur* continued to prepare for a real shooting war, to defend American colonists against hostile natives. The ship was anchored "off Seattle Town," as Dallas put it, "moored head and stern, guns shotted, loaded with grape, shell and canister, and trained" on the shore. The sailors were divided into four divisions, plus the howitzer's crew and the company of marines—six fighting units. On shore, the divisions and marines drilled with cutlasses and small arms. Daily, at unpredictable times, the ship beat to quarters and exercised the gun crews, shooting round shot, grapeshot, and delayed-fuse shells. The *Decatur* offered theatrical displays of power from the fixed anchorage in Elliott Bay, as though from a floating stage. But the ship itself was virtually an immobile battery: Puget Sound waters were difficult for a warship under sail to manage. Writing to Mervine, Sterrett argued for a "good steamer of some description [to be sent to Puget Sound] for in a sailing vessel, dispatch is out of the question in consequence of the strong tides, frequent calms and uncertain winds." Until a steamer could be spared, he planned to arm several of the *Decatur*'s small boats and station them far from the sloop of war at "several points on the Sound." Making a virtue of necessity, Sterrett was convinced that the *Decatur* needed to remain in Elliott Bay. "The Indians," he informed Mervine, "have repeatedly threatened to destroy [Seattle]. As this ship is here, the town is safe."[22]

Reading Sterrett's dispatches at anchor off San Francisco, Mervine concluded that the *Decatur* was in the midst of what he called a "general Indian War, the declared object of which is the extermination of all the white population," which called for a substantial steam naval force on Puget Sound. But Mervine was at a loss for a steamer to send north. The *Massachusetts* was on urgent duty in the guano islands off Peru and scheduled to head to San Juan del Sur to investigate William Walker's ongoing filibuster of Nicaragua— Walker's "unwarrantable outrage," in Mervine's view. Then James Alden, commander of the *Active,* which was refitting at San Francisco, volunteered to return the survey steamer to Puget Sound as a warship. Relieved, Mervine ordered Alden to prepare for sea and to load as large a supply of food as possible. Mervine also ordered Alden to requisition from U.S. Army ordnance at Benicia as many pistols, muskets, and cutlasses as could be spared and to "proceed to Puget Sound . . . to act in concert with the Sloop of War *Decatur* and the [U.S. Army] Forces. . . affording aid and protection to the inhabitants residing on the Sound." Then Mervine summarized Sterrett's report for Dobbin and reiterated his own longstanding request for a second steamer. The *Active* was a survey ship, undergunned and undermanned to be a fighting ship, the commodore wrote, and had to be crewed up to be effective as a warship. Mervine had authorized Alden to hire seamen at the rate being paid by the merchant marine at San Francisco. The commodore hoped that Dobbin would not disapprove the expense, which seemed essential to prepare the steamer for war on Puget Sound.[23]

At about this time, U.S. Army lieutenant Henry Crosbie proposed an audacious scheme to Sterrett. He suggested that most of the *Decatur*'s crew join him and his men in a large expeditionary force, leaving the ship at Seattle manned by just enough sailors to fight the starboard carronades. Crosbie planned to march east to Lake Washington and construct a strong blockhouse on the western shore. Using that blockhouse as a base, he proposed sending armed sorties to capture or kill the hostile Indian force reported by friendly Indians to be camped on the lakeshore. Meanwhile, Crosbie planned to garrison Seattle with the civilian militia, supported by the *Decatur*'s fire. He argued that Seattle would be adequately protected if the town was attacked while the expeditionary force was away. Sterrett's response to Crosbie's bold plan is unknown but the logbook records no such expedition.[24]

Once Seattle's blockhouse was complete and the volunteers armed, Sterrett gingerly sailed the *Decatur* south down Puget Sound, to consult with the army officers at Fort Steilacoom. Captain Keyes begged for reinforcements, and Sterrett detached Master Francis Dallas to Keyes as his aide-de-camp and Assistant Surgeon John Taylor to accompany the U.S. Army punitive expedition led by Lieutenant William Slaughter against the Indians up the White

River. Learning that the volunteer militia had also left Seattle to support Slaughter, Sterrett hastily sent Lieutenant Drake with a company of marines back to Seattle to garrison the blockhouse.[25]

On November 25, a group of settlers visited Sterrett and asked his help in dealing with some Alaska Indians who were "troublesome, and refused to go away, though threatened with violence." Sterrett described the outcome in a letter to his old friend David Farragut. Anchored off Steilacoom and "waiting for a wind to get underway for Seattle," Sterrett wrote "Dear Farragut" that he had barely dissuaded the settlers from shooting the Indians down, right on the beach. But, unarmed, Lieutenant Hughes "walked boldly" up to the chief, who had leveled his gun at him. After parlay, the Northern Indians left. Sterrett wrote Farragut that if inflamed local sentiment had prevailed, "we should have had our hands full. In less than ten days, every person living in the lower part of the Sound would have been murdered." The military men were in agreement: the ignorant brutality of territorial colonists heightened the risk of war.[26]

In his letter to Farragut, Sterrett continued that news had just come in of an attack on Slaughter's company. After midnight, the party found itself surrounded by more than two hundred territorial Indians, an unexpected force, "for every person supposed the Indians more scattered." Surgeon Taylor was all right, Sterrett wrote, but one settler had been killed. The Indians captured three dozen horses and cattle, and Sterrett feared that the armed, provisioned Indians would ambush "the Seattle volunteers; if so, we shall have dreadful accounts." He continued, "This war has barely commenced yet, and I regret to say that we are totally unprepared." At Steilacoom, Keyes had passed over "forty good rifles" to the *Decatur,* and Sterrett wrote that these were the only decent weapons on the ship. Once again, Sterrett asked Farragut to send food to Puget Sound and, even more important, rifles, small arms, shot, and powder.[27]

By then, Sterrett knew that he would soon be removed from command of the *Decatur,* and he opened his private heart to Farragut. One of the recent mailbags from San Francisco had included a copy of the *New York Herald* listing the plucked officers: Sterrett's name was on the list, "but I did not believe it." Then he received a letter from his wife confirming this "severe blow" that drove him "almost crazy." He tried to joke: "I have supplied the whole country with arms and ammunition for which I suppose the Late Board would certainly place me on the dropped list." Sterrett wrote that he was "in hourly expectation of my relief," probably Lieutenant Guert Gansevoort, and closed his letter.[28]

'Northern indian canoe.'

FIG. 25 *Taylor's drawing of Northern Indians—possibly Haida—shows an elite family being transported in an oceangoing canoe. From the John Y. Taylor Sketch Books, Western Americana Collection, Beinecke Rare Book and Manuscript Library, Yale University.*

Seattle. W.T. in 1855.

The Plucking Board's actions were common knowledge in Washington Territory, though poorly understood: Seattle's citizens met on November 13 in Fort Decatur to draft a resolution of support for Sterrett and mailed copies to Acting Governor Mason and President Franklin Pierce, "earnestly solicit[ing] reconsideration of that decision . . . that our nation not be deprived of so able a commander." The colonists were consumed with curiosity to meet the man who would replace the *Decatur*'s lame-duck captain. Guert Gansevoort received his orders on October 30 to take command of the *Decatur*, "supposed to be at Seattle, Washington Territory," and sailed from San Francisco in the merchantman *Leonesa*, arriving on November 27. But the ship ran aground off Port Townsend and Gansevoort waited restlessly, impatient to assume command.[29]

Meanwhile, Captain Sterrett sailed the ship back to Seattle from Steilacoom, his ears ringing with the grateful settlers' cheers. They had turned out to watch the *Decatur* depart "in gallant style with the wind from the southward. We could not but admire the graceful figure of the noble vessel as she glided onward under the propelling power of every inch of canvas that she could spread," wrote the local newspaper editor. After briefly anchoring off Seattle,

FIG. 26 Taylor's unfinished pencil drawing of Seattle, looking east in 1855, is an interesting contrast to Phelps's similar view. Each offers details that the other does not. Here, Yesler's sawmill belches smoke skyward, and a brig waits to load lumber alongside the mill wharf. The Decatur *is anchored in the foreground, partially concealing the merchantman. From the John Y. Taylor Sketch Books, Western Americana Collection, Beinecke Rare Book and Manuscript Library, Yale University.*

Sterrett sailed the *Decatur* across Elliott Bay to Port Madison in response to another plea for protection against the Alaska Indians. Sterrett wrote to Dobbin that he held "several interviews with the Northern Indians" and invited some on board to witness timely exercises of the *Decatur*'s great guns. The captain continued to be worried by the "imprudence of some of the Whites," which he feared would precipitate violence with these "numerous, brave, athletic and revengeful" Indians. Though this band left and promised to stay away for the duration of the local troubles, Sterrett reminded Dobbin that without a "large naval steam force," determined raids by the Northern Indians would "result in the destruction of every settlement on the Straits of Fuca and Puget Sound."[30]

Sterrett wrote directly to Dobbin because he considered the situation on Puget Sound to be worsening daily. Perhaps he hoped, too, to impress his name and his duty on the secretary in the wake of the Plucking Board action. Writing that he did not know where Mervine was, Sterrett provided Dobbin with a concise review of events and then he prepared his dispatch for the letter bag, to be sent to San Francisco on a merchant ship and then on to Panama and Washington, DC. Hours later, he added a tense postscript. Lieutenant Drake had just rushed an urgent message to the *Decatur* from Seattle, sending an Indian canoe racing across Elliott Bay to Port Madison, to inform Sterrett that a band of well-armed Indians had attacked Slaughter and Hewitt's combined force at the forks of the Green and White Rivers, about eighteen miles from Seattle. Slaughter, two corporals, and one private had been killed in this attack and five other men were seriously wounded. Taylor was with the company, tending the wounded. Sterrett concluded his hasty postscript warning Dobbin that "war in this Territory [has assumed] a most serious aspect," in part because "the valor and prowess of the [hostile territorial] Indians have been greatly underrated." Sterrett judged the military forces totally inadequate to win the war, which would require "regiments instead of companies and years instead of months to conquer these tribes." At anchor off Port Madison, Sterrett knew that Seattle was unprotected except for Drake and the handful of marines. It seemed likely to him that the victorious Indian band would sweep down the Duwamish River, burning houses and barns in their path, and attack the settlement. Sterrett prepared the *Decatur* to return, fortify Seattle, and then take the wounded to Steilacoom for treatment and the dead for burial.[31]

At first light, Friday, December 7, 1855, the *Decatur*'s crew hoisted the anchor and unfurled the sails, beating for Seattle against moderate southerly winds. Guided by local pilot William Webster, the *Decatur* ran aground at about two in the afternoon on an uncharted ledge of rocks off Restoration Point, on the southeast tip of Bainbridge Island. The ship erupted with frantic energy. The launch's crew rowed out a kedge anchor on the port quarter. Sailors raced aloft to furl the sails, ran the first two starboard guns aft, and then ran in the entire port battery, shifting the *Decatur*'s weight to free the ship. Letting go the starboard anchor, the crew hoisted out all the small boats to try haul the *Decatur* off but the ship was stuck fast. The desperate scene was swept by a sudden squall and then a steady downpour set in.[32]

As winter darkness fell, the ship was left stranded on the rocks by the receding tide. At ebb, the stern floated in three feet of water, the starboard bilge from the gangway to the bow rested on a long ridge, and the keel balanced on a sharp rock ten inches to the rear of the foremast. Just after dark, the *Decatur* cracked at this point, breaking apart under its own weight: "a loud, sharp report was heard," Phelps remembered, "accompanied with a severe trembling of the vessel." The keel had snapped; the ship's back was broken. Under lantern light, all hands worked to empty the ship of everything heavy that could be removed. Two seams had sprung open where the starboard bilge was stove in and the carpenter's gang went over the side to try to "stop them up" with blankets. But despite their efforts, "water was flowing into the ship," and the sailors worked the pumps throughout the night. When the tide turned, the ship slowly rose and righted itself, grinding and twisting on the rock ledge, opening new seams to the water. At three in the morning, Sterrett ordered the men to "splice the main brace," rest for a few minutes, and then get back to work.[33]

Before dawn, December 8, leaking badly, the *Decatur* was backed off the rocks at high tide, driven by a gusting rainstorm. Once afloat, the crew let down the anchors and turned in watch by watch to get some sleep. Because the ship was perilously close to the island shore, just after noon the ship's boats towed the *Decatur* out into deeper water, leaving behind on the rocks the kedge, starboard anchor, thirty fathoms of chain, and much heavy tackle and rigging. "Endeavoring to get to Seattle," the ship lofted sail in the afternoon and limped slowly across the bay in a harrowing voyage against contrary winds, through heavy rain squalls. Despite almost constant pumping, the ship was making one foot of water per hour. Midmorning, December 9, 1855, the *Decatur* let down its anchors off Seattle.[34]

Captain Sterrett ordered Carpenter Miller to conduct a quick survey of the damage. An hour later, Miller reported that some frames under the starboard bilge and a set of string timbers had cracked, and a few outside planks were broken off. Seams were open to the water on both port and starboard. After hearing Miller's report, Sterrett asked that it be entered in the Logbook and wearily sat down at his desk to draft his own dispatch to the squadron commodore and the secretary of the navy. It was Sterrett's "painful duty" to report that the *Decatur* had struck on "a reef of rocks off Point Restoration, not laid down on the Chart." "The ship," Sterrett stressed, "was at the time under the charge of a pilot, who repeatedly assured me that there was no danger whatever off the point." Fifteen minutes before the *Decatur* struck, Sterrett took command and ordered the helm down "against the remonstrance of the Pilot." The ship then missed stays. As soon as the ship had headway, the helm was again ordered down, and the *Decatur* came about but struck the rocks. "The ship was high and dry on the starboard side from abreast of the gangway to the bows, and lay with her bilge on a projection of the ledge . . . [she] struck very easy and during the time she was ashore, did not thump," wrote Sterrett, "the sea being very smooth."[35]

By the time Sterrett completed his report, Guert Gansevoort had finally arrived in Seattle, with orders. One was dated September 28, 1855, in Washington, DC, more than two months earlier. Dobbin informed Sterrett that he had been placed "on furlough pay" after evaluation by the Efficiency Board. In a second dispatch, Mervine ordered Sterrett to turn over command of the *Decatur* to Gansevoort and to transfer all books, papers, and orders to him. These orders were Sterrett's first official notice that he had been plucked.[36]

The following day, Gansevoort formally relieved Sterrett, who said farewell to his officers, mustered the crew, and transferred command of the ship. The *Decatur*'s officers and crew, reported the *Evening Post*, unanimously protested Sterrett's removal and intended to petition the secretary of the navy for his reinstatement. A *New York Herald* correspondent reported that "the petty officers and seamen" of the *Decatur* signed a resolution that condemned the board's "egregious error" in furloughing Sterrett and that endorsed him "as among the most able, skillful and efficient seamen in our Navy." George Davis, born in Finland, a seasoned captain of the foretop, headed the list of ninety signatures. Many local people were convinced that Sterrett had been disciplined for sailing to Seattle's relief "on his own initiative" and flew to his defense; the territorial legislature passed a memorial expressing gratitude to Sterrett and regret at his "degradation." In the meantime, Gansevoort had his baggage moved into the captain's cabin and greeted his new officers. Duty required that they face the present emergencies together, regardless of personal feelings.[37]

Sterrett and his son Jimmy boarded the *Leonesa*, to sail to San Francisco and begin their long journey home to Maryland. Three months later, from

Baltimore, Sterrett directed a tart inquiry to Samuel Francis Du Pont himself: "Having been placed on the 'Reserved List' on furlough pay, by action of the Board of which you were a member, and being unable to learn from the Department any cause, I have now to request that you will inform me from what reason in your judgment, I have become inefficient." Du Pont's reply was dismissive: "the action of the Naval Board" had been submitted to the secretary of the navy and the president and was "by them approved." The board, Du Pont informed Sterrett, had dissolved, and "I am not at liberty to reply to your inquiry." Judged unfit in a military star chamber, Sterrett had been placed on a naval "black list," the decision made public but not the cause. Publicly identified as a failure, Sterrett's pride was wounded and his sense of fairness offended. Like many other plucked officers, he decided to seek reinstatement.[38]

Back in Seattle, Gansevoort brought his own reputation on board with his baggage: the news traveled quickly through the *Decatur* that the new skipper had been the sole lieutenant on the training brig *Somers* during the tragedy of 1842. When that ship returned from an Atlantic cruise, three crewmembers had been hung for mutiny, including the son of the secretary of war. Throughout the public firestorm that followed, Gansevoort stood by his embattled captain and staunchly defended the executions, but he developed a lifelong pattern of heavy drinking, alternating periods of abstinence with binges. In fact, Gansevoort had been reviewed by the Plucking Board and was "believed to be a drinking man." Some members who knew Gansevoort were "fearful as to his habits," but the lieutenant was cleared of any charge of inefficiency and retained on the active list, poised for promotion. Gansevoort took command of the *Decatur* in the midst of an Indian war, determined to distinguish himself as he had done during the war with Mexico. He began by organizing emergency repairs to the ship.[39]

Captain Gansevoort reported to Mervine that the *Decatur* was "very much injured." The ship was making six inches of water an hour "in perfectly smooth water" off Seattle. He immediately ordered "a strict and careful survey upon the hull of this ship" to plan "what will be necessary in the way of repairs and the manner they should be made to render her sufficiently seaworthy to proceed to San Francisco." Gansevoort assigned Executive Officer Lieutenant Middleton, Lieutenant Phelps, and Carpenter Miller of the *Decatur*, Captain William Pease of the revenue cutter *Jefferson Davis*, and Captain Thomas Coupe of the bark *Success* to the task. The findings of their extensive survey were alarming.[40]

The keel and keelson were broken, and the starboard bilge stove in. On the starboard side, the *Decatur* had suffered five broken frames, and the lower deck clamps were broken in three places; many stringers had snapped and several hanging knees were broken. Five outside planks were torn away, and the futtocks separated from the floor timbers, opening seams on the berth deck. The ship was wrenched "6″ out of true for more than 20′," and Gansevoort concluded that the *Decatur* was "entirely unseaworthy, and even unfit to cruise in the Sound." The surveyors recommended replacement of some timbers and planks and extensive heavy bracing throughout, with recaulking and recoppering of the hull. But they ominously noted for the record that "many of the timbers are rotten," and they feared that they had not seen the worst of it. Once they got into the ship's bones, the surveyors expected to find more problems, and this proved to be true. After the water tanks were removed, a note was added to the survey that the stringers "were found to be completely rotten, and the frames at the fractured places rotten nearly through." Later, Phelps recalled that the survey found that the entire starboard side was completely dry-rotted except for the outermost inch, next to the water. The surveyors recommended that the ship be towed into shallow water alongside Henry Yesler's wharf and careened for repairs.[41]

Gansevoort had hoped that the ship could be quickly patched up, but the survey made it plain that the *Decatur* required extensive repairs to sustain firing the battery, let alone to be seaworthy. The ship would be stranded in Seattle for weeks to come, and repairs began at once. The men of the *Decatur* moved off the ship into Yesler's cookhouse, which became the barracks of an occupying force, living on shore. Each evening, Gansevoort stationed armed seamen along the beach with their commanding officers, as well as the marine guard, to garrison the town. Every night or two, the Logbook noted a new alarm—distant campfires, hooting owls, mysterious musket shots. Garrison duty took on real meaning as the divisions defended the ship's supplies of arms and food, stored under canvas on shore. It was essential that hostile Indians not capture or set fire to the ship itself, and Gansevoort decided to mount the howitzer in the launch to create a mobile waterborne battery while the warship was helpless. The navy men were sobered by the war canoes of the Northern Indians but equally alert to the saltwater canoes of territorial Indians. The *Decatur* had been driven from its commanding position in Elliott Bay, and rather than defending American settlement on Puget Sound, the crippled ship itself needed defense.[42]

The ship was secured to the wharf on the starboard side and to the shore on the port side with chains and hawsers to keep the stove-in starboard bow above water. A "pair of sheers"—a primitive crane—hoisted the ship's guns to the wharf; they were then moved to shore. Next, the yards, masts, sails, and standing rigging were sent ashore; then the hold was completely unloaded. The sail room had leaked badly, and all the stored sails were soaked and in danger of rotting—they were dried out in Yesler's cookhouse, then stored above the rafters. While the crew emptied the *Decatur*, Carpenter Miller, the armorer, and the sailmaker planned the repairs. Their principal task was to strengthen the ship to remount and fight the battery as quickly as possible. Some of the broken timbers were hoisted away to be replaced, but the keel and keelson and most broken futtocks, stringers, and clamps were left in place, heavily reinforced with new lumber and iron strapping secured with bolts. The *Decatur*'s side was jacked into place to be refastened and replanked with new wood. Yesler's sawmill provided the lumber, but repairs on this distant beach were frustrated by "the want of many necessaries," and the workers were forced to use "materials that were unfit for the purpose."[43]

Gangs of carpenters, armorers, and sailmakers put in fifteen-hour days, and on many nights, men worked by lantern light until well after midnight and then were up at dawn to start again. Local carpenters and laborers were hired to work on the ship, including Indian people. Acting Governor Mason had declared that all "friendly Indians" at Seattle should be sent to the reservation at Port Madison, pointing out that every Indian on Puget Sound had been relocated "with the exception of a small band at Seattle." But like Yesler, Gansevoort depended on Native labor, and he refused Mason's request, demanding that "such a number of the Indians as I deem necessary for my use may be allowed to remain here until I have completed the necessary repairs, to make the ship effective."[44]

The U.S. steamer *Active* arrived on December 15 and became indispensable, steaming back and forth to Victoria to fetch sheathing nails, rod iron, sheet lead, oakum, and sheet copper. The busy ship zipped around the Sound, carrying volunteers and soldiers, supplies of arms and ammunition, mail and messages, and civilian passengers of every sort. A navy war steamer was essential to Puget Sound defense, however. David Farragut, at Mare Island, had been hastily fitting out the *John Hancock* for service on the Sound but the war steamer's boiler "had collapsed" and the steam plant was inoperable. To defend and supply the settlements on Puget Sound, Mervine had to either hire a private steamer into the navy or summon the *Massachusetts* from pressing duties in Peru and Nicaragua. He had already stretched the budget, hiring sailors for the *Active* at merchant marine rates, and he chose to order the *Massachusetts* to steam to Seattle.[45]

In Elliott Bay, the weather worsened throughout the short, dark days of

December and January as windstorms plowed through Puget Sound, always blowing hard from the southwest. On Christmas Eve 1855, the *Decatur*'s thermometer registered 7°F. Icy tools were hard to grip and metal was difficult to work on the forge; the wharf and ship's timbers became slippery with snow and frost. Heavy winds thwarted efforts to keep the ship in place. On December 18, during a storm, the hawsers that held the ship upright parted at the dock and the ship fell over onto the port bilge, only righting with the rising tide. Two days later, the crew lashed a spar across the pilings of Yesler's wharf and chained the starboard side of the ship to the spar. But three attempts to keep the ship upright failed when hawsers snapped or chains broke in windstorms, and the carpenters finally gave up and loosely secured the *Decatur*, allowing the ship to fall over onto the port side at low tide and right itself at high tide, twice each day. At high water, the ship was tipsily afloat, and at low water, it rested in the mud, "inclining so as to render it impossible to walk on her decks."[46]

While the ship was under repair, Gansevoort continued to supply the community with food, but he was far less open-handed than Sterrett had been with arms and ammunition. And, despite heartfelt pleas from local army officers, he insisted that Surgeon Taylor and Master Dallas rejoin the ship. Likewise, he recalled Lieutenant Drake, whom Sterrett had detailed to command the volunteers at Luther Collins's farm on the Duwamish River. Gansevoort dismissed William Webster and hired a new pilot, who was not only "the best pilot on the Sound" but also had "an intimate knowledge of the Indian language and character" and could act as liaison between the officers and the Indians on the navy's payroll. *Decatur* carpenter James Miller was joined by Hans Jacob Jepsen, a Danish-born ship's carpenter on loan from the *Active*, in directing the repairs. Jepsen's journal described the *Decatur* as a ship in disrepair and disarray, its poor discipline aggravated by an extraordinary series of events: the mutiny at Santa Cruz, the passage through the Strait of Magellan, the debilitating outbreak of scurvy, the death of a shipmate who fell to his death in a storm, the heavy drinking of Gunner Stocking and other officers, the loss of Captain Sterrett, and the ship's grounding and forced occupation of Seattle.[47]

Jepsen met three Danish-born seamen on the *Decatur*: a boy of eighteen and two men "who had sailed most of their lifetimes on American men o'war . . . between 60 and 70 years old." The four men worked side by side, chatting in Danish, and the *Decatur* sailors confided to Jepsen that if "hell was worse [than the *Decatur*], it must be a bad place." In contrast to the *Active*, Jepsen noticed that between three and six men were punished daily on the *Decatur* for drunkenness and insubordination, chained under the forecastle, and that half of the sloop of war's "miserable crew" were "drunkards, officers and all." The Danish sailors told Jepsen the ship had run aground through "the negligence and incapacity of the officers of the deck." When the *Active* was in harbor, Captain Alden asked Jepsen how things were going, and the carpenter told his captain that he hated working on this ship. He said that *Decatur* carpenter Miller was a drunk who was forbidden to go ashore because he could not be trusted; instead, Miller paid sailors to steal or buy whiskey for him and spent many days blind drunk, passed out in the hold. Alden told Jepsen that "he knew what kind of ship it was" but that their duty required that he return to work on the *Decatur,* to get the warship seaworthy.[48]

Alden and Gansevoort were already at odds. While the *Decatur* was under repair, Gansevoort fought an unseemly contest with Alden and with army captain Erasmus Keyes, stationed at Fort Steilacoom. Alden had learned from Indian spies that forty warriors had crossed Puget Sound in canoes to "tamper with four or five hundred friendly Indians on the reserve." The hostile group included Leschi, principal strategist for the Native war effort west of the mountains, who hoped to persuade the reservation Indians to join the revolt. Army captain Maloney had heard the same news and he asked for a lift out to the *Active* on board the Hudson's Bay Company steamer *Beaver* to meet with Alden. Maloney and Alden then traveled to Fort Steilacoom to consult with Captain Keyes. All three believed that capturing Leschi would deal a death blow to Indian strategy on Puget Sound. Keyes and Alden decided that Maloney should remain behind and keep watch on the Indian party. The two men planned to steam up to Seattle in the *Active* and borrow the *Decatur*'s howitzer-armed launch and one of the cutters, both boats manned by trained, armed boat crews. Then they would return quickly and lie in ambush near the reservation. Arriving in Seattle in the early evening, the two men excitedly told Gansevoort about this remarkable opportunity and their plans to capture Leschi.[49]

To their shared "disappointment" and Alden's "mortification," Gansevoort "unhesitatingly refused to lend the arms, men and boats, alleging the necessity of keeping his whole crew about him for self-protection and that of the town." The three men argued heatedly, their voices rising. Likely, they were meeting in Gansevoort's temporary housing, either a room in Yesler's cookhouse or a tent. Finally, Alden pleaded with Gansevoort to lend the launch alone, armed with the single howitzer and ammunition but without any marines or sailors. He would find the men somehow. Gansevoort again refused, saying flatly and finally, "You can't have her. That settles the matter."[50]

Furious, Alden and Keyes steamed back to Steilacoom, arriving to find that "the enemy had escaped with an additional fifteen Indians obtained at the reserve, at the times and in the directions anticipated." They were gone. If Gansevoort had loaned them the means, Alden and Keyes believed they could have captured Leschi and his party, "so rare and excellent an opportunity for capturing the originators and instigators" of the Treaty War. Alden and Gansevoort wasted no time writing to Mervine and Dobbin. Their first dispatches were reasonably measured but the war of words escalated into an increasingly nasty series of letters. Throughout most of January 1856, as the *Decatur* lay crippled in a territory at war, the commanders of the two U.S. Navy vessels in Puget Sound feuded, insulting each other's honor, bravery, and suitability for command.[51]

Gansevoort argued that the *Decatur* needed its men, guns, and boats to defend the settlers and refugees at Seattle, "because it is the nearest point to the Snoqualmie Pass, and has no military force to protect it, as Steilacoom has." And why in the world, asked Gansevoort rhetorically, did Alden waste all that time steaming to Seattle? "This seems to me," he wrote with emphasis, "an arrangement well calculated to *ensure* the escape of the hostile Indians," a delay which did not "reflect much credit on [Alden's and Keyes's] military character," who should have set up their own ambush. Additionally, Gansevoort condemned their involvement of the *Beaver* as a "humiliation," accepting help from the Hudson's Bay Company.[52]

Alden wrote snidely that Gansevoort "preferred . . . to adopt the more passive pastime of culpable inactivity and . . . either inexcusably failed to comprehend our plans or willfully distorts and ridicules them to divert attention from his unpardonable delinquency." He explained that he needed the heavy boats of the *Decatur* and the launch-mounted howitzer, not the light, unarmed "whaling boats" of the *Active*. Captain Keyes agreed that the *Decatur*'s howitzer was essential to a successful ambush and echoed Alden's insinuation that Gansevoort was overly concerned for his own safety. In Keyes's opinion, Seattle was protected by a "first rate blockhouse with two guns mounted in it and a company of volunteers, about eighty strong, for its defense." Keyes unforgettably noted—and documented in writing for the secretary of the navy—that he "considered the catching of Leschi alone as of far more value to the Government than this whole ship and all the property on board of her." Keyes would rather have seen the *Decatur* at the bottom of Elliott Bay than to lose Leschi.[53]

Gansevoort disclaimed any "disposition to prolong this controversy, which has been forced on me in a most unwarrantable, wanton and indecent manner, and was totally unprovoked on my part." Then he angrily rebutted each of Keyes's and Alden's points at considerable length, in eight closely written pages. Gansevoort was especially offended by Alden's approval of Keyes's preference to see the *Decatur* a loss rather than miss a chance at Leschi, who was, after all, just one "ignorant savage," in Gansevoort's view. Seattle was, argued Gansevoort, at *considerable* risk. Slaughter and his men had died within a day's march of the settlement. Since Gansevoort's arrival, he claimed to have seen nothing of Hewitt's volunteers; the town was entirely defended by the *Decatur*'s guns, sailors, and marines.[54]

Though Gansevoort and Alden disputed the details of the plan and its likelihood of success, the root of the conflict really lay in whether Guert Gansevoort was in command of James Alden. Gansevoort put it bluntly, with heavy emphasis: "Since Commander Alden's arrival here in the *Active*, he has exhibited a disposition to assume an independent position and *co-operate* with me instead of *obeying* me." From Gansevoort's point of view, Mervine had put the *Active* under his orders, ordering the steamer to Puget Sound to "report to [Gansevoort] for duty." Alden, on the other hand, retorted that his own orders from Mervine stated that he was to "cooperate with [Gansevoort] and . . . to act in concert with him."[55]

Throughout January 1856, Gansevoort's notes to Alden became briefer and increasingly vicious. On January 16, Gansevoort wrote, "I have taken no pains [in my reports to the department] to repress the indignation I feel at the gross and wanton injustice, intended to be perpetrated on me." This seems to have been the last communication between Alden and Gansevoort for some time—the two commanders were no longer on speaking terms. Driven to conflict by uncompromising codes of manliness, duty, and honor, Gansevoort and Alden's poor discipline threatened their mission and crippled their ships' efficiency at a time of great risk.[56]

While the *Decatur* remained helpless on the beach, the officers and crew became part of the daily life of the settlement. Seattle was an occupied village under siege, ringing with practice rounds of pistols, muskets, and howitzer and filled with refugees living on ship's rations. The ship's trained and armed garrison provided security, and that is how the *Decatur* was recalled in reminiscence. Settlers remembered the gallant officers and a charming young "midshipman" who would one day return to the settlement as a Baptist minister. They remembered friendly marines who adopted a local boy as a mascot and gave his mother an old uniform to cut down for him. But navy records fully document a darker beach experience shared between ship and shore, of local economic opportunism and widespread violence and vice among *Decatur* sailors, demonstrating the officers' inability to project the ship's hierarchy and routine to the beach. While the officers hunted, competed at target practice, studied the Chinook trading jargon, and attended dinner parties, the men were to work and drill and to conform to ship's discipline on shore. The officers had forbidden contact between sailors and Seattle's respectable settlers. But seaman John Drew kept getting drunk on liquor bought in the woods and broke all the rules.[57]

At about midnight on January 18, sentries heard a musket fired in town, and the Decaturs beat to quarters on shore. Many of the settlement's women, children, and—as Phelps disdainfully put it—"others" raced to the safety of the blockhouse. The marines were detailed to guard the wharf and protect the warship. On patrol, alert for Indians, one of the sentries stumbled over a body in the dark. John Drew, thirty-six years old, born in Ireland, had been shot to death not by an Indian but by Milton Holgate, a thirteen-year-old Seattle boy, when Drew tried to break into his fifteen-year-old sister's bedroom. The sailor had a long history of trouble on board ship, starting with his role in the mutiny at Santa Cruz, and he was punished three times for drunkenness in the month before his death. The Logbook noted that Drew had been "shot through the head and killed while attempting to enter the window of a house in the town of Seattle, having been already warned off twice." Barred from association with the respectable Holgate family, Drew crossed the line in an attempted rape of Olivia Holgate. The sailor was buried without ceremony, and the Decatur's officers emphasized the lesson by inviting Milton Holgate, "the brave boy, with a number of ladies and gentlemen," to a dinner party in celebration of his valor for "saving his sister from a midnight assault by two desperate drunken deserters, one of whom was trying to force an entrance."[58]

The day after Drew's death, the Decatur was towed out to an anchorage in Elliott Bay, and the crew moved back onto the disciplined island of the ship. Over the next week, the ship's cutters towed the scow from the wharf to the ship, fetching the carronades and their carriages, the masts, yards and spars, sails, and stores of every sort. The ship's battery was set up and able to fire a fifteen-gun salute to honor the visit of Governor Stevens on January 24, 1856, as he passed through Seattle on his way back to the capital at Olympia, concluding months of treaty negotiations east of the Cascades. Traveling on the Active, Stevens invited Gansevoort to join him in a triumphal tour of Puget Sound. When he refused, noting Seattle's vulnerable situation, Stevens privately accused the Decatur officers of fostering panic. The governor then addressed the assembled colonists at Seattle, reportedly remarking, "I believe that the cities of New York and San Francisco will be as soon attacked by Indians as this town of Seattle." Anxious that the territory not lose population,

Stevens argued that settlers should stay put, that they were perfectly safe. As soon as Stevens steamed away, the *Decatur*'s great guns were reloaded with shell, round shot, and grape and directed to cover the shore, ready for the anticipated Indian attack.[59]

Gansevoort ordered the *Decatur*'s boats out on limited sorties, carrying stores up the Duwamish River for the civilian volunteers at the blockhouse at Collins's farm and later to a second blockhouse farther up the river. The *Decatur*'s skeptical officers were convinced that the volunteers enjoyed the navy rations of meat and whiskey much more than they enjoyed drilling and fighting. To Phelps's utter disgust, the civilian militia disbanded on January 22, 1856, when "these worthies declared that 'they would not serve any longer while there was a ship in port to protect them.'" Phelps spluttered with contempt for these eighty "embryo soldiers"; he had never seen "a more reckless, undisciplined set of men" in his life. After much "rough argument," thirty of them reluctantly agreed to form a company assigned duty on shore between the *Decatur*'s second and third divisions. But by ten that night, they had all abandoned their guns. Their captain gave up in disgust and volunteered to join the *Decatur*'s third division.[60]

Life on the newly refloated *Decatur* was extraordinary, outside the experience of its officers or crew. Each night, while the divisions patrolled the shore and bivouacked in Yesler's cookhouse, about forty women and children slept on the ship. During the day, most of the sailors and marines returned to the ship and most of the civilians returned to shore. However, the town's Methodist minister, David Blaine, moved on board the *Decatur* full-time with his wife, Catharine, and their newborn son. The ship's life went on all around the refugees: drills, offenses and punishments, wooding and watering parties, inspections at quarters, ongoing repairs, illnesses and even death. On January 25, Hans Carl, captain of the afterguard, died. Carl had been one of Jepsen's Danish confidants; he was sixty-three and diagnosed with *catarrhus senilis*, an acute bronchitis that the surgeons associated with Carl's age. The medical journal had charted with resignation his steady decline over the previous month.[61]

The day Carl died, Chief Tecumseh, so named by Arthur Denny, brought a group of Lake Indians into Seattle, seeking protection behind the lines. They were assigned ground at the south of town. Later that day, Gansevoort wrote to Dobbin that he had just learned that "a large number of Indians had crossed Lake Washington . . . for the purpose of attacking the place." Yarkeke-e-man Jim—a "particular favorite"—told Gansevoort that many hostile warriors had crossed the mountains from eastern Washington and intended to break into two forces to attack Steilacoom and Seattle. But once they had learned that the *Decatur*—the "Boston warship"—was aground, they abandoned the goal of Steilacoom and combined forces to attack Seattle, planning to seize the food, ammunition, and arms that the *Decatur* had unloaded on the beach. Though the Indians were a week late, the "Battle of Seattle" was about to begin.[62]

The garrison was put on heightened alert, its four divisions led by the *Decatur* lieutenants. Dallas's division, the fourth, was armed with muskets, rifles, and pistols and stationed at the southeast end of town. Drake's division, the first, was stationed on the extreme south side. North of Drake, the second division, under Hughes, was armed with rifles and carbines and occupied a Seattle store. The third division, under Phelps, was armed with muskets and held the position east of Yesler's cookhouse at the head of the wharf, facing the mouth of the trail to Lake Washington. Passed Midshipman George Morris commanded the nine-man howitzer squad, the howitzer now dismounted from the launch and placed "across the street" from another store, pointing east at the woods. The marines, commanded by Sergeant Corbin, were stationed at the blockhouse and manned the old ballast cannon. The officers dressed like their men so that they could not be distinguished and picked off by Indian sharpshooters. Phelps detailed the *Decatur* getup as flannel underclothing, heavy marine trousers, high cowhide boots, a slouch hat, blue flannel shirt, and an "Indian blanket" secured by a cartridge belt—a Western filibuster or miner's costume.[63]

Trusted Indian spies continued to bring in news of hostile warriors gathering east of town. Dallas wrote that, during the day, he could glimpse Indians "prowling in the . . . forest" and, at night, he could hear them in the woods. As darkness fell on January 25, the men of the *Decatur* stood to their stations, "every man a sentry." The weather was too overcast for stars or moon; it was damp and cold. No one spoke above a whisper as all listened almost breathlessly for the enemy's approach. The air was calm and still, filled with night noises: waves rushed up and down Seattle's pebbly beach, twigs snapped back in the brush, dogs barked, and a few drunken former volunteers caroused. The hours passed very slowly.[64]

Phelps later claimed that two Indians wrapped in blankets against the chill walked south from Suquardle's camp toward the new encampment of Lake Indians. As they passed his station, Phelps stepped out of the darkness and asked them in the Chinook trading jargon who they were and where they were going. One replied that they were: "*Lake Tillicum*"—"Lake friends"—and that they had been to visit Curley, the settlers' name for Suquardle. Phelps

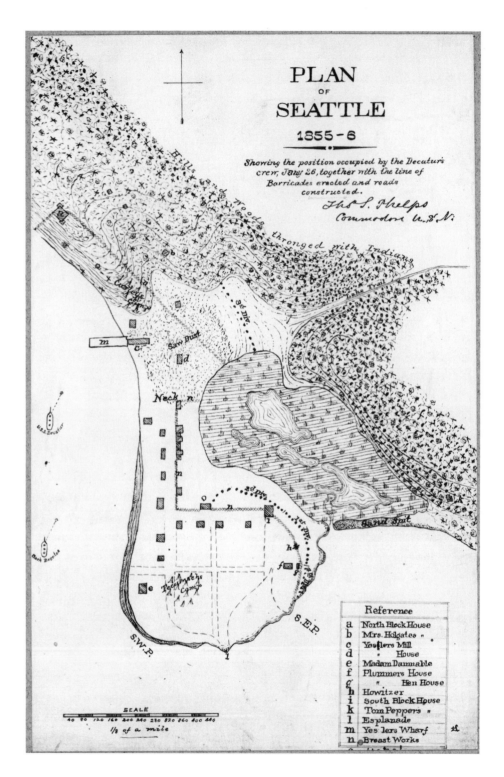

PLAN
OF
SEATTLE
1855-6

Showing the position occupied by the Decatur's
crew, Jany 26, together with the line of
Barricades erected and roads
constructed.

Thos S. Phelps
Commodore U.S.N.

	Reference	
a	North Block House	
b	Mrs. Holgates	"
c	Yeslers Mill	
d	" House	
e	Madam Dammable	
f	Plummers House	
g	" Hen House	
h	Howitzer	
i	South Block House	
k	Tom Peppers	"
l	Esplanade	
m	Yeslers Wharf	
n	Breast Works	

SCALE
40 80 120 160 200 240 280 320 360 400 440
1/8 of a mile

FIG. 27 *Phelps dated this bird's-eye view of Seattle to the morning of the battle, January 26, 1856. However, the south blockhouse, drawn here, was not built until the spring. Likely redrawn and re-inked for publication in the early 1880s, this drawing is packed with information about the settlement at war. Phelps shows us the sawdust filling in the wetlands north of the saltmarsh. Henry Yesler's mill is at the heart of town, his dock extending into Elliott Bay, and just north is the camp of Suquardle or "Curley," father of Yesler's "country wife," Susan. "Tecumseh's" camp is south, behind Madame Damnable's place. The* Decatur *is anchored in the bay, north of the lumber bark* Brontes. *Courtesy Museum of History & Industry, SHS 1116.*

warned them that the Decaturs were on a hair trigger, and the two walked away, down to Tecumseh's camp. An hour later, Phelps heard an owl's hooting in the woods behind the center of town, answered immediately by hootings to the north and south. Alarmed, he roused Suquardle and sent him out to scout nearby. Returning two hours later, Suquardle irritably reported that there were no Indians in the woods and he wanted to return to bed. Phelps was suspicious and followed him. Suquardle stopped on the trail and paced back and forth, gesturing and muttering angrily to himself. Then he turned abruptly and headed for Tecumseh's camp, passing Phelps hidden along the trail. The two blanketed Indians, Phelps wrote, were the hostile warriors Leschi and Owhi, and they met with Suquardle, Yark-eke-e-man Jim, and Tecumseh. Leschi proposed a predawn attack by the Indians quartered within Seattle to kill every settler and every sailor. Suquardle asked that Henry Yesler be spared, the American who was the father of his daughter's child, and his request was denied. Intending to warn the settlers, Jim bought time by suggesting an alternative plan: to attack the village in the morning just after the Decaturs returned to their ship. This plan was agreed to and Leschi slipped away, returning to his camp in the woods. Presumably, the hootings that alarmed Phelps were the signal to Indians in town that the Indians in the woods understood and agreed to the first-thing-in-the-morning plan.[65]

At first light, January 26, 1856, the garrison returned on board for breakfast and to get some sleep. Yark-eke-e-man Jim slipped away from Suquardle and passed his information on to the settlers, and Yesler was rowed out to the *Decatur* and awakened Gansevoort to tell him that he had just learned "from a private source . . . worthy of attention" that many hostile Indians had gathered in the woods close to town, planning to attack at once. Gansevoort leaped from his berth, yelling, "John, bring me my boots!" An allied Indian force estimated at about 750 warriors was ranged thinly through the woods along the east side of town. At once, Gansevoort ordered 119 officers, sailors, and marines rowed from the *Decatur* back to shore, without sleep and without breakfast, to defend a line in an arc from the blockhouse to the southeast point of Seattle. Gansevoort joined his men on shore; Gunner Stocking, Carpenter Miller, clerks Francis and Ferguson, and fifteen men remained on board under the command of First Lieutenant Middleton to guard the ship and fight the great guns.[66]

Friendly Indians loaded their canoes and paddled away from Seattle's beach, headed to the Port Madison reservation. Ki-cu-mu-low, Yark-eke-e-man Jim's mother, ran from Curley's camp to a canoe, yelling, "*Hiu Kliktat copa Tom Pepper's house! Hi-hi hiu Kliktat!*" (There are many Klickitat Indians at Tom Pepper's house! Many, many Klickitat!).[67]

Gansevoort set up his command post at Yesler's bunkhouse and assembled a staff composed of Surgeons Jeffery and Taylor, Purser Jones, and Sailmaker Warren. He turned to Phelps and said, "Get your men under cover and to sleep, so they can be rested and ready when the Indians appear, and I will have their meals sent to them on shore; first, however, I will go to the south end and have the howitzer lodge a shell in Tom Pepper's house to see if they (the hostile Indians) are there." While Gansevoort made his preparations, the Decaturs crammed into Yesler's bunkhouse, weapons at their sides, to snatch such sleep as they could. The volunteers who had deserted three days earlier were now bustling around, talking excitedly. Phelps shushed them—cowards and delinquents—and warned them away; then, out of patience, he ordered the sentry to shoot them if they did not leave. They damned Phelps with "such oaths and curses as would have shamed the Dutch in Flanders." Then the howitzer was fired, immediately followed by a thirty-two-pound shell from a carronade on board ship, aimed at Pepper's house. The navy fired the first shots in the Battle of Seattle.[68]

The Indians yelled defiance from the woods and fired muskets and pistols into the town. As the sailors raced from Yesler's bunkhouse to their stations, Phelps noted with contempt the former volunteers sprinting for the safety of the blockhouse, running "as men never ran before . . . so that the very bones in their legs bent under them . . . to cower behind the wooden bulwarks." The women and children who were not on board the ship fled to the blockhouse, too, babies in their arms and fresh-baked biscuits in their aprons.[69]

Although ranged throughout the woods east of town, a body of Indians had massed at the trail that led to Lake Washington. According to Phelps, his division charged toward them and found stumps to crouch behind and support their rifles. Then the Decaturs "cooled down to their work," shooting into the woods along the trail. The firing was constant: the rattle of small arms, the whistle of bullets, the sharp crack of the howitzer, and the booming of the great guns. Dallas's division came under fire by Indians on the high ground east of the marsh. Half of his men were in a hencoop; the other half were divided between a woodshed and a hayloft, shooting up into the woods. At the south end of the peninsula, Taylor and some Port Madison sawmill workers joined the line, aiming their hunting rifles across the marsh, into the brush.[70]

Throughout the morning, the Indian attack slowly moved northward, sending "a sharp and steady fire" into the settlement. From time to time, a band would sally out to attack the American position: "down came the Indians, like so many demons," as Phelps put it, "tearing through the bushes and filling the air with frightful yells [taking cover to] deliver a terrific volley." The *Decatur*'s gun crews directed the carronades with deadly efficiency, firing shell, round shot, and grape into the woods. A couple of settlers thought that "Captain Gansevoort aimed rather low," though it was Middleton directing the *Decatur*'s battery; one ball drilled clear through a building.[71]

The Indian force was a confederation and the warriors did not speak one another's language: the only way they could coordinate the attack was to use trading jargon to shout to one another, communication easily understood by all, including their enemies. Most of the Indians had old-fashioned muskets rather than rifled guns. The Indian Phelps called "Klakum" was an exception and was an excellent shot with his rifle. He was likely the war chief identified as "Claycum" by historians Thomas Prosch and Frederic Grant, in command of a small group of insurgent Duwamish Indians. Phelps asked Morris to load the howitzer with a delayed shrapnel shell and aim it into Klakum's well-screened sharpshooter nest. The shell burst, sending shrapnel "around the corner," so to speak, and driving Klakum out. Phelps also wrote that he watched a shell with a fifteen-second-delay fuse land in a group of ten Indian warriors. As it rolled, seemingly inert, they trapped it with blankets and had just joined hands to dance around the shell in triumph when it exploded and killed them all.[72]

In the late afternoon, the Indian fire diminished and Gansevoort brought the Decaturs on board for rest and food. At this time, all the women and children who were in the blockhouse were rowed out to the lumber bark *Brontes* and the *Decatur*. There was scattered musket and pistol fire from the Indians throughout the growing January darkness, and the *Decatur* carronades continued to sweep the woods, ending the bombardment at ten that night. At dawn, the *Decatur* fired a shot that went unanswered. The battle was over.

No Decaturs were killed or injured in this engagement. Two Americans died: one was young Milton Holgate, shot as he stood in the door of the blockhouse, backlit by a fire. Holgate, that fated boy, had shot John Drew to death less than two weeks earlier. The second dead man was a footloose drifter whom no one seemed to know very well—he was variously named in reminiscences as White, Pocock, and Wilson. The Indian attackers took their dead and wounded with them at day's end. Although some Indians claimed that no attacker had been wounded, an eyewitness later wrote that the Indians admitted that twenty-eight warriors had died and eighty were wounded. "The chief of a friendly tribe" reported to Gansevoort that he thought "a great many" warriors had been killed. The battle was a real fight in which people lost their lives.[73]

The Decaturs celebrated their victory; the men enjoyed their extra grog and retold the day's adventures to each other. The officers did the same: fighting in a real battle was a professional achievement, demonstrating "martial manhood" in pursuit of their duty. The officers exaggerated the number and skill of Native attackers to balance their technological advantage—rifles, carronades, delayed-fuse shells, shrapnel shells—over their Indian opponents, who were mostly firing "flint-lock muskets . . . of an inferior quality." In addition, Phelps stressed his enemy's strategic abilities, describing Leschi as one of three Indian "generals-in-chief," noble and manly, proficient in navy-style fighting; after the battle, Lieutenant Philip Johnson, of the *Active,* claimed that Leschi boldly sent Gansevoort a personal challenge: that he would return in force to destroy the town. Gansevoort wrote to Secretary Dobbin of the "gallant and energetic behavior of the officers and men who, although they had been out for several nights, at this inclement season, obeyed every order promptly and with the greatest alacrity." In praising the bravery and skills of both sets of adversaries, the officers refashioned the battle as an honorable passage at arms.[74]

In Phelps's memory, navy men were brave and true, declaring, "Never fear for us, sir; we will stand by you or die in our tracks." A "colored boy" who had nursed Hans Carl in his last illness begged for a rifle to come ashore and fight, and "a braver man never endured Indian fire in battle." As Phelps contructed the battle's imperial meaning, he wrote that "the fate of Seattle hung by a thread" and the *Decatur* "was the salvation of every white inhabitant in the Territory." The siege and battle provided stages in a theater of bravado in which the opponents mounted displays of power. The *Decatur* had been staging theatrical demonstrations of the great guns and the men's shore drills for weeks. The officers' costume was dashing: one of the *Decatur*'s young officers, George Morris, was "a perfect brigand in appearance," parading the single street of Seattle in a poncho, slouch hat, and high leather boots, draped with a cutlass, revolver, and rifle. Likewise, Suquardle emerged from his camp in the afternoon of the battle "arranged in his war dress and smeared with paint," holding a bow in one hand and a musket in the other, yelling words incomprehensible to Phelps and dancing to and fro across Yesler's sawdust. His dance built to a climax: a great leap in the air and a "frightful whoop." To Phelps, this was simply "a ludicrous exhibition of Indian bravado, beyond description." The lieutenant would not draw comparisons between naval exhibitions of bravura and those of Native warriors.[75]

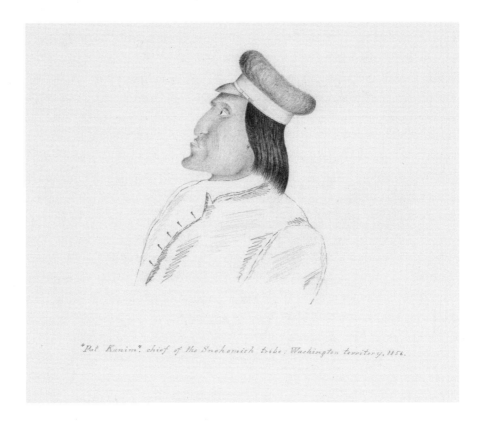

FIG. 28 Taylor sketched this portrait of Snoqualmie chief Patkanim, who was hired as an auxiliary by Washington's territorial authorities to identify, hunt, and kill hostile Indians. The severed heads were stored on board the Decatur until Patkanim and his men could take those trophies to Olympia, to be paid their bounty. From the John Y. Taylor Sketch Books, Western Americana Collection, Beinecke Rare Book and Manuscript Library, Yale University.

"Pat Kanim" chief of the Snohomish tribe; Washington territory, 1856.

We see all Indians dimly through the eyes of American observers, whether officer or colonist, whose understanding was poor and motives suspect. Certainly, the Treaty War forced many Native people to define themselves with respect to the American newcomers: Leschi, Seattle, Suquardle, Yark-eke-e-man Jim, Susan (Yesler's "wife"), Tecumseh, Patkanim, Klakum, and thousands of others. And each American developed a different test for deciding which Natives were "friendly" and which were not, imperfect insights into the Indian world. Phelps never trusted Suquardle but had confidence in his nephew, Yark-eke-e-man Jim; he judged Chief Seattle's friendship to be genuine and Chief Patkanim's alliance to be expedient. And although officers and settlers depended on some Indian people to defeat others, on "friendly" Indians to police "hostile" ones, Alexandra Harmon, Coll Thrush, and Brad Asher have shown that Indian roles were far more fluid and motivations more subtle than Americans understood.[76]

In the battle's aftermath, territorial and military authorities continued to rely on Native people. For instance, Chief Seattle "informed the whites" that a hostile warrior had come to the Port Madison reservation, prompting the fugitive's arrest. Additionally, Governor Stevens directed the Indian agent at Port Townsend to raise one hundred warriors from the "Clallam and McCaw" tribes to act as auxiliaries "under an efficient white man to lead." Instead, Snoqualmie chief Patkanim and fifty-five warriors were hired to hunt down hostile Indians, receiving an $80 bounty for each head brought in of a "chief" and $20 for lesser warriors. The *Decatur* was the collection site for these grisly trophies, acquired without arrest or trial. Patkanim spent the bounty on clothing—to turn "from a dirty savage to a pattern citizen," Phelps mocked— climbing the *Decatur*'s gangway wearing gaiters, white kid gloves, a white shirt with high standing collar, and a red necktie. Patkanim had spent blood money to assume the American uniform of power. In 1901, Thomas Prosch claimed that Patkanim became "chief among the friendlies" because he had once traveled to San Francisco and been overwhelmed by American strength—"the ships, the houses and the vast number of people." However, Patkanim's understandings remain hidden, as do those of John Decatur, whom the officers decked out in motley off Tierra del Fuego, underlining their conviction that assuming a costume would never remake the Native person. In 1856, Surgeon Taylor sketched Patkanim in profile, a navy regulation cap partly disguising his flattened forehead, the result of a procedure performed on babies of high birth among the Snoqualmie. Patkanim was ashamed of what had once been an honor—or rather, Taylor believed that Patkanim should be ashamed and so drew him in disguise.[77]

Seattle is a city on Indian ground but we are reduced to American memories of Indian people, the archaeological record, and a slender Native oral tradition. In 1940, Frank Allen, a Skokomish, related his family's oral history of "Leschi's war":

I never saw Leschi, but my great-uncle was a Nisqually fighting man, and I have heard him tell about Leschi's war. Leschi went to the Yakama, to ask them to fight the whites with him. I don't know who the head fighter was there, but they were all willing, and they told Leschi they'd fight with him. Leschi said to them, "The white men burnt my village. I was out on the bay fishing, and they burnt my village. That's why I'm going to fight."

Now Leschi and his people came home, and they went toward Seattle, to White River, and all over where there were settlements, killing. Old Seattle came to Leschi and said, "No, Leschi, don't kill these white people. Yesler and others of them have Indian women. Don't kill them. Take my word." Well, Leschi said to Seattle, "All right, we'll take your word. We won't kill them."

So . . . Leschi and his fighters showed themselves to the soldiers.

Indian fighters had indeed shown themselves to the soldiers, attacking

Slaughter's company and then mounting an assault against a fortified town that was defended by a well-armed force of sailors and marines, backed up by a warship. This alliance of Native people had prepared an unprecedented attack on Seattle, to resist American conquest in armed rebellion.[78]

As the Indians withdrew, they ransacked abandoned farms for provisions and then burned the buildings; smoke rose along local river valleys. The newspapers reported that the rural countryside was "utterly depopulated . . . literally used up and rubbed out," and Puget Sound editorialists anguished over the setback to territorial growth. King County—"one of the best counties in the Territory"—had been "all laid in ashes by the savages." According to the *Pioneer and Democrat,* three-quarters of the businesses in Washington Territory had been destroyed, half the population had been driven away, and the remaining settlers were crowded into blockhouses. To observers, Seattle itself looked deserted, and one noted ominously that "many of the best citizens are leaving the place," packing up and heading for San Francisco or Portland, increasing the local percentage of tough drifters. But some of the founding settlers stayed: David and Louisa Denny's daughter was born in the blockhouse in March, and she was named Madge Decatur Denny to honor the warship.[79]

Some jittery colonists went about their daily activities armed, jumping at every noise. On February 22, the *Decatur* celebrated George Washington's birthday with a blank salute and then reloaded all the guns with grape and round shot, just in case. In March, local newspapers reported skirmishes south of Seattle that left one soldier dead, a dozen wounded, and at least thirty Indians killed. The ship's crew remained on a war footing and continued to garrison Seattle every night during February, March, and April 1856, receiving their meals and grog on shore. There was no casual strolling around: when one of the *Decatur*'s marines needed a bucket of water from the creek, he was assigned an escort. *Active* lieutenant Philip Johnson was convinced that the Decaturs were playing at war. He considered the nightly garrisoning of the town "farcical" and satirized the defense of "the important city of Seattle against the threatened attack of about fifty miserable Indians." Johnson wrote in his journal that Gansevoort—whom he termed "the Big Indian"—was "a d—d fool" and that "nothing but fear actuates him."[80]

Gansevoort insisted that Indian threats be taken seriously and ordered that the *Active* either remain anchored in Elliott Bay or place its fieldpiece on shore. Alden chose the latter, and Johnson, the steamer's junior lieutenant, was assigned to the Seattle garrison. He reluctantly pitched his tent on the beach, furnished with a table, chair, toilet-stand, and woodstove, and brought

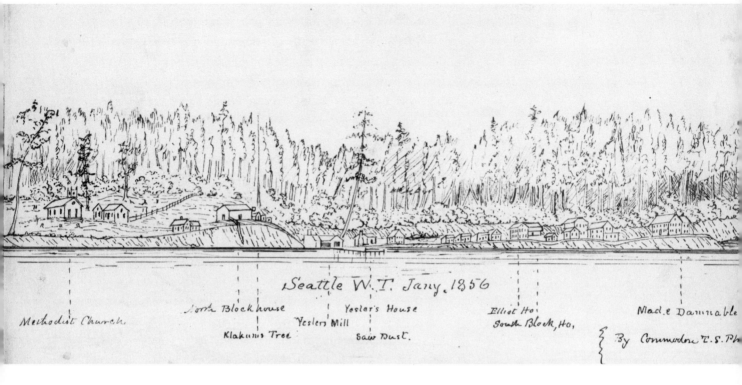

Seattle W. T. Jany. 1856

Methodist Church.   North Blockhouse   Yesler's House   Elliot Ho   Mad.e Damnable
                     Klakums Tree   Yesler Mill   Saw Dust.   South Block Ho,   By Commodore T. S. Ph

"a box well stowed with little niceties for the inner man." Late one February night, a sentry heard whooping in the woods and raised the alarm. Johnson wrote that he "had my boots and arms on in a very short time, for these are the only things I take off when I go to sleep." The incident proved to be a false alarm; at least, when the detail searched the woods, they found nothing except an abandoned campfire. In another February alarm, Indian spies brought the news that seven canoes had crossed Lake Washington from the east and that the warriors intended to attack Seattle. Gansevoort sent every available man on shore and ordered Phelps to keep rat-tail files ready to spike the shore guns if the force had to retreat quickly to the ships.[81]

Rattled by weekly alarms, the *Decatur* officers expanded the settlement's defenses. Work parties built a second blockhouse in Seattle on a low ridge in the southern part of town, using Yesler's donated lumber. One of the old ballast cannons was moved outside the south blockhouse, and the crew also built a long line of five-foot-high barricades, made from two rows of poles eighteen inches apart filled in with rammed earth and sawdust, to encircle the town on the south and east sides. But most of the settlers were not frightened enough to defend themselves, and the *Pioneer and Democrat* wondered why none of the volunteer militia companies were at full strength. Phelps wrote in disgust that it proved impossible to "induce the floating population of the town to

FIG. 29 *Phelps's 1856 drawing of Seattle's waterfront is signed by "Commodore" T. S. Phelps, a rank not achieved until the 1880s. The pencil sketch was re-inked and some details have been added or changed. Nevertheless the settlement is clearly a sawmill port bracketed by a church to the north and Madame Damnable's house to the south. Phelps confidently sketched the rough little colonial town, clinging to the beach at the edge of the forest, out at the western edge of the continent. Courtesy Museum of History & Industry, SHS 2761.*

organize for the field." Johnson and Phelps agreed that "the only ones who are doing anything [to defend Seattle] are the Decaturs; the citizens take no part in the defenses." Johnson described Seattle's settlers as "a set of good-for-nothing and cowardly rascals," and Phelps despaired of "the vicious element overrunning the place." In February, an exasperated Gansevoort reduced the number of Decaturs assigned to shore duty "on account of the men getting drunk. If the inhabitants insist upon selling them liquor," Lieutenant Johnson observed, "[Gansevoort] says they may take care of their own property." But Seattle's merchants sold liquor to anyone willing to buy it, apparently unconcerned by danger to themselves or to their property, and sailors in the garrison continued to sneak away from their duty into the woods, paying top dollar for every drop of liquor that locals could provide.[82]

Mervine dispatched the *Massachusetts* north, informing Alden and Gansevoort that the war steamer's commander, Samuel Swartwout, would "assume the command of the naval forces now in Puget Sound." In the same dispatches, Gansevoort was ordered to sail the *Decatur* to Mare Island for repairs as soon as possible. Once those were complete, he was to take the warship south and investigate the situation of eighty Americans who had sailed on the *Archibald Gracie* from San Francisco, intending "a filibustering expedition at La Paz" in Baja California. They had been captured by the Mexican army and sent to Mazatlan for trial. Mervine noted that the filibuster violated the laws of the United States and Mexico—"which precludes the right of making a demand for their release"—but he hoped Gansevoort's good offices might ameliorate the "unhappy condition" of these "deluded Young Americans." Gansevoort's second mission was to cruise among the American guano vessels in the Chincha Islands off Peru. Reading these orders in Seattle's chilly drizzle, Gansevoort may have felt restless indeed.[83]

But the settlers did not want the naval force to diminish and circulated a petition for presentation to the *Decatur*'s captain. Nearly every man in Seattle signed the document.

We the undersigned citizens of Seattle, W.T., having heard of the expected arrival of the United States Steamer Massachusetts in these waters, and that she is intended to relieve the Decatur under your command, beg leave to convey to you our earnest hope that you will not abandon us. . . . You have fought for us and we all have confidence in your zeal, energy and talents; and you are perfectly advised of our exposed situation and the absolute certainty that exists of our being destroyed if left to defend ourselves, without assistance. You also know that there is a good trail leading from this place, without obstruction, to the camp of the hostile Indians, who are known to number many hundreds. . . . In expressing our personal confidence in you and your ship we are far from wishing to depreciate the merits of others. We merely give utterance to our undivided sentiments as a community in thus declaring our preference for you and your officers and men, over all others.[84]

Settlers at Seattle depended on the *Decatur* for protection, as a source of cash for a variety of goods and services, and for supplies of weapons and food. Gansevoort's crucial December report that the *Decatur* had only two months' supply of provisions had gone astray, taking six weeks to reach Mare Island. The shipyard worked round-the-clock to prepare the *Massachusetts* to supply Puget Sound. Farragut loaded the steamer with muskets, carbines, pistols, a ton of cannon powder, and a thousand cartridges, as well as tons of food. On February 24, 1856, the *Massachusetts* finally arrived and remained for more than a year, long after the *Decatur*'s departure. Commodore Mervine had concentrated more than half of the Pacific Squadron in Puget Sound: the *Decatur*, the *Massachusetts*, the *Active* (on loan), and soon the *John Hancock*. Without this show of force, Mervine believed that the Sound's "Emigrant Settlers" would have been massacred.[85]

On arrival, Swartwout reported that he had engaged a pilot, yet another local man on the navy payroll, noting that the same practice was followed on the *Decatur*, the *Active*, and the revenue cutter *Jefferson Davis*. The pilot customarily "took charge" in the Strait of Juan de Fuca and his stint continued until the ship left the strait. The local going rate was $125 per month—a princely sum—and budget-minded Secretary Dobbin balked, suggesting that $25 per month was reasonable. Swartwout tartly replied that a skilled Puget Sound pilot would not work for that money. And if, he continued, Sterrett had spent a little more and "if the *Decatur*'s pilot had possessed . . . experience and judgment, that vessel would not have been run upon rocks and the government have been saved several thousand dollars expense." Swartwout got his high-priced pilot and also hired eight Indian people for "special services."[86]

Swartwout requested that another survey be completed on the *Decatur*. The carpenter and steam engineer of the *Massachusetts* took borings of the frame and hull in the area of the damage and found "this part of the ship is considerably affected by dry rot, and . . . the natural inference is that other parts are affected in like manner." However, the basic repairs were judged adequate to make the *Decatur* seaworthy for a trip to San Francisco, and the surveyors recommended that the ship sail in June, waiting for the best possible weather.[87]

After settling in, Swartwout reviewed the litany of summary courts-martial, desertions, and subjudicial punishments and wasted little time before deciding that the Puget Sound naval forces were in disarray. He took firm command of the feuding naval commanders and then published two general orders on March 1, 1856, which were read to all hands, on all three ships:

General Order No 1

The sailors and marines attached to the vessels composing the U.S. Naval Forces in Puget Sound are strictly forbidden from purchasing or otherwise obtaining liquors from any of the inhabitants of the town of Seattle, and I expect that the commander of each vessel will make every exertion to enforce this order as necessary for the preservation of discipline.

General Order No 2

No person attached to any of the vessels composing the U.S. Naval Forces stationed on Puget Sound will be permitted to discharge any fire arms outside of the fortified precincts of the town without my permission. Officers who wish to practice may fire from 10 to 11 every day on Commercial Street, south of Mr. Chase's store, but at no other time or place. In case of an attack of Indians at night, a blue light will be burned at the two blockhouses when I shall expect the commander of each vessel to repair on shore with all dispatch accompanied by as many of the officers and crew armed and equipped, as can be spared from the defense of the vessel.

Swartwout's orders suggest the ironies of the occupation: some settlers claimed that they feared Indian attack and needed navy protection while other settlers freely sold liquor to sailors and marines, befuddling the wits and spoiling the aim of their defenders. Likewise, while officers diligently drilled in anticipation of the "attack of Indians at night" on Seattle, most sailors behaved as though attack was highly unlikely. Melville noted the basic antagonism between the interests of officers and of enlisted men: combat offered the sailors nothing but "hard work and harder usage" but held the promise of honor and promotion for their officers. Phelps remembered a heroic crew bravely following their officers to fulfill dangerous duty on the beach at Seattle, but the evidence of the punishment record, the medical log, and Swartwout's General Orders suggests otherwise. The crews of the *Decatur* and the *Active* were now joined on Puget Sound by the crew of the *Massachusetts*, and these hundreds of enlisted men shaped a primitive sailor town in the woods behind the beach despite Swartwout's General Orders.[88]

The occupation of Seattle continued to allow easy contact between men from the three navy ships and the local community. Work parties cleared the area within the barricade and built a street through town, burning stumps and leveling the grade. As Phelps put it, by the time the navy was finished, "Seattle assumed the appearance of a well-laid out town," designed in precise military fashion and distinguished by two blockhouses. Then the town's eastern edge was cleared of brush between the barricade and the woods, to discourage Indian attack but also to establish a perimeter of discipline. Nevertheless, as many as six Decaturs were daily ordered confined as "drunk on duty," having crossed the barricade to slip into the woods. Writing of Fort Steilacoom soldiers in the 1850s, a settler recalled many "hard characters . . . whose proper place was the penitentiary" and mentioned that they indulged their "vicious proclivities" late at night when they were drunk. Phelps wrote contemptuously of "certain dealers [who were] bent upon selling liquor to our men and in trading with the savages," selling "rifle whisky"—a kind of moonshine, with a kick like a rifle.[89]

Officers exhibited an amused, exasperated tolerance for the "recklessness of the sailor who only looks to present enjoyment regardless of the future." The officers *expected* men to have a wild time on liberty, to drink too much, to gamble all their money away, to fight with the locals, to have sex with prostitutes, and to try to smuggle liquor aboard. They expected a wave of punishments after liberty as the boats returned filled with bruised drunks; they expected to treat outbreaks of venereal disease after visiting port. But the *Decatur* was not at sea, stopping in liberty ports for a spree. Instead, the long occupation of Seattle brought daily temptation, and the men's constant, casual disobedience defied their officers' command and undermined officer and settler narratives of danger. Navy officers despised most Seattle settlers as venal cowards and disobedient sailors as thoughtless fools, but perhaps the officers missed the point in their own eagerness for distinction. Perhaps the sailors and settlers were realists rather than cowards, well informed by Indians of any pending danger. The Old Navy record of summary courts-martial for ongoing liquor offenses documents occupied Seattle and suggests complicated relationships among sailors, settlers, and Indians.[90]

Patrick McCann, an Irish-born ordinary seaman on the *Decatur*, was accused of leaving a Seattle work party that was under orders of Sailmaker Warren. The cutter was loaded with firewood and water, and the oarsmen sat in the rain waiting impatiently for McCann. Warren called him repeatedly but McCann had bought a bottle of liquor and was "talking to one of his friends" under the sheltering roof of Yesler's sawmill. McCann finally sauntered down to the cutter and the crew pulled away. Warren told the sailor that he intended to report him for disobedience of orders, and McCann threatened the warrant officer, "I will meet you after this, back in the states, when I will be as good as you are. If you had not been a damned shit, you would not have reported me." McCann was found guilty at a summary court-martial.[91]

John Ryan, another Irish-born ordinary seaman, was charged with disobedience; the specifics were that Ryan, ashore in Seattle with a firewood party from the *Decatur*, had refused to obey an order given by the boatswain's mate and "cursed the ship, the flag and the country." He had been drinking, witnesses testified, but was not so drunk that he did not know what he was saying. Standing on Yesler's wharf, in Washington Territory, on Washington's birthday, Ryan told the world that he was an Irishman and that he "wanted to get out of this damned ship!"[92]

The second charge against Ryan was that he had used "provoking and reproachful words," specifically calling Robert Shorter "a black son of a bitch." Shorter testified: "We were on the wharf at Seattle, and . . . boatswain's mate was hurrying us. I told [Ryan] to get out of the way. He said, 'You damn black son of a bitch, I'll kick your head off you.' Brennan and Sprague caught hold of him as he picked up a stick of wood to strike me with." As an experienced seaman, Shorter earned $18 per month. Ryan, ordinary seaman, earned $14, and likely resented Shorter for his race and his position. Convicted of all charges, Ryan was lightly punished. Despite the similarity to John Peckham's outburst the previous fall, Ryan was far from dishonorably discharged; instead, he was disrated to landsman and lost three months' pay. It is likely that the *Decatur*'s discharged sailors had become troublesome to shore discipline, discouraging additional dismissals.[93]

In another case, two *Massachusetts* sailors, William Flynn and Robert Logan, were charged with getting drunk while on garrison duty. Late at night, Flynn bought a bottle of liquor at the barricade or in the woods and chugged it down. Drunk, he reeled into Suquardle's camp, "a part of the said town of Seattle which was interdicted," and "went into an Indian hut and molested its inmates." Suquardle approached one of the *Decatur*'s officers to complain that there was a "Boston sailor in his hut." Flynn was found unconscious on a bed and carted off to the blockhouse. Logan also bought a bottle and went into Suquardle's camp and into his hut. According to testimony at his summary court-martial, after a few moments all the Indian women ran outside and sat along the path. Logan staggered out of the empty hut and entered a second hut and then passed out. One of the lieutenants detached a marine guard to fetch Logan and sent for Charles Curley, Suquardle's son, to identify the marauding sailor by lantern light. Logan was still so drunk the next morning that the quartermaster refused him his grog at breakfast.[94]

Swartwout's General Orders had placed Curley's camp off-limits, but

Flynn and Logan displayed considerable familiarity with the camp and its residents. It is also clear that Suquardle was confident that the officer would remove Flynn from his hut and put an end to Flynn's "molesting the inmates." "Molesting" was the navy's term and it may not mean that Flynn tried to rape an Indian woman or that he tried to assault an Indian man—we cannot be sure what the verb means. And, Flynn and Logan were not tried for breaking into the Indian dwellings; their punishable offenses were getting drunk on duty and violating Swartwout's General Orders.

In another case, a thief on the *Massachusetts* who had stolen a $20 gold piece from a shipmate went to the forbidden Elliott House to buy a bottle of brandy. By the time one of the marines spotted him, he was leaning on the bar, very much "in liquor." Challenged, he claimed that he had gotten the money from "some Indians who were playing cards" at the Elliott House, and that he had stolen their tin box of coins. The marine sentry replied, "That's false; you didn't take it off of no Indians." Testimony in this case offers evidence that seamen spent money on liquor in the Elliott House, that the establishment was managed by a woman, and that Indian men played cards at a table in the barroom there. The thief lied that he had paid for his bottle with money stolen from the Indians, as though their presence, their money, and his theft were convincing commonplaces. The sentry did not raise an eyebrow at the theft; instead, he disbelieved the thief because of the amount. Questioned by the marine sentry, the Elliott House landlady replied that the seaman had paid $10 for his bottle, about five times its market value in Seattle. The marine commented, "Well, you did not lose any money here," and she frankly admitted, "No, we did not." The shrewd landlady spoke not only for herself but for all the merchants of Seattle, vicious and virtuous alike.[95]

Throughout the spring, the record documents one case after another of men getting drunk on shore while on duty, their testimony opening windows on a forgotten Seattle. Charles White was a member of a work gang rowed to the beach at dawn to repair the little civilian steamer *Water Lily*. Three hours later, a dinghy from the ship brought breakfast and grog to the men. White, a member of the carpenter's gang, had gotten drunk in the woods and became increasingly unruly until he was clapped into irons to sober up. Michael McCann was so drunk that he could not stand, but from his supine position on Seattle's beach, he loudly accused an Alabama lieutenant on board the *Massachusetts* of being a Southerner, of not being a real American. George Smith walked out of the woods drunk late one night and was hailed by the sentries at the north blockhouse, "Who is there?" He answered, "Friend," and was told, "Stand, Friend." Smith ignored the order and staggered up to the blockhouse and leaned against it. The lieutenant on duty had heard all the commotion and asked Smith what in the world he thought he was doing. Smith told him, "I am pissing!" Since he did not say, "I am pissing, *sir,*" he faced charges of insubordination. Benjamin Lenz, on garrison duty, bought a bottle and told the world that he was a Virginian, that he hated the ship and everybody in it, and that he did not give a damn what they did with him. On shore at midnight, Lieutenant Young was awakened by sailors Arthur Dixon and Peter Cochrane, who were on duty but drunk and quarreling outside the south blockhouse door. The officer ordered them disarmed and confined and went back to bed in his tent. He was awakened by a loud commotion and found that Dixon had tripped over the blockhouse doorsill, struggling to walk in his leg irons. He could see that Dixon had a bottle under his pea jacket; it looked very familiar. In fact, it was the lieutenant's very own bottle of brandy, which Cochrane had earlier stolen from his tent.[96]

Seattle had developed a lucrative trade meeting the liquor cravings of the thirsty Decaturs, now joined by the crews of the *Active* and the *Massachusetts.* It is reasonable to assume that these hundreds of men also presented a market for sex—for "vicious proclivities"—and that Seattle met the needs of that market. Aside from John Drew's abortive attempt to climb into Olivia Holgate's bedroom window, no records remain of sexual encounters between navy men and settlers or Indians. However, no records remain of the sexual encounters of the Decaturs at other ports except the undeniable evidence of rampant venereal infection among the crew. Nearly 30 percent of the men in the *Decatur*'s crew were diagnosed with venereal disease and had presumably been infected in sailor town brothels. The building designated as Madame Damnable's on Phelps's drawings of Seattle has long intrigued local historians—was it a brothel?[97]

Lieutenant Phelps's memoir subtly suggests that Mary Ann Boyer, also known as Mary Ann Conklin and as Madame Damnable, was more than a hotel manager in Seattle. She was, he wrote, "a stout coarse Irishwoman"; her language was vile, and she screamed curses at the sailors and so earned her name. But there was a prototypical Madame Damnable, a Frenchwoman living at Callao, Peru's port city, who may have run a bordello there. Also, Quartermaster Sam Silk—"a veritable old-time salt"—recognized Seattle's Madame Damnable from Baltimore's red-light district. On shore in Seattle, Silk scolded her for yelling at the *Decatur* sailors: "What do you mean, you damned old harridan, raising hell this way? I know you. . . . Many's the time I've seen you howling thunder around Fell's Point, Baltimore. You're a damned pretty one, ain't you?" Men who had paid for sexual encounters in

Baltimore and Callao certainly expected to pay for them in Seattle, whether in the comfort of a hotel room or back in the woods.[98]

Swartwout's General Order 5 had placed Curley's camp, the Elliott House, and the "south end of the said town of Seattle," including Madame Damnable's, off-limits to men from the *Decatur, Active,* and *Massachusetts.* Testimony from Peter Lines's summary court-martial clearly shows the resistance of the hands during this long occupation of Seattle to Swartwout's efforts to impose ship's discipline on men on liberty. Rowed ashore in the cutter, Lines and a friend scaled the barricade and sneaked south down the beach through the cloaking secrecy of the trees. But they did not head into the woods; instead, they cut west to town. There they broke Swartwout's order and entered the barroom at the Elliott House. Under arrest, Lines protested that, if a man had to obey such commands, he was no free man. Lines asserted himself as the officers' equal, saying that he considered himself as good as any person on board "except," he admitted, "in property, where he was not as well off in the world as some." Lines said that, on liberty, navy men should be allowed to go anywhere they pleased, and he defied the officers' right to command the men's behavior off duty. Like many *Decatur* sailors, he was an egalitarian, resisting the ship's hierarchy as oppressive, unfair, and un-American and arguing that only the marines enforced the authority of officers, who were well-to-do, unskilled at sea, and physically weak and flouted the very rules of behavior to which they held enlisted men.[99]

Not all naval officers were models of temperance, and alcohol was a comfort and a risk for officers just as it was for enlisted men. When the *Massachusetts* arrived, the *Active*'s officers sent over a "demijohn of cocktails" as a welcoming gift. On another occasion, Lieutenant Johnson, of the *Active,* described a gloomy party given by the settlers for the naval officers, which included "four married ladies . . . each of whom had about three babies." The lieutenant lamented these slim pickings in an uncivilized backwater, but "fortunately, some of the officers of the *Decatur,*" continued Johnson, "were thoughtful enough to take something to drink with them or we should have suffered much." Lieutenant Young brought a bottle of brandy into his tent on shore, and Lieutenant Johnson mentioned packing a bottle of whiskey and a book for a pleasant afternoon off duty. Liquor was essential to naval officers' routine sociability and also one of the comforts for Johnson's "inner man," but Jepsen's diary accused the *Decatur* officers of hard drinking: Gunner Stocking would soon be dismissed from the service for his binges, and Captain Gansevoort frequently drank to excess in Seattle. As Lieutenant Johnson wrote,

"It does seem that the Big Indian is always drunk or has drank so much as to have lost all common sense."[100]

Nevertheless, the *Decatur* continued to respond to Indian threats. In fact, when Governor Stevens suggested that the navy build a blockhouse on Lake Washington and patrol the lake in armed cutters, Swartwout declined to move men inland because springtime alarms were so frequent. In March, gunfire was heard up the Duwamish, and the Decaturs beat to quarters. Gansevoort took men upriver in the gig to investigate, accompanied by the howitzer-mounted launch. Sentinels at the blockhouse at Collins's farm had fired at Indians seen approaching an army encampment on the riverbank. One April night, *Decatur* lookouts spotted a large fire at Alki Point. Gansevoort commanded the gig and Phelps commanded the launch, and both boats crossed the bay to investigate the blaze. The anxious officer of the watch noted in the log that he heard the howitzer repeatedly fired just before midnight. When the party returned, they reported that a sawmill on the point had been burned to the ground, "fired by hostile Indians." On more than one occasion, anxious settlers rowed out to Gansevoort with news of another force of hostile Indians massed east of Seattle, planning to attack the settlement. Local editorialists heatedly rebutted General John Wool's opinion that the war on Puget Sound "has been greatly exaggerated" with these local alarms. Wool wrote dismissively to Governor Stevens that five companies of regular army infantry and three navy warships ought to be enough to "bring to terms two hundred Indian warriors." Stevens complained to Jefferson Davis, then secretary of war, that Wool would neither act decisively against the Indians himself nor allow others to do so. But the general's decision was based on information provided by Lieutenant Colonel Silas Casey, commander of the U.S. Army's Ninth Infantry in the Puget Sound District. In May, Casey informed the general that there had been no "depredations" in the area since March 7 except for acts of private revenge against Indian people, and that Puget Sound was "pacified."[101]

Some settlers did indeed exact "private revenge," and others continued to treat Indians brutally. For instance, the Indian whom Chief Seattle had pointed out as hostile was arrested and taken to Olympia, where he was shot to death by Joseph Brannan in revenge for his brother's family, murdered on the White River. Thomas Prosch noted that, throughout the spring of 1856, "Indians were caught from time to time, some being brought in and others shot on the spot." In May, disgraced pilot William Webster and former volunteer commander C. C. Hewitt hired five Snoqualmie Indians to paddle their

"Mount Rainier," from the mouth of Duwamish river. W.T.

FIG. 30 As tensions eased in the spring, Taylor sketched duck hunters at the mouth of the Duwamish River, looking southeast toward Mount Rainier. Guided by a Native paddler, the two Decatur officers prepare their weapons. From the John Y. Taylor Sketch Books, Western Americana Collection, Beinecke Rare Book and Manuscript Library, Yale University.

canoe up to Collins's blockhouse. While waiting for Webster and Hewitt to return, three of the Indians went berry picking and were murdered by two white men "whose names," wrote Phelps, "I forebear to mention." Lieutenant Drake, of the *Decatur,* took a party up the river to bury the Indian men, but no action was ever taken against the murderers, who, according to Brad Asher, included settler Luther Collins.[102]

As spring warmed Elliott Bay, an Indian attack seemed decreasingly likely, even to the most bellicose officers and alarmist settlers. Swartwout wrote to the secretary of the navy that the two steamers under his command were adequate for the territory's defense, and he directed Gansevoort to take the *Decatur* on a cruise to Port Townsend and then to Esquimalt Harbor, off Victoria, on Vancouver Island. The object was twofold, explained Swartwout: to test the repairs on the *Decatur*'s hull and to "intimidate the hostile Indians and keep under subjection those tribes who profess to be friendly." He was nervous about the *Decatur*'s seaworthiness, warning Gansevoort, "I would much rather your cruise should be prolonged than to have you run any risk by keeping your ship underway at night or during a fog."[103]

The *Decatur* weighed anchor on April 14, 1856, with a fresh breeze from the south. It was the first time the ship had been under sail since December 9, and the *Decatur* tiptoed nervously out of Elliott Bay and into Puget Sound. By evening, the ship was off Port Townsend under squalls of wind and rain, but on April 20 the *Decatur* anchored off Victoria in bright sunshine. The crew had manned the pumps almost constantly, but the battered sloop of war made it. James Douglas, governor of Vancouver Island, visited the *Decatur* and was saluted with seventeen guns and the English ensign at the fore.[104]

And the Decaturs finally went on proper liberty. Gansevoort inspected the crew at quarters and then turned them loose on Victoria, eager for the delights of a real harbor town. The officers saw the sights and went fishing and hunting and bought toothbrushes, books, and shoes. For a week, the cutters carried the sailors and marines to town watch by watch—combed, clean-shaven, and wearing their best—and then carried them back—broke, bruised, and exhausted. On May 3, the *Decatur* headed south and sailed into Elliott Bay four days later. Gansevoort was jubilant, pleased that the *Decatur* had handled the cruise so well, "though we had the wind fresh and considerable sea," and he was able to report that the *Decatur* could manage the long trip from Puget Sound to Mare Island Navy Yard.[105]

While the *Decatur* was away on the Victoria cruise, Swartwout informed Dobbin of a few decisions he had made. He had armed his sentries and instructed them to shoot men attempting to desert into the woods at Seattle. And, since he found it "impracticable" to complete the *Massachusetts*'s depleted company of marines by local recruitment, he had asked Gansevoort to detach six marines from the *Decatur* for his use. Additionally, the newly arrived *John Hancock* lacked a lieutenant, and with the new commissions, the *Decatur* had six, so Swartwout ordered Dallas reassigned to the *Hancock*. Swartwout was grateful for the *Hancock*—"a very great acquisition to the Naval Force under my command"—arguing that one steamer was more useful in Puget Sound than three sailing ships. Swartwout intended to deploy the ships as a squadron, keeping the *Hancock* or *Massachusetts* constantly cruising in Puget Sound as "an exhibition . . . to intimidate the hostile Indians and prevent the Northern Indians . . . from cooperating with the hostile tribes [in the territory]." Swartwout set himself up as a mini-commodore, and his busy plans for his "Naval Force" on Puget Sound antagonized squadron commodore Mervine, as we will see.[106]

Swartwout ordered the *Decatur* to lighten ship, hoping that "the weight taken from the ship will make her more light and buoyant, particularly forward of the center of gravity, where the injury has been sustained." The Decaturs wooded and watered their ship for the cruise to San Francisco while the carpenter's crew strengthened Yesler's wharf to receive everything the sloop of war could do without, including the warship's carronades. The ship supplied Luther Collins with powder "for the defense of his farm" and transferred the howitzer, rifles, rockets, blue lights, percussion caps, cartridges, and remaining powder to the wharf.[107]

Some Decaturs did not want to leave. As the ship prepared to head south, William Price slipped away from the north blockhouse one night; William Bass and John Mason did not show up for their muster. They were never found. At least eight Decaturs successfully deserted in Seattle, and two were dishonorably discharged. A few who had completed their term of service asked to be released and calmly walked away. They left the *Decatur* with at least $50 back pay in their pockets; their skills were much in demand on Puget Sound, where wages for skilled laborers ranged from $3 to $5 per day. Between 1853 and 1855, fresh beef sold for an average of 18¢ per pound, potatoes never cost more than $3 per bushel, and a gallon of whiskey ranged from $1.25 to $2. Sailors were well-off in the territorial economy. One such sailor, Humphrey Davis, was honorably discharged from the *Decatur* and found "dead in his bed" three weeks later, at Port Townsend. A native of Massachusetts, Davis was about fifty years old and had joined the *Decatur* in Boston. Punished for occasional drunkenness during the cruise, Davis drank himself to death on shore: the coroner's inquest found that he had died "by too great an indulgence in spirits." Enforced moderation on board the *Decatur* kept Davis alive; freed of that discipline, he lived less than a month. Men who were not dominated by their vices found other opportunities to pursue in the Pacific Northwest. They may have headed for Vancouver Island or the Colville goldfields, signed on to a merchant ship, or stayed in the territory, established an alias and an alibi, and become "founders" themselves.[108]

The siege and battle at Seattle were contests at arms but they also became contested ground for memory as officers and settlers made their own meanings of events, understandings that were further refashioned by succeeding generations. The *Decatur* defended Young America's mission of Pacific colonization, enforcing federal treaties and protecting American settlement on Puget Sound. Indian people fought to drive American settlers from Washington Territory, resist the treaties, revenge settler crimes, and restore their familiar way of life. Only the *Decatur*'s superior firepower and the divisions' practiced skill during the battle trumped the crew's poor discipline during the siege. But the imperial context, Gansevoort's operatic quarrel with Alden, the one-sidedness of the battle, the navy's dependence on Indian labor, information, and goodwill, the ship's disorder, and the criminal underworld back in the woods—all were forgotten when Phelps created the Battle of Seattle in his memoir. Instead, Phelps stressed the blunders that led to the war and blamed the colonists, from the stubborn governor to thuggish settlers to cowardly militia. Above all, to Phelps, the battle was a real fight in a shooting war and the navy had saved Seattle in an honorable contest. But the American imperial narrative was decentered in Seattle, as both civilian sawmill owner and *Decatur* captain insisted that Native people not relocate to reservations because they were indispensable, and a navy warship became the repository for burlap sacks of severed Indian heads gathered by other Indians under contract.

Seattle settlers and their descendants constructed a history that selectively emphasized some people and events to vindicate conquest. The bravery of steadfast settler families, especially of pioneer women, grew in the retellings while officer accusations of settler cowardice were rejected and the navy's vital economic role in Puget Sound was ignored. Hostile Indians were "race-conscious" and bloodthirsty, and settler brutality was forgotten. Friendly Indians were weak, almost childlike, in need of American guidance and protection, but the resilient agency of Indian interpreters, workers, lovers, spies, and fighting men was forgotten. Henry Yesler was remembered as Seattle's first industrialist, but his "country wife" and her new baby were forgotten, and Catharine Blaine, the minister's wife, and her new baby were remembered—

Blaine became the battle Madonna and Susan Suquardle did not. Seattle became not a hardscrabble beach mill town filled with "rough characters" but a colonial town of respectable families on the knife edge of the frontier— "enterprising pioneers in that distant and very sparsely settled region," as Dobbin put it. Seattle's nameless drifters, not remembered clearly in either life or death, disappeared from settler memory, as did the deserters, offenders, and dishonorably discharged Decaturs.[109]

The Old Navy punishment records describe a place in Seattle ignored by officer memoir and settler reminiscence, where sailors and drifters shared forbidden space to shape an outlaw society that welcomed them, underscoring the economic opportunism of local residents, from respectable carpenters and pilots to disreputable purveyors of vice. The *Decatur* officers drew lines in the sand to try to extend the ship's command to the beach, issuing orders designed to segregate marines and sailors as social inferiors who defended Seattle but were not part of it. Swartwout's General Orders set out more lines, physically barring sailors and marines from most of town: settler homes, hotels, stores, taverns, and Native camps. The barricades marked another line on the beach, between the orderly ship and settlement and the disorderly woods, the "paradise for lazy people who were content to live like Indians." The majority of the *Decatur* crew crossed these lines, and Seattle took its place on the littoral of the Pacific West along which footloose opportunists drifted in search of their next chance—a beach underworld that stretched from Chile to Alaska and included the lawless woods back of Seattle.[110]

On June 2, 1856, the *Decatur* hoisted anchor. A few passengers were bound for California, including the three children orphaned by the Indian raid on the White River cabins. Towed to the Strait of Juan de Fuca by the *John Hancock*, the ship was accompanied by canoes of Northern Indians—"our Indian friends" from the Tongas, Haida, Stickene, and Tsimshian tribes, "with whom [the *Decatur*] appeared to be an especial favorite." The *Decatur* parted company and sailed west and then south, to Mare Island.[111]

6

San Francisco

"This Reckless Life"

In the [northern California mining district], the surface diggings are not
so generally exhausted as further south, [and] are paying well. . . . To a
man of small means, desirous of procuring a claim that can be worked
with little capital, this is, perhaps, the best place to go. . . . The diggings
in Coffee Creek . . . are turning out rich. The gold is coarse; pieces being
taken out weigh from eight to one hundred and twenty-five dollars. The
miners are all doing well.—*San Francisco Daily Evening Bulletin,* August 5,
1856

[Sailors in San Francisco] reason among themselves in this way: "the value
of my labor when I entered the service was only eighteen dollars a month,
but now it is fifty or seventy-five. . . . What a fool I am to remain here under
such circumstances! . . ." gold has turned their heads, and they have gone
off in crowds . . . some of these desertions have surprised me, these men
were so respectable. . . . It was only to be accounted for by this extreme
infatuation about getting gold, and this reckless life without a conscience
or restraint, which characterizes California.—DAVIS, *Life of Charles Henry
Davis, Rear Admiral*

In his final communication to Secretary Dobbin concerning the *Decatur,* Samuel Swartwout judged that dry rot permeated the ship's entire
frame and that the main timbers were nailsick from frequent replanking.
He was convinced that the ship would be condemned upon survey at Mare
Island. John Lenthall, the *Decatur*'s designer, had already gone on record as

saying that there was no advantage in continuing the sloop of war in service when extensive repairs were required. As the ship sailed south, the hull seams worked open, and each officer of the watch carefully noted how much water was in the bilge. Confronted by a storm off northern California, the *Decatur* heaved to, to ride out the gale, and the sailors pumped round the clock. The storm passed and the *Decatur* limped south, anchoring off the Mare Island Navy Yard on June 13, 1856.[1]

Commander Guert Gansevoort reported his arrival in San Francisco to Commodore William Mervine, informing him that the *Decatur* must be surveyed to determine the ship's condition. Then the report had to be forwarded to the Department of the Navy for approval before repairs would begin. And Gansevoort was afraid that, despite all the work in Seattle, it would take two months to properly refit the ship. There was tremendous pressure not to condemn the *Decatur* but to patch the ship up and send it back to work. Writing from Callao, Mervine expressed great regret at the delay in returning the *Decatur* to full service. The Pacific Squadron was still concentrated in Puget Sound but the commodore hoped to redirect those resources to prevent ongoing Central America filibuster landings on the Pacific coast. He ordered Gansevoort to "do everything in *your* power" to facilitate the ship's repairs.[2]

On his arrival, Gansevoort was pleased to find mail waiting for him that had not been forwarded to Puget Sound. Perhaps he read for the first time a clipping from the *New York Times* that praised him as "as good a general as he is a thorough sailor." Also in the letter bag was a warm letter from Secretary Dobbin quoting "several kind and complimentary expressions" included in a note from Secretary of War Jefferson Davis. Davis applauded "the very efficient aid to the military in their efforts to protect the inhabitants of the Territory of Washington from the incursions of the Indians." Davis's compliments took the sting out of Captain Keyes's official complaint that Gansevoort "refused to co-operate properly with military forces" on Puget Sound. Also, the mailbag contained his commission as commander and Phelps's and Dallas's commissions as lieutenants. Carpenter James Miller and Sailmaker Augustus Warren received their warrants in the same mailbag; they were all no longer "acting."[3]

Since the *Decatur*'s last visit, many of the Mare Island buildings had become fully operational; the sawmill and dry dock were now in full use. Shortly after the *Decatur*'s arrival, the marine railway was used for the very first time; steamers ran special excursions from San Francisco to see the event, and surely the Decaturs watched, too. Onlookers marveled as the sloop of war *Warren* was towed into dry dock and ended the day "sitting high and dry, like a duck on a fence." By summer 1856, Mare Island Navy Yard could provide most of the services found in one of the established eastern yards, an inestimable asset to the navy in the Pacific West.[4]

After navy authorization, the *Decatur*'s crew took down the warship's sails, rigging, spars, and masts and emptied the hold of all remaining provisions, water, and small arms. Shipyard work crews came aboard every day to undo the work the Decaturs had been at such pains to accomplish in Seattle; they cleared out Yesler's timbers and the Victoria bracing and began to rebuild the ship. But repairs were halted by a shoreside crisis.[5]

The brig *Merchantman* had arrived from Seattle with the *Decatur*'s battery, and the ship hastily remounted the carronades in late July 1856, loading them with man-killing grapeshot, directed at the shore. Farragut had directed that the *Decatur* be immediately "fitted for service" to combat the "insurrection of San Francisco's Committee of Vigilance." After a long period of unrest and controversy, a newspaper editor was shot and mortally wounded in a city street on May 14, 1856. More than a thousand men marched on the jail to demand the accused murderer's release to their rough justice. Following a "trial," he was executed by the Vigilance Committee. As vigilante activity increased, California's governor declared San Francisco "in a state of insurrection," and the so-called law-and-order party, with ties to institutionalized crime and political corruption, appealed to David Farragut, the commandant of Mare Island, for arms and men to arrest the Vigilance leaders. Maintaining that the ongoing uproar was a California state matter, Farragut refused to intervene but sent the sloop of war *John Adams* to anchor off San Francisco, with its twenty-gun battery loaded and run out, ready to fire. The commander of the *Adams* was the excitable Edward Boutwell.[6]

When the *Decatur* arrived from Seattle, the Vigilance Committee held a number of prisoners, including David Terry, chief justice of the Supreme Court of California, and naval agent Richard Porter Ashe, Farragut's brother-in-law. After the committee lynched two more accused murderers, the governor of California, Terry's wife, and other interested parties besieged Farragut and Boutwell with pleas for intervention, claiming that the Vigilance Committee members intended to capture the navy vessels in the harbor, seize the federal armory and treasury, and secede California from the United States. The committee, Boutwell wrote, was "in open rebellion against the laws of our country . . . under a suspension of the laws of California." He demanded Justice Terry's release and threatened to turn the *John Adams*'s guns on San Francisco and "batter the city down."[7]

Farragut's son and biographer, Loyall Farragut, pointed out that the commandant, like many solid citizens, had some sympathy for the Vigilance Committee because "of the outrages perpetrated by the desperate and lawless characters who infested San Francisco." In describing the situation to the secretary of the navy, Farragut—owner of considerable local property—at first characterized the Vigilance uprising as "done with perfect organization and deliberation." He repeatedly counseled patience to Boutwell, who continued to threaten to "fire on the City" and punish the California rebels. But by mid-July, six thousand Vigilantes were under arms and Farragut grew alarmed by the apparent slide toward civil war. In an early August letter, Farragut told Dobbin that "the people have been running riot, and setting all law and the Constitution at defiance, and I did not know at what moment they would seize the money at the branch mint." Once federal property was at risk, Farragut's duty became clear to him. He met with the mint superintendent "to consult as to the safety of the funds, papers, etc. of the United States." They agreed to convey $4 million in gold to Mare Island Navy Yard for safekeeping and readied the batteries of the *Warren* and the *Decatur* with "plenty of ammunition."[8]

Farragut prepared his little armada, outfitting the tiny revenue schooner *Fenimore Cooper* with a fieldpiece lashed in place with rope. The *Alta California* published local rumors that the *Decatur* and the *Warren* would join the *John Adams* in the harbor, and the three men-of-war would level their guns and "demolish San Francisco, a la Greytown." The *Daily Evening Bulletin* satirized Farragut's defenses, marshalling "big guns and little guns, and mortars and carbines, and cutlasses and pistols, and shot and shells, and proclamations, and gin and water, and the *Decatur* and *Warren* and *John Adams*," to prevent the Vigilantes from blowing up the warships in the harbor and destroying every building on Mare Island. "Little men in big cocked hats ran wildly about, and big men with little regulation caps looked very fierce," snickered the editor, and the Vigilance Committee was thus prevented from "taking possession of everything," at which outcome "we may all with gratitude and joy, join hands and sing." But Farragut maintained that the warships' show of force preserved the treasury, curbed Vigilance excesses, and calmed San Francisco. On August 7, Judge Terry was released and crowds of onlookers watched the *John Adams* sailors man the yards and fire a salute in his honor. Farragut reported his satisfaction to Dobbin that "preparation at the yard of the vessels of war for such service as might be required of them" had contributed to Terry's release from the "canaille."[9]

Once the Vigilance crisis had passed, Gansevoort was free to complete the refitting of his ship and head south to duty in Mexico and Central America. But something interfered—likely, preparation of the *Decatur*'s hold for painting uncovered further, more extensive damage—and the ship was readied for major repairs. Mervine bitterly regretted this setback to the navy's response to "the many calls for protection within the great extent of [his] command."[10]

While the *Decatur* was being stripped, five days before the ship was scheduled to enter dry dock, David Farragut encountered Guert Gansevoort reeling drunk on the Mare Island Navy Yard wharf, at eleven o'clock in the morning, August 16, 1856, and suspended him from duty. The two men were members of a party gathered to see off Lieutenant Aaron Hughes—who had walked boldly up to the Northern Indians in Washington Territory—as he joined the *John Adams*. In informing Dobbin of the suspension, Farragut noted that the commander's intemperance was "commonly known" but that the public incident forced his official notice of Gansevoort's intoxication in "uniform both on the wharf and the steamer, much to my mortification." The *Decatur*'s logbook quietly noted, "Commander G. Gansevoort was suspended from duty by Captain Farragut." Farragut, whose first command had been the *Decatur* and who was Isaac Sterrett's friend, appointed Lieutenant Edward Middleton as the *Decatur*'s acting commander.[11]

Gansevoort appealed to Farragut to withdraw the suspension, and Farragut wrote that Gansevoort "made the most solemn pledges that he never will be found again in the state for which I reported him." But the commandant was convinced that he did not have the authority to overturn the suspension and left the decision to Dobbin. The disgraced commander remained on board the *Decatur* for seven weeks, hoping to gain reinstatement. Gansevoort's brief appeal to the secretary was, in the parlance of the day, manly and forthright: "Having been reported by Commodore Farragut to the Department, I beg leave to request that you will not push the charge. For the first time in my career, I am suspended from my official duties, and feel not the less acutely this punishment because it is a just one. I promise that if this charge be withdrawn, that my future conduct shall justify the course."[12]

The charge was never formally withdrawn nor was it pressed; rather, Gansevoort was officially described as "detached and placed on furlough." Some Plucking Board members had voiced concerns about his heavy drinking, and he passed their review but failed in his command. Chair of the U.S. Senate Committee on Naval Affairs Stephen Mallory successfully moved to halt an inquiry into the "causes of the return from the Pacific squadron of the . . . commander of the sloop-of-war *Decatur* . . . and whether any and what action was taken by the President or Secretary of the Navy in relation to Captain Gansevoort." Silence cloaked Gansevoort's suspension. In fact, his family went to great lengths to conceal his lapse and the suspension itself. His letter books donated to the Navy Department Library omit the notes to Farragut and Dobbin and all other documents that mention the suspension. In fact, the letter book for this period is so organized as to disguise Gansevoort's removal altogether, concluding with the rousing February 1856 petition from Seattle citizens.[13]

Farragut copied Mervine on his suspension of Gansevoort, and Mervine in turn commented to Secretary Dobbin that he was not surprised, "having long known indirectly that his habits in this respect are bad." Mervine lamented that many officers conspired to "screen such acts" from view. Because of this whitewash, navy men who habitually drank to excess were seldom brought to "a proper accountability." As if on cue, the *Decatur*'s officers directed a carefully worded petition to the secretary of the navy: "In consideration of our private friendly feelings toward Commander Guert Gansevoort, we hope you will excuse the liberty we take of addressing you in his behalf. He states this to be the first time that he has been suspended for the charge now made against him, and we trust that you will . . . allow him an opportunity of proving that it will be the last." The petition was signed by all the lieutenants and midshipmen who had served with Gansevoort in the Battle of Seattle—Middleton, Drake, Phelps, Hughes, Morris, and Dallas—as well as Purser Jones, Surgeon Jeffery, and Surgeon Taylor. The delicate wording that referred to Gansevoort's assertion that he had never been suspended "for the charge now made against him" begs the question of whether his statement was accurate and whether he had been previously disciplined for that charge by some punishment short of suspension. Dobbin's secretary jotted on the margin of the petition, "He will consider himself as detached from the *Decatur* and on general furlough until further action can be had in his case." Two days later, a still-hopeful Gansevoort dashed off a breezy note to Dobbin, acknowledging the receipt of his commission as commander.[14]

Confident that his Seattle service would stand him in good stead, Gansevoort did not act on his detachment until October 16, when he finally turned over to Middleton "all the papers and instructions which [he had] received." And whatever his hopes or schemes, Gansevoort cooled his heels on shore for a long time. In December 1856, writing from New York, Gansevoort thanked Dobbin for the order that placed him on the active list "awaiting orders." But Gansevoort remained without a command, and he wrote humbly to the secretary of the navy in 1858, requesting "the command of any seagoing ship that the Honorable Secretary may think proper." He waited until the Civil War began.[15]

Two weeks after Gansevoort's suspension, Middleton suspended Gunner

Robert Stocking from duty for habitual drunkenness. As executive officer, Middleton had frequently warned Stocking for intoxication both on and off duty but there had been no change in his behavior. Stocking was drunk on duty in Norfolk, and after only a few days on board ship with the gunner, Captain Sterrett begged for a substitute. In California, Stocking had been publicly intoxicated in the streets of Vallejo, frequently observed by the *Decatur's* officers and enlisted men. The last straw was Stocking's absence from the ship, overstaying his leave by nearly three days, an offense punishable as desertion for an enlisted man. The ship's gunner, wrote Farragut, "is of all officers the last who should be a drunkard." Stocking left the *Decatur* in disgrace, "dismissed from the service by the Secretary of the Navy" and set on shore in California.[16]

In the summer of 1856, San Francisco was a teeming crossroads of land and water pathways to local mining districts, to Mexico and Nicaragua, to China, Oregon, and the Sandwich Islands. All the editions of the local newspapers posted jobs for sailors and laborers and touted dubious opportunities to invest or join in new ventures. William Walker's filibuster recruiter "Captain" M. E. Bradley hired rooms at the Rassette House, offering "restless, ambitious adventurers" a quick steamer trip to San Juan del Sur, good wages, and the opportunity to regenerate Nicaragua and gain a *rancho* in Central America. Nearly every mail steamer that left San Francisco carried $2 million in gold; in 1855 alone, more than $44 million in California gold went south to the transits and then on to New York and London. But viewed through its 1856 newspapers, San Francisco was a violent and disorderly city, its boom-and-bust economy in recession and characterized as much by auction sales, failed partnerships, and shady investments as by sudden wealth. The *Alta California*—a Vigilance advocate—worried about the hundreds of "shiftless idlers," "good-for-nothing vagabonds," and "suspicious characters" who hung around, out of work and looking for trouble. San Franciscans read daily accounts of their opportunistic, heterogeneous, and dissolute society: black and white Americans, Mexicans, Indians, Kanakas, and Chinese and Jewish shopkeepers, Brazilian hoteliers, and Swiss restaurateurs knifed one another, fell drunk into the bay and drowned, shot each other from ambush or in duels, gambled their money away or were robbed, were savaged by wolves "in the hills," and "were on conditions of intimacy" with women other than their wives.[17]

The comfortable, familiar sailor towns in Vallejo and San Francisco offered the saloons and brothels that accommodated seafaring men. The *Decatur's* stay in port resulted in hard-fisted, hard-drinking offenses—old Sam Silk,

FIG. 31 *In 1855, San Franciscans crowded the waterfront every two weeks to watch the steamers depart for San Juan del Sur or Panama. As Frank Soulé wrote in his 1855* Annals of San Francisco, *"Steamer-Day in San Francisco stands alone. . . . Every body, man, woman and child, native and foreigner, merchant and miner, general dealer, laborer and nondescript adventurer, old resident and recent immigrant—every body is deeply interested in this day." Steamers like this one carried filibuster recruits south to Nicaragua. Courtesy University of Washington Libraries.*

now rated boatswain's mate, ended up in double-irons for a day after he returned from liberty drunk and noisy. Archibald Sprague, Martin Walsh, and John Brennan got into a rousing fistfight on shore and were returned to the ship black-eyed, bruised, and sullen. Dennis McCarty was double-ironed for smuggling liquor on board ship, James Daily for attempted desertion, and Isaac Williamson for drunkenness. No day off Mare Island passed without subjudicial punishments for the Decaturs as the logbook recorded offenses typical of sailors on the beach.[18]

However, seaman James Simpson was brought before a summary court-martial on the serious charge of insubordination. Simpson had joined others waiting on shore for the sundown boat, including Lieutenant Drake, who had successfully handled a series of detached commands in Seattle. The visibly intoxicated Simpson was armed, alarming Drake, who asked the sailor to hand over his weapon. Simpson coolly replied, "Mr. Drake, go and get your uniform on, and then I will obey your orders—without your uniform, I will knock you to hell in a minute." At trial, Drake indignantly testified that Simpson was "under the influence of liquor, but not so much as that he did not know what he was about." The court found Simpson guilty, and he lost three months' pay and was reduced in rating. A week later, undaunted, he was confined in double-irons for disobedience of orders and "being noisy" and disrespectful.[19]

A few Decatur sailors became involved with local police, and some of their violence made the San Francisco newspapers. Marine sergeant Charles Corbin was badly beaten on shore by three sailors who settled a shipboard score and were never identified or arrested. Corbin, thirty-two, Irish-born, had testified at the Norfolk trial of the Santa Cruz mutineers and was the principal policeman on board the Decatur throughout the ship's turbulent stay in Puget Sound. When Corbin was brought on board the ship by the police after his beating, he was unconscious and vomiting. His nose was broken and his eyes were swollen shut, his lips were cut, and many teeth were knocked out or broken. He had been beaten and kicked and suffered severe internal injuries. The surgeons kept him under sedation for many days and he barely survived. Eventually, Corbin recovered sufficiently to be sent ashore, and he left the Decatur for good.[20]

Marine corporal Coon was also badly beaten in San Francisco by seaman William Fredericks, likely another revenge attack. After Coon's recovery, he deserted the Decatur and reinvented himself as a "desperado," taking the alias "L. Van Rensselaer," the name of the sickly lieutenant who had been invalided off the ship back in Rio de Janeiro. "L. Van Rensselaer" quickly became notorious for numerous local assaults and robberies. Finally, in Vallejo's sailor town, he attacked and robbed former *Decatur* shipmate Edwin Brown, who was "much intoxicated," and then pushed the sailor into deep water off the end of the wharf "with the intent to kill." Brown was rescued by passersby who dove into the bay, and the police took "Van Rensselaer" Coon into custody, a failed opportunist in the reckless life of San Francisco.[21]

Decatur sailors were also drawn into the city's disorderly urban politics, becoming involved with a local criminal and political hack, the very sort of man that the Vigilance Committee hoped to drive from the city. William H. Werth was a "notorious" member of the "Chivalry" faction of the Democratic Party—a "son of the sunny South," "petted and lionized by a certain clique, who falsely pretend to represent high-toned southern chivalry." The *Daily Evening Bulletin* freely termed Werth a murderer, responsible for the death of a political opponent. In another incident, Werth had attacked *Evening Journal* editor Joseph Kingsbury for his editorial comment on a letter Werth published in a Tuolumne paper. Werth beat Kingsbury to the ground with a heavy cane and struck him repeatedly as he lay in the street. Convicted of Kingsbury's assault, Werth was imprisoned in the county jail. A few days after his release, on November 5, 1856, Werth rounded up six American-born *Decatur* sailors in a waterfront tavern, bought them drinks, and handed out ballots marked for the Democratic ticket. Drunk, Werth drove the sailors to the second-district polls in a carriage, shoved them to the head of the line, and loudly demanded that they vote at once. Members of the Vigilance Committee at the polls shouted that Werth was trying to "stuff" the ballot box with "illegal votes." The sailors were denied and Werth burst into a profane tirade against the "Vigilant police." Charged with "violent and indecent conduct," Werth was arrested, tried, and pled guilty.[22]

Werth represented the persistence of San Francisco's corrupt and violent politics, and Mervine grew concerned that the Vigilance Committee would revive. The commodore ordered Middleton to detain the *Decatur* "so long as there shall be any indication of further domestic troubles." Mervine directed Middleton that, once he was convinced that the committee had disbanded, he was to head south. With an eye on Panamanian unrest and the Nicaragua filibuster, Mervine warned Middleton not to delay longer than necessary because "important events are daily transpiring in this quarter which may require the service of the ship under your command."[23]

The dry dock was sunk and removed from beneath the *Decatur*. Four days later, the ship mounted its masts and became a beehive of activity: it was caulked and painted inside and out, the riggings and sails were run up, and

FIG. 32 At Mare Island Navy Yard, in San Francisco Bay, the Decatur underwent major repairs to replace the Seattle bracing and timbering. The hull was recaulked and recoppered—in other words, the space between the ship's planks was packed with oakum and the hull below the waterline sheathed with thin copper sheet. Harper's Monthly, April 1862. Courtesy University of Washington Libraries, Special Collections, UW 27977z and UW 27976z.

FIG. 33 *This 1854 mining scene, from Soule's* Annals of San Francisco, *is not unlike that of the Coffee Creek diggings. When the* Decatur *was at San Francisco, men of little means still believed that they could strike it rich and deserted the ship with that hope. Courtesy University of Washington Libraries.*

furniture and galley equipment were installed. However, once the *Decatur* was ready to sail, the crew remained at about half-strength. Like Sterrett a year earlier, Middleton found it impossible to enlist a full crew and keep them on board in San Francisco. Despite the raises and reenlistment bounty, nearly two dozen men whose "time was up" received their honorable discharges and left the ship. Plenty of Decaturs had had enough and wanted to take advantage of other opportunities. A man "ran" from nearly every cutter sent to shore, and *Decatur* officers went armed at all times to prevent desertion; nevertheless, about twenty Decaturs deserted at San Francisco. Middleton was able to offer sailors the same wages as in 1855: Swedish-born seaman Hendrik Guy still earned $18 per month, Irish-born ordinary seaman Michael Thompson $14, and a landsman like Edward Fletcher, a black man born on the island of Jamaica, earned $12. Sailors could easily double their pay on a merchant ship or in a filibuster, or they could head to the Coffee Creek diggings, described in the epigraph at the head of this chapter in a typical mining news item, where miners "of small means" were said to be daily turning up gold pieces of greater value than months of navy wages.[24]

FIG. 34 This 1857 engraving from Harper's Weekly *(March 28) shows a bearded soldier of fortune in the Pacific West. Leaning on his rifle, the opportunist is weary, sockless, and out-at-the-knee, but he remains hopeful. Courtesy University of Washington Libraries, Special Collections,* UW 27978z.

In October, Middleton took the ship from Mare Island to San Francisco to try to enlist more sailors. Farragut wrote to Mervine that Middleton was "shipping a crew as fast as he can, [and] how much longer he will take, I know not, as seamen are scarce." Seamen were not so much scarce as they were active agents on their own behalf, pursuing their best opportunities all along the Pacific coast. The difficulty of recruiting sailors was just as bad in Panama as it was in San Francisco, and Mervine wistfully asked Middleton to bring extra men with him from California. Although Middleton "used exceptions" to rate ordinary seamen as seamen and pay them higher wages, the *Decatur* remained short twenty seamen, six ordinary seamen and landsmen, and nine marines. Middleton gave up and decided to put to sea; they would have to manage as best they could.[25]

On January 8, 1857, the *Decatur* set sail after six months in San Francisco, finally back in service in the Pacific Squadron. The ship's order had been challenged by the removal of Commander Isaac Sterrett and by the suspension of both Commander Guert Gansevoort and Gunner Robert Stocking for drunkenness. San Francisco's crime and disorder had involved the ship's company as well. And dozens of ambitious or restless sailors had been discharged or had deserted, compelled "by this extreme infatuation about getting gold, and this reckless life . . . which characterizes California." The sailors had entered the beach borderland of "Californio," which was peopled by a "floating population" of "landless men of no fixed dwelling place, trappers, deserters from ships," and "adventurous rascals of various sorts." They were all perfectly at home in the continuous Pacific West. At San Francisco, John Drinkhouse was one of many men who deserted the *Decatur*, visiting Walker's recruiter at the Rassette House and signing on to the filibuster adventure to "see the elephant" in Nicaragua.[26]

7

Episode 3. Nicaragua
"Seeing the Elephant"

We Americans are the peculiar, chosen people—the Israel of our time. . . .
God has predestinated, mankind expects, great things from our race; and
great things we feel in our souls. . . . We are the pioneers of the world; the
advance-guard, sent on through the wilderness of untried things, to break
a new path in the New World that is ours. In our youth is our strength, in
our inexperience, our wisdom. . . . And let us always remember that with
ourselves . . . national selfishness is unbounded philanthropy; for we can
not do good to America but we give alms to the world.
—HERMAN MELVILLE, *White-Jacket*

After scrutinizing the elephant without glasses and to his heart's content,
James Ryan, [a deserter], found himself ready to retire from [Walker's]
service, though he still likes the cause and would espouse it under more
auspicious circumstances.—*New York Times,* March 21, 1857

For two months, the *Decatur* sailed south, quiet and busy, enjoying the
blue-water routine. The new men learned to sail the ship, and the divisions were put through timed practice drills for the first time, pitting
one division against another in competition. For instance, on February 2, the
ship beat to quarters at 9:30 a.m. and the divisions reported ready: the first
division at 9:33, the second and third at 9:34, and the fourth at 9:40. Ordered
to "secure the foremast," this action was completed by 9:43. Called to fire stations, the crew practiced the fire drill. The divisions also practiced daily with

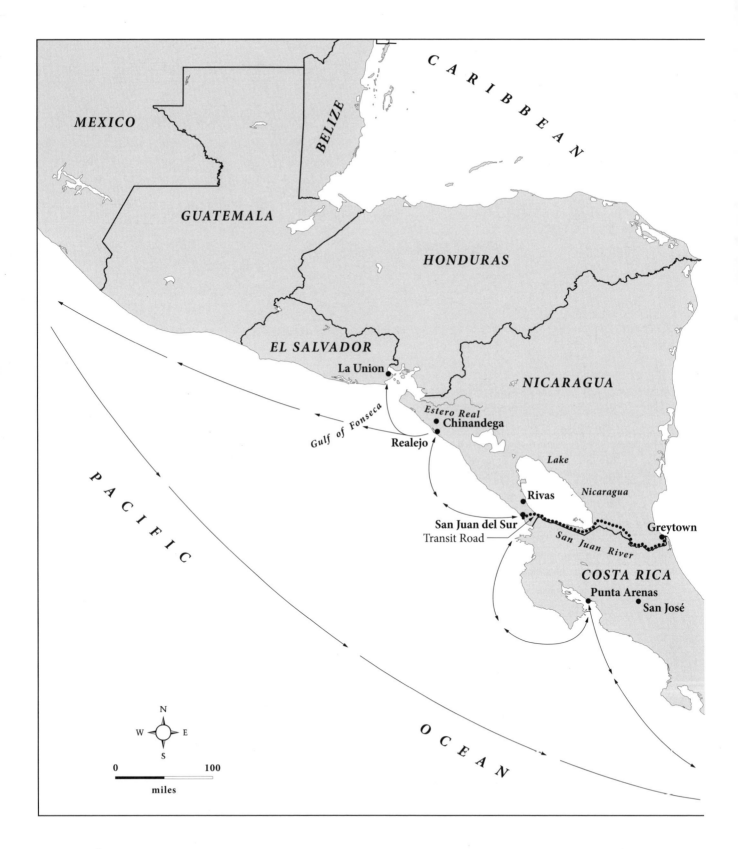

ECUADOR
Guayaquil

Payta

PERU
Callao
Lima

Bay of Casma
Chincha Islands

Caldera

Pacific

Ocean

Valparaiso
Santiago

CHILE

Atlantic

Ocean

N
W   E
S

0   1000

miles

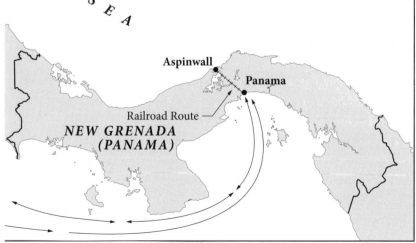

S E A

Aspinwall

Panama

Railroad Route

NEW GRENADA
(PANAMA)

*Map 4. Panama, Costa Rica,
and Nicaragua*

small arms, making and trimming sail, and shooting at floating targets with the great guns. Melville described these drills on board his fictional man-of-war, the *Neversink*:

> it was terrible work to help run in and out . . . that amazing mass of metal, especially as the thing must be done in a trice. . . . We were made to rush from our guns, seize pikes and pistols, and repel an imaginary army of boarders. . . . After cutting and slashing at them a while, we jumped back to our guns. . . . Meantime a loud cry is heard of "Fire! fire! fire!" on the maindeck; and the entire ship is in as great a commotion as if a whole city ward were in a blaze.

By March 7, 1857, land was in sight and the *Decatur* entered Panama Bay. The crew withdrew the shot from the carronades, and the *Decatur* saluted the broad pennant of Squadron commodore William Mervine in the flagship *Independence* with thirteen guns. The sloop of war furled the sails, warped into the harbor, and let down the anchors. The officers, marines, and a few enlisted men prepared to leave the ship, their terms of duty over. Once that was accomplished and the new men mustered in, the *Decatur* would be ready for new assignments in the Pacific West.[1]

In his final annual report as Franklin Pierce's secretary of the navy, James Dobbin again recommended that the Pacific Squadron be doubled in size and broken into northern and southern squadrons to effectively protect growing American interests of commerce, transportation, and settlement across the enormous distances of the Pacific. When the *Decatur* anchored off Panama, the Pacific Squadron faced a variety of challenges throughout this cruising ground, including in Hawaii, Samoa, and the Chincha Islands and other guano islands. In 1856, hundreds of American merchant ships visited the Sandwich Islands carrying an estimated $20 million in cargo. Americans in the islands and expansionists at home continued to agitate for Hawaii's annexation to the United States, and filibusters were frequently rumored. The secretary judged it prudent to station a warship at Honolulu. In Samoa, there existed "a state of society that beggars all description, composed of . . . the most immoral and dissolute foreigners that ever disgraced humanity," who had utterly debauched the Native population, according to Mervine. He believed the U.S. Navy was duty bound to enforce morality in Samoa.[2]

And in the mid-1850s, guano—the droppings of fish-eating birds—was one of the most valuable substances in the world, an unrivaled fertilizer. The imperial Guano Island Act of 1856 stated that any unoccupied "island, rock, [or] key" that had a deposit of guano could be claimed by the United States;

the *St. Mary's* would soon seize the islands of Jarvis and New Nantucket. The squadron was under orders to identify additional guano islands to be claimed as U.S. territory in the Pacific. In addition, ongoing revolutionary ferment in Peru threatened the lucrative shipping of guano from the Chincha Islands. In May 1857, sixty masters of American guano vessels petitioned for a U.S. man-of-war to be permanently stationed at the Chinchas.[3]

But in 1857, the principal concerns of the Pacific Squadron were Nicaragua, Panama, and Washington Territory, and the ill-feeling among officers in the squadron. Under Mervine's leadership, the squadron was plagued by a series of distasteful feuds. The nasty exchanges between Gansevoort and Alden in Puget Sound were a smaller version of those between Mervine and Swartwout, Tatnall, Ritchie, Boutwell, and many other junior officers in the squadron. For instance, Samuel Swartwout had offended Mervine by corresponding directly with the secretary of the navy, trumpeting his engagement with the Northern Indians at Port Gamble on Puget Sound that left twenty-seven Haida men and women dead. The officious Swartwout had even suggested that the secretary communicate directly with him rather than waste time routing dispatches through the commodore. Mervine found Swartwout's "language and tone" rude and accused him of the "desire to make [himself] independent in [his] command." On another occasion, frustrated by the refusal of a lieutenant to sign a court-martial decision, Mervine branded the recalcitrant as "one of a class of young officers banded together to break down the old usages and discipline of the Navy." He complained that the Plucking Board had advanced "a large number of young officers . . . so inflated with their own importance and attainments as to foster a belief that they are the soul of the [service]," and he advocated the "entire dissolution and reorganization of the Navy" with stronger subordination and an end to naval officers lobbying their legislators. In reply, Secretary Dobbin rebuked Mervine for the "unhappy state of feeling between yourself and many of the officers."[4]

Mervine irritably ordered Swartwout out of Puget Sound in March 1857. But in mid-April, Washington territorial governor Stevens wrote to an unspecified "captain" at Mare Island, begging for a steamer to protect "our citizens and the Indians of the Sound" against raids by the Northern Indians; the letter came to Farragut, who passed it along to Mervine. Hudson's Bay Company representatives, Stevens wrote, had urged Americans to leave San Juan Island for their own safety. The situation seemed dire to Stevens, but Mervine bridled at taking orders from this pushy territorial appointee. Convinced that the danger was exaggerated, Mervine informed the secretary with emphasis in June 1857, "*I* do not deem it necessary to dispatch any Naval force thither at present." But on August 11, 1857, customs inspector Isaac Ebey was beheaded by Northern Indians on Whidbey Island. Navy men considered this an act of revenge by the Haida for the death of their chief and of other men, women, and children killed by the men of the *Massachusetts* at Port Gamble. The Northern Indians, claimed Phelps admiringly, had "traveled two thousand four hundred miles to comply with the demands of a principle." By October, Mervine became convinced that Ebey's murder was the prelude to widespread "depredation and violence" and decided that a warship was needed on Puget Sound. But the *Massachusetts* was unavailable, put out of commission. Mervine authorized Farragut to hastily ready the *Massachusetts* for duty and furnish the steamer with the *St. Mary's* crew—both ships were at Mare Island at the time—and send the *Massachusetts* back to Washington Territory. His desperately limited resources reduced him to robbing the crew of a sloop of war to man a war steamer.[5]

While the *Massachusetts* steamed to Puget Sound, Mervine turned his attention back to Central America, specifically to Panama. The first train on the Panama Railroad ran on January 28, 1855, replacing two and a half days of travel by donkey cart with a daily train trip of five hours. The train transported passengers, mail, and gold between the Atlantic and the Pacific far more quickly, safely, and cheaply than did the sea journey around the Horn. From the Atlantic side, the railroad crossed the isthmus on tracks supported by pilings driven deep into the marsh, then up through jungle and across the Chagres River on a six-hundred-foot-long bridge. American travelers found "the luxuriance of the [jungle] vegetation beyond the powers of description." In fact, travelers ran out of superlatives to describe the foliage that arched over the rail line, the passionflowers and orchids accented by the flashing brilliance of the parrots and toucans. Heading down on the Pacific side, the land opened up into mountainous terrain, and the little train plunged down the forested hillside into the city of Panama.[6]

In 1857, the Panama Railroad station was spacious and comfortable, its grounds luxurious with flowers. Travelers could glimpse the cathedral towers, the tiled roofs, and the ancient fortifications of the Old City to the southeast and, to the west, the wharves of the railroad's steamship line. Coastwise steamers carried indigo, cochineal, coffee, rosewood, and other products, as well as passengers and freight, to and from the Pacific ports of Central America. California-bound travelers were eager to board the next steamer to San Francisco, dreading fever, the curse of "this pestilential climate." Six thousand men had died to lay fifty miles of track across the isthmus, and the very climate seemed sickly to North Americans: tropical heat throughout the

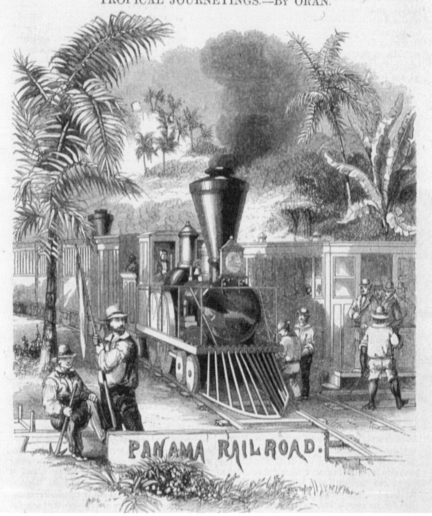

year and torrential rains from May through December. No precautions had proven effective against illness on the isthmus: visitors, workers, and locals fell ill, and no one understood why. Some journalists advised travelers to stay in the train cars and not breathe the "miasma" of the jungles. Others warned that one should avoid alcohol when the weather was sultry or recommended against eating fresh fruit, so cheap and abundant.[7]

At every rail stop, hawkers sold mangoes, oranges, and watermelon, cut and ready to eat. On April 15, 1856, while the *Decatur* lay off Seattle, a drunken American railroad traveler took a slice of watermelon from a vendor's tray at Panama and refused to pay for it. This arrogant refusal to pay a few pennies for a slice of watermelon touched off a struggle between street merchants and California-bound adventurers. A mob erupted from the impoverished Cienega district and ran from hotel to hotel, beating and robbing Americans. There were about three thousand travelers in Panama, waiting to board northbound steamers to San Francisco or to catch the train to Aspinwall, the Atlantic terminus of the railroad. That night, fifteen Americans died and sixteen more were badly beaten; two Grenadians also died in the night of violence. In the aftermath, 160 sailors and marines from the *Independence* and *St. Mary's* occupied the railroad station for three days. After their withdrawal, Mervine remained convinced that there was "no safety for Americans resident at Panama . . . without the presence of a restraining military force" and described for the secretary of the navy the "terrible calamity of a city sacked, a train robbed and its passengers indiscriminately murdered." In his official report on the riot, U.S. consul Amos Corwine recommended that the United States occupy New Grenada—today's Republic of Panama—"from ocean to ocean," a proposal viewed by Central Americans as a signal of aggressive expansionism from the new administration of President James Buchanan. When the *Decatur* arrived, the situation in Panama was tense. According to Dallas, the crew of the *Independence* "was prepared to resist an attack upon the Railroad and Buildings of the Panama R.R. Company and American Citizens," and the *Decatur* became part of the commodore's plans "to take possession of the town at any moment."[8]

The *Decatur* was anchored right under Mervine's gimlet eye, and the commodore's orders and remarks were communicated by almost continual signals from the flagship. On March 31, Commodore Mervine himself inspected the ship and observed the men execute Middleton's timed drills. After his departure, the *Decatur*'s crew was mustered at quarters and Lieutenant Middleton read his order of detachment. The tour of duty for the officers and men who had come together through the Strait of Magellan, the Battle of Seattle, and

FIG. 36 *Steel rails thread the lush jungle and workmen trim the roadside foliage at the site of Stephens's Tree, which was named in honor of John Stephens, former president of the Panama Railroad, who died in 1852. This exotic paradise was within easy sail of U.S. ports.* Harper's Monthly, *January 1859. Courtesy University of Washington Libraries, Special Collections, 27546z.*

San Francisco's civil unrest was at an end, and the new officers were rowed out to the *Decatur* from shore. Middleton and his officers awaited their arrival, lining the starboard side—the honor side—of the quarterdeck in full-dress uniform, and the crew was arrayed in ranks. Captain Henry Knox Thatcher and Lieutenants John Clitz, David Harmony, and Edward Stockton, Surgeons John Ward and Levi Cooper Lane, and warrant officers Boatswain Jasper Coghlan, Gunner James Lilleston, Sailmaker John Chevalier, and Carpenter William Hyde, all climbed on board the *Decatur*. Thatcher stepped up to Middleton and said, "I relieve you, sir," and Middleton replied, "I stand relieved." The remaining Decaturs warily inspected the new team. Commander Thatcher conducted a lengthy inspection of the ship on Sunday, April 5, 1857, after mustering the crew and reading them the Articles of War. Then Middleton, Drake, Phelps, Dallas, and Morris went down over the side. So did Surgeons Jeffery and Taylor, Carpenter Miller, and Sailmaker Warren. They likely all remained in town for a few days, then boarded the train to head to their homes in the eastern states after more than three years of distant duty.[9]

Thatcher put the crew to work at once "setting the ship to rights" and putting "her all ataunto." The crew holystoned the deck and retarred the rigging and then once again began the familiar naval drudgery of scraping and painting the iron work and repainting the spars, mast, and hull. The ship sent the market boat to the wharf for fresh meat and fruit, and the cutters rowed men over to the islands to load firewood and water. Soon, three more *Decatur* officers brought the ship to its full complement: Lieutenants Joseph DeHaven and Robert Scott and Purser Felix Senac. Then, despite shoreside tensions, the Decaturs were released on liberty.[10]

Panama was a city of ten thousand in 1857, where modern residential, warehouse, and shopping districts surrounded the bustling railway and steamship terminus, adjacent to the romantic and picturesque Old City, "deserted, crumbling and grass-grown, [and] 'mellowed into harmony by time.'" In new Panama City, narrow cobbled streets wound between stone houses, three and four stories tall, each with a graceful balcony. Visitors bought souvenirs in the market and saw the sights and people of this intersection between the Atlantic and Pacific oceans. One Panama traveler remembered stepping from the dazzling sunlight down into a dim, cool saloon, where Frenchmen were playing dominoes, Indians were shooting billiards, and the bartender was mixing a sherry cobbler for a fever-stricken Yankee. Looking out the window, another visitor recalled, a black woman walked by in the shade of the buildings, carrying her baby on her hip. Indian farmers bore sacks of corn on their backs, heading in from the countryside to market. An old Spanish

Cathedral, Panama. N.E.

FIG. 37 *When Taylor left the* Decatur *at Panama, he brought his sketchbook into the city and sketched this view of the great cathedral. From the John Y. Taylor Sketch Books, Western Americana Collection, Beinecke Rare Book and Manuscript Library, Yale University.*

padre strolled along, puffing a cigar, wearing his black surplice lined with pink satin. Germans, Frenchmen, and Americans chatted in the shade. A mother and daughter passed, hand in hand, wearing bright calico dresses and broad-brimmed Panama hats. A beautiful Indian girl threw her *rebozo* over her head and glanced dark-eyed at her laughing friend. The water carrier rode his mule through town, carrying spring water to refill his customers' water jars. An elderly Spanish lady clad in black from head to toe entered the church for mass. Panama was a wonderful city to see with an artist's eye, and Surgeon Taylor used his few days there to sightsee and sketch.[11]

Some Decaturs never left Panama's sailor town, and the logs document the usual run of liquor smuggling, fights, and complaints of venereal infection, as the men spent time in the beachfront brothels and taverns. Rum was the ubiquitous drink of Central America—*aguardiente*—potent and cheap in taverns, dancehalls, and theaters. In Panama, most *Decatur* officers and enlisted men would have paid to see a cockfight, the great national spectator sport. Male aficionados gathered in smoky theaters, standing in a circle around the fighting stage to drink and bet on their favorite of the two fighting cocks, the

FIG. 38 Men of every sort join in the rough fun of an antebellum cockfight in Central America except, perhaps, the fever-stricken, threadbare fellow in the foreground who has lost his bet. Harper's Monthly, January 1860. Courtesy University of Washington Libraries, Special Collections, 27970z.

birds' feet bound with razor-sharp knives. As their partisans shouted them on, the cocks' fight was fast and furious: "a fluttering of cropped wings, a shaking of scarlet crests, a cross-fire of murderous glances, a sudden spring, a bitter tussle, fuss and feathers, [and] a pool of blood." Afterward, visitors strolled along the esplanade and leaned on the parapet, listening to street musicians and looking out at the islands in the harbor, the old pirate haunts. In 1857, California-bound steamships rocked on the Pacific swell, and "the dark hulls and tall tapering masts of several American men-of-war swung lazily at their anchors," including the *Independence* and the *Decatur*.[12]

According to Dallas, Mervine ordered the *Decatur* to reload the carronades with shot and shell, to arm the sailors who were on duty, and to prepare the small boats to convey landing parties at a moment's notice. The commodore feared that Panama was on the edge of explosive violence, convinced that the riots he anticipated would demand marine-style shore fighting with the new minié rifles as well as bombardment with the great guns. The crews of the *Independence* and the *Decatur* practiced "infantry and artillery drills" almost daily, and the seamen became "nearly as effective as marines in the use of small arms." At Mervine's order, Thatcher had the launch "fitted for action," mounting the howitzer to create a gunboat just as Gansevoort had done in Seattle. The captains of the two warships afloat and Consul Corwine ashore

FIG. 39 *This 1855 engraving shows Panama's rampart, where locals and visitors strolled in the evening, gazing out at the Pacific. Commodore Mervine prepared the sailors of the* Independence *and the* Decatur *for marine-style shore actions here in the event of revolution in Panama.* Harper's Monthly, *October 1855. Courtesy University of Washington Libraries, Special Collections, 7972z.*

agreed upon flag signals for communication in the event of trouble. However, the *Decatur* had not been adequately resupplied at Mare Island with weapons and ammunition, and the ship arrived at Panama with just a handful of muskets, three rifles, and a few double-barreled shotguns. It was a pathetic arsenal; Puget Sound settlers likely shot deer for many years with the *Decatur*'s firearms. Sterrett, grumbled Mervine, "had parted with a large portion of her muskets to volunteers in the late Indian disturbances, and those arms are irrevocably lost to the Navy." Writing to Duncan Ingraham, chief of the navy's Bureau of Ordnance, Mervine complained that he been forced to reduce target practice because the *Decatur* had arrived virtually unarmed, and he requested that the ship be supplied at once with a "full complement of small arms" and an extra supply of Sharps rifles. In the intervening two weeks, Mervine carefully doled out ammunition, thinking it wise to "retain an ample supply for contingencies not wholly improbable."[13]

FIG. 40 In 1855, Harpers New Monthly Magazine *published this provocative engraving of a Native Nicaraguan woman, said to be the Mother of the Tigers—the wild "model of female loveliness." Western opportunists sought not only fame and fortune but also the companionship of a woman like this one, so clearly untamed.* Harper's Monthly, *September 1855. Courtesy University of Washington Libraries, Special Collections,* UW 27974z.

Aside from crises in Puget Sound and Panama, William Walker's filibuster to Nicaragua claimed the squadron's attention and threatened to raise the "contingencies" Mervine feared. When Gansevoort was in Puget Sound, Mervine had ordered him to investigate the imprisonment of eighty filibuster soldiers from San Francisco held for trial at Mazatlan, "doubtless many deluded Young Americans among them." Wrecked on the beach at Seattle, Gansevoort missed this chance to rescue these Mexico filibusters. However, other adventurers were inspired to take up arms—self-interested mercenaries, idealistic crusaders for manifest destiny, and footloose soldiers of fortune—as the Young America expansionist movement pressed along the coasts of the Pacific West. Each filibuster soldier and supporter had his own set of motives, and manifest destiny's lush rhetoric equated conquest and liberation and was easily borrowed to describe freebooting expeditions as "regeneration." American agents, including those of the navy, both encouraged and discouraged, aided and thwarted, filibuster crusades in Central America. The *Decatur* played a minor role in the Nicaragua filibusters of "General" William Walker and in the career of William Carey Jones, the diplomat who was sent to clean up the filibuster mess but who made matters so much worse.[14]

William Walker captured the imagination of the nation, which became fascinated by this small, slim, quiet man. Stubborn and ambitious, inspired and delusional, Walker became for a time Young America's quixotic knight-errant. Born in Tennessee in 1824, Walker studied first medicine and then the law and edited the *New Orleans Crescent*, promoting a progressive agenda that included the gradual abolition of slavery. He courted Ellen Martin, who died of cholera during the 1849 epidemic, and he was undone by her death. The Pacific West called him as it did many men who were despondent or at loose ends, and Walker traveled to gold rush California via the Panama transit to make a fresh start. His new San Francisco friends included men interested in soldiering for manifest destiny and personal gain. Backed by such prominent Californians as the Young America senators William Gwin and John Weller, Walker took a leading part in an 1853 freebooting adventure to Sonora, in Mexico; his men were recruited from "unemployed veterans of the Mexican War and down-on-their-luck gold seekers," the opportunists of the Pacific West. Walker proclaimed himself president of Sonora but shortly thereafter barely escaped with his life. Tried in San Francisco for violation of the Neutrality Act, Walker was easily acquitted and began to raise an army for another expedition, this time to Nicaragua.[15]

The Panama transit is familiar to us, but in the 1850s an alternative transit route across Nicaragua was equally appealing. Cornelius Vanderbilt's Accessory Transit Company negotiated concessions with the Nicaraguan government for a transit corridor and explored the possibility of digging an isthmian canal, which was abandoned as too costly. Instead, the company developed a segmented passage from Greytown on the Atlantic side to San Juan del Sur on the Pacific by steamer most of the way and stagecoach the rest. Opened in 1851, the Nicaragua route cut 700 miles off the Panama route and was advertised as the cooler, healthier, and more comfortable alternative. During the first years of the Nicaragua transit's operation, an average of two thousand Americans made this crossing each month, mostly heading westward to California. The travelers had "ample time to admire the splendid country through which they passed, to look with utter contempt on the natives, and to speculate on what a country it would be if it were only under the stars and stripes." Whether their California dreams succeeded or failed, many remembered Nicaragua. Once, Nicaraguan mines had yielded gold, silver, copper, lead, and iron; its plantations had shipped mahogany, cedar, rosewood, indigo, cotton, sugar, rice, coffee, and tobacco. But the two governing parties, Liberal and Conservative, had vied for power for more than a decade, and during the long period of civil disorder, exports had fallen to nearly nothing. Stateside journalists usually concluded their catalog of Nicaragua's resources by reminding readers that the "present inhabitants are so low in the scale of intelligence and morality, that there is scarcely any hope for them" and that "unless foreigners settle in the country," these opportunities would remain undeveloped.[16]

Amy Greenberg has described this "Latin American booster narrative . . . steeped in Manifest Destiny": that Nicaragua was a paradise within easy reach of Americans. E. G. Squier, Young America spokesman and former ambassador to Nicaragua, published ten books and dozens of articles and pamphlets extolling the nearby exoticism and exciting potential of Central America. Other journalists wrote delightedly of the dramatic volcanoes that rose out of Lake Nicaragua and exclaimed over the oranges, guavas and pineapples and the parrots, palm trees, and orchids. They wrote of cooling breezes off Lake Nicaragua and the Pacific Ocean and praised Nicaragua's temperate climate, pronouncing it "extremely favorable to the general health of natives, as [it was for] foreigners." They described beautiful Nicaraguan women, who had "an infinite fund of animal spirits," and promised four women for every man. Many stateside writers casually assumed that Nicaragua's conquest by the United States or by Great Britain was inevitable and spun racist generalizations in justification. The Nicaraguans were "a mongrel race," wrote one journalist; the "languor and ignorance of its inhabitants, who are of mixed races, keep [Nicaragua] in a semi-barbarous condition." Nicaraguans were described as lazy, violent, passionate, and childlike and had "managed to reduce themselves and their country to such a wretched state of misery that it really appeared to be the duty of some civilized nation to step in and keep them all in order." To expansionist Americans, Nicaraguans could not look out for themselves. Above all, they could not manage the transit so vital to American interests. Nicaragua hung ripe for the picking when William Walker raised a filibuster army of adventurers under contract with the Liberals to fight the Conservatives.[17]

Under the Neutrality Act, U.S. citizens were forbidden to mount such private military expeditions against nations at peace with the United States, and the filibuster was clearly illegal. However, especially during the first year and a half of Walker's invasion of Nicaragua—during the first filibuster—he had the support of many Americans in and out of government. When Walker first prepared to sail from California, he met with U.S. Army general John Wool and described his Nicaragua contract. The old soldier reportedly shook Walker's hand and told him that he would "not only not interfere with the enterprise but wished it entire success." In May 1855, while the *Decatur* was at Honolulu, Walker sailed from San Francisco on the *Vesta*, landing at Realejo, Nicaragua,

with sixty filibusters, later known as The Immortals. By October, his army had swelled to about four hundred men, and Walker had virtually ended armed resistance in Nicaragua. The young man from Tennessee became Generalissimo Walker, the power behind a puppet president, Patricio Rivas. Soon, the transit in his hands, Walker revoked the Vanderbilt charter and awarded it to the financier's rivals to cement a new alliance with them. In his early successes, Walker was portrayed stateside as an advance agent of "Anglo-Saxon Manifest Destiny." The Young America organ *New York Herald* gave Walker "prominent and favorable display in both news stories and editorials, comparing his victories with those at Marathon, Yorktown and Waterloo."[18]

The "grey-eyed man of destiny" created or capitalized on a Nicaraguan folk belief that one day a man with gray eyes would liberate Nicaragua. From the point of view of *DeBow's*, Walker's Nicaragua filibuster was not merely predestined in Central American folktales: the "general" was an agent of the United States, and the filibusters had the "good-will of the majority of the American people, [and] they represented the nation as truly as [President] Pierce and his cabinet." Nicaragua's Americanization—its "regeneration"—would soon be complete, the magazine confidently continued, and that beachhead represented just the beginning of "occupation by Americans of all the Central American states, and, in due course of time, of Mexico and Cuba." In October 1855, when the *Decatur* was anchored off Seattle, large crowds turned out in San Francisco to cheer on the *Uncle Sam* as it steamed out of the harbor with more new recruits to join Walker in Nicaragua. The ship carried away not

FIG. 42 The widely read Frank Leslie's Illustrated Newspaper *published this engraving of Walker's men smoking, drinking, playing cards, and relaxing after the successful battle to take Granada, encouraging enlistment in the filibuster. May 3, 1856. Courtesy University of Washington Libraries.*

only hundreds of eager filibusters but the entire armory of the Sacramento Rifle Company. U.S. Navy efforts to prevent the sailing and landing of the *Uncle Sam* and other filibuster ships from San Francisco during the first filibuster were halfhearted at best; they were certainly ineffective.[19]

Walker's message of recruitment called to a generation of Young Americans eager to be both heroic and successful and to act out bold exploits that merged the mission of Pacific maritime expansion with pursuit of personal advantage, combining new notions of nationhood and manhood. One starryeyed recruit wrote that Walker had the "iron will and reckless courage of the true man of destiny," who with just a few words could inspire his men with the glory of their mission. But it was a glorious mission with self-interested outcomes: camaraderie with a band of brother knights, fabled passages at arms, and the reward of a beautiful woman and one's own *rancho* in the West. Walker and his recruiters moved men to extraordinary commitment by appealing to both their idealism and their opportunism, promising both fame and fortune, helped along by lavish publicity. The early Nicaragua crusade was a highly publicized success, and one enthusiastic filibuster observer noted that the streets of Granada, Nicaragua, were soon "thronging with the representatives of 'Young America.'" Stateside newspapers breathlessly reported Walker's lavish entertainments, his "groaning" table and "elegant" ladies. Walker's agents found no difficulty recruiting men for the effort, and

FIG. 43 *The San Juan River,*
pictured here in 1853, was a
vital link in the Nicaragua
transit. Though the river
was navigable by shallow-
draft steamers, here men
row upriver. J. M. Letts,
California Illustrated.
Courtesy University of
Washington Libraries.

thousands steamed to Nicaragua from San Francisco alone. Young American adventurers spoke of "seeing the native Nicaraguan elephant" in 1856 just as they had spoken of seeing him heading to Sutter's Mill in 1849, the Queen Charlotte Islands in 1851, or Puget Sound in 1853.[20]

One eager recruit to the Nicaragua filibuster, John C. Drinkhouse, deserted the *Decatur* to sign on for the Great Adventure as a private in Walker's army. Raised in Pennsylvania, Drinkhouse had headed West to fight in the Mexican War and was discharged at Vera Cruz. He made his way to San Francisco, sailed in the Royal Navy and on whaling ships, and joined the *Decatur* to sail to Puget Sound and then back to San Francisco. In the U.S. Navy, Drinkhouse was ranked an ordinary seaman; filibuster recruiters doubled his wages, offering $25 per month, plus a land grant of 250 acres. Once in Nicaragua, Drinkhouse soon left the army ranks to join the filibuster navy on its single schooner of war, the *Granada;* he was promoted to seaman and earned even more. It is highly likely that other "sailors of manifest destiny views" deserted the U.S. Navy and signed up, making their way to Nicaragua; nearly three hundred filibuster recruits steamed south from San Francisco on the *Orizaba* on November 20, 1856, just as the *Decatur* was suffering through waves of desertion and Middleton was unable to crew up.[21]

San Francisco steamers carried the filibusters and their gear to San Juan del Sur, the terminus of the Nicaragua transit on the Pacific; these soldiers of fortune mingled with ordinary passengers who were simply homeward bound. Other filibusters entered the Nicaragua transit at Greytown on the Atlantic side, coming from New York and Mobile. The typical recruit arrived well-armed and tested his marksmanship on the transit, shooting monkeys in the trees as the steamer chugged up the river. Then it was off the boat and across the portage to reboard at Lake Nicaragua and finally land on the dock at Virgin Bay. There, it was hoped, a few Americans could beat any number of "greasers" and mestizos and live happily ever after in the Pacific West.[22]

Following a few executions and a dubious election, Walker became president of Nicaragua in July 1856 and authorized a "crash program" of Americanization. Strapped for cash, the cocky filibuster levied "forced contributions" on American citizens living in Nicaragua, including U.S. consul John Priest, who indignantly refused to pay his $150 "assessment." When Walker's officers threatened to imprison him and seize his property, Priest paid up under protest with sacks of dimes. Corresponding with Secretary of State William Marcy, Priest begged for a man-of-war off San Juan del Sur to protect American interests from Walker's marauding filibusters. In the meantime, the U.S. ambassador to Nicaragua, Young American John Wheeler, had endorsed Walker's efforts by recognizing the pirate government, giving it credibility. Known in Central America as *el ministro filibustero*, Southern expansionist Wheeler regularly supplied copies of Walker's propaganda newspaper, *Il Nicaraguense*, to Wheeler's hometown North Carolina newspaper, the *Raleigh Weekly Register*, which applauded Walker's plan of "regeneration": democratic reform, economic development, public education, and free trade. Then, in September 1856, William Walker reinstituted slavery in Nicaragua.[23]

The reestablishment of slavery was the opportunist's strategic bid to tap the resources of the American South to filibuster the Pacific West. Writing in early 1860, Walker recalled the proclamation of the slavery decree as both principled and pragmatic: "calculated to bind the Southern States to Nicaragua, as if she were one of themselves" and to identify "the naturalized Nicaraguans"—the filibusters—as the "champions of the Southern States of the Union in the conflict truly styled 'irrepressible.'" Walker praised the "superabundance of intellect and capital" in the South, which was crippled by a shortage of slave labor, and he argued that Southern expansion to Nicaragua and beyond might be "the only way to avoid revolution" in the United States. Walker contended that Central American slavery was an essential element of the region's Americanization and regeneration and called for a renewal of the slave trade, defending human bondage as a benefit that brought the African man from his "native wastes" to the New World, teaching him the "arts of life" and "true religion" and allowing him to join the dominant white race as a "useful auxiliary" in subduing the American continent. Walker claimed that his goal had always been to provide slavery with a refuge—a tropical empire "beyond the limits of the Union"—and that Nicaragua was just the beginning. *DeBow's Review* praised the "glorious acquisition" of Nicaragua as "a new State to be added to the South, in or out of the Union," which Walker had taken "possession of in the name of the white race." Now "the darling of southern slave expansionists," Walker issued a clarion call to Southern men take up arms in Nicaragua.[24]

Ambassador John Wheeler was a committed Walker partisan and his support did not waver. It is likely that Wheeler helped convince Walker to reestablish slavery; a recent historian has termed Wheeler a staunch white supremacist. The ambassador thoroughly admired Walker's "daring and romantic adventure," hailing the filibuster as an "ardent Anglo-American" who wished to introduce to Nicaragua "a new civilization by a race whose destiny was to found new nations" through regeneration of the "mongrel races." In his outspoken approval of Walker's government, *el ministro filibustero* ignored the instructions of Secretary of State Marcy, infuriating the secretary. "Old Fogy" Marcy called for Wheeler's resignation in cabinet discussions, but Secretary of War Davis and Secretary of the Navy Dobbin both defended the ambassador for reasons of friendship and principle. According to one historian, Dobbin had secured Wheeler's appointment, and Wheeler's biographer claimed that Dobbin and President Pierce were the ambassador's close friends; he was not recalled until the final days of Pierce's administration, as a personal favor to the dying Marcy. In 1856, Wheeler and Walker enjoyed support at the highest levels of government, including from the secretary of the navy.[25]

While the *Decatur* was at Seattle, "spread-eagle expansionist" Lewis Cass drafted an enthusiastic letter urging U.S. recognition of Walker's government that was read to a New York crowd of twenty thousand, gathered to support "Liberty and Nicaragua": "The heroic effort of our countrymen in Nicaragua excites my admiration while it engages all my solicitude. . . . He who does not sympathize with such an enterprise has little in common with me. The difficulties which General Walker has encountered and overcome will place his name high on the roll of the distinguished men of his age. . . . A new day, I hope, is opening upon the States of Central America." However, as Buchanan's secretary of state, and after Walker's institution of slavery, Cass either became less candid or changed his mind, and he ordered U.S. marshals to use all means at their disposal to prevent such illegal expeditions. Cass was not alone in this change of heart. Robert May has argued that the record confirms the growing antifilibuster convictions of both the Pierce and Buchanan administrations. Many Americans initially hailed Walker as an "advance agent of Manifest Destiny" because they were convinced that he intended to bring Nicaragua into the national fold. However, once Walker unveiled plans for an independent slave republic, his popular support became largely sectional, and the filibuster lost its appeal for men in uniform, at least for Northern men. Additionally, the crusade grew less appealing to footloose Pacific West opportunists when the Nicaragua filibuster faced a series of disastrous setbacks.[26]

With hindsight, a journalist wrote that "nothing is more deceptive and fallacious than the first successes of a tropical buccaneer war." By January 1857, Walker's cheap and easy romp was over. British warships blockaded the Atlantic side to prevent supplies and reinforcements from reaching the filibuster from the American South. Supported by a vengeful Vanderbilt, Costa Rican general Joaquin Mora rallied troops from Costa Rica, Honduras, El Salvador, and Guatemala into an allied army to drive the invaders from Nicaragua. Fighting the Costa Rican–led allies, the filibuster army encountered a determined and well-armed enemy. One of Walker's Rangers wrote that at one time each filibuster could handle seven or eight "greasers," but now, "greasers" and filibusters were matched man for man and "it became apparent that the filibuster day was over." Starving men ate their horses; cholera wracked the ranks. In December 1856, Juan Rafael Mora, the president of Costa Rica, issued an amnesty to be circulated among the men in "Walker's Army." The proclamation claimed that Mora sympathized with the soldiers, who by then surely realized that they were fighting against people "who were only defending their country, their rights, liberties and homesteads." If they would desert Walker, the "Scourge of Humanity," Mora guaranteed their safe passage to Panama, to cross the isthmus and board a steamer bound for New York. The Costa Rican president's promise marked the downfall of Walker's first filibuster, as "large parties" began to desert, slipping away at night. Plagued by desertion, disappointment, illness, hunger, and fatigue, Walker's army was "driven back step by step into a corner at Rivas," and U.S. representatives prepared to negotiate a settlement in Nicaragua and to rescue American citizens among the filibusters.[27]

In February 1857, Commodore Mervine ordered Commander Charles Henry Davis to sail the sloop of war *St. Mary's* from Panama to San Juan del Sur, joining the filibuster schooner *Granada* in the harbor. Mervine's orders to Davis left much to the commander's discretion but clearly express the commodore's wary distrust of Walker:

> You will prepare the U.S. ship *St. Mary's* [and] proceed to San Juan del Sur, Nicaragua, where the presence of a man-of-war is necessary in consequence of the unsettled state of public affairs. The precarious and straitened conditions of the forces under Gen. Walker may induce him to attempt depredations upon American citizens in that State, which you will prevent and restrain. In the event of the expulsion of Walker and his forces from Nicaragua by the allied armies, and his departure to adjacent territory in Central America for the purpose of hostile and aggressive operations, you will take such further measures with the force under your command as circumstances shall require for the adequate protection of American citizens.

Davis met with senior officers of the Walker camp and the Costa Rican high command and expressed to Mervine his frank admiration for the filibusters and his sympathy with their crusade. Speaking with the confident racialism of Young America expansionism, Davis wrote: "The truth is, Commodore, if the Americans establish themselves here [in Nicaragua], it will be by the same laws that the Turks govern the effete races of Asia Minor, the Tartars the Chinese, [and] the British the wealthy but enervated nations of India—a law of nature." Davis contrasted the manly countenances of Walker's men with the "mild unthoughtful faces" and "large womanly eyes" of the allied Costa Ricans, Guatemalans, and Nicaraguans, the masculine heroes contrasted with "these effeminate people." The *St. Mary's* commander admired the "real ability" and "moral and physical strength" of Walker and his officers, who "have staked their own fortunes upon his." Amy Greenberg has argued that these filibusters embodied American masculine virtues of fearlessness, self-reliance, and independence and were the "true men of the 1850s"; they were E. Anthony Rotundo's "self-made men" of achievement—the ultimate Young Americans, even in defeat—and Commander Davis admired them as such. Commodore Mervine did not agree.[28]

William Mervine had been a Whig, he called himself and was called by

FIG. 44 Frank Leslie's Illustrated Newspaper *published this engraving of the western boomtown of San Juan del Sur, the Pacific entrance to the Nicaragua transit, where Commander Henry Davis later negotiated Walker's surrender. November 29, 1856. Courtesy University of Washington Libraries.*

others an Old Fogy, and he was vehemently opposed to Walker's piratical adventurism: this "damned Southern, pro-slavery movement," as he put it. The *New York Herald* called Mervine a "pretty consistent Black Republican," or abolitionist, and Secretary of War Jefferson Davis excoriated such Northern Republicans for their support of the Costa Rican–led alliance against Walker. William Walker considered Mervine an "intimate friend of Secretary Marcy"—himself a Fogy—and he was convinced that Marcy had given the commodore secret instructions, passed along from Mervine to Commander Davis, to destroy the Nicaragua filibuster at all costs. But on at least one occasion in the recent past, according to the *New York Times*, Davis had permitted the landing of eighty Walker filibuster reinforcements from the Pacific steamer *Sierra Nevada* "without inquiry or the least objection." The *Times* correspondent concluded that both Mervine and Davis deliberately ignored the filibuster landings, aware that "the Government at Washington did not wish the neutrality laws enforced in the case of Nicaragua." The motives of federal agents and military officers during Walker's Nicaragua filibusters are very difficult to ascertain, and since newspaper reports of the events were highly partisan, they are unreliable as evidence.[29]

As the *St. Mary's* lay at anchor, Commander Davis found that he was uniquely placed to negotiate a ceasefire, and he arranged the evacuation of the filibuster women and children from Rivas, who marched out of town under escort of marines from the *St. Mary's*. Davis contacted Mora with the message that, if the filibusters were allowed to leave unharmed, the naval officer believed he could persuade Walker to surrender. In discussions on board the *St. Mary's*, one of Walker's officers claimed that if worse came to worst, they could flee on board the schooner *Granada*. However, convinced that his rank-and-file army would be starved out, Walker surrendered to Davis. On May 1, 1857, the navy commander and the filibuster general signed an agreement in which William Walker surrendered to the U.S. Navy rather than to the Costa Rican alliance. Walker and his senior staff boarded the *St. Mary's* for the sail to Panama. Once on board, Walker balked at turning over the *Granada,* and Davis manned the *St. Mary's* yardarms with armed marines and turned the ship's broadside toward the schooner. Walker capitulated and ordered the filibuster schooner's commander to hand over the *Granada* to the U.S. Navy, who then turned the schooner over to the Costa Rican navy. *Granada* seaman John Drinkhouse, once of the *Decatur,* appealed to Davis for help; the commander left the deserter to shift for himself in the chaos,[30] remarking that he had once deserted the U.S. Navy and now sought to desert yet another cause. Drinkhouse was merely an opportunist, his self-interest no longer clothed by any greater mission.

And so Walker's first filibuster in Nicaragua came to a conclusion, ending hopes for riches and an easy life, for honor and glory, for the expansion of American territory or the creation of a slave republic. Walker's crusade had ignited virulent anti-American sentiment in Central America and led to the closure of the Nicaragua transit by the Costa Rican–led alliance, which triggered a diplomatic initiative involving the *Decatur.* Finally, Walker abandoned the least fit of his men, who began a long and miserable chapter of the filibuster story that also involved the *Decatur.*[31]

When the *St. Mary's* arrived at Panama, Mervine hoped to rush Walker and his officers across the isthmus in a closed train and so be rid of them. But in the tinderbox atmosphere of 1857 Panama, he changed his mind, fearing a riot and mass murder of the surviving filibusters as well as other American travelers and residents. Mervine informed Bartolomé Calvo, governor of New

Grenada, that Walker and his staff had arrived on the *St. Mary's* and that the remainder—more than three hundred men—were soon expected in Panama on the *J. R. Mora* and other ships. He wanted them all to pass across the isthmus quietly and quickly and assured Calvo that their passage was "wholly of a peaceful character."[32]

Mervine coordinated the landing of the filibuster officers with the Panama Railroad's train departure and detailed the marines of the *Independence* to be stationed fully armed in the flagship's cutters when the filibuster group was rowed to shore. He ordered the marines who had been relieved from the *Decatur* and who were headed home to form an escort across the isthmus for the senior filibusters. Walker and his officers walked from the dock into town between files of marines, who shielded them from the hostile Panama crowd. Ushered into the railroad office, the little filibuster general settled down with a newspaper and waited to board the train. Crossing the isthmus, Walker and his officers were seated in the same railroad car with the *Decatur*'s marines, with John Kelly and John Maher from Ireland, Matthias Senn from Switzerland, and a dozen others. Though Mervine reassured Calvo that the marine guard was as much to prevent the filibusters from breaking out of the train as to prevent the populace from breaking in, the governor was furious. The *New York Times* had just reported that a filibuster was mustering in New Orleans against the New Grenada province of Veragua, and such rumors were frequent, almost weekly, occurrences. The last thing Calvo wanted was Walker's senior command loose in Panama, looking speculatively for their next big adventure, but Walker and his senior officers headed stateside in an uneventful passage. Landing in New Orleans, Walker was met with "almost frantic enthusiasm" and went to work planning the second Nicaragua filibuster.[33]

St. Mary's Lieutenant David McCorkle was given the assignment of marching three hundred filibusters from Rivas to San Juan del Sur and then south to Punta Arenas in Costa Rica, more than a hundred miles. Those who could walk formed a dreadful parade of the "most miserable specimens of humanity that it is possible to conceive," as McCorkle described them, staggering mile after mile toward the sea and then down the coast. At Punta Arenas, they waited for days and then crowded on board the *J. R. Mora* for a twelve-day passage to Panama. McCorkle, himself sick with fever, called the trek and the voyage the "most arduous and trying duty I have ever been engaged in during sixteen years service in the Navy." Men endured the most awful suffering; Virginian Andrew Johnson, died of chronic dysentery on board the *Mora* within sight of Panama. When the survivors finally arrived, Mervine described their condition to Buchanan's new secretary of the navy, Isaac Toucey:

The men were not only destitute of money but even of comfortable and decent clothing; many of them were extremely emaciated from fatigue, exposure and the want of sufficient and wholesome food, and many were suffering from dysentery and inveterate ulcers. They presented a revolting spectacle of squalor and suffering, the more pitiable because the subjects were young men who had been reduced to this condition by famine and exposure.[34]

The navy and the State Department had ordered the Pacific Squadron to help these American citizens reach their homes, but they had not provided the means. Mervine was at a loss as to how to get the filibusters across the isthmus on the train, let alone to New York. The intention of the department, Mervine reasoned, was to assist these survivors, and the only way to do that was to send them stateside, so he booked passage for those fit to travel, hoping for the "justice of our government" to compensate the carriers. Mervine gave the Panama Railroad Company a draft on the navy for the huge sum of $7,474 to cover the party's passage. The filibusters crossed the isthmus and arrived at Aspinwall, where they were joined by a group who had been detained at Greytown in Nicaragua, on the Atlantic side, and sent down the coast. The filthy, emaciated, sickly filibusters were unappealing traveling companions. The private steamers refused to transport them, and the suffering men were shared out among navy ships: the sloop of war *Cyane*, the steam frigate *Roanoke*, and the flagship *Wabash*. When the survivors arrived in the States, the public was appalled by their physical condition, and Northern newspapers published shocking tales of their suffering and of Walker's incompetence and inhumanity. *Decatur* deserter John Drinkhouse made his way to New York on board the *Roanoke*, listed among the sick.[35]

Meanwhile, on June 3, 1857, Mervine ordered Thatcher to prepare the *Decatur* for sea to transport William Carey Jones—"a gentleman who has some commission from our Government to the States of Central America"—to Punta Arenas, in Costa Rica. Mervine asked Thatcher to station the *Decatur* there in case Jones needed further transportation. In fact, the *Decatur*'s primary mission became "the conveyance of Mr. Jones" wherever he needed to go. Mervine further instructed Thatcher to visit San José, Costa Rica, to investigate the complaints of American citizens impressed into the Costa Rican army in the "national war" against Walker in Nicaragua. Consul Corwine, at Panama, had also requested that Thatcher bring along Young Anderson, a "Costa Rican gentleman," as a passenger. By the late 1850s, Anderson had built a "beauteous English home, deepset in the heart of the mountains," surrounded by his coffee plantations. Often visited by journalists, English-born

Anderson was a prominent member of the expatriate European community and had a financial interest in the Nicaragua transit. Also, when Jones's mission permitted, Thatcher was instructed to sail the *Decatur* on to San Juan del Sur, in Nicaragua, and check on the American consul, John Priest, who was rumored to be dissipated. And Thatcher was finally ordered "to render assistance to American citizens who have been connected with the expedition of Gen. Walker in Nicaragua." Secretary Toucey had ordered Mervine to "direct the commander of the *Decatur* that should any American citizens who have been connected with the expedition under General Walker in Nicaragua present themselves on board the vessel for protection, to receive them and carry them to Panama."[36]

In the meantime, Thatcher awaited the arrival of William Carey Jones, who had been appointed a "special agent" by newly elected president James Buchanan and was to report to Secretary of State Lewis Cass. Jones was delegated to "negotiat[e] between the hostile parties [in Nicaragua], and assist to end the contest." He had agreed to this difficult and dangerous assignment, expecting to "enter the camps . . . of belligerent forces" and to carry "weapons of defense" while sustained by, at the very least, a sloop of war. Jones hoped, however, that a war steamer could be assigned to either side of the isthmus in his support. At $8 per day plus expenses, Jones was to "visit the states of Central America for the purpose of observing and reporting upon the condition of affairs in that quarter, and of preventing, as far as possible, the recent occurrences there from affecting injuriously the interests of this country." The "recent occurrences" were the activities of Walker's filibuster army, the involvement of the British, and the surprising successes of the allied Central American armies, as well as whatever resentment Ambassador Wheeler's partisanship for Walker might have caused in Costa Rica. The "interests" included the safety of American citizens residing or passing through Central America and assurance of an open transit through Nicaragua. At the time Jones received his orders, Walker had not yet surrendered to Commander Davis.[37]

Jones was an attorney in his midforties; he was the son-in-law of Missouri senator Thomas Hart Benton and the brother-in-law of California settler and politician John C. Fremont. Jones had achieved notice in the early 1850s with publication of his *Report on the Subject of Land Titles in California,* a study conducted at the request of the secretaries of state and the interior. The *Report,* soon discredited, defended the dubious land titles of Fremont and other early Anglo settlers in California. Marrying Benton's daughter, Jones smoothly entered the world of political patronage, and his appointment depended on

FIG. 45 (Facing page) *Young Anderson, English expatriate, built this Costa Rican hacienda in the midst of his coffee plantations, surrounded by gardens "surfeited with pineapples, oranges, quinces and mangoes." This* Harper's *engraving continued to encourage dreams of "pioneering" on the Nicaraguan "frontier."* Harper's Monthly, *February 1860. Courtesy University of Washington Libraries, Special Collections,* UW 27968z.

the support of President Buchanan and the consent of Secretary of State Cass. Benton's secretary, Frank Blair, angrily asserted that Jones earned his "roving commission" in Central America as an "administration hireling" by "lying on his brother-in-law [Fremont] . . . during the last Presidential election." Blair also accused Jones of lying when he claimed during the campaign that the aged Benton had come to support Buchanan's pro-Southern policies, declaring that Jones was willing to "sell the ashes and reputation of Col. Benton to the Administration for an office for himself." Like Wheeler, Jones had parlayed political influence to gain a diplomatic appointment.[38]

Jones was an unlikely diplomat to send to Central America, and he seemed destined to become as unpopular as Wheeler had been. In May 1856, a number of stateside newspapers published Jones's open letter to Young America senator John Weller of California, calling attention to the plight of "our brave countrymen in Nicaragua," who must be protected "to the extent of war if necessary." Walker had broken no laws, argued Jones, and had instead shown a "pacific, statesmanlike and commendable character" in the betterment of Nicaragua. In fact, Jones continued, that country had not in twenty years been "so quiet, order so well maintained, the laws so well administered, property so secure and business so safely conducted." Jones argued that Costa Rica had invaded Nicaragua to attack American citizens and, in doing so, had in effect declared war against the United States. In conclusion, Jones identified himself as a western man: he deplored the disregard that the federal government showed for the interests of "us settlers on the Pacific" and called for repeal of the Clayton-Bulwer Treaty and for war with Costa Rica to protect the filibuster "settlers" on the Nicaraguan Pacific West frontier.[39]

James Buchanan was a far more experienced diplomat than Franklin Pierce and had fewer illusions about the redemptive expansionism of Young America. However, Central Americans who feared American interference, occupation, or outright invasion found much in Buchanan's administration to alarm them. Buchanan's Democratic Party platform had emphasized the overriding importance of "the great highway which nature . . . has marked out for a free communication between the Atlantic and the Pacific oceans" and further resolved: "That, in view of so commanding an interest, the people of the United States can not but sympathize with the efforts which are being made by the people of Central America to regenerate that portion of the continent which covers the passage across the Interoceanic Isthmus." Although Buchanan's platform made no mention of Walker by name, support for the filibuster and its relationship to the transit is quite clear. Indeed, "regeneration" was Walker's own term for his Nicaragua venture, and the plank had been written by Young America filibuster enthusiast Pierre Soulé. Like Jones's open letter, the plank was written before Walker issued the slavery proclamation. Nevertheless, Buchanan's appointment of an outspoken Young America expansionist like Jones, who had advocated going to war to protect the American beachhead in Nicaragua, was not reassuring to the Costa Rican officials with whom he would be dealing.[40]

On May 20, 1857, William Carey Jones took the mail steamer from New York to Aspinwall and then crossed the isthmus by train. Once at Panama, Cass instructed Jones to consult with Mervine and then to embark on an unnamed sloop of war (a space was left in Cass's orders where the ship's name was to be filled in), whose "commander will be instructed to receive you and convey you to the port of San Juan del Sur" in Nicaragua. Jones ended up on board the *Decatur*. Writing to Jones before Walker's surrender, Cass worried that "much must be left to your discretion, because it is impossible to foresee what precise condition of affairs may exist" in Nicaragua. The latest intelligence then available indicated to Cass that a great many U.S. citizens were stranded in Nicaragua "who ha[d] participated in its local controversies and [were] left by the reverses of war without the means of returning home." Cass directed Jones to obtain the release of "Walker and his friends" if they had been captured and to get them to Greytown or Aspinwall on the Atlantic side or to San Juan del Sur or Panama on the Pacific side, to then be taken home on an American navy ship. Thus, the U.S. State Department and Navy assisted in the retreat of Walker's army.[41]

Cass carefully instructed Jones that the evacuation of Walker and his men—so easily perceived as a rescue—was officially on humanitarian grounds and in no way intended to "express an opinion concerning the Nicaraguan controversy." Indeed, the official position of the State Department was that Walker and his army were only in Nicaragua at the "invitation of one of the native parties, whose leader claimed to be the rightful President of the Republic." Cass reminded Jones that Costa Rica and Nicaragua had a longstanding border dispute, and the alliance was not really intended to get the Yankees out of Nicaragua but was rather a cynical scheme to seize the transit and distribute the rest of Nicaragua to the adjoining republics. Costa Rica, Cass continued, had artfully whipped up "the prejudice of the Spanish-American races against alleged aggression of foreigners from the North." Jones was to reassure the Central Americans he encountered that the United States had absolutely no intention to colonize, annex, or occupy Nicaragua but instead hoped to help that republic maintain its independence.

In the tradition of the Clayton-Bulwer Treaty, Cass stressed that the Nicaragua transit "should be kept open and secure for the travel of the world"; he was concerned by American citizens' complaints "of serious injuries . . . to their persons and property and of the seizure of their [transit] boats" on the San Juan River and Lake Nicaragua. Finally, Cass ordered Jones to travel as a private citizen, reasoning that he would have access to information that would be unavailable to a "public functionary." However, Cass provided a passport:

> To all to whom these presents shall come, Greeting.
>
> Know ye that the bearer hereof, William Carey Jones, a distinguished citizen of the United States, is proceeding to Central America as a Special Agent of this government.
>
> These are therefore to request all whom it may concern to permit him and his suite to pass freely without let or molestation, and to extend to him such friendly aid and protection as would in like cases be extended to similar officers of foreign governments in this country.[42]

Intending to travel light as a simple American tourist, Jones purchased a saddle and saddlebags for inland travel. Except for the support of the *Decatur,* he was on his own in an unpredictable situation. As Cass pointed out, the United States had no dependable diplomatic representatives in Central America: Wheeler had been withdrawn; Amos Corwine was too far away in Panama; William Edward Venable, minister in Guatemala, had not yet reached his post (once he did, he died of cholera in the summer of 1857, when Jones had barely begun his mission). Cass did not mention the U.S. consul at San José, Costa Rica, Marquis Hine. John Priest, U.S. consul at San Juan del Sur, was reputed to be both venal and dissolute and more partial to "Spanish Americans" than to American citizens. Rather than expecting any help from Priest, Jones, like Thatcher, was ordered to investigate him. Cass could only advise Jones to "improve any opportunity" that presented itself and send frequent reports back to Washington.[43]

Cass had charged his special agent with negotiating the reopening of the transit with whomever was in power in Nicaragua. On May 1, 1857, before Jones even left New York, Commander Davis had accepted Walker's surrender. Had events moved a bit more slowly, Jones, rather than Commander Davis, would have treated with Walker and General Mora, and Commander Henry Knox Thatcher would have conveyed Walker to Panama on the *Decatur,* rather than Davis on the *St. Mary's.* Commodore Mervine had planned to order Davis to sail from San Juan del Sur to claim the guano islands Jarvis and New Nantucket and had intended the *Decatur* to replace the *St. Mary's.* But in

May, the *Decatur* was still at Panama awaiting arms and ammunition and the full complement of officers, Jones did not arrive in time, and Commander Davis was on the scene and in the hot seat.[44]

Writing to Cass after the surrender, Jones foresaw that, when Walker returned to the United States, he would be lionized by the Southern press and lavished with sympathy and support. Jones also predicted that Walker would turn on Commander Davis and claim that, if Davis had not tricked them, he and his senior staff could have sailed away in the *Granada*. Once back in the States, Walker met for three hours with President Buchanan and accused Davis of betrayal as part of an antifilibuster conspiracy that originated with former president Pierce's Secretary of State William Marcy and included Commodore William Mervine. Buchanan was reported to "disapprove as strongly as Walker himself the intervention of Davis" and to have told Walker that he would initiate a formal investigation of the naval officer's actions. The president was said to have encouraged Walker to "make another attempt to conquer Nicaragua," reinforcing the popular sense that he was the consummate "doughface": a Northern man with Southern principles, in secret sympathy with the proslavery filibuster whatever he might say publicly. Certainly, Commander Davis received scant support from President Buchanan or from the secretaries of the navy. From retirement, Dobbin claimed that he had simply directed the *St. Mary's* to "protect the person and property of American citizens," and certainly not to negotiate the filibuster surrender. Secretary of the Navy Toucey noted in his first annual report that the department, "as a measure of humanity and policy," had intended to offer Walker's men "an opportunity to retreat from Nicaragua" and had directed Commodore Mervine accordingly. However, Mervine had acted before receipt of those instructions and sent Davis to San Juan del Sur with orders "to protect the person and property of American citizens," and "with this authority only," Davis had "negotiated with General Walker terms of capitulation." Toucey approved Davis's actions "so far as he aided General Walker and his men . . . to retreat from Nicaragua and return to the United States . . . but his interference with the *Granada* and her transfer to the Nicaraguan authorities was not approved." Damned with faint praise by the president and the secretary, Davis was honored in the North and vilified in the South.[45]

Cass had instructed Jones to take ship at Panama for San Juan del Sur and then to continue inland to Rivas to meet with representatives of the contending armies and negotiate a settlement to reopen the transit. But the war in Nicaragua was over, and Jones decided to start his mission in Costa Rica, now master of the Nicaragua transit. At Panama, Jones informed Cass that he planned to head out on the *Decatur* for Punta Arenas, Costa Rica, and then travel inland to San José, where, he wrote confidently, "the leading minds of all Central America are to be found." Jones also requested of Cass that "any private hostile expeditions" be delayed "at least" until he had gotten a foothold in Costa Rica. His clear implication is that Secretary of State Cass or agents of the U.S. government were aware of pending filibuster ventures and able to advance or hinder them at will. As for Jones himself, the envoy reiterated his sympathy with the mission of "General Walker and his brave command," as he termed them. As Jones began his mission, his success depended on his discretion and common sense, but he got off on the wrong foot at the very start, encouraging "a thousand and one rumors to circulate" by brushing off every inquiry with the facetious claim that he had been sent to investigate the headwaters of the Amur River, located in Manchuria. Jones thrived on theatrical secrecy, on the role of a man of mystery, the "mysterious stranger," as he came to be called derisively.[46]

On June 3, Jones and his baggage were loaded on board the *Decatur*. He wrote directly to his patron, President Buchanan, reminding him that Central American affairs were "a good deal complicated" and changing by the moment. Jones requested that a steamer be made available at Greytown so that he could communicate directly with Buchanan in Washington, DC, and urged the president to take "no important step" with regard to Central America without receiving "a statement" from Jones. On June 5, champing at the bit but still awaiting "the first favorable wind, for the *Decatur* to sail," Jones again wrote to Buchanan reiterating the need for swift communication. The private mail company steamers made monthly circuits of the Central American ports on the Pacific, to and from the Bay of Panama, but Jones considered that frequency by no means adequate. At just this time, *Decatur* surgeon Levi Cooper Lane signed on as correspondent to the *New York Herald*, and his articles provide a firsthand account of Jones's mission as seen from the water and the beach and the deck of the *Decatur*.[47]

On June 9, the *Decatur* finally put to sea, beating north against contrary winds and through extended calms. Nearly three weeks later, June 28, the ship finally anchored in the protected harbor of Costa Rica's principal seaport. About 2,500 people lived in Punta Arenas in 1857, many of them European and American expatriates. The town was built on a sandy spit, baking in the tropical sun between the sea and an estuary and reminding one reporter of a "miniature Sahara," the "last place a man would select for a pleasure residence." The town boasted "a lighthouse, a town clock and . . . a railroad of some ten miles . . . drawn by mules." Commander Thatcher visited Colonel Canas, commandant of Punta Arenas, to propose a salute to Costa Rica, which protocol required be returned gun-for-gun. Canas apologized that he had too few guns in working order to respond to the *Decatur* and that the last such salute—to celebrate the expulsion of the Walker filibuster—had resulted in the death of two soldiers. Instead, Canas suggested, he would inform his government that the national salute had been duly fired and that each had responded appropriately. Both men agreed to this face-saving fiction.[48]

The *Decatur*'s crew immediately went to work scraping and painting, preparing the ship to celebrate July 4, and the warship was dressed with bunting and flags to honor the eighty-first anniversary of U.S. independence. "Our little man of war arose that morning gay as a bride," Lane reported, "in honor of the birth of Young America." After Executive Officer John Clitz inspected the crew at quarters, the *Decatur* battery fired a salute, answered by a Chilean warship. As the celebration continued, many of the *Decatur*'s crew were released watch by watch on liberty, and the deck officer noted eight attempted desertions and a dozen drunk and disorderly. While at Punta Arenas, a drunken *Decatur* marine was jailed by the civil authorities for breaking down a door. The local judge forwarded a report to San José, complaining about the behavior of the *Decatur* sailors and marines on liberty, but Surgeon Lane derisively excused "whatever indiscretions our men may have been guilty of" by the money they had spent on liberty, their "spare change" creating a "grand era in the financial status of the town."[49]

Jones was eager to get started on his mission. From his reading, Jones was impressed by the progressive ideas of Costa Ricans; he considered them "a much superior people to the Nicaraguans." Stateside writers had termed Costa Rica "the New England of Central America," happily "free from revolution" and inhabited by an industrious people protected by a standing army of nearly five thousand men. By the summer of 1857, Costa Rican forces had established military bases along both sides of the San Juan River to guard the transit. Early in his mission, Jones argued to Cass that Costa Rican domination of Nicaragua might actually *further* U.S. interests in Central America because the Costa Ricans would be more likely than the Nicaraguans themselves to encourage modernization and, ultimately, Americanization of Nicaragua. Now that Walker had failed to regenerate Nicaragua, Jones saw Costa Rica as the best alternative. Jones and Thatcher packed their bags, preparing to visit San José and engage in delicate negotiations: Jones to liberate the transit and Thatcher to liberate American citizens impressed into the Costa Rican army.[50]

Commander Thatcher and Lieutenant Robert Scott joined Consul Hine,

Jones, and Anderson to travel inland from Punta Arenas. They rode on the mule-drawn railway to its terminus, paused for lunch, and then mounted mules and led a pack train carrying their baggage twelve miles farther inland. The party stopped at sunset to pass the night in a bamboo hut. The next morning, they began again, climbing uphill—"up, up and up," as Thatcher remembered. A heavy rain began "as usual" in the midafternoon, and they ended their second day of travel at a "rancho," eating beefsteak and "tortillos" for dinner and sleeping uncomfortably in flea-ridden cots. Jones continued to tell everyone they met that he was bound for the Amur River. Then, "some of the company," including Jones, fell sick and were left behind. Continuing on, Thatcher, Scott, and Hine entered the city, "completely worn out with this tedious journey, particularly those unaccustomed to the saddle." The officers recovered at the comfortable Costa Rica Hotel, kept by an expatriate German.[51]

The commander's first meeting in San José was with President "John" Mora, as Thatcher styled Juan Rafael Mora, on July 7. Thatcher and Scott were prompt, attired in full-dress uniform and soon joined by Consul Hine. The Americans were "received by his Excellency very politely," and after an exchange of compliments, the four men talked for half an hour. Then the two naval officers and the consul visited the residence of General Joaquin Mora to complete Thatcher's "important business"—the investigation of American citizens' forcible detention—but found the general to be out of town. Hine squired Thatcher and Scott around the city to see the sights and invited the officers to dinner. That evening, Hine's wife and sister-in-law, "both natives of the country," sang and played Nicaraguan music to entertain their guests. As the officers prepared to return to the Costa Rica Hotel, the kindly consul pressed on them a bottle of oil of anise to drive the fleas from their bedding.[52]

The following morning, Thatcher and Scott visited a San José distillery, enjoyed an anise cordial, and then strolled back to the hotel. Informed that Joaquin Mora had returned to the city, Consul Hine and Commander Thatcher met with the general. Thatcher later summed up Mora's remarks for Commodore Mervine: "No American citizen has at any time been forcibly detained on the San Juan River or Lake steamers. All the engineers, officers and hands employed or occupied on said steamers at any time were paid by the government of Costa Rica, and no men were forced to remain." Thatcher's mission had been modestly successful. As he and Scott rode their mules down to the ship, the commander noted that the "country around San José is the most picturesque I have ever beheld," and he wrote admiringly of it once back in his cabin on the *Decatur*.[53]

FIG. 46 *San José, the capital of Costa Rica, was a modern, thriving city when* Decatur *captain Henry Knox Thatcher and agent William Carey Jones visited in the tense summer of 1857.* Harper's Monthly, *January 1860. Courtesy University of Washington Libraries, Special Collections,* UW27971z.

Off Punta Arenas on July 16, waiting for Jones, Thatcher received a note from filibuster surgeon R. J. Royston indicating that he had just arrived from Rivas with two dozen men from Walker's army who had been unable to walk out with McCorkle's group. Royston told Thatcher that he had left "no Americans in Nicaragua except those who chose to remain." The invalids were "wretched and helpless," wrote Royston to Thatcher, begging him to find a way to send them to the States. "A speedy removal to a more bracing climate," the surgeon continued, "together with the comforts of home and friends can save the lives of a large portion of them." Thatcher visited Royston and the filibusters onshore and wrote to Mervine that "more complete destitution and misery, I have never witnessed or conceived."[54]

Captain Thatcher's orders were clear. He had brought Jones to Punta Arenas, and the diplomat was believed to be gainfully occupied at San José. He had traveled to San José to discuss complaints made by American citizens against Costa Rica and had received a satisfactory reply. Thatcher had been ordered to "render assistance to American citizens who have been connected with the expedition under General Walker in Nicaragua" who might present themselves for protection—they were to be rescued and brought to Panama. Thatcher decided to bring Royston's patients on board the *Decatur*, where Surgeons Ward and Lane would join Walker's medical men in caring for them.

On the following day, July 17, Thatcher jotted a brief note to Colonel Canas, repeating the substance of Royston's petition and mentioning that one of the filibusters had died during the night. Thatcher informed Canas that he intended to take the survivors to Panama and the general readily agreed. Over the next ten days, the ship was prepared to house and care for the invalids. On July 27, twenty-five survivors of Walker's army were brought on board. According to the logbook, the filibusters included Surgeons R. J. Royston and G. B. Bouton, Major Dolan, Captains West and Rayburn, and twenty privates, including men from Ireland, Poland, Sweden, and Germany, as well as deluded Young Americans.[55]

The *Decatur*'s logs do not include descriptions of the injuries of the former filibusters, but the *New York Times* published the names and homes of the survivors, as well as the nature of their wounds and illnesses. Fourteen of them suffered from disabling wounds, at least one was an amputee, three had severe infections, and four suffered from chronic disease, or "debility"—likely dysentery or malaria. Assistant Surgeon Lane's *Herald* articles and a later account published in the *Journal of the American Medical Association* detailed his experience with Royston's filibusters. After their surrender, these young men had been given a *rial* (twelve and a half cents) each day by the Costa Rican government; all they could afford to eat was bread, bananas, and plantains. They were starving, Lane wrote, pale and cadaverous. Some had walked barefoot from Rivas to Punta Arenas, and their feet were lacerated and infected. Many were syphilitic, he added, but all had malaria. Lane observed that, in his experience, every American or European immigrant to Central America eventually contracted malarial fever and became "emaciated, bloodless and spiritless." Confined to hammocks on board the *Decatur*, the filibusters—these "poor wretches"—suffered from infected wounds that created "offensive stenches on board." These large ulcers, wrote Lane, resulted not only from bullet and knife wounds but from a tiny thorn prick or insect bite that became the center of a large and spreading growth.[56]

In the *Herald*, Lane reported that there were about sixty men in this condition at Punta Arenas, and the ship could not accommodate them all. "A considerable company took a large boat" and rowed alongside the *Decatur*, begging to be taken aboard. When Thatcher refused them, the filibusters called down curses on his head that shocked "ears obtuse to marine blasphemy." Thirty or forty were left behind and they likely soon died, thought Lane. Thatcher put to sea for Panama and anchored in the bay on August 5. Commodore Mervine described these men as "the only remaining sick in the hospital at Rivas and the last from Punta Arenas (Costa Rica), formerly belonging to the Army of General Walker," omitting the dozens left stranded at Punta Arenas. The *Decatur*'s surgeons were overwhelmed by caring for these men, and "this small vessel" was overcrowded with the sick men, whose "groans and cries" could be heard throughout the ship. The commodore took twelve invalids on board the flagship.[57]

Mervine was winding up his command of the squadron and would soon head home around the Horn on the sloop of war *John Adams*; he hoped to take as many filibusters as possible with him. The Panamanian government had forbidden the landing of any former filibusters unless they were bound across the isthmus and ticketed for a steamer on the other side. Mervine convened a medical board to examine the invalids, and medical officers from the *John Adams* joined *Decatur* surgeons Ward and Lane, identifying only one man who would be "able to endure the passage around the Cape." In fact, only five of the filibusters were judged fit even to travel by steamer to San Francisco. The others were simply too ill to be moved and remained on board the *Decatur* after Mervine sailed south. The surgeons noted in their report that "some of their diseases are extremely . . . prejudicial to the health of the crew."[58]

Writing to Toucey, Mervine called the men left behind on the *Decatur* at Panama "inveterate invalids." Thatcher appealed to Secretary Toucey as well: Private Call had lost a leg in action; Private Madison the use of his arm; these men could not, Thatcher pointed out, ever earn their own living in Central America. What was to be done with them? For the time being, at least six invalid filibusters remained on board the *Decatur*, confined to their hammocks in the berth deck, cared for by the ship's surgeons, and eating by the wardroom's generosity. Back in Washington, Toucey's clerk jotted on Thatcher's note that the department was "at a loss" to find the funds to pay for the filibusters' maintenance or their transportation and that Thatcher must exercise his best judgment. In October 1857, the *New York Times* reported that the officers and enlisted men of the *Decatur* had passed the hat to buy passage to New York for some of the "twenty or thirty filibusters" on board, certainly an exaggerated number. Although some filibusters left the *Decatur* at that time, a few invalids who were too sick to travel stayed on board, and thus the *Decatur* remained a hospital ship until the departure of the last filibuster, John

Frizzell, in June 1858, nearly a year later. As Mervine prepared his final dispatches, the Pacific Squadron commodore singled out Commanders Charles Davis of the *St. Mary's* and Henry Thatcher of the *Decatur* for rare "unqualified approbation," commending their "great professional ability and discretion."[59]

Meanwhile, William Carey Jones was fuming in San José. He had been robbed of $700 in gold by Tom Edwards, identified by the *New York Times* Costa Rican correspondent as a "notorious sharper." Surgeon Lane wrote for the *Herald* that the thief was a man of "uncertain morals," "known here by the name of Tom Edwards," who had fled California to escape the rough justice of the Vigilance Committee and joined Walker's filibuster army. Charmed by the filibuster veteran, Jones had chosen Edwards as a traveling companion from Punta Arenas to San José and then as a roommate in the city. Jones accused Edwards of stealing the money from his trunk, and Edwards accused Jones of libel. "Tom Edwards" was a likable Pacific West rogue who freely admitted to cheating at cards but claimed to be above robbing a man of cash money. However, Edwards had easy access to Jones's trunk containing Secretary of State Cass's instructions and was now "blabbing them all over the country." Jones mentioned nothing of this to Cass, referring vaguely to "an illness which overtook [him] on the road"; however, Jones's misfortunes were publicized in Central American and then stateside newspapers.[60]

The Edwards incident was a most unfortunate beginning to Jones's diplomatic mission—his cover had been utterly blown in San José. Costa Ricans freely discussed Jones's orders from Secretary Cass and pointed at him in the streets, saying, "There he is; there is the American agent." Long before Jones's arrival in the city, Costa Rican newspapers had already published the news that "an agent of the government of the United States" was on his way. It had taken the *Decatur* three weeks to sail from Panama to Punta Arenas; the mail steamer left Panama twelve days *after* the *Decatur* sailed and arrived seven days *before* the sloop of war. Jones complained about the interminable passage, against unfavorable winds. "This fact shows," he wrote, "how necessary it is that steam should be employed in place of sails for the service of our government on this Pacific Coast." Under the circumstances, Jones confessed to Cass that it was no longer possible to "hold here the character of a simple traveler." He decided to visit President Mora and candidly explain his mission in Central America, initiating discussion of the Nicaragua transit. Jones remained confident "that the authorities and people of Costa Rica are . . . exceedingly disposed to cultivate the good will of the United States," but this ham-handed agent of manifest destiny strode without self-control into a world where too many Americans had already ridden roughshod.[61]

San José had none of the picturesque melancholy of Old Panama but was a bustling city of 15,000, founded about eighty years previously. High above sea level, the climate was cool and dry, delightful after the sultry sea-level weather—"delicious," as one reporter put it. In this spreading city of white brick and red tile roofs, the Palace of the Government, where Jones first presented himself, was an impressive structure. Passing through a wide-arched gateway, he entered a spacious hall surrounded by a second-floor gallery, where government officials, including the secretaries of foreign relations and state, had their offices. Beyond this office court was the Hall of Congress, very "American" in its design. Next door was the city barracks, which Jones likely did not see. Inside, the Costa Rican army exhibited a collection of "relics and trophies" from the war in Nicaragua, arranged in an ornate glass case. The label on the case referred to the "happy issue of the Holy War, sustained by the Republics of Central America against their invaders," reflecting Costa Rican pride in repelling the filibuster invasion.[62]

When Jones called at the residence, President Mora was said to be unavailable because he had been "obliged to go to the country [for] his health." That, wrote Jones to Cass, was on July 15. On July 27, the president had still not contacted Jones, though it was widely known that Mora had returned to the city. Jones then wrote to the Costa Rican secretary of foreign relations to request an audience with President Mora, which was immediately granted. Mora finally met with Jones on July 29, and the American diplomat wrote to Cass that he was "received with apparent warmth" in a pleasant but inconclusive meeting. However, the *New York Times* reported a far-different encounter. According to the Nicaraguan correspondent of the newspaper, Jones's instructions for his assignment were "written on one sheet of paper," which he thrust impatiently into Mora's hands at their meeting. Jones reportedly told Mora to read only the paragraph that referred to Costa Rica. But the "President replied that if he read any, he must read the whole" because both he and Jones were concerned with all five states of Central America. Jones then "snatched the paper, telling President Mora that he should read nothing." What had been described as a mission of "a most friendly character" had turned out quite differently. If the *Times* correspondent was at all accurate, it is difficult to understand how any diplomat who was sober and earnest could bungle a conference so badly.[63]

The *New York Times* and the *New York Herald* published numerous reports from Central American correspondents, who were trying to figure out Jones's purpose. Antagonistic to the Buchanan administration, the *Times* enjoyed Jones's blunders to the utmost, though the *Herald* was not far behind. The

Times's knowledgeable "UNO" telegraphed from Washington that Jones had been sent to Panama to board the *Decatur* and then sail on to Nicaragua to recognize Walker's government and negotiate the transit's opening with the filibuster general. If Walker had capitulated, Jones was to negotiate the opening of the Nicaragua transit with the Costa Rican victors. Another correspondent agreed that Jones had been sent to reopen the Nicaragua transit by negotiating with "whatever power might be in the ascendancy," but that he was regarded in San José as a spy, that he cultivated a foolish air of mystery, and that his manners did not "command respect." The affair with Edwards marked him as a naïve tenderfoot, and the incident with Mora was ludicrously inept. Over the months, Jones became a public figure of fun in the *Times* and *Herald* columns, satirized as "Mr. Buchanan's secret agent," thin-skinned, bibulous, and bumbling, a kind of comic ambassador, his Young American mission a caricature of diplomacy.[64]

Jones's initial enthusiasm for Costa Rica as a potential American ally in Central America faded rapidly. The *Times* reported a series of unfortunate incidents which led to Jones's departure from Costa Rica "in high dudgeon" after the "bust-up" with President Mora. Rid of the disreputable Edwards and established in a San José hotel, Jones hired as cook a man he described as a "destitute fellow countryman who had been the baker" for Walker's army. Then Jones struck up an acquaintance with another former filibuster, a naturalized German American citizen named Stroebel who had been one of Walker's topographical engineers. Stroebel and his American-born wife had walked out from Rivas to San Juan del Sur, where they boarded a ship chartered by the Costa Rican government. Landed at Punta Arenas, they decided not to head to Panama but rather to try their luck in San José. Jones became friendly with the couple and hired the engineer to make some sketches of the city to accompany his reports to Cass.[65]

Jones had not written to Cass about Edwards but he did voluminously report his side of *l'affaire* Stroebel. According to Jones, on August 18, 1857, while Stroebel sat in San José's central plaza, sketching "the Cathedral and the mountains," he was roughed up by some militia and then imprisoned. Stroebel was charged with "speaking in favor of William Walker, late president of Nicaragua, and against the government of Costa Rica, and of having been an officer in the army of General Walker." Jones immediately went to the presidential residence and filed a protest, claiming that Stroebel was a member of his diplomatic "suite" and should be released into his custody. Mora was said to be unable to read the note, which was written in English, because there was no translator present. Jones rewrote the note in Spanish, and the president was said to be unable to read it because he was sick in bed. Snubbed, Jones seethed in the lobby of the residence and eventually returned to his hotel, to fire off a volley of irate notes to Costa Rican officials. According to Jones, Joaquin Calvo, secretary of foreign relations, responded by rudely disparaging his diplomatic credentials as "a simple passport," which Jones was improperly trying to use to free Stroebel. Jones replied to Calvo with thirteen pages of long-winded indignation, to which Calvo returned a dismissive note, affecting surprise that Jones seemed to expect "attentions and immunity" that his credentials did not merit. Calvo requested that the correspondence come to an end. Jones found the secretary's tone so insulting that he wrote to Cass that he could hardly bear to translate it.[66]

According to the *Times*, Stroebel was a dodgy character who "used to get intoxicated, and go reeling and swaggering through the streets of San José . . . proclaiming his earnest desire that Walker might return, take the country, confiscate the property, and chop its inhabitants into inch pieces." Stroebel was "insufferable," wrote the *Times* Costa Rican correspondent, and was legitimately arrested as a disturbance to the peace. Then Jones—the "quasi-ambassador"—arrogantly demanded Stroebel's release, sending his passport as his only authority. The request was politely denied, according to the *Times*, and Jones stormed out of San José. The correspondent concluded that Jones was incompetent, tactless, and ignorant of the language and customs of Costa Rica. Surely, he wrote snidely, Secretary Cass would be wiser to find his diplomats in the Republican Party if Jones was the best he could offer from his own.[67]

As a "special agent," Cass had intended Jones's civilian status to be an asset: he could ask questions freely and travel quickly and quietly. But Jones did not have the diplomatic status to intervene on Stroebel's behalf; by doing so, he invited the Costa Ricans to call his bluff. Certainly, Jones was indiscreet to deal so openly with these former filibusters, who had been banished from Costa Rica by decree on August 9, 1857, in reaction to repeated rumors of a filibuster landing. Consul Hine distanced himself from the Jones's "imbroglio," which made his position awkward in San José. Far from securing an agreement with the Costa Rican government to reopen the Nicaragua transit, Jones had become *persona non grata*.[68]

When Jones returned to the coast, he found that the *Decatur* had sailed for Panama with Royston's patients. In Punta Arenas, Jones encountered more survivors of Walker's army. Everywhere one turned in Central America, there seemed to be more ragged, starving, feverish scarecrows who had deserted Walker, former loyal soldiers who had walked away from Rivas or men, women, and children who had been left behind for a variety of reasons. The Punta Arenas survivors were, Jones wrote, "sick, many; wounded, some; nearly naked, without shelter day or night. They wound the sight wherever one turned in Punta Arenas. They are under banishment . . . without any possible means of getting away [and] they are mostly Americans by birth." Two dozen Americans at Punta Arenas gave Jones a petition to be presented to President Buchanan, begging to go home. These filibusters had been unable "by fevers and other complaints" to go on the long march and had been left behind by the *Decatur*. Referring to President Mora's December 1856 amnesty proclamation, they charged that "the government has fell short of their promises" and that they were "in the most unhappy condition that men could be placed in upon the earth." And if they were deserters, they would hardly have been welcomed by the loyal survivors of the Walker army, like the two dozen who had returned to Panama on the *Decatur* with Surgeon Royston. Despised by the Costa Ricans, by the loyal filibusters, and perhaps by the navy and William Carey Jones, the filibuster deserters were in despair. Jones forwarded their petition on to Cass.[69]

Hundreds of former filibusters who had gambled on the Pacific West haunted Central America, desperate for a new start. In San José alone, Consul Hine calculated that there were about three hundred deserters from Walker's army—"these unfortunate and misguided men"—who had responded to the amnesty. Many who were able to leave did so, but of those who remained, many were "pitiful, in the extreme," too sick to travel. A mere trip from Nicaragua or Costa Rica to Panama would not improve their situation much. They were marked men in Panama, where Mervine was convinced they would experience "violence at the hands of the populace who are not kindly disposed towards Americans."[70]

Petitioned by desperate Americans and stinging with his San José rebuke, Jones made a formal application to the State Department to be appointed minister to Nicaragua or Costa Rica, with "powers of commissioner" to the other Central American states. One month later, Jones directed the same request to President Buchanan. There appears to have been no response to either application. Instead, Cass instructed the special agent to take a firm stand against Costa Rica's apparent "war of conquest" because the United States would not tolerate the Nicaragua transit's continued closure. Cass was worried that Costa Rica would repudiate the "transit grants" made to American investors and urged Jones to remind the Costa Ricans that their president had declared in March 1856, "Ours is not a fight for a piece of land, not to secure ephemeral powers, not to achieve wretched conquest" but rather to drive out "the freebooters now attempting to usurp the territory, and the independence and liberties" of Nicaragua. That goal had been accomplished, Cass wrote, and now it was time for Costa Rica to withdraw.[71]

In the fall, Jones resumed his tour by the mail steamer, north to San Juan del Sur in Nicaragua. An American resident of that town lamented that, since the departure of the transit passengers, the filibusters, the deserters, the warships, and the Costa Rican troops, the little Pacific West boomtown had fallen on hard times. The "few white people here," wrote the *Herald* correspondent, "having nothing else to do, have taken to quarrelling with each other." On Jones's arrival, a number of American residents presented him with a petition demanding the removal of beleaguered consul John Priest, who was accused of favoring the locals over Americans. Priest retorted that his enemies were all Walker partisans. Jones passed along the file of pros and cons to Cass, dispiritedly remarking that the only real government in Nicaragua was that maintained by the Costa Ricans. General Tomas Martinez of the Legitimist Party and General Maxime Jerez of the Democratic Party had just been elected copresidents of Nicaragua, but the transit remained closed by the Costa Rican army to prevent access to Nicaragua by the "highway of filibusterism." Jones wrote to Cass that he had urged President Martinez to trust American good intentions to prevent any filibuster and that he was met with "insolence and . . . disbelief in the good faith of the United States." Rumored sightings of William Walker or his senior officers were almost daily occurrences on both coasts of Nicaragua.[72]

Walker toured the American South to the strains of "Yankee Doodle Dandy," speaking to enormous crowds to raise recruits and money for his second expedition to Nicaragua. He claimed that he had been forced from Nicaragua by Northern abolitionists because of his reinstatement of slavery, and Southerners flocked to his banner, eager to build a Central American refuge. John Richmond, Walker's "sub secretary of state," wrote to a Kentucky sympathizer to encourage "gentlemen from southern states, wishing to emigrate to this country [Nicaragua] with their slaves." The *New Orleans Delta* reassured slaveholders that they could soon safely head for Nicaragua "to cultivate sugar, coffee, rice, indigo or chocolate plantations." All that remained to be done, the *Delta* concluded, was to regain and parcel out Nicaragua and then restore the African slave trade to the Atlantic coast. Whether Walker was a genuine advocate of slavery expansion or a glib opportunist, he convinced American slaveholders to embrace the second filibuster. Young America's hope that manifest destiny would somehow heal sectionalism failed as western expansionism became an aggressive Southern crusade in Central America.

As David Potter remarked, by late 1857, antebellum American nationalists were no longer expansionists, and expansionists were no longer nationalists.[73]

In the second Nicaragua filibuster, the steamer *Fashion* outfitted at New Orleans and left on November 14, 1857, with about two hundred Southerners drawn by the filibuster's frank mission of slavery expansion. Once a beachhead was established, "many thousands of young southerners" planned to follow Walker to Nicaragua. No act was ever more anticipated than the *Fashion*'s departure and yet the steamer easily eluded federal pursuit. One of the best-known public figures of the day, Walker had himself jumped federal bail to board. The steamer ran down the coast past Greytown to disembark a company of men to advance overland into Nicaragua, and then the *Fashion* itself headed into Greytown harbor. The steamer landed one hundred and fifty filibusters on shore right under the nose of the warship *Saratoga,* commanded by Frederick Chatard, who made no effort to prevent the landing of this illegal expedition.[74]

The filibusters hastily made camp on Nicaraguan soil. Then Commodore Hiram Paulding turned the *Wabash* broadside against the encampment and ordered three hundred marines and sailors rowed to shore to arrest Walker and his men. Outflanked and outgunned, the filibuster army surrendered, and so ended Walker's second filibuster to Nicaragua. Central Americans were relieved that Paulding had intercepted the invaders but irate that he had landed an armed force on the Greytown beach to do so. In fact, they were indignant that the filibuster had taken place at all. If the U.S. government sincerely wished to put an end to these illegal expeditions, they argued, surely it would be prudent to arrest, try, and imprison their mastermind! The second filibuster generated considerable controversy concerning the navy's response, affecting the ships in the Pacific Squadron, including the *Decatur.*

Paulding defended his apprehension of Walker and his men on the Greytown beach to Secretary Toucey, writing that he regarded the filibusters as "outlaws who had escaped from the vigilance of the government." But to his wife, Paulding privately admitted he had taken "strong measures" to force Walker from "neutral territory" in Nicaragua; his actions might make him president, he wrote, or they might cost him his commission. Once Walker was back in the states, Cass reportedly told the filibuster in a face-to-face meeting that he was free to go about his business and that he disavowed Paulding's actions as "illegal, inexcusable and unauthorized." After the meeting with Cass, Walker was said to have gone "on his way rejoicing." Buchanan sent a message to Congress that condemned filibustering in strong terms but charged Paulding with a grave error in landing an armed force on Nicaraguan soil. Secretary Toucey suspended both Chatard and Paulding from command: Chatard was disciplined for permitting Walker to land on Nicaraguan soil and Paulding was disciplined for arresting him there. Public opinion about the navy's actions and inactions divided along sectional lines.[75]

Isaac Toucey, Buchanan's secretary of the navy, was a Buchanan protégé—a political appointee with little experience in naval matters and a Northern man with Southern sympathies. It is uncertain to what degree Toucey favored the Americanization of Nicaragua in 1857, but historians have criticized his "vague suggestions for preventing the landing of invaders on any of the coasts [the Navy] patrolled" and characterized his orders to squadron commodores and commanders as "ambiguous, perhaps deliberately so." Toucey's orders regarding Walker seem particularly confused and confusing and placed complete responsibility for their interpretation on the shoulders of naval commanders. Officers were to use "all lawful means" by sea to prevent filibusters from landing, but they were not to land on sovereign soil, interfere with legitimate vessels at sea, or act on "mere suspicion."[76]

In October 1857, navy commander John Almy requested that Toucey clarify these instructions, but the secretary's reply simply emphasized their uncertainties:

> You will not seize an American vessel, or bring her into port or use the force under your command to prevent her landing her passengers upon mere suspicion. . . . But where you find that an American vessel is manifestly engaged in carrying on an expedition . . . against the territories of Mexico, Nicaragua, or Costa Rica . . . you will use the force under your command to prevent it and will not permit the men or arms engaged in it or destined for it to be landed in any port.

Barred from suspicion or interference, it is difficult to see how an officer could determine whether a ship was "manifestly engaged in carrying on an expedition." Commenting on Toucey's note, one historian joked that naval commanders could prevent the landing of filibusters "only by chance." Robert May has argued convincingly that many federal authorities mounted "a determined effort to get filibusters behind bars" that was compromised by the lack of "vigor with which military and civil officers implemented presidential policy." It is undoubtedly true that some navy officers sympathized with Walker's filibuster and admired the filibusters as martial men; they were responsible for the "half-hearted enforcement of neutrality laws." However, Secretary Toucey did not provide clear, unequivocal direction, and his evasions seem deliberate. In San José, Commander Thatcher accepted at face value Mora's glib assurances that the Costa Rican army had in no way interfered with American citizens, let alone pressed them into service. But a commander might be pardoned for going through the motions of his duty when the secretary concealed his convictions behind mealy-mouthed double-talk. In its ambiguous response to Walker, the leadership of the antebellum navy expressed the nation's growing inability to pursue a foreign policy in Central America that was free from sectional influence.[77]

For his part, Walker styled himself as an outraged citizen of Nicaragua seeking innocently to return home with a group of pioneer settlers, and his supporters claimed that he was "as legitimately President of Nicaragua as Buchanan of the United States." In an open letter to President Buchanan, published in the *New York Times*, Walker complained that the navy's interference had twice forced his removal from his own country, first at the hands of Commander Davis and then at the hands of Commodore Paulding. Walker's arrest at Greytown also posed further challenges to William Carey Jones's discretion. Nicaraguan president Tomas Martinez and Jones were in conference on board the steamer *San Carlos* on Lake Nicaragua when the urgent message arrived reporting Walker's landing in the *Fashion* and Paulding's capture of the filibuster army. Both Jones and Martinez learned of these events simultaneously. The Nicaraguan president questioned Jones "pretty closely" as to whether Paulding had really "captured" Walker's force and why the U.S. government believed it had the "right" to seize prisoners on the shores of a foreign state. Annoyed, Jones retorted that if President Martinez wished to appeal the filibuster arrests, doubtless the U.S. Navy could return the prisoners to the "place from which they had been taken," armed and ready to go, and that he would be happy to be Martinez's messenger in the matter. Jones's thinly disguised advocacy for either Walker's filibuster or American annexation of Nicaragua alienated the presidents of both Costa Rica and Nicaragua; the *New York Times* reported that Jones had "succeeded in getting upon nearly as bad terms with President Martinez as he did with Mora in Costa Rica."[78]

Jones had reached the end of his rope by January 1858. "First," the *New York Herald* commented derisively, "he lost his baggage, now it seems he has lost himself." He had suffered constant misadventures: it had become public knowledge in the States that the ingratiating thief Tom Edwards had bestowed Jones's stolen wedding ring on a prospective bride at San Juan del Sur. Jones had been embarrassed by the *Decatur*'s painfully slow progress up the coast; his cover was blown, he was robbed, he "quarreled with everybody," he was reported to be "seldom sober," his travel plans were frustrated by "sinister controlling influences," he fell ill, and he was insulted, almost mocked. He was undone by simple deception. He was deeply offended by theatrical displays of insolence, and he could not keep his temper. He was convinced that his correspondence was being opened and read. He was irritated with Cass and with his assignment: he had "all the duties and more than the responsibilities of a diplomatic minister, without his power, privileges or position." His bids to be appointed ambassador had met with stony silence. Once Jones left the *Decatur* behind, there was no navy ship to support him, let alone the attentive war steamers he had hoped for. He was disappointed by the pending Cass-Yrissari Treaty to reopen the transit, and he hoped it would not be ratified by the U.S. Senate; he thought it was high time that Costa Rica and Nicaragua were punished for their "outrages on our citizens."[79]

The most foolish element of Jones's bumbling diplomacy was his continued relationship with filibuster veterans, which contributed to Central American suspicions that he and his superiors in Washington, DC, supported Walker's plans. On the heels of taking up with Edwards and hiring two former filibusters in San José, Jones hired a third in Nicaragua—a Mr. Fields—to serve as his private secretary, "who told me very frankly that he had been in the army of Walker . . . the fact of [which] was not a crime and to have continued until the capitulation rather a virtue." President Martinez specifically mentioned Fields during the Lake Nicaragua conference, remarking that he considered him a potential collaborator with any future filibuster. It is possible that Jones agreed. In one of his final letters to Cass, Jones suggested that five hundred armed men could easily seize the Nicaragua transit if the force could "escape the vigilance of the authorities of the United States." If, as Jones was convinced, his mail was being intercepted, this inflammatory suggestion was deliberately written to be read by Martinez, Mora, and their staffs.[80]

William Carey Jones had done nothing to calm Central American fears that every American representative was a proponent of filibuster, annexation, or colonization. A *Times* correspondent wrote, "It is lamentable that at such an important period [Jones] should have been sent here by our government; for he has, by his exceedingly eccentric conduct, greatly depreciated the good opinion entertained of Americans." According to the *Herald*, Jones loudly remarked while drunk in the Rivas public square that he was all for American interference in Central America, that he advocated "no milk and honey policy," and, if Walker's filibusters could not hold Nicaragua, that he would see to it that "Brother Jonathan" (a personification of the United States) did. "Damn all diplomatic missions!" Jones was reported to have continued, "Nicaragua for ever! Boys, let's have a drink!" The *Herald* correspondent looked forward to the arrival of former Texas governor Mirabeau Lamar, newly appointed U.S. minister to Nicaragua.[81]

Stateside journalists casually reported that Cass was "puzzled to know how to get [Jones] home." The secretary flattered Jones by saying that he wanted the agent to brief President Buchanan in person, but it is likely that Cass simply wanted to get him out of Central America before more harm was done. The secretary dashed Jones's career hopes by informing him that Lamar had been named "Envoy Extraordinary and Minister Plenipotentiary" to Costa Rica and Nicaragua, and, to make matters worse, Jones read about the appointment in the newspaper before Cass's dispatch reached him. Stung, Jones reminded Cass how difficult his mission had been and recommended that the newcomer be "a man of courage," backed by a navy war steamer on each coast.[82]

In the States, Walker organized the third Nicaraguan filibuster and worked on the manuscript of *The War in Nicaragua* to "recapture his own myth, to vindicate his own heroism," as Richard Slotkin put it. He had been driven against his will from Nicaragua, Walker wrote, and compelled to return by "honor and duty." He wrote of the gallantry of his men, who won eternal glory on the battlefield, "like the knights of feudal times." Framing the filibuster as a noble quest on the South's behalf, Walker paid tribute to the martyrs who left their homes "in defense of slavery [and] yielded up their lives for the interests of the South." In their memory, he vowed "never to abandon the cause of Nicaragua." As Walker raised money and recruits, Southerners continued to "regard General Walker as the great agent for the Americanization of that region and the reinstitution of slavery," and Southern newspapers trumpeted, "We are Walker, Nicaragua, Pro-Slavery Men," above the fold. In May 1858, representatives of Virginia, South Carolina, Alabama, Georgia, Mississippi, Louisiana, Tennessee, Texas, and Florida met in the Southern Commercial Convention, at Montgomery, Alabama. The delegates "repudiated" the "grievous wrongs" of navy commanders Davis and Paulding. Though they voted at the last moment to strike the threat that any further similar federal act would "certainly dissolve the Union itself," the convention passed the following resolution: "Resolved, That we regard the establishment of the Americans in Nicaragua as a work of duty, no less than of honor and interest, on the part of the Southern people; and that this enterprise, tending as it does to the increase of Southern commerce and Southern power, is of paramount importance to all other questions now before the American people."[83]

As Southern extremists embraced Walker's obsession, resistance to anticipated filibusters and resentment of seeming federal complicity solidified pan–Central American nationalism. Walker's easy access to the president and the secretary of state, the apparent support of navy secretaries James Dobbin and Isaac Toucey, and the belligerent diplomacy of John Wheeler and William Carey Jones crippled American interests in Nicaragua. Consul Hine reported to Cass that Costa Rica's president Mora was furious that William Walker was being publicly fêted in the United States, openly planning a third invasion. While U.S. policy condemned the filibuster's "illegal expeditions," U.S. practice furthered his successes and softened his defeats. Horace Greeley editorialized that the government had alienated Central Americans by its "open sympathy with and aid to William Walker's butcheries in Nicaragua," and *Decatur* surgeon Levi Cooper Lane—who was there in person—maintained that Walker's "freebooting expedition . . . had the sanction of President Buchanan's administration, and the aid of the Navy, as far as it was possible to go without arousing international suspicions." The *Decatur*, the *St. Mary's*, and the *Merrimac*, Lane continued, "quietly acted their respective parts" in supplying this aid. A contemporary naval officer, Seth Ledyard Phelps, agreed that Walker would have been long dead if "left to his fate," but instead of "stringing them up as pirates are usually treated," the navy transported these "dainty pirates" to safety with "all possible care." Robert May concluded that the U.S. Navy "was riddled with officers who at best felt ambivalent about implementing their orders to repress the filibusters" and that the navy helped to rescue "hundreds of filibusters from life-threatening situations." As a result, in 1858, the Nicaragua transit—the filibuster highway and the great isthmian strategic link—remained closed because Central Americans mistrusted naval and diplomatic representatives of the United States.[84]

Martinez and Mora jointly signed a May 1, 1858, proclamation condemning all the "official agents of the United States at Nicaragua [to date]" as "accomplices and auxiliaries of the invaders . . . openly menac[ing] Central America with inevitable annexation," clearly referring to Borland, Wheeler, and Jones and perhaps to U.S. naval officers. Jones waited to leave Nicaragua until Lamar arrived and then handed the ambassador a copy of the Monroe Doctrine and a "long string of complaints" against the Costa Rican and Nicaraguan governments. Trying to redeem the situation from Walker's violence and Jones's bluster, Lamar held his post for nearly two years. The *New York Times* considered the ambassador "an amiable old gentleman of insinuating manners," likely to win the Costa Ricans' affection. Lamar deplored "every scheme of filibusterism," but after another rumored American landing at Greytown, he was treated with "coldness and neglect" in Nicaragua. Flirting with French development of the Nicaragua transit, President Martinez prevented the ratification of the Cass-Yrissari Treaty and then proposed a second treaty unacceptable to the United States. Discouraged and ill, Lamar returned home in October 1859 and died within two months.[85]

In American westering slang, adventurers had "seen the elephant" when they had seen all there was to see of something strange and wonderful—and when they had had enough hardship and were beat and ready to go home. Everyone saw the elephant in Nicaragua, the most deadly and compelling attraction at the circus. Men who saw the Nicaraguan elephant reported wryly that "he looms up of magnificent proportions, [and] that whoever has walked all around him, and seen all his points, has of necessity an enlarged experience." William Carey Jones saw the elephant and his failure was complete. The *Decatur* became a hospital ship, filled with men who had come too close to the elephant. And John Drinkhouse, who represents so many Naval deserters, saw the elephant, too. A sailor of manifest destiny views, Drinkhouse was likely convinced of the logical progression from fighting Mexicans to fighting Indians to fighting Nicaraguans. He had signed on to Young America's dream in the Pacific West: to pursue his country's advantage and to make a killing for himself. In the end, he was sick and scared; once a western opportunist, he had become a defeated sailor in the Southern cause. Drinkhouse died at home in Pennsylvania, victim of the "fatal disease" he had contracted in Nicaragua. William Walker chased the elephant, too; he returned again and again to the circus until his execution by a Honduran firing squad in 1860. American slavery expansionists saw the elephant in Nicaragua and so did antislavery American nationalists. For one faction, it was the golden future; for the other, it was the betrayal of Young America's hope: that aggressive expansion could somehow heal the United States.[86]

8

Episode 4. Panama

"All the Subtle Demonisms of Life and Thought"

We are all most earnest in our wishes to leave this inhospitable climate [at Panama] at as early a date as possible, since if a prolonged residence in these latitudes does not prove at once fatal, it is certain to lay the foundation of numerous organic derangements of the system in most persons, which require a long period to eradicate.—ASSISTANT SURGEON LEVI COOPER LANE, *New York Herald,* February 17, 1858

As we near the vortex of ruin, events will hasten.—*Manifesto,* League of United Southerners, 1858

The new commodore of the Pacific Squadron, John C. Long, anchored off Panama in his flagship, the *Merrimac,* a 275-foot screw-propeller steam frigate.[1] The *Merrimac* was almost brand new, one of six war steamers proposed by Secretary Dobbin, and signaled a major addition to the resources available to the squadron: the old flagship, the *Independence,* had been launched in 1814, the first ship of the line commissioned in the U.S. Navy. After the *Merrimac*'s arrival, the *Independence* sailed to San Francisco to be put out to pasture as a receiving ship. The *Saranac,* a side-wheel steam sloop of war, soon joined the squadron, which also included the sailing sloops of war *St. Mary's, Decatur,* and *Vandalia.* Secretary Toucey enjoined Long to the strictest economy in the use of coal by both his steamers. Long, in turn, dutifully wrote to the *Saranac*'s commander as the steamer prepared to round Cape Horn for the Pacific, recommending as much reliance on the ship's sails as possible, but he made no suggestion of gathering "Patagonia coal" in the Strait of Magellan, as Surgeon Taylor had once dreamed.[2]

Commodore Long planned to send the *Saranac* on a "weary round" of cruising patrol among the ports from Peru to Mexico, looping back to Panama once a month and coaling at Acapulco, Panama, and Callao. Long intended to keep the *Merrimac* centrally located at Panama but had to abandon this plan almost immediately. The flagship steamed out of harbor bound for pressing distant duty and left the *Decatur* anchored in the bay, "held in readiness for any immediate call, should it be necessary either for shore or sea duty." No such call came and the *Decatur* began a long and increasingly troubled stay off Panama as a floating battery and hospital ship, in the "notorious idleness" of a man-of-war in port. The effects of equatorial weather were well known among navy surgeons: men became "much enervated from several months continuous residence in this warm climate," breathing the "poisonous exhalations arising from the [damp] soil." In December 1857, Surgeon Lane's *New York Herald* columns first referred to the "debilitating influence of this prostrating climate" on the health of the *Decatur*'s crew, noting that the ship's sick list had doubled since he joined the ship in the spring.[3]

The *Decatur*'s surgeons were trained and equipped to treat shipboard injuries and the wounds of battle—broken bones, sword thrusts, bullet wounds, and bodies mangled by splintered wood from cannon fire. Their goal was to get sailors and marines back to work and back in the fight, but no man on the *Decatur* was wounded in battle in the course of the ship's five-year cruise in the Pacific Squadron. Instead, at Panama, the surgeons treated infections and contagious diseases on the crowded ship. The head at the ship's bow served as the *Decatur*'s open-air toilet; in harbor, only the tide washed away the pall of fetid water around the ship. Though the *Decatur* was kept spotless to the naked eye, its warm, moist belowdecks offered an excellent environment for pests of all sorts to multiply. The men of the *Decatur* waged constant warfare against rats, fleas, mosquitoes, and cockroaches, as well as body lice, one of the complaints against the filibuster invalids. Enlisted men scrubbed their hammocks and laundered their clothes once a week in warm climates like Panama, but it is doubtful whether their hammocks, blankets, underwear, shirts, socks, and pants ever were truly clean or dry. Certainly, the berth deck was never dry: it was sluiced and mopped nearly every day and poorly ventilated, the damp air fouled by dirty water in the bilge and by unwashed men "living almost like kenneled dogs," their hammocks slung elbow to elbow. The men easily passed their contagions around the ship by sneezing and coughing, sharing tools, and touching the same surfaces. Although many Decaturs suffered from the

FIG. 47 The Decatur *was a sloop of war and did not have a gun deck, like the one shown here in J. G. Heck's engraving, from the 1851 Pictorial Archive. However, this image of men asleep elbow to elbow in their hammocks illustrates the close quarters experienced by the Decaturs and suggests how easily communicable illness could spread in the ship. Courtesy University of Washington Libraries.*

pretubercular condition phthisis, the most common shipboard epidemics at Panama were fever, diarrhea, and bronchitis.[4]

Surgeon Lane reported in the *Herald* the rising incidence of fever and how much he wished the *Decatur* could "leave this inhospitable climate at as early a date as possible." Navy medical officers agreed that Panama duty put men's health at risk. In 1857, Pacific Squadron fleet surgeon William Ruschenberger reported to the chief of the Navy Bureau of Medicine and Surgery that the *Independence* had suffered more than fifty cases of dysentery in four months, including one fatality. In the harbor off Panama, the immune systems of European and American sailors were unable to withstand opportunistic bacteria, a reversal of the usual biological assault in the Pacific. Tropical illnesses afflicted nearly two-thirds of the *Decatur*'s crew at Panama, although the record underreports the actual incidence of infection. To be entered in the Medical Log, a man had to present himself to the surgeons and complain of his symptoms; for a variety of reasons, men often kept their illnesses to themselves. Additionally, the first notation of an illness often indicated that the patient had been complaining of it "for some time" before it was severe enough to take official notice. Finally, the medical register did not log the illnesses of either the commanding officer or the surgeons. Nevertheless, the number of men on the *Decatur*'s sick list continued to climb, and sick men suffered in the constant sultry heat, alcohol and shore leave their only relief.[5]

On liberty at Panama, men drank in local taverns, gambled at faro, bet on cockfights, and visited brothels. Those sailors already afflicted with venereal disease infected their sexual partners, who in turn passed infection along to others. Averaged over the cruise, nearly 30 percent of the *Decatur*'s enlisted men reported a venereal infection to the surgeon. That is, the symptoms were so severe that the sufferers voluntarily went to the surgeons. But many men concealed their syphilis, hoping against hope, but there were no antibiotics and there was no cure. Once their syphilis reached a debilitating point, men were dismissed from the navy, losing their livelihood. Consequently, at least two sailors, George Neal and James Devlin, kept their illness to themselves and were completely untreated until their secondary syphilis was systemic, including virulent skin abscesses, eye infections, and ulcerated tonsils. When Bernard Dougherty finally went to the surgeon, he was immediately admitted to sick bay—afflicted with orchitis, one of his testicles was swollen to five times its normal size. At a less dramatic stage of the disease, the surgeon's primary treatment was to cauterize the venereal chancre with a caustic agent. For instance, when Robert Hicks presented the chancres of syphilis, the surgeon cauterized the sores with silver nitrate. It was believed that venereal tumors—termed "bubos" in the ship's records—needed to "brought out" so that they discharged. Ebenezer Cumberland complained of painful buboes in his groin, and the surgeon applied an irritant poultice to "bring them out." However, such symptomatic treatment was ineffective against the disease, and most men diagnosed with venereal infection eventually became too sick to work and fight. The *Decatur*'s records sometimes document the entire course of disease. In 1854, a ship's boy contracted gonorrhea on liberty, in 1856, he was diagnosed with syphilis, and in 1858, he was sent home from Panama, insane with syphilitic paresis. Many of the men suffering from secondary syphilis, which would likely take their minds, their livelihoods, and their lives, were under thirty. In one of many examples, William Gray was only twenty-one when he was condemned as unfit and dismissed from the service because of his venereal infection.[6]

Dozens of sick men were "surveyed and condemned," as the phrase went, sent away from the ship because they were judged too ill to serve. Sending the sick to shore not only was intended to rid the ship of invalids but was sometimes a compassionate act to send men home or to a naval hospital. At Panama, Seaman W. H. Wright was surveyed and condemned; he suffered from chronic diarrhea and had not responded to treatment. Surgeon Ward wrote that "there [was] little hope of recovery as long as [Wright] remains in this debilitating climate." Because medical science did not understand infection as such, naval surgeons treated symptoms or prescribed environmental change: Ward and Lane were convinced that sending Seaman Wright to a cooler climate would give him a better chance at recovery. Likewise, an old sailor who had joined the ship in San Francisco was surveyed at Panama by a group of surgeons and condemned according to the naval practice of the time. Arkansan George Raymond was the wardroom cook and very likely an African American man; Raymond was then seventy-five years old and the oldest man to serve on the *Decatur*. Captain Thatcher had requested the survey after the *Decatur* surgeons diagnosed the poor old man with epilepsy or with an illness that was perceived as epilepsy. The Medical Log noted that he developed seizures because of his long "exposure to intense heat, as a cook." Based on Raymond's statements and the opinions of the *Decatur*'s medical officers, the board concluded that the condition had "originated in the line of duty," entitling Raymond to a highly unusual medical pension, the only one awarded in the five-year cruise of the ship, and a ticket home to a healthful climate.[7]

The surgeons devoted compassion and professional skill to the treatment of illness; however, they had little patience with men who were injured or fell ill through dissipation, violence, or stubbornness. Charles Mason, a Prussian seaman, passed out drunk on shore and lay immobile for hours; the surgeons were unsympathetic to the temporary paralysis of his hand and arm and simply prescribed a strong purgative. Half a dozen Decaturs over a five-year period suffered such severe delirium tremens that they were admitted to sick bay while they withdrew from alcohol, and the surgeons' disapproval is clear in the record. When James Dougherty came back from liberty in Panama with a sprained wrist, and Robert Foreman, John Hays, Charles Kelly, and dozens more got badly mauled in sailor towns from Victoria to Valparaiso, they were patched up, but censorious little notes were jotted in the Medical Log: "Not duty—received while ashore fighting." William Fredericks returned from liberty sick with Panama fever, but the surgeons noted in the log that he became ill because he had fallen asleep on the beach in the open air and morning dew, after a debauch. Similarly, Timothy Harper could not bear the heat of the berth deck one night in August 1858 and climbed up to sleep on the open deck, which was against ship rules. Notes in the Medical Log and Journal make it clear that the surgeons were convinced that it was unhealthy to sleep outside in the morning dew, and from their perspective, Harper deserved the Panama fever he got. So did James Lanther deserve his injury when he cut his foot badly while running away from the marines down a Panama side street, attempting to desert.

Throughout the fall of 1857 and into 1858, the *Decatur* continued to play its part in the rescue of William Walker's filibuster army. On October 25, five

American filibusters—John McCall, John Frizzell, Columbus Cason, George Ide, and Charles Madison—were returned to the *Decatur* by the *John Adams,* which was about to sail for Norfolk. These men either were too ill to endure the trip around Cape Horn or wished to remain in the Pacific West, and they joined an unknown number of filibuster invalids on board. In November, the *Decatur* sent two filibuster veterans ashore who had found work in Panama and were permitted to move to town. Then Cason left, fit to work his passage up the coast on the steamer *Golden Age* and try his luck in San Francisco. Surgeon Lane accompanied an unnamed filibuster across the Isthmus of Panama on December 18, 1857. But two or three invalids remained on board, unaccounted for in the Logbook or the Medical Log, ghost men, living on wardroom charity and spreading the stink of misery and failure throughout the *Decatur*'s stifling berth deck.[8]

The *Decatur* was the visible representation of U.S. military power in Panama, and it was essential that the sloop of war look shipshape. So the sailors continued to scrape, repair, and repaint the vessel, and the Logbook recorded almost daily, "Crew variously employed about ship." Thatcher made sure that the *Decatur* was a treat for the eyes, a beautiful little warship fit to play its role in the customary round of diplomatic visits. The American and English consuls both visited, and in December the governor of Panama toured the ship with pomp and ceremony. In February 1858, the *Decatur* marked George Washington's birthday with seventeen guns, answered by the French frigate

FIG. 48 This March 1857 engraving shows the filibuster hospital at Granada. Some of the Decatur *invalids may have been treated here before they began their long retreat to Rivas, to San Juan del Sur, and finally to Punta Arenas, in Costa Rica.* Harper's Weekly. *Courtesy University of Washington Libraries, Special Collections,* UW 27979z.

Perseverante and the English frigate *Havanna*. Before his contretemps with William Walker at Greytown, Commodore Paulding passed by on a civilian steamer and received a salute. New Grenada's anniversary of independence was November 28, and the *Decatur* fired a twenty-one-gun salute in honor of the day. Such salutes and ceremonial visits became the principal occupation of the *Decatur* while it was at anchor in Panama Bay.[9]

One of the few advantages of stationary duty at Panama was quick access to news from the States. Surgeon Lane was a correspondent for the *New York Herald,* and that newspaper as well as a dozen others arrived daily in Panama, just a few days behind the stateside news. Nearly everyone on board the *Decatur* was interested in the naval courts of inquiry that had convened to review appeals to the Plucking Board decisions. There was general agreement that naval reform was essential but the board's hasty, clandestine deliberations were widely condemned in the press and had offended popular opinion. As well, a few celebrated errors in judgment encouraged accusations of bias and sectionalism and tainted all of the board's decisions. Congress bowed to overwhelming political pressure and passed the awkwardly worded Act to Amend an Act Entitled "An Act to Promote the Efficiency of the Navy." Any officer who had been dropped, furloughed, or retired could request a court of inquiry, and if he successfully established that he had "the physical, mental, professional and moral fitness of [an] officer for the naval service," he would be restored to his rank and seniority with full back pay. Three courts ran simultaneously and convened on January 20, 1857, to hear first the cases of those officers who had been dropped from the rolls, next those placed on the reserved list with furlough pay—like Commander Isaac Sears Sterrett and Lieutenant Van Rensselaer Morgan—and finally those placed on leave-of-absence pay.[10]

Secretary James Dobbin had defended the "delicate task" accomplished by these "men of high reputation" on the board, who had struggled between "duty and feeling." And though Dobbin was convinced that "this work of reform reinvigorated the Navy," he recognized that the board was "not infallible" and that, if "the sword of any one of those gallant men has been incautiously taken from him, all right-minded men will say, let his country restore it to him with all the honors and reparation due to injured merit."[11]

Sterrett had been relieved of command, wrote his loyal lieutenant, Thomas Phelps, "in consequence of false charges having been preferred and the defendant adjudged guilty without a hearing." But the Efficiency Board was not a naval court of inquiry or a court-martial—rather, it was a closed-door hearing by a handful of Sterrett's peers in which his honor as an officer and a gentleman was as much at stake as his livelihood. Given the chance to vindicate his reputation, the disgraced commander provided the court with a list of witnesses who had agreed to testify on his behalf—from naval luminaries such as old-timers from the War of 1812 to newcomers of the 1850s. Among the three dozen were Captains Thomas ap Catesby Jones, Isaac Mayo, Josiah Tattnall, Silas Stringham, Franklin Buchanan, and Matthew Calbraith Perry, as well as nearly every officer from the *Decatur:* Surgeon Jeffery, Purser Jones, Lieutenants Morgan, Drake, Hughes, Phelps, Morris, and Dallas. During the deliberations, the *New York Herald* reported that Sterrett had "been furloughed on the charge of dissipation," and William Kane, steward at the Philadelphia Naval Asylum, was called to rebut the charge that Sterrett had drunk too much there; other witnesses testified specifically to his sobriety at sea.[12]

Commodore Perry was called before the court of inquiry "to establish the charge of drunkenness against Commander Sterrett," according to the *New York Herald,* but he testified instead that he had sailed with Sterrett from 1824 to 1848 and "never saw him intoxicated." Perry stoutly maintained that he "never listened to the tattling among the officers, that if every slander was to be believed, no man was safe." Purser Jones testified that in twenty-three months on board the *Decatur,* he had never seen Sterrett under the influence of liquor. The *Herald* concluded that, far from proving Sterrett was dissipated, "the government has failed to prove that he was ever inebriated." In addition, Sterrett placed in evidence the commendation for his actions in Puget Sound, in which Dobbin had particularly approved "the protection afforded by you to the citizens of Washington Territory against the incursions and threatenings of the Indians of that country." Sterrett was "triumphantly vindicated" before this "proper tribunal" and restored to the active list, per Phelps, who dubbed him "one of the most genial and efficient officers of the Navy." In Washington Territory, settlers greeted the news with delight that this "meritorious naval officer has been restored," overturning the decision of the "iniquitous Court of Inquiry." Though Senate action promoted Sterrett to captain, he was not restored to command of the *Decatur* or to any other ship. Instead, he languished on shore, writing letters and awaiting orders.[13]

Lieutenant Van Rensselaer Morgan, the *Decatur*'s 1854 executive officer, had also been plucked and placed on furlough pay because of chronic illness. At the court of inquiry, he, too, was reinstated. In fact, one-third of the officers who were disciplined by the Plucking Board were restored. The board had doubtless made some mistakes: they missed Guert Gansevoort, who had endured the firestorm of the *Somers* affair but whose career was always shadowed by drunkenness. Sterrett had probably been removed unfairly, but Morgan was too ill for sea duty. Most historians of the Efficiency Board have considered its action necessary but a "rough pruning knife," as Charles Paullin put it, which worked too quickly, after too long a delay, and on too large a scale. Alfred Thayer Mahan, near contemporary to its actions, judged that "in very few instances had injustice been done"; a second contemporary, *Decatur* commander Henry Knox Thatcher, praised Du Pont's "severe struggle for the honor and dignity of the service." Thatcher and Mahan disapproved of the 1857 boards of inquiry on principle and were disappointed that the secretary of the navy had been browbeaten into retreat. As plucked officers were restored, those officers promoted as a result of the Plucking Board's actions were not demoted. The "jackass officers," as they were termed, kept their rank though their pay was reduced. On the *Decatur* in the Bay of Panama, Joseph DeHaven and David Harmony were "jackass lieutenants," and the ship's captain, Henry Thatcher, was himself a "jackass commander."[14]

After the excitement of this news wore off, the *Decatur* lay anchored off Panama week after week, rocking slowly in the blood-warm water in the "intolerable" heat of this "unchanging summer." Thomas Labey and William Jarvis suffered sunstroke while scraping the hull. Painting inside the hot, poorly ventilated berth deck, Peter Conlan became violently ill from the fumes. Jeff Dubrow was one of a dozen sailors to be so badly sunburned that he was admitted to sick bay. After the turn of the year, scraping and painting became more desultory, and drills and ceremonial visits infrequent. Lane complained in the *Herald* of the monotony, in which "every reef and incurvation [of Panama Bay] as well as . . . the surrounding hills have become . . . familiar" from the *Decatur*'s deck. Lane reported that the health of everyone on board had suffered by the "protracted sojourn in this debilitating climate," aggravated by the presence of four remaining filibuster invalids. Reported illnesses continued to increase, by February 1858 having nearly tripled since the ship's arrival. Over the same period, *Decatur* punishments more than doubled, and a causal relationship between illness and offense emerges clearly in the record. The incidence of diarrhea, infections, and fevers at Panama skyrocketed, and it is possible to identify by name many men who were consistently too ill to work and who broke the rules because they were too ill to care. At times, a majority of the crew seemed close to despair, as dozens of sailors and marines were confined for insolence, sleeping on post, smuggling liquor, and disobedience of orders; men attempted to desert almost daily. The *Decatur* descended into a disorder that was statistically twice as bad as that off Seattle, became far more violent, and eventually involved warrant and commissioned officers as well as

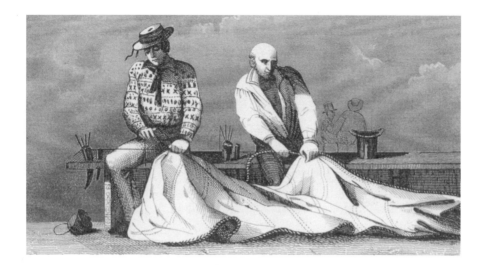

FIG. 49 *Captain Thatcher despaired of finding a skilled sailmaker in antebellum Panama. Here, J. G. Heck shows sailors doing the hard work of making or mending sail and rigging, their awls and heavy needles at their sides. Courtesy University of Washington Libraries.*

enlisted men. Not only did 1858 offenses dramatically increase over the level of offense on Puget Sound, but most offenses took place, not on the beach, but on the ship or in the small boats. Men in Seattle had claimed the woods behind town as a criminal space in 1856; in 1858 and 1859, the ship itself became a criminal space.[15]

At Panama, attempted desertion accounted for more courts-martial than any other crime as men tried to flee the ship. In the Pacific West, where seamen were in high demand, commanders shipped footloose opportunists who were just hitching a ride from San Francisco to Panama and would run at the first opportunity. The *Decatur* sailed from San Francisco without a full complement and remained undermanned off Panama, within sight of land. Dozens of Decaturs overstayed their leave, and two dozen more deserted successfully, disappearing altogether from the record. The ship's corporal, master-at-arms, and marines were as often on shore as they were on board, prowling the dives of Panama to arrest deserters. Other offenders were captured by the police on shore and brought back on board to face their punishment. But the many successful desertions from the ship encouraged men who had failed to bide their time and try again. The entire crew of the first cutter abandoned it in November 1857; a month later, the dinghy was found empty on shore: both crews had walked away and disappeared into the West. Thatcher was hard put to recruit in Panama. When acting sailmaker Chevalier left the ship, Thatcher begged for a stateside replacement because he could not find a seaman in Panama with such specialized skills, and the *Decatur* no longer had "a man on board capable of cutting or even properly repairing a sail."[16]

The quality of the *Decatur's* crew declined. As desertions continued, new men joined the crew nearly every week, and the constant turnover caused disruption. Though the punishment records and Logbook fully document the troubled ship, another source confirms problems of discipline and skill among even the most experienced sailors on board, the seamen. In the summer of 1857, three ailing seamen underwent a medical survey and were duly condemned and ordered to be sent home. Highly competent, at least on paper, these men would prove difficult to replace at Panama, but Captain Thatcher's frank characterization of the sick men is revealing:

Samuel Mahoney (seaman) long in service and a very excellent man

James A. Lowther (seaman) insubordinate and troublesome

Nicholas Andrews (seaman) a very short time in service and worthless

If the survey proportion held true, Thatcher would have judged two-thirds of the *Decatur*'s skilled seamen to be insubordinate or worthless by the summer of 1857. It is tempting to speculate that some of the *Decatur's* healthy and ambitious sailors were more likely to desert the warship for other opportunities, leaving behind an increasing percentage of the ill, who were "troublesome" and "worthless." However, a solid core of capable, longtime, man-of-war sailors and marines remained on the *Decatur,* including Sam Silk, Robert Shorter, Charles Cloyd, and about thirty others—the "sober, steady men."[17]

As the *Decatur* descended into disorder, most enlisted men committed offenses that were considered subjudicial, given punishments that could be reckoned at or below the old standard of twelve lashes: drink, insolence, or neglect of duty. The *Decatur*'s confinement area had been under the forecastle or on the berth deck in the port steerage, but First Lieutenant John Clitz seems to have introduced the innovation of "tricing" men between the guns, up on the deck. The specifics of this punishment on board the *Decatur* are unclear, but Peter Karsten described a man "triced up by the wrists . . . with his arms fully extended laterally." Confinement was the usual punishment levied on the *Decatur* in this period, although a man's pay was sometimes forfeited as well. In general, men charged at Seattle had received a more severe punishment than men charged at Panama with the same crime. Even mutiny and desertion were more lightly punished in 1858 than in 1856. The *Decatur*'s crew was well under strength, and the monotony of the duty, the sickness on board ship, and the constant heat and humidity further encouraged leniency.[18]

A step up from subjudicial punishments were summary courts-martial, which increased dramatically. Three cases will suffice to represent many others. First, George Charles, ordinary seaman, was charged with drunkenness

FIG. 50 J. G. Heck's 1851 Pictorial Archive *shows sailors punished by confinement, locked in leg irons belowdecks. Courtesy University of Washington Libraries.*

on duty and assault of a shipmate. He had come back from liberty "drunk and riotous, from the town of Panama." Charles and Robert Ramsey had quarreled on shore and argued all the way back to the *Decatur* in the sundown boat. Charles told Ramsey he would knock his teeth down his throat, and Ramsey responded that he would be happy to meet him on shore any time. Once on board, Charles struck Ramsey on the head with a belaying pin, knocking him unconscious. Convicted, Charles was confined to double-irons for thirty days and lost his pay for two months.[19]

In a second case, seaman Henry Williams looked Lieutenant David Harmony right in the eye and kept swigging the bottle of liquor he had smuggled on board the *Decatur*. When Harmony ordered him to stop, Williams said, "No, and you may put me in *triple* irons, if you like!" Williams was lightly punished. He was docked $25 in pay, reduced to ordinary seaman in rank, and had extra police duties for three months.[20]

In a third case, Irish-born landsman James Wilson deserted from the market boat at Panama, trying to disappear into town. Most men who committed an offense serious enough to merit a summary court-martial were drunk but Wilson was sober. He had planned his desertion carefully, hiding clothing on shore. When he was caught by the marines, he was dressed as a civilian. Wilson pled guilty and was punished by solitary confinement in double-irons on bread and water for thirty days and loss of pay for three months. A month later, barely out of double-irons, Wilson refused to obey a direct order on deck, saying to the officer, "[I have] been treated like a dog since [I have] been in the ship and [I] intend to act like one." Forbidden to desert, Wilson refused to do any more work and went back into double-irons.[21]

At the time of their offenses, all three men—Charles, Williams, and Wilson—had been ill for months, and their light punishments show the typical leniency of this period. One of the very infrequent dishonorable discharges punished an attempted murder and rid the shorthanded ship of a violent and dangerous man. James Daily had been in trouble since he boarded the *Decatur* in 1854, at Boston, and he was not much of a sailor either: four years after joining the ship, he was still ranked only as a landsman. He had sailed with the *Decatur* to Santa Cruz and Norfolk, through the Strait of Magellan, to Honolulu and Seattle, and on to San Francisco and Panama. Along the way, Daily had contracted venereal disease. On January 13, 1858, he got drunk on smuggled liquor and quarreled loudly with ordinary seaman Augustus Furlong. Marine Thomas Seely, one of the ship's police—"stationed at the fore hatch for the purposes of suppressing disorder in that part of the ship"—ordered Daily to shut up. Daily grabbed Seely by the throat and wrestled him down to the deck. Furlong, Seely, and Daily were ordered to the mast to explain themselves to Boatswain Jasper Coghlan, officer of the deck. Instead, Daily punched Furlong in front of Coghlan, who ordered Master-at-Arms Peter Conlan to confine Daily in double-irons. Daily then drew his sheath knife on Conlan and threatened to kill him. A group of marines wrestled Daily down and carried him below, to be double-ironed. As he went, Daily yelled that he would get them all one way or another, one time or another. The next day, as the prisoner was being taken to the head, he passed Seely at his post and told him that he planned to slit his throat. Seamen carried sheath knives to do their duty in the rigging, and Daily posed a constant, unpredictable threat. He was dishonorably discharged at Panama.[22]

But mutiny was the great nightmare of command, and the *Decatur* experienced its second mutiny during a breathless Panama night, when a dozen members of the crew made common cause against illness, boredom, and authority. At about midnight on February 23, 1858, Lieutenant David Harmony was the officer of the deck; behind his back, the men called him "his lordship" because of his affected British accent and mannerisms. Harmony himself was sick with fever, miserable in the sticky heat, and exhausted from sleeplessness. The officers' berths, like the men's hammocks, were "stew-pans" in which they simmered in their own sweat. In a sour mood, Harmony could hear the men returning from liberty yelling and singing as their cutter drew near the *Decatur*.[23]

Joseph McDonald climbed on board drunk and riotous, howling a bawdy song. A drunken sailor was hardly unusual on board ship, and Harmony wearily ordered that McDonald be confined to sleep it off. But McDonald violently resisted being ironed, biting and kicking; he was remarkably strong, and the master-at-arms and three marines struggled to subdue him. Then a chain reaction of angry resentment began among men in the crew who were sick, who were fed up with "nothing to do and nowhere to go," who felt unmanned by rigid naval discipline, and who had been drinking all night, both on shore and on the ship.[24]

Robert Watson lay on the floor of the berth deck near the brig; perhaps he was hoping for a breath of fresh air down the hatch. But he did not get out of the way quickly enough during McDonald's struggle, and he was kicked by marine private Thomas Bulger while he was trying to confine McDonald. Watson sprang up, bruised and furious. Bulger was kneeling, his hands holding Joe McDonald's feet so that he could be ironed. Watson reared back and kicked Bulger as hard as he could in the mouth. Through his blood and broken teeth, Bulger cursed Watson.

Lieutenant Harmony ordered Watson to be confined for his attack on the marine, and as the lieutenant walked forward, Watson yelled to his mates, "I have done nothing and that son of a bitch has ordered me to be put in double irons." Beyond caring, Watson insulted the officer as a "son of a bitch." Harmony again ordered Watson put into irons. The angry voices brought Lieutenant Clitz out of his bunk, who in turn called Watson and other members of the crew sons of bitches. In 1858, those were fighting words among men, but the officers behaved as though the sailors were not men like themselves. Navy discipline required enlisted men to stand still and take the abuse of a superior officer, swallowing insults to their manhood without response.

Lieutenant Clitz ordered Gunner James Lilleston to see to Watson's confinement, and the sailor's wrists and ankles were locked none too tenderly in double-irons. Watson kicked and yelled, bit and head-butted, cursing the ship and the officers. Several seamen had by now gotten out of their hammocks and crowded around the prisoners, muttering. Charles Boland was lying on a mess chest, taking it all in, and "insolently" refused Lilleston's order to move along and go back to his hammock, saying that if Watson was to be ironed then he should be ironed, too. Boland claimed that Watson was being punished for nothing. Four or five marines were still roughly trying to iron Watson, and Boland yelled, "Don't hurt that man so!" and walked back toward the brig to intervene. Bulger grabbed him and shoved him down, hard. Lieutenant Harmony, standing nearby, ordered that Boland be manacled, too. So once Watson was ironed, the group of marines turned to Boland and wrestled him down to the deck.

The marines were holding the sailors at bay. After McDonald, Watson, and

Boland were ironed, seaman Hendrik Guy challenged Private Bulger to a fist-fight on the forecastle, saying, "Bulger, you're one of the sober, steady men, ain't you? Come up on the forecastle with me, and I'll let you know what you are. I can lick you any way you are amind to try me. I'll pay you off for this yet." Bulger turned away, wiping blood from his mouth.

George Harris came up to Gunner Lilleston at the mast and waited to be recognized. When he was, he walked forward and told Lilleston that he had seen Bulger hit Boland when the sailor was ironed and helpless; Lilleston brushed off the complaint and told Harris to go below. He did, muttering that Bulger was a bully and a coward. Later, Harris was overheard down on the berth deck saying loudly to his friends, "Boland is not a bit to blame and ought not to be confined." Marine sergeant Robert Small told Harris to shut up and turn in to his hammock. Harmony nervously asked what the sailor was saying, and Small told the officer that Harris "was trying to vindicate the cause of Boland," and then Harmony ordered Harris confined, too. So far, McDonald, Watson, Boland, and Harris were locked hand and foot in irons.

Later that night, one of the marines went forward to use the head and found "sea-lawyer" Augustus Furlong sitting amidships, making "a kind of speech to a circle of seven or eight men." On navy ships, the "sea-lawyer" was an enlisted man who was an articulate critic and had earned the crew's respect; he was dangerous to discipline. The marine heard Furlong say that it was a great shame for officers to treat the men in such a beastly manner and they should not be allowed to do it, and if the officers called the men sons of bitches, they did not deserve any better language themselves. Were they not free men? Furlong asked rhetorically. "Is that the way you use men on board a man of war?" He spent the rest of the night in double-irons.

Joe McDonald, the seaman who had come to the ship from Panama drunk and rowdy and set the whole chain of events into motion, was twenty-eight years old, born in Maine. Lieutenant Harmony was four years younger than McDonald, and he had been sick ever since he set foot on the *Decatur*. He came down with cholera when the ship was taking William Carey Jones to Punta Arenas and then progressed through a series of illnesses until that hot night in February 1858: fever, diarrhea, herpes, and boils. Harmony suffered from "irritatio nervosa," the surgeon wrote; he could not sleep and he was not in command of himself. Boatswain Coghlan was forty-six, born in Ireland and an experienced veteran of British merchant ships in the East Indies. Lieutenant Clitz was alternately ill with Panama fever and with constipation; the treatment for the diarrhea of the one apparently causing the blockage of the other.[25]

Peter Conlan, master-at-arms, was thirty and born in Ireland; he had syphilis and he, too, was suffering from chronic diarrhea. Like many of the marines, "sober and steady" Tom Bulger was also born in Ireland; he was twenty-eight and under treatment for primary syphilis. Seaman Hendrik Guy—who challenged Bulger to fight it out—was born in Sweden; he was thirty-eight, an elder statesman by the *Decatur*'s standards. Guy was sick, like so many of the *Decatur*'s officers and crew, with Panama fever and chronic diarrhea. George Harris was twenty-seven, an ordinary seaman born in England; he, too, was ill with fever and was still healing from a deep gash he had received while running on deck "in a gale" while the ship was sailing south from San Francisco. Charles Boland, landsman, was new to the ship, having been recruited to replace a deserter, and no one knew much about him. Robert Watson, who kicked Bulger in the mouth, was twenty-one and from Delaware; he had been at sea for at least two years and was classified as an ordinary seaman. Sea-lawyer Augustus Furlong was also twenty-one—sometimes he told the surgeons he was from Boston and sometimes he said North Carolina. He, too, was sick was fever and with syphilis. Most of the sailors and marines accused of mutiny on the *Decatur* in the Bay of Panama were sick men, and they were commanded by sick men.

At the summary court-martial, Joe McDonald pled guilty to coming aboard drunk and riotous. He was confined for two weeks in double-irons and lost $10 in pay. George Harris pled not guilty to charges of disorderly conduct; he was found guilty and sentenced to solitary confinement in double-irons for thirty nights, to be confined after supper and released at daylight. In addition, his pay was stopped for two months. Charlie Boland also pled innocent to the charge of disobedience of orders, to interfering with Lilleston, and refusing to go on deck. He was found guilty but Thatcher pardoned him because he was inexperienced in a man-of-war, having so recently enlisted. Bob Watson pled not guilty to the charge of mutinous conduct. He was found guilty of calling Lieutenant Harmony a son of a bitch and of kicking Tom Bulger in the mouth. Watson was confined in double-irons for thirty days and lost two months' pay. Hendrik Guy admitted that he had challenged Bulger to fight but argued that he was not guilty of mutinous conduct. He was found guilty of both charges and ordered to be confined in double-irons for thirty days on bread and water and to lose two months' pay. Augustus Furlong pled not guilty to the charge of mutinous language, for his little speech to the circle of admiring shipmates. One of the marines called to testify, Louis Celagi, was born in Poland and admitted to the court that he did not really understand much of what Furlong was saying. But Celagi did not like the sound of it and called the master-at-arms over to listen. Found guilty, Furlong was put into solitary confinement on bread and water, in double-irons, for thirty days, and his pay was docked for three months. The 1858 punishments were lighter than those levied at Norfolk in 1854 for a very similar "mutiny" in Santa Cruz. The 1858 cases were tried in a summary court-martial; the 1854 cases were tried before a general court-martial. And instead of being imprisoned or discharged, the *Decatur*'s 1858 mutineers were briefly confined, docked pay, and released back to duty. The lenient punishments did not discourage continued offenses among these sick, desperate men.[26]

Seaman John Coulyer was twenty-two, born in Philadelphia, and he usually pulled the after oar on the port side of the second cutter. He suffered from primary syphilis. One night, the cutter was headed back from Panama to the *Decatur* with Purser Felix Senac, Assistant Surgeon Lane, Gunner James Lilleston, and several others, after a day ashore in Panama. Coulyer was in charge of the sail, in the offshore breeze. One of the oarsmen accidentally knocked his hat off, and he jammed it back on his head, complaining drunkenly. Purser Senac first asked him to be quiet and then ordered him to shut up and head forward, away from the sail. Coulyer threw his hat down in the cutter and went forward, rocking the boat, and saying, "A man cannot do or say anything without having his head knocked off." He loudly complained, "A person was not allowed to speak in an American man-of-war, but he would be damned if he would not speak." Senac ordered Coxswain Thomas More and oarsman Charles Kelly to gag Coulyer, to shut him up. Coulyer resisted violently and spat out the gag; he tried to tip the boat over, threatening to knife Kelly—"to run a knife through his heart." Senac asked Edward Murphy to help hold Coulyer's arms, and Murphy refused. While More and Kelly were gagging Coulyer, Murphy rose from his seat to defend Coulyer, protesting angrily, "That's a damned pretty way to treat a drunken man. There are too many men on him already." Gunner Lilleston warned him, "I am listening to every word you say, Murphy." Murphy rebelled against Lilleston's threat and against manhandling a helpless shipmate: "Don't hurt that man. I'll be damned if three or four of you shall use a man in that way." At the summary court-martial, Lilleston testified that Murphy was trying to organize the men in the cutter to mutiny against the purser and the gunner. Both Coulyer and Murphy were found guilty and both suffered the same light punishment: loss of pay, extra police duty for three months, and no liberty for six months.[27]

As offenses escalated, the *Decatur* was no longer an orderly, disciplined island. The log entries became brief, almost perfunctory; there were no enemies to fight and few visitors to the ship. Just as the drills became pointless, so did maintenance. Despite liberal applications of putty and paint, the ship was rotting at anchor; the damp, hot Panama climate ruined rigging and sails and accelerated rot. The ship's carpenter discovered that the planking in the port bends was badly decayed; sails were found to be rotted in the sail room. The heat spoiled ship's stores—one barrel of salt beef burst and contaminated more than two hundred gallons of drinking water stored beneath it. Bread, rice, cheese, and other foodstuffs were surveyed and condemned as spoiled and dumped overboard into Panama's harbor. And a few sick filibusters remained on board, bedridden and stinking. The hands' offenses reflected, too, the loss of purpose on board this warship, the absence of coordination, subordination, and balance. The men's behavior displayed mounting illness, despair, and violence, and the malaise soon spread to their officers.[28]

A Pacific Squadron commander had suggested that tours of duty be reduced from three years to two because of the "hard service" on the Pacific station. Even at sea, the enlisted men, the commander continued, "get tired of being cooped up in a small vessel . . . so long on salt provisions, and the monotonous life. Exercise guns and sails, eat and sleep, and day after day this is the routine until they become so tired that good men desert often for no other reason than the want of a change." And the commander noted that officers themselves lost interest in "the order, discipline and efficiency of the ship" and soon "get sick, break down and go home." Mental problems were associated with the tropical climate. *Decatur* seaman Thomas Bradley, twenty-one, tried to commit suicide at Panama by slitting his wrist; the surgeons sewed him up and sent him back to work. However, in May 1858, Surgeon Ward sent John Adams home, judged insane at twenty-two. William Jarvis, who had suffered sunstroke in December 1857, was soon "laboring under mental derangement," which was "daily growing worse." Ward wrote that Jarvis needed order and quiet, not the daily "excitement and noise" of shipboard life, and the sailor was sent stateside. In May 1858, Surgeon Lane reported in the *Herald* that not just the *Decatur* enlisted men but their officers had become "greatly prostrated by their prolonged stay in this debilitating climate." At the time, *Decatur* Lieutenant Edward Cantey Stockton was under the surgeons' treatment for chronic Panama fever and diarrhea, and he was also an alcoholic.[29]

The previous fall, Lieutenant Stockton's behavior had become increasingly erratic. First, he announced to the wardroom that the Navy Department had authorized him a leave of absence from the *Decatur*. The leave was to run for two months, noted the ship's log on September 30, 1857, but Stockton was back on board signing the Logbook on October 3. Then, on October 20, the note "Lieutenant Stockton having obtained a leave of absence for two months from the Honorable Secretary of the Navy, he left the ship," was written into the log but then lined through with a heavy pencil. However, this time, Stockton did stay away, crossing the Isthmus of Panama and catching a steamer to New York, then traveling to his home. Stockton returned to the *Decatur* on January 14, 1858, but he was soon away from the ship again on a leave beginning in mid-April. His frequent furloughs were authorized by Commander Thatcher either because Stockton was too ill for duty or because he was drinking too much, or both.[30]

Shortly after his return to the ship, on May 9, 1858, Stockton spent the day in Panama and joined Surgeon Lane and Commander Thatcher in the sundown boat, to return to the *Decatur*. The officers found that two of the gig's crew, Tom Berry and Bill Martin, were absent. It was almost impossible to keep men waiting at the boat with the temptations of town so close at hand. Irritated, Thatcher sent two men to hunt for them, who returned "after a long absence" to say that Berry and Martin were drinking at a tavern in town and refused to come down to shore. Sometimes, if men had strayed from the waiting boat, the coxswain would send a runner to get them, saying, "The captain is in sight!" and it was just a ruse. So, because they were having too good a time, Berry and Martin preferred to believe that Thatcher was not really at the cutter. Eventually, they came down to the dock with Lieutenant Stockton, and the sundown boat headed out to the *Decatur*. What was said en route was not recorded. Berry was "excited with liquor," remembered one of the boat's passengers, "but not intoxicated."

Seaman Thomas Berry was in his thirties, born in England, and ordinary seaman William Martin was twenty-four, from Delaware. Berry had been oarsman for thirteen months and was ashore almost daily in the line of duty. Commander Thatcher considered him experienced and trustworthy—"one of the best men on the ship"—and had appointed him acting coxswain of the gig. Like nearly everyone on board, Berry and Martin had been ill throughout the spring: Martin with chronic diarrhea, Berry with Panama fever. They had rowed the gig side by side, they were drinking buddies, and now they were in trouble together.

Berry and Martin pulled their oars, as usual, and Lieutenant Scott was officer of the deck when the gig was made fast to the *Decatur*'s side. On boarding, Martin surprised him by saying, "Mr. Scott, you see I am not drunk, sir." As Scott later said, he judged Martin and Berry to be "under the influence of liquor, but not drunk." Once everyone was aboard, Commander Thatcher ordered Berry to be put in irons. Then, Scott said, Berry's language became profane and mutinous; Lieutenant Harmony heard Berry say that he "would be goddamned if he would allow any drunken lieutenant to lead him down to the boat, that he intended to see the commodore if he could and let him know how things had been conducted on board this ship."

William Martin and Thomas Berry were brought before a general court-martial and charged with disobedience of orders, abusive language, and assault on a superior officer. The general court-martial required the presence of a captain, two commanders, and three additional officers. On May 22, 1858, Captain Thatcher was too ill to leave his cabin, and the court-martial was adjourned until he could attend. When the trial began, both sailors pled not guilty; in the end, both were found partly guilty. But as the trial unfolded, its emphasis shifted as the testimony moved from the sailors to Lieutenant Stockton himself.

Two weeks earlier, while the sundown boat awaited the two tardy sailors, Stockton had volunteered to go up into Panama, find them, and bring them down to the boat. Thatcher agreed. "I found them in a drinking house in Panama City," testified Stockton. "I ordered them to the boat and accompanied them down, holding each by the collar of the frock" (in other words, by their shirt collars). At the beach, both men wanted to roll up their trousers to keep them dry and Stockton refused permission. Martin bent to roll his trousers anyway, Stockton testified, continuing, "I having both hands occupied, used my foot to prevent his doing it. As my foot was raised, Martin caught hold of it and tripped me up, [and] as I was struggling to regain my feet, the prisoner pressed me down." But Berry claimed that Stockton had fallen and that he had lifted the lieutenant to his feet, saying, "Mind, Mr. Stockton, I did not trip you." After the three men regained their footing, Stockton hailed the boat and they headed out to the *Decatur.*

Questioned in Berry's court-martial, Martin testified that Lieutenant Stockton "was in liquor," and that as the three men walked down to the gig, Stockton "leaned pretty much all of his weight on my shoulders [and] when we got to the beach, he fell, and he could not get up himself. He lay so long, we had to lift him up. After he got up, . . . he said, 'Thank you, Berry.' I thought he said so because Berry helped him up." No one tripped or pushed Stockton down, Martin testified; he had fallen down all on his own: the lieutenant could hardly walk because he was so drunk. But Assistant Surgeon Lane and Commander Thatcher did not support Martin's testimony, and both officers claimed under oath that Stockton was perfectly sober that night. Lieutenant Harmony testified that after Berry had been ironed, he yelled, "I have been thirteen months in this ship and I'll tell the commodore what I have seen and what I know!" No one asked Berry what he had seen and what he knew about the *Decatur* during that long, hot stay in the Bay of Panama. Both sailors were found guilty of the lesser charges—disobedience of orders and abusive language—but not of assault on a superior officer, not of "placing . . . hands willfully upon Lieutenant Edward C. Stockton and pressing him down." That far more serious charge was held "not proven." Stockton's sworn testimony, even with the support of Lane and Thatcher, did not convince the general court-martial. Berry's punishment was six weeks of solitary confinement on bread and water and loss of pay; Martin's was four weeks of each.[31]

U.S. naval officers were expected to be able to hold their liquor; it was part of the gentlemanly sociability expected in the wardroom, an attribute of midcentury masculinity. But drink was very easy to come by, and drunkenness and alcoholism were systemic problems in the officer corps. Sick men of every rank in Panama's sultry climate used alcohol to feel a bit better, for a little while. In May 1858, general courts-martial at Panama tried and convicted two *Merrimac* officers for public drunkenness on shore and on duty, and Commander Thatcher served at both trials. The officers were tried for violation of the Act for the Better Government of the Navy, which required that "all officers of the Navy . . . set an example of morality, subordination and attention to duty," and continued, "If any officer in the Navy shall be guilty of . . . drunkenness, profane swearing or any other scandalous or dishonorable conduct unbecoming an officer, . . . he shall, on conviction therefore, be cashiered."[32]

On June 9, 1858, less than two weeks after Berry and Martin were sentenced, Surgeon John Ward filed a report with Commander Thatcher that formally charged Lieutenant Stockton with "scandalous and dishonorable" conduct. Ward detailed a series of encounters with Stockton the previous day. While in town at Panama, Ward was paying his bill in a shop when the clerk pointed out Stockton "staggering across one of the streets" in the afternoon. He joked, "Look, Doctor, what is the matter with Mr. Stockton? Is the poor [fool] drunk again?" Surgeon Ward replied tartly that there was nothing wrong with Stockton except too much to drink.[33]

An hour later, the sundown boat was waiting at the quay to return to the *Decatur*. Although ranking lieutenant Joseph DeHaven was on board, he was too sick with fever to command the boat and Stockton took charge. Ward wrote that Stockton was "very much intoxicated," judging by his "general demeanor and language." Stockton pretended to run the gig up onto a rock and to ram another small boat, he insulted and threatened Purser Felix Senac, and he insulted and then physically attacked Surgeon Ward. High words were exchanged on board the little boat as Stockton called Ward a "damned son of a bitch." Surgeon W. A. Nelson, of the *Saranac,* was also on board—Stockton's condition was no longer a *Decatur* secret. The incident was reported in the *New York Times,* and according to that newspaper's Panama correspondent, there was long-standing bad blood between Lieutenant Stockton and Surgeon Ward. The reporter was sympathetic to Stockton, commenting that the officer had been ill and was not yet recovered and "got a little exhilarated over a bottle of wine." The correspondent continued that Stockton leaned out of the sundown boat to "wash a sponge which he had purchased." Ward ordered Stockton to sit up straight, and Stockton replied, "Dr. Ward, I have been in the Navy long enough to know what to do without your instructions." After an angry exchange, the correspondent reported that Stockton slapped Ward's face. On board the *Decatur,* Ward refused to accept Stockton's apology, "which would have satisfied any honorable man," according to the *Times* correspondent.[34]

Thatcher could not ignore Ward's formal report on the Stockton affair, and he suspended the lieutenant from duty and informed Commodore Long to that effect. He enclosed a copy of Ward's charges and initiated an inquiry of his own. Thatcher wrote: "Since this report has been made to me, it has come to my knowledge that Lieut. E. C. Stockton has been drunk at other times; on one occasion so recent, within the last eight or ten days, he has been asleep on his watch, said watch being a night watch . . . and that he has been repeatedly asleep during his watches and further that he has been repeatedly drunk since he has been under my command." Ward had attached a list of officers and enlisted men to his report whom he called as "witnesses" and who would testify to the serious charges he was making against Stockton. The list included Executive Officer John Clitz, Lieutenants Scott, Harmony, and DeHaven, Assistant Surgeon Lane, and Purser Senac. But the list also included warrant officers, petty officers, and enlisted men: Boatswain Jasper Coghlan, Quartermasters Cloyd, Knight, Frost, and Rath, Robert Manchester of the gig's crew, and William Keith, coxswain of the gig. Thomas Berry and William Martin were not named as witnesses; they had been sacrificed when the cloak of official silence had been thrown around Stockton. But Stockton had gone too far with Ward.[35]

A general court-martial was convened on board the *Decatur* on June 11, and Thatcher was one of the senior officers who tried the case. Commodore Long delayed the *Merrimac*'s departure from Panama because of the gravity of three of the charges against Stockton. The first charge was drunkenness and the specifications were

1. On June 8, 1858, Stockton was drunk on shore in the streets of Panama.

2. On June 8, while in charge of one of the boats of the Decatur, on her passage from Panama to the ship, [Stockton] was drunk and unfit for duty.

3. That while the said United States ship Decatur has been lying in the port of Panama, he has repeatedly been drunk both on duty and off duty, on board said ship and ashore.

The second charge was assault of an officer, and the specification was Stockton's attack on Ward. The third was neglect of duty and showed the results of Thatcher's investigation:

1. Between May 25 and June 9, 1858, Stockton grossly neglected his duty by sleeping under the top gallant forecastle, while keeping a night watch on board said ship.

2. While the ship has been lying in the port of Panama, Stockton has repeatedly neglected his duty by sleeping while in charge of the deck of said ship during his night watches.

The fourth charge was unofficerlike conduct, and the specification was Stockton's calling Ward "a damned son of a bitch" on the boat and thus behaving "in a manner unbecoming an officer and a gentleman." Stockton pled guilty to all charges, and as a result, no testimony was taken. The lieutenant was sentenced by the court to be cashiered, to return to the United States, and to report to the Navy Department. Stockton arrived in Washington, DC, on June 27 and penned his resignation from the navy on the following day. He was not replaced, and the *Decatur* continued its tour of duty with four lieutenants. Writing to Toucey after the trial, Commodore Long sadly observed that "the officers of the *Decatur* are much debilitated by long detention in this port, so as to be frequently unfit for duty."[36]

When the Stockton general court-martial concluded, the *Decatur* had been at anchor in the Bay of Panama for ten months, since August 1857. The *Decatur* was nominally effective as a hospital ship, a floating battery, or a base for shore actions, but the ship had to put to sea to restore good order. Flag Officer Long ordered Thatcher to prepare the *Decatur* for an extended cruise to the south, turning over Panama duty to the *Vandalia*. Three American merchant vessels, Long explained to Thatcher in his orders, had been seized as prizes during the previous year and sent into ports in Chile and Peru, "for want of protection from our ships of war." The commodore ordered Thatcher

FIG. 51 The Illustrated London News (February 21, 1863) published this engraving of the harbor off the Chincha Islands, crowded with schooners and brigs loading guano. This was the vital trade that the Decatur and the Merrimac headed south from Panama to protect. Courtesy University of Washington Libraries, Special Collections, UW27981z.

to watch over Americans engaged in the guano trade in the Chincha Islands but also in the "large American trade growing up with the Port of Caldera in Chile." The presence of a ship of the line, Long continued, would discourage interference with these merchantmen. But he also gave Thatcher more general instructions, ordering him to extend protection to American vessels and citizens "as circumstances may require" and encouraging him to "exercise . . . discretion under extraordinary exigencies." Those "exigencies" might arise in services requested by John Clay, U.S. minister to Peru, and John Bigler, U.S. minister to Chile.[37]

Long struggled, as had Mervine, to balance the responsibilities and resources of the five-ship Pacific Squadron. A warship had to be stationed off Nicaragua to discourage renewal of the filibuster there. Another, of course, needed to be anchored permanently at Panama to protect the transit railroad. The coastal states and territories and the Sandwich Islands and "the various islands of the South Pacific Ocean" should also be visited frequently. Long had once hoped to keep the *Merrimac* at Panama, where it would receive orders from Washington as quickly as possible, but the ship proved essential for "general supervision of the whole cruising ground." The debilitated, rotting, unhappy *Decatur* was a vital member of the squadron.[38]

Before sending the *Decatur* south, Long ordered another hull survey, and the surveyors concluded that the ship was in a "defective and unseaworthy condition," leaky and dry-rotted. The *Decatur*'s very gun carriages functioned poorly. Commodore Long recommended that the *Decatur* be ordered to Mare Island as soon as possible for "thorough repairs." In the meantime, he told Thatcher that the storeship at Valparaiso was holding a supply of planks, set aside for the *Decatur*'s carpenter and his gang. The port bends, afflicted with dry rot, twice repaired after the ship's collision with rocks off Restoration Point in Puget Sound, needed immediate strengthening to make the ship "seaworthy for another season." But Secretary Toucey was on record as saying that sailing frigates were so old-fashioned that they should be downgraded to sloops of war and eventually retired from active service as stationary store-ships, but that sloops of war built before 1840, like the *Decatur*, were not even worth repairing.[39]

As the *Decatur* prepared to put to sea, whatever injured filibusters remained on board had to be dealt with; they had been on the ship for more than eleven months. One, John Frizzell, had suffered a wound that shattered the femur of his right leg; he could not walk and was "sick all the time . . . a great annoy-ance to the officers and crew." The surgeons found Frizzell to be permanently disabled "in consequence of gunshot wounds received in the employment of General William Walker" and recommended that he be sent to the United States "as an act of humanity." Thatcher asked Long for help, and the com-modore requested of Toucey that Frizzell be sent home as a charity case. In June 1858, twenty-five chronic invalids were taken by train across Panama and then traveled on the navy storeship *Relief* from Aspinwall to New York City, some from the *Decatur*, including John Frizzell. He was the last filibuster to leave the *Decatur* as the ship readied for sea.[40]

Long decided to accompany the *Decatur* in the *Merrimac*, convinced that rising tensions between the United States and Peru over the guano trade called for a considerable show of force, but the commodore also intended to shepherd the troubled vessel. As battered as the *Decatur* was, while blue-sea sailing on a following wind the sloop of war easily outsailed the clumsy steam frigate in an exhilarating display of speed and skill. The *Decatur* always rose to the occasion at sea and under sail, where the warship's seamen were at home. Once at sea, Surgeon Lane happily noted the rapid reduction of the sick list, although there were plenty of workplace injuries—burns, sprains, fractures, bruises, and cuts. One old hand, Francis Purcell, London-born captain of the foretop, fell from the rigging and cut and bruised his head and sprained his wrist. Practicing with his gun crew, Joseph Jenkinson's foot was run over by the carriage, crushing it. John Johnson tripped and fell from the forecastle clear down the hatch to the berth deck. As the *Decatur* pitched and rolled, the ship's cook was badly scalded by boiling water when a pot on his stove slid forward. Hauling up the anchor, William Edwards was heaving as hard as he could on the capstan and slipped; he broke a number of teeth and laid open his cheek. Strains and hernias were common as men heaved, pulled, or lifted too much weight.[41]

Such injuries were commonplace under sail but during the cruise to Peru, wardroom steward Joseph Hombra died and was buried at sea, one of only two sea burials during the *Decatur*'s five-year cruise in the Pacific Squadron. Born at Mahón, on Minorca off the coast of Spain, Hombra died far from home. He had been seriously ill for only three weeks with catarrh and asthma, and finally with "hydrothorax," or pleurisy. Surgeon Lane's minutely observed description of pleurisy may describe Hombra's last hours in sick bay:

> The inspiratory act is made with effort, and it is accompanied by a hissing sound from the air being sucked through the narrowed canal; and at the same time, from the vibration of the vocal chords, a hoarse or croaking sound is produced. . . . From an insufficient quantity of air reaching the lungs, the blood is imperfectly oxygenated, and that venous blood is circulating in the arteries is apparent in the cyanosed or purplish hue of the lips and cheeks. . . . The patient is in a state of great restlessness, throwing his limbs hither and thither . . . seeking a position in which he can breathe more easily. In his efforts to get more air, he tries to catch or seize it with his mouth.

Lane found Hombra's case fascinating; and he noted in the log that the interested reader should turn to the ship's journal for a fuller discussion; that volume of the Medical Journal is now missing. Hombra's body was sewn by the ship's new sailmaker, Ware Branson, into his canvas hammock, his bed becoming his shroud, and the canvas was weighted at the foot with two thirty-two-pound shot. The flag was lowered to half mast and Captain Thatcher likely read the service before the silent, assembled crew—"Unto Almighty God we commend the soul of our brother departed and we now commit his body to the deep"—and the corpse was tipped feet first into the Pacific Ocean.[42]

The *Merrimac* and the *Decatur* arrived together at Payta, in Peru, on July 7, 1858. The *Decatur*'s log recorded the usual hustle and bustle of a man-of-war in a distant port. As always, the *Decatur* looked beautiful from a distance, rocking gently in the harbor; the tidy little sloop of war reminded viewers of the sailing navy of their youth. But sailing south alongside the *Decatur*, Long had studied the hull survey and observed the sail and gun drills and reaffirmed his earlier judgment, "The *Decatur*, having been so long at Panama, [has] become next to useless in the debilitated state of her officers and crew."[43]

The two ships left Payta together and sailed on. By July 24, they were anchored in the Bay of Casma, and by August 2, in the harbor of Callao. Here, both ships engaged in a busy round of formal visits and salutes. The *Decatur*'s officers exchanged dinner invitations with a British warship; a week later, the *Decatur* hoisted the French flag to commemorate the birth of Napoleon I. The provincial governor visited on August 24, and the ship fired a salute for him, returned by the Peruvian navy's flagship. Two days later, the *Decatur* was dressed to honor Prince Albert's birthday with the English ensign and a twenty-one-gun salute. On August 30, the ship flew the Peruvian flag and fired a twenty-one-gun salute to honor General Ramon Castilla, who visited the *Decatur* on Sunday. The following day, the ship again honored Castilla, celebrating his birthday by dressing the ship and firing a salute. Then, the U.S. Commission to the Sandwich Islands, in Peru on their way to Hawaii, visited the ship. Finally, American minister John Clay met with Captain Thatcher on board, honored with dinner and a salute. July and August 1858 seemed to be good months for the *Decatur*, once again at sea and paying calls in port.[44]

But no cruise or round of official visits could cure the poisonous feeling on board the ship. In Callao, a court of inquiry was convened to investigate Surgeon John Ward's allegations against Purser Felix Senac. On July 9, Ward, who had filed the official complaint against Edward Stockton, filed one against Senac. When the *Decatur* was at anchor off Payta, Senac was at work on his accounts. His body and the open purser's chest blocked one passageway from the open deck down into the wardroom. Rather than walk around to the other side and come down through the pantry, Ward chose to step over and around Senac. He may have pushed him; he certainly touched him as he squeezed past. Words were exchanged, words so heated that Ward wished to challenge Senac to a duel. But "as officers of the Navy are prevented by the rules and regulations of the service from demanding personal satisfaction from each other," Ward wanted Commander Thatcher to address the serious issues "affecting the discipline and harmony of the Navy" that he had raised about Senac. Ward wrote it all up for Thatcher and formally requested that his complaint be forwarded to the commodore for investigation. Reluctantly, Thatcher did so; he had no choice.[45]

The court of inquiry met on board the *Decatur*, and Ward's report was read aloud to the court, and the witnesses called. Lieutenant Harmony, sworn, testified that he had been seated at the wardroom table and could easily see Senac sitting before the purser's chest, blocking the passage. Ward came down the passageway into the wardroom, stepping over the purser, saying, "Purser, let me pass," and walked into his own tiny room. Senac finished what he was doing, locked the chest, and went into his own compartment. But he immediately came out, saying,

> Dr. Ward, you have frequently done this before. I will not submit to such indignities any longer. I believe you do it to annoy me.
>
> [Ward replied,] Am I to inconvenience myself for you on all occasions? I have always gone around the mast when you were busy at your chest.
>
> No, sir, [said Senac,] you have frequently done this before . . . and I'll not submit to it.
>
> It is not so, you are mistaken, and you have no right to construe my intention.
>
> Dr. Ward, I do not want a war of words with you. I have the right, and I'll use it when and where I choose.

Harmony, questioned, said that Senac's manner was calm and that Ward's was excited and harsh. Purser Belknap of the *Merrimac* was sworn and testified that Dr. Ward visited him on the afternoon of the incident with Senac. Belknap returned to the *Decatur* with Ward, hoping to act as peacemaker, but "the statements of those two officers differed so materially that one would hardly suppose they had reference to the same transactions." Belknap decided that both men should apologize to one another, shake hands, and forget about the incident. Senac agreed but Ward refused and instead filed his report with Commander Thatcher, precipitating the court of inquiry. The rules governing disagreements between officers were designed to encourage cordial relationships among professional gentlemen and specified that an apology for an offense, freely given, should be freely accepted, with no loss of honor by either officer. Belknap's recommendation was sound; he had tried his best to mediate in the spirit of fraternity. In fact, he pleaded with Ward, "Doctor, there is no harm in your making this apology—the terms will compromise no one." But Ward did not want peace on these terms. The surgeons did not log their own illnesses, but one may safely assume that Ward was as sick as everyone else. Senac had survived a bout of cholera the previous summer and was under medical treatment for fever and chronic diarrhea. Lieutenant Harmony, who had walked out of the wardroom to get a little peace and quiet, had been sick with cholera when Senac was and was also currently under treatment for chronic diarrhea. The ailing officers were thoroughly tired of one another, and little idiosyncrasies became infuriating as the *Decatur* seemed to grow smaller every week.[46]

After Ward wound up his case, Senac declared to the court that the surgeon's "malicious, unfounded and puerile" report was unsupported by the very witnesses he himself had called to testify. After wasting the time of Commanders Thatcher and Hitchcock and Lieutenant Daniel Ammen, the court of inquiry concluded that there was insufficient cause to call upon the flag officer for his interposition and that they did not recommend any further action. Long wearily agreed, recommending "to both parties more circumspection in their intercourse hereafter." Senac and Ward, now bitter enemies, had to continue to work and live together on board the *Decatur.* The enlisted men, who were forced to arrest, subdue, and double-iron each another and then to testify against one another at courts-martial, also had to continue to live and work together. The enlisted men let off steam in fistfights; the officers were not permitted to duel. But Surgeon Ward could make other arrangements. He soon left the *Decatur* for the *Saranac,* and Assistant Surgeon Lane took sole charge of the ship's medical duties.[47]

After Commodore Long sailed for Honolulu in the *Merrimac,* Philo White, U.S. minister to Ecuador, handed Thatcher an urgent dispatch for Long and asked the *Decatur* captain to read it. The letter indicated that the Ecuadorian government believed that Peru was about to send a naval force to take the port of Guayaquil, the "commercial metropolis" of Ecuador. Guayaquil had been under blockade by three Peruvian steamers for more than a month, and White was concerned for the safety of American citizens there. He urged the squadron assign a warship to "keep an eye upon movements of expeditionary enterprise against the port" and to offer help to Americans living in the area. Before departing, Long had briefed Thatcher on these developing problems between Peru and Ecuador and ordered him to be prepared to act as necessary. However, on the same day that he received White's note, Thatcher also received a direct order from Secretary Toucey to sail at once to Realejo, Nicaragua, with dispatches for Ambassador Mirabeau Lamar. Toucey also ordered Thatcher to be vigilant against the rumored landing of more filibusters in Nicaragua from California. Thatcher had intended to sail to Valparaiso, pick up his lumber from the storeship, stock up with everything from whiskey to candles, and to follow up on Minister White's urgent dispatch for Long. But with his new orders to sail to Nicaragua, Thatcher had to hastily replenish ship's stores at Callao, where "provisions are scarce and not always of the best quality." The *Decatur* was short on powder to fight an engagement; powder was contraband in Peru and could only be acquired directly from the government. The *Decatur* gratefully borrowed one thousand pounds of cannon powder from the Peruvian authorities in September 1858, and the officials "would not be induced to receive pay."[48]

Thatcher hastened north from Callao "under royal and flying jib" and made a steady eight knots heading north to Realejo, a glorious run, exhilarating to the seamen on board. Lane wrote enthusiastically to the *Herald* about exercising the carronades at sea and about how accurate the gun crews' firing was despite the "ship's active motion." At sea, under sail, firing the great guns with Peruvian powder, the *Decatur* was still a real, fighting warship, with duty to fulfill. Two weeks after leaving Callao, the ship glided into the harbor off Realejo. Ambassador Lamar proved to be away in Costa Rica, and Thatcher anxiously awaited his return, composing a brief on local conditions.[49]

"The small village of Realejo," Thatcher began, "is situated on a low, unhealthy spot" on the river, about six miles inland from the *Decatur*'s anchorage. Though Thatcher remarked that "the rain is almost incessant," he enjoyed a pleasant visit with longtime resident John Dothan, an "American gentleman from Connecticut," who noted that it took about four days to travel by land from Realejo to San Juan del Sur and that the journey was far quicker by sea. Dothan also warned Thatcher that the public mails were routinely opened in Nicaragua and Costa Rica and to be careful what he wrote and sent. Taking Dothan's advice, Thatcher held on to Lamar's dispatches from Washington until the diplomat's arrival.[50]

At anchor in Realejo's bay, the *Decatur* dealt with the aftermath of murderous violence on board ship. Though Ward, Senac, and Stockton were all Southern men, seaman Thomas Murray's attack on Henry Lewis, captain of the main top, had sectional, perhaps racial overtones. On the day the *Decatur* sailed north from Callao, Murray stabbed Lewis with the intent to kill.

On shore at Callao, Lewis had threatened him, "It's time for you yet, you Virginia son of a bitch." Murray replied, "I am no son of a bitch, but a white man," and then Lewis struck Murray repeatedly in the face. Both men were in their thirties; Murray was from Virginia, and Lewis from New York. When they were waiting for the cutter to return to the ship, sailors testified that Lewis had knocked Murray down on the beach and kicked him. Lieutenant Harmony had charge of the deck and kept an eye on Lewis from the time he stepped on board the *Decatur* because he so clearly was "under the influence of liquor." Both Murray and Lewis, the marine corporal testified, were "more or less drunk." Boatswain Coghlan agreed; he was taking roll as the men returned from liberty and noted down their condition. At the ship, Lewis continued to insult Murray, calling him a damned son of a bitch and saying that he had licked Murray before and he would lick him again.

Then Harmony heard "a noise" and turned to see Murray with his clasped hand against Lewis's chest, near the heart. "Someone cried out, 'He is stabbed,'" and blood poured around the knife from a deep wound. Enraged,

Murray pulled the blade out and braced himself to stab Lewis again, but Sam Silk and others held him back. One of them grabbed the clasp knife and threw it overboard. Dragged away to be ironed, Murray bellowed that he had been beaten on shore, that he was a Virginian and would be goddamned if he would not have his revenge on Lewis. Assistant Surgeon Lane rushed to Lewis, who was lying in a pool of blood on the deck. Lewis's wound was severe: "dangerous and almost fatal," Lane testified. The sailor had been stabbed between the second and third ribs, with profuse internal hemorrhaging. In the *Herald,* Surgeon Lane reported that after stanching the external bleeding, he had suctioned nearly a "wash basin full of semi-coagulated blood" from Lewis's chest cavity. Lane saved Lewis's life.[51]

At Realejo, rejoined by the *Merrimac,* a general court-martial was convened on the *Decatur* to try Murray, who pled not guilty to premeditated assault with a deadly weapon. By then, he had been confined in irons for nearly two months, awaiting a time when enough officers could be brought together for his court-martial. Murray's statement to the court was prepared by his counsel, *Merrimac* Chaplain Charles Davis, but beneath the flowery language, one can hear the seaman's perspective in sober retrospect:

> May it please the court I am a poor frail man. My advantages have been few. I have no doubt on many occasions been betrayed into errors. . . . The charge preferred against me is simply that of "an assault of a petty officer with a deadly weapon." If the specification had not gone beyond the charge . . . I should not have hesitated to plead guilty . . . and should have contented myself with an attempt to show that the assault was one purely of self defense following a series of most wanton and unprovoked injuries. [But] where is the evidence of premeditation? The possession of a knife at the time was purely accidental. It was one of six which I had purchased that morning and which I was examining at the time. . . . I used the knife which I happened to have in my hands as the only means of defense against this infuriated madman, whom I had not strength to contest.

Murray was found guilty and sentenced to be held in irons until the *Decatur* put in at Mare Island; then he was to be turned over to civilian justice to be tried for attempted murder.[52]

On Sunday, November 27, 1858, at Realejo, Minister Lamar finally visited the ship. He met with Thatcher, and the commander passed along the dispatches that had been entrusted to him at Callao. As well, the *Decatur* was carrying a mysterious passenger—"a supernumerary"—Jacob Weckell. Perhaps Weckell was yet another wandering filibuster; perhaps he was just a friend of

Lamar's. On December 18, President Martinez traveled from Managua with the members of his cabinet to stay with Lamar at his home at Realejo. Martinez was welcomed aboard the flagship and the *Decatur* with all due ceremony: the Decaturs manned the yards, then beat to quarters for inspection and offered a twenty-one-gun salute to honor the Nicaraguan president.[53]

Commodore Long decided to delay the *Merrimac* at Realejo, awaiting action of the U.S. Congress on the amended Cass-Yrissari Treaty with Nicaragua, which would reopen the transit. Anticipating that the treaty would not be ratified, Long helpfully informed Toucey in December 1858 that "military operations in this region can only be favorably undertaken during the dry season," November through May. Additionally, Long recommended that, if a blockade of Nicaragua became necessary, a warship should be stationed at San Juan del Sur or Realejo but a steamer should also be assigned to patrol the Gulf of Fonseca. Communication was very slow, Long continued, and there was only one monthly commercial steamer out of Panama that stopped at Realejo. In fact, he had decided to send this note to Toucey via Panama on a British steamer, the *Vixen*. Long feared that he would not long command the squadron because his own health had broken; after a medical examination, the assembled surgeons recommended that he be sent home via the isthmus. "I should be afraid," wrote the fleet surgeon, "of his doubling Cape Horn." The *Merrimac* surgeon also reported to the chief of the Navy Bureau of Medicine and Surgery that a wave of "fever and influenza . . . invaded us upon our arrival" at Realejo.[54]

Lane combated the same epidemic on board the *Decatur* at Realejo but also traveled inland to Chinandega to perform a delicate operation on a woman suffering from a goiter. Forty years later, Lane reminisced about this operation, likely typical of a number of his "compassionate surgeries" on civilians:

This operation was performed on a woman in Chinandega, Nicaragua in 1859; and as aids were a German and an American physician, residents of that city. As it was thought possible that the woman might die during the operation, the priestly official with his tapers and other appanage in use there in the death ceremonial, stood near by to perform the last offices, should the knife render them necessary. The patio of the Spanish house, and the street in front, were crowded with curious spectators. . . . The operation was a very bloody one, and midway in the work, the bleeding was so profuse that one of the assistants was seized with panic, and begged that the work should cease there. These remonstrances were not heeded; the patient could not have run more risk from concluding the work than from leaving the half-enucleated tumor in her neck. By the careful ligation of vessels, and dissection of the growth from the parts to which it was attached, the work of removal was brought to a fortunate issue. The patient soon recovered, and was amply repaid for the risk of submitting to an operation which had rarely been done, risks here augmented through submitting to a knife which had been disciplined by but little experience.

A consummate medical observer and bold experimentalist, Surgeon Lane enjoyed himself so much on board the *Decatur* that he requested reassignment to the warship. He sent a letter to the head of his bureau on December 20, 1858, asking that, if the *Decatur* was continued in commission in the Pacific Squadron, he "beg[ged] leave to tender [his] services as her senior medical officer, if it be consistent with the usage of the service." Studying a wide variety of injuries and diseases on ship and shore, Lane was surely the happiest man on board.[55]

Though it was the dry season, Realejo's heat was unrelenting, and the water in the bay stood at eighty-seven degrees. The epidemic of influenza and fever was compounded by an outbreak of ophthalmia—shipboard eye—on board the *Decatur*. Complaining of infected eyes, Gunner Lilleston left the ship to "reside on shore for the benefit of his health." Purser Senac also left the ship "for his health"; he had been treated for cholera, chronic diarrhea, and fevers since entering duty on the *Decatur*. Perhaps both officers stayed with Lamar, at his residence. The *Decatur*'s sailors and marines continued to suffer a great deal of illness, reporting frequently to the ship's surgeons; an analysis of these medical records allows us to sketch the demography of the ship's crew in 1858 and compare it with the crew of 1854.[56]

One interesting change is that, while most foreign-born sailors who shipped in Boston in 1854 were from northern Europe and Canada, the 1858 muster included numerous sailors born in Italy, France, Jamaica, the West Indies, and Mahón—a more multinational crew, recruited in the Pacific West. Of the seamen on board the *Decatur* who reported sick to the surgeon in 1858, 63 percent were American-born, compared with less than 50 percent in 1854. In an even more dramatic reversal, in 1854, six of the ship's seven petty officers, the most experienced seamen on board ship, had been foreign-born sailors, but in 1858, only Captain of the Hold Robert Cammon and Captain of the Maintop William Fredericks were foreign born, from Ireland and Scotland respectively. The other petty officers, captains of the three tops and the forecastle, as well as the coxswain, were all born in the United States. The data suggest that an increasing percentage of the better-paid skilled seaman and petty officer positions went to American-born sailors. It is possible that, as the

U.S. Navy embraced steam in the late 1850s, experienced American sailors became concentrated on a decreasing number of warships under sail. Wherever they were born, man-of-war seamen had fewer options in the modernizing navy, and they constituted an enduring core of skill in a troubled crew on this sloop of war.[57]

At Realejo, with easy access to liquor, the *Decatur*'s litany of smuggling, brawling, and insolence began again. Two months earlier, men were first ironed to stanchions out on deck for days on end, an extension of the tricing to deck guns that Clitz had introduced to the *Decatur*. Perhaps this was an act of compassion because of the heat and poor ventilation on the berth deck. The only surviving bimensal (bimonthly) punishment record for the *Decatur* during the 1854-59 cruise is for November and December 1858, when the ship was in the harbor off Realejo. Prepared by Commander Thatcher to be reviewed and then forwarded by Commodore Long to the secretary of the navy, this document recorded only subjudicial punishments, which did not require the convening of a summary or general court-martial and were administered by the officer of the deck. The logbook also recorded subjudicial punishments; however, neither document is complete, as each noted punishments missing from the other. The following analysis merges the two.[58]

Of the thirty-one subjudicial punishments recorded during November and December 1858, eleven were for insolence or disrespect, six for violence, eight for drunkenness while on duty, five for neglect of duty, and one for mutinous language. Of the punishments, six were given to marines. Those punished included petty officers, such as the wardroom cook, the coxswain, the captain of the main top, and one of the quartermasters, not just marines and sailors. Two confinements were ordered by Lieutenant Joseph DeHaven, but First Lieutenant Clitz was the principal disciplinarian on board the *Decatur.* Clitz ordered landsman Charles Ellis confined twice, in the first case for disrespect to Surgeon Lane and in the second for fighting with Edward Fletcher in the wardroom; for the latter offense, the men were double-ironed daily for thirteen hours for four days. Later in the same two-month period, Fletcher was confined for theft. Coxswain James Dougherty and ordinary seaman John Williams ended up ironed for riotous conduct and drunkenness on duty; it is likely that they were fighting. Two marines, Peter Kennedy and H. B. Chamberlain, were found asleep at their posts on different nights, and each was double-ironed for nine hours. Edward Murphy was gagged and confined in double-irons because he had returned drunk and disorderly in the gig after rowing the president of Nicaragua to shore at Realejo. George Roe, ship's yeoman or clerk, was classed as a prisoner at large after having an open flame in the forepeak, risking fire or explosion and strictly forbidden on board ship. George Ensign, wardroom cook, was double-ironed twice for insubordination, first for two hours and then for nine hours.

Confinement while the ship was at sea was a miserable punishment. One of the men confined while the *Decatur* was en route from Callao to Realejo described it in his trial:

> I was in double irons under the forecastle, port side, the ship at sea, rolling heavily and the water rushing through the hawse holes, wetting me completely through, not being allowed a hammock or change of clothes and compelled to sleep on the wet deck. [Then] my feet irons were removed but I was still kept confined, removed from the forecastle to the berth deck, just abaft the ship's galley where the heat is almost insupportable. Upon a representation of my condition to Captain Thatcher, he, with great humanity, ordered a change in my condition for which I shall not cease to be grateful.

Confinement on deck exposed the prisoner to the elements but confinement belowdecks was stifling. Commodore Long, on reviewing *Decatur* summary courts-martial, moderated a sentence: John Murphy, convicted of insulting Lieutenant Harmony, was given a sentence of six months' confinement, on bread and water on alternate weeks, and to be dishonorably discharged at the end of his term of service. Long reduced Murphy's confinement to three months, in consideration of "the climate where the ship is at present employed."[59]

The *Decatur* returned to coastal patrol, detailed to prevent filibuster landings under Toucey's ambiguous orders. In December 1858, Walker mounted his third filibuster against Nicaragua in the schooner *Susan,* which sailed out of Mobile, Alabama, and ran aground off Honduras. Back in the United States after the failed filibuster, Walker prepared a fourth expedition, returning to the West to recruit. Reports reached the Pacific Squadron of an "illegal expedition from California, with the design of invading the Territory of Nicaragua" through the Estero Réal on the Gulf of Fonseca, and the Congress of Costa Rica met to discuss "the anticipated invasion of Walker." One of the most persistent rumors claimed that five hundred filibuster recruits were expected to steam south on the *Hermann* from San Francisco to Panama, there to be joined by Walker and his senior officers. The filibuster army would then head for the Gulf of Fonseca and enter Nicaragua from the north; these were Western men recruited to a Southern quest. A Democratic journal scolded Californians for their willingness to support "private military expeditions against Nicaragua and New Grenada," admitting that while these "States must be Americanized," this must not be done at the expense of forcing Costa Rica to close the Nicaragua transit, one of only two Central American "highways to California."[60]

Long ordered the *Decatur* to sail north to find a position from which to observe the entrance to the Gulf of Fonseca, to prevent any filibuster ship from entering the gulf and also to resist any Royal Navy effort to exercise the "right of search" against the *Hermann.* Chastened by the experiences of Davis and Paulding, Thatcher asked Commodore Long to clarify his responsibility and authority: if the *Decatur* should encounter the *Hermann,* what exactly should Thatcher do? Long inquired of Lamar and then of Toucey for "definite instruction" whether Thatcher was authorized to board and detain ships in which the filibusters arrived, and if they had already landed, whether he was authorized to send marines and sailors to shore "to oppose their progress and compel their withdrawal from the soil."[61]

President Buchanan had issued a recent proclamation concerning illegal expeditions, which continued to suggest an equivocal policy toward the filibusters in which their safety was of as much concern as prevention of their "illegal enterprises":

> for the purpose of saving American citizens who may have been honestly deluded into the belief that they are about to proceed to Nicaragua as peaceful emigrants, if any such there be, from the disastrous consequences to which they will be exposed, I . . . have thought it fit to issue this my proclamation in enjoining all officers of the Government, civil and military, . . . to be vigilant, ACTIVE and faithful in suppressing these illegal enterprises.

In reply to Long's request for specific instructions, Lamar simply provided the commodore with a copy of this proclamation, telling Long that "he had no other official information." In turn, Long seems to have asked his clerk to copy Buchanan's proclamation and sent it out to Commander Thatcher, by way of clarification of his duty. Long directed Thatcher to patrol the gulf and prevent the landing of any filibuster ship, and then leave in time to visit La Union, El Salvador, and return to Realejo by February 15, 1859. Like other navy commanders, Thatcher was left on his own to translate federal policy into on-the-spot practice concerning the filibusters. There is no record of what Thatcher thought of his situation or of the discussions he may have held with his officers. His surviving journals do not cover this period.[62]

Sailing north, the *Decatur* briefly put in to San Juan del Sur, Nicaragua. Embattled American consul John Priest visited the ship, and the *Decatur* carpenters set up a flagstaff at his home to distinguish the U.S. consulate. Additionally, three more "distressed Americans"—Hugh Rush, Richard Shay, and William Wells—begged for sanctuary and were brought on board the *Decatur* as passengers. They were almost certainly desperate survivors from Walker's filibuster army who were down on their luck. The ship then sailed north past Realejo and into the Gulf of Fonseca to guard against a filibuster landing.[63]

Thatcher reported to Long that it was impossible to find a place from which the gulf could be commanded where the *Decatur* could safely anchor. The *Decatur* "rolled very deep . . . in heavy ocean swells," and the gravelly bottom would not hold an anchor under the strong prevailing winds. Thatcher moved the ship to a sheltered spot where he had a clear view of the channel to La Union, but to survey the entire gulf entrance, Thatcher sent Lieutenant DeHaven ashore with "17 picked men" in the launch, to set up an observation post that would command the entrance to Estero Réal. DeHaven's squad was equipped with minié rifles, and the howitzer was mounted in the launch as a

FIG. 53 The Decatur *was assigned patrol duty to prevent the San Francisco steamer* Hermann *from entering the Gulf of Fonseca and landing filibusters for an invasion of Nicaragua from the north, down the Estero Réal, depicted here. Squier, Nicaragua, 1852. Courtesy University of Washington Libraries.*

mobile battery. Whatever his precise orders from Thatcher, DeHaven was prepared to threaten or attack the *Hermann* on the bay to prevent the steamer's landing or to pursue the filibuster passengers on shore or up the river.[64]

On January 27, 1859, the heavy launch headed to shore under sail. Determined to be comfortable, the group set up camp with tents and tarps and fortified themselves with beef, beans, bread, and six gallons of whiskey. Within days, Sailmaker Branson returned to the ship for more whiskey, camp stools, hammocks, a lantern, and boards to make a table. The men on the beach were divided into watches, scanning the bay night and day for incoming vessels.[65]

Two weeks later, DeHaven jotted a note to Thatcher on the conclusion of his shore duty: reporting that he had used "all vigilance to execute the duty assigned me but failed to discern any vessel with the exception of boats plying daily in these waters." In his report to Long, Thatcher noted that between the *Decatur* and DeHaven's outpost, they had been able to observe the entrance to the Gulf of Fonseca and the channels to the ports of Nicaragua, San Salvador, and Honduras but spotted nothing out of the ordinary; indeed, they saw no seagoing ships at all except the *Carlotta*, innocently inbound with a cargo of coffee beans. The *Decatur* then sailed up the Gulf of Fonseca to La Union in El Salvador.[66]

The *Decatur* was the first U.S. Navy ship to ever visit La Union, and it fired the first national salute ever received by the flag of El Salvador. Thatcher noted that the "compliment was gratefully received by all classes" and could not fail "to have a beneficial effect upon the interest of our country." The governor and military commander of La Union and their families were invited to visit the *Decatur*, observe a "display of Yankee arms," and enjoy a formal dinner. In turn, the ladies and gentlemen of La Union organized a dance for the *Decatur* officers as well as "a sumptuous breakfast," at which Captain Thatcher, inspired by the sight of the U.S. and Salvadoran flags hanging side by side, pledged: "As the two flags are thus intimately joined, so may the two republics they represent remain in everlasting unity." Thatcher concluded the visit with a graceful note to the governor, thanking him for his "kind attentions."[67]

Sailing south to San Juan del Sur, Thatcher found specific orders from Commodore Long to intercept the *Hermann* if it attempted to land an expeditionary force. Long was convinced that the steamer's arrival was imminent and that its passengers intended an "illegal expedition." The *New York Times* correspondent from La Union had written that anxious eyes observed the arrival of every steamer and schooner. The fact is, he wrote, "the name of Walker and *Filibustero* is a perfect night-mare to these people, and it will take a long while to remove the impression that all Americans are in some way connected with some filibustering movement."[68]

On March 2, 1859, while anchored in a cove near San Juan del Sur, the *Decatur* sent two small boats ashore for water. The warship was mistaken by Nicaraguan lookouts for a filibuster ship and the sailors in the ship's boats for the advance party of an invading force. The *Decatur* was a square-rigged man-of-war, flying the U.S. flag, and had been stationed in Central American waters for two years. The *Decatur* did not look in the least like a civilian schooner or steamer, and the lookouts' alarm suggests that the Nicaraguans were convinced that the U.S. Navy was acting in support of a Walker filibuster. Notified inland, President Martinez declared martial law, ordered that the three principal bridges along the transit route back to Lake Nicaragua be burned, and led out an army of three hundred men to prevent the feared filibuster landing from the *Decatur*. The *Decatur* carried no filibusters, but Martinez's defensive destruction dealt the final blow to the Nicaragua transit. American interests in Nicaragua were finally "annihilated, defunct, dead and buried," by the landing of a *Decatur* shore party to load drinking water.[69]

Two weeks later, Thatcher again reported to Long that the *Hermann* had not arrived at San Juan del Sur. Ordered back to Realejo, the *Decatur* rejoined the *Merrimac*. Commodore Long, accompanied by his suite of officers, came aboard to observe the *Decatur*'s exercises at small arms, great guns, and "all the minutiae of naval engagement." After lunch, they inspected the ship. During the afternoon, the *Decatur*'s crew demonstrated target practice from different distances and in timed drills. The flag officer and suite left the ship in the late afternoon. The *Decatur* was surveyed once again in the next few days, and some of its rigging and cables was condemned and replaced. The *New York Times* had reported months earlier that the *Decatur* would be put out of commission at Mare Island at the end of the cruise and dismissed the ship as "a small old-fashioned vessel . . . not of the class of ships required in modern service."[70]

On the night he received the survey, Long ordered Thatcher to prepare the *Decatur* for sea and to report to the commandant at Mare Island Navy Yard, "who has been instructed by the Department to put the *Decatur* out of commission." Once the *Decatur* was at Mare Island, Thatcher was to take command of the *Warren*. Those sailors and marines who wished would be discharged at San Francisco, and the remainder were to be transferred to the *Warren*, sail to Panama, disembark, and head east via the isthmus railroad. Captain Thatcher was instructed "to unbend [the *Warren*'s] sails and make her snug" for use as a storeship at Panama and remain on board, awaiting further orders.[71]

The *Decatur* transferred nearly all arms and ammunition to the sloops of war *Cyane* and *Vandalia*. On April 2, 1859, the last cruise of the *Decatur* began at Realejo, Nicaragua. Heading to San Francisco, the *Decatur* averaged six knots, sailing through schools of dolphins and flights of boobies, overarched at night by fields of stars, surrounded by the shimmering sea, and looking north to the aurora borealis. As always, at sea, there was a long blissful period of pure joy. Melville remembered looking down at his ship from the maintop on "a moonlight night . . . going large before the wind. . . . That immense area of snow-white canvas sliding along the sea was indeed a magnificent spectacle." Aged and leaky, the *Decatur* was a fine old warship under sail, flying north before the wind some days and tacking leisurely against the wind on others. The ship came into its own and so did the sailors: the angriest and sickest among them were at their best at sea, and it was a solemn thing to take a ship home for the last time.[72]

Then the Farallon Islands were in sight, marking the entrance to San Francisco Bay, and the pilot came on board. By May 24, 1859, the *Decatur* was anchored off Mare Island Navy Yard and then docked, ready for the end. The

men stripped the masts of sails and rigging and emptied the hold. The yards came down, then the masts. The old familiar ship came undone: workplace, prison, man-of-war, home. So much had happened on board. "The men," as the Logbook put it day after day, "are employed in stripping the ship. . . . [we] spliced the main brace."[73]

Thomas Murray, who had knifed Henry Lewis, was delivered to civil justice. Fifty men received honorable discharges from the *Decatur* in one day and left the ship, followed by another dozen over the next week who chose to be discharged in San Francisco. They either reenlisted on another man-of-war or left the navy behind to take their chances in the Pacific West. The *Decatur*'s remaining crewmen went on liberty, watch by watch, including old shipmates Louis Celagi, Thomas Bulger, Thomas Berry, and Henry Lewis, who were all sailing south to Panama with Thatcher on the *Warren*. Lewis, captain of the foretop, had recovered from his stab wound. Berry was the English seaman who had either pushed Lieutenant Stockton down or pulled him up to his unsteady feet; he had served his sentence. Bulger was the Irish marine kicked in the mouth by Robert Watson. Celagi was the Polish marine who could not understand what Augustus Furlong was preaching to his messmates but knew he did not like the sound of it.[74]

And there were two dozen "silent" men on board the *Decatur*, silent because we know little more about them than their names, ranks, and origins: such as Captain of the Afterguard William Brislin from Pennsylvania, Scottish seamen William Burnet and Robert Foreman, New York cook Adolph Duncan, Canadian seaman James Hughes, Swedish seaman John Lind, New York coxswain Thomas Moore, Prussian seaman Theodore Ohlsen, Maine seaman William Riley, and four John Smiths hailing from Florida, Pennsylvania, Maryland, and France. A few of them had seen it all, the entire cruise of the *Decatur* from Boston through the whole Pacific West: the terror of the strait, the siege of Seattle, the excitement of "Californio," the elephant in Nicaragua, and the dark descent of the last eighteen months.

The men who had stayed with the *Decatur* for the five-year cruise had lost their first officers—first Sterrett and then Gansevoort; then Middleton, Phelps, Dallas, Drake, Hughes, Dr. Jeffery, and Dr. Taylor—and gained a new set. They knew which three shipmates beat Sergeant Corbin within an inch of his life in San Francisco. They knew that Lieutenant Phelps and Surgeon Taylor made sketches and collected specimens. They knew Lieutenant Stockton was a drunk, Surgeon Ward was ill-tempered, and Lieutenant Clitz was a hard-horse disciplinarian. They had been struck silent by the awful misery of the filibuster survivors, and they had hunted fresh filibuster adventurers along the coast of Nicaragua. They had seen six men die throughout the cruise. Robert Hamilton fell from the yardarm during a storm in the Strait of Magellan. John Drew was shot to death while breaking into a house in Seattle to rape a young woman. Hans Carl died of catarrh in Seattle, and Charles Francis died of hepatitis there. Joseph Hombra died of pleurisy while the *Decatur* was at sea, cruising from Panama to Payta; a sixth, Pomeroy Edwards, died of a carbuncle—a massive skin infection—off Nicaragua. Carl, Francis, and Hombra died slowly, over the course of weeks while the medical team tried to keep them comfortable. Many more would have died during the *Decatur*'s cruise, but they were weeded out: surveyed, condemned, and sent ashore.[75]

Some *Decatur* sailors who made it all the way through the five-year cruise elected to remain in the Pacific West rather than return to the eastern seaboard. They had not deserted for western opportunities, but they were eager to take their pay and try their luck. Robert Cammon was born in Ireland and sailed the whole commission; he was captain of the hold when he left the *Decatur* in San Francisco. He was never punished and seldom ill—once he reported with fever, another time with hemorrhoids. He did his job and he stayed in the West.

William Brown, an ordinary seaman from Boston, made it all the way; he had been busted in rating, beginning the cruise as a seaman at forty and ending it as an ordinary seaman at forty-four. He had reenlisted with Sam Silk at San Francisco back in 1856, eager for the bonus. He was punished for a half-hearted "desertion" attempt and for a few incidents of drunk-and-disorderly. Brown had been sick quite a bit—treated nine times by surgeons on board the *Decatur* for a workplace injury (a badly cut finger) and also for the diarrhea and fever typical of the ship during its Central American duties. He, too, asked to be discharged in San Francisco.

William Fredericks, captain of the mizzen top, was from Scotland and in his late thirties, and he also made it all the way through and managed to earn an honorable discharge. A brawler and a boozer, Fredericks had been in plenty of trouble over the years. He suffered delirium tremens in Seattle right before the battle and had passed out on the beach at Panama, contracting fever. Clitz punished him severely in November 1858, ironing him to the stanchions for four days, thirteen hours each day. Fredericks was prone to fever and was treated for it throughout 1857 and 1858, and he had suffered a dislocation on the cruise to Callao. But as a leader of the topmen, he was a member of the shipboard aristocracy of skill and experience. He asked to be discharged at San Francisco.

Augustus Furlong, ordinary seaman, gave his birthplace at different times as North Carolina and Boston; his name suggests a German heritage. He was a boy of twenty in 1856, already an ordinary seaman; he had grown up on board sailing ships. In 1856, Furlong was diagnosed with primary syphilis; by 1857, the surgeons were treating his symptoms of secondary syphilis. He battled through Panama fever with everyone else. He was the sea lawyer who argued to an admiring circle that his mates should not be double-ironed. He, too, was discharged in San Francisco.

New Yorker Charles Cloyd was thirty-two when he was honorably discharged in California. Like Sam Silk, he had joined the ship in January 1854 when the *Decatur* was first sent out of Boston in a snowstorm to hunt for survivors of a disabled steamship. Cloyd was one of the quartermasters, and a steady, quiet sailor, seldom seen by the surgeons. He was a friend of Silk's, and he was to have been one of the witnesses against Lieutenant Stockton at his 1858 general court-martial for drunkenness on duty.

When Sam Silk left the *Decatur*, he was rated boatswain's mate. Early in the cruise, he claimed to be born in New York, but after 1856, Silk usually gave his birthplace as Ireland. In their reminiscences, Phelps and Taylor celebrated Silk for his brogue, sea lore, and wit; he was a genuine old salt. As Melville put it, he was one of the fellows "who spin interminable yarns . . . who officers never pretend to damn . . . that it does your soul good to look at. . . . grim sea grenadiers." He almost certainly explained to Taylor that "them catamarans" sailed right in the wind's eye, and the "picalilly went up the spout," and he recognized Madame Damnable in Seattle from her hell-raising days in Baltimore. Silk reenlisted in San Francisco in 1856 to qualify for Dobbin's bonus. Honorably discharged at Realejo, Nicaragua, in 1859, at his request, the 1860 census found Silk already back East, at the Naval Asylum in Philadelphia, for "the worn-out veterans of the Navy." He declared to the enumerator that he was fifty-three, that he had been born in Ireland, and that he could read and write. Silk lived out the rest of his days an Atlantic man.[76]

It is important to remember these enlisted men who worked and fought the ship, whose lives on shore were so hard that life on board a man-of-war looked good to them. They are almost beyond our grasp, so that one Irish seaman seems much like another, one drunkard much like another, one offender much like another. And yet, of course, each man had a unique past and future. They were individuals in an organization that turned the ship into a dynamic machine of great and deadly beauty, almost independent of the land, tracing pathways through the waves. Many enlisted men regarded themselves as members of a group distinct from the officers and tried to protect one another. They had clear ideas about what was fair and what was cruel. They were not slaves, they said; they were free men. Many of them were proud of their skills and proud of their home, whether they hailed from Ireland or Virginia, from Massachusetts or Denmark. Most of these men were strong and tough; some of them were brawling brutes. Most of them drank too much; some were drunks. None of them were choirboys, and many turned every liberty into a violent spree. Some of them were thieves who stole from their shipmates; some had long-standing quarrels with one another. Some of them were married, with wives far away; many of them paid prostitutes for sex in liberty ports, and many became infected with venereal disease, infecting their future partners in turn. Many deserted: some became "pioneers" in Chile, Hawaii, or Washington Territory; others raced for the golden opportunities of "Californio"; and others joined Walker's filibuster navy. They all came together on the deck of the *Decatur* in the West, their lives intersecting there for a time and then moving on.

At the very end, there were two weeks of uneventful watches on board the nearly empty ship. The *Decatur* was a quiet place in a busy harbor, echoing with twenty years of man-of-war life. And then the remaining sailors were released—they walked away from the *Decatur*, heading for the *Warren* or heading into the West. On June 20, 1859, the *Decatur*'s flag and pennant were hauled down; Boatswain Jasper Coghlan wrote, "At 2 p.m., put this ship out of commission," and signed the final entry in the *Decatur*'s Logbook. The *San Francisco Times* doubted that "this venerable craft will ever leave California again." Across the bay, the *Saginaw* was on the ways, the first U.S. Navy warship constructed at Mare Island Navy Yard, a side-wheel steamer built "entirely of California wood."[77]

In the final two years of the *Decatur*'s commission, 1857-59, the ship endured its most difficult duty, at anchor off Panama much of the time, deprived of a real mission and descending into illness and disorder. Finally, the ship participated in a disastrous comedy of errors, pursuing filibuster steamers under ambiguous orders and then itself mistaken for a filibuster ship, causing the decisive destruction of the Pacific-side bridges of the Nicaragua transit. Back in the States, the nationalist impulse that had powered Young America initiatives in the Pacific West died, consumed by sectional controversy. The misguided hope that outward aggression could somehow heal inner conflict failed in Nicaragua, and the nation's knives turned inward as events hastened toward the vortex during the *Decatur*'s Central American commission. The Kansas-Nebraska Act, an 1854 compromise between incompatible principles, unfolded over the years in bitter bloodshed. The U.S. Supreme Court handed down the 1857 Dred Scott decision, which effectively put an end to free soil under the American flag. In 1858 and 1859, Southern extremists vowed that their states would leave the union if a Republican were elected to the presidency in 1860. At the Naval Academy, a Southern midshipman offhandedly remarked to an acquaintance that James Buchanan would be the last president of the United States, in calm anticipation of the secession of the South. On distant Puget Sound, Washington territorial governor Richard Gholson, a Buchanan appointee, took an extended leave of absence to return home to Kentucky and agitate for secession, then resigned his office in February 1861, "unwilling even for a day to hold office under a (so-called) 'Republican' president." Events had hastened as the nation and the navy fell apart.[78]

9

The Civil War and Beyond

I respectfully resign the position which I hold in the Navy of the United States. No official act of my life has ever been performed with as much pain, but believing it due to myself and to the service, it must be done, though it removes me from association of a most happy character and from many of my most cherished friends.—RICHARD JEFFERY, Surgeon, *Decatur*, 1853–57

My sympathies are with the Southerners . . . I still look upon [South Carolina] as my home and shall never feel elsewhere other than as a stranger [but] I hold that in times of revolution an officer bound by his oath is not at liberty to throw off his allegiance. . . . He may resign, but he cannot be held free from disloyalty. . . . Such I consider to be the delicate nature of the obligations due by naval and military officers to the government.—EDWARD MIDDLETON, First Lieutenant, *Decatur*, 1854–57

The Civil War reinvented the U.S. Navy. Between 1861 and 1865, annual naval expenditures grew from $12 million to $123 million, and the number of enlisted men increased from just over 7,000 to more than 50,000, and officers from 1,300 to nearly 7,000. Journalists pointed out that control of the military had passed to Young America—the Civil War drove the Fogies into silence or retirement. The number of warships climbed more than tenfold, from sixty-one to nearly seven hundred—

and Alfred Mahan carefully noted that the prewar figure included three dozen "worthless scarecrows," sailing ships like the decommissioned *Decatur.* In 1861, Congress established a retired list to which an officer automatically passed at age sixty-two. In 1862, the navy created the ranks of ensign between midshipman and master and of lieutenant commander between lieutenant and commander and of commodore and rear admiral above that of captain. By the end of the war, a naval examining board reviewed each officer's promotion before it was made, on the basis of merit. And in 1862, the "spirit ration in the Navy of the United States . . . forever cease[d]," and grog came to an end. The Old Navy slipped into the past.[1]

Management of these dramatic changes fell to President Abraham Lincoln's new secretary of the navy. Gideon Welles was a veteran of the navy's Bureau of Provisions and Clothing, and made no pretense to a technical or strategic understanding of a fighting navy. But he brought intelligence and energy to the task of growing the navy quickly in a nation at war. When Welles took over the office from Isaac Toucey in March 1861, he found that the secretary "had failed to place the Navy in a posture of defense," as though there were no unfolding civil war. Pensacola Navy Yard had been taken by Confederate forces without a shot fired, and it was feared that the navy yard at Norfolk would go the same route.[2]

In 1857, the steam frigate *Merrimac* was the brand-new flagship of the Pacific Squadron, accompanying the *Decatur* to Callao and Realejo while squadron commodore John Long worried about the debility of the sloop of war's officers and crew. Three years later, the *Merrimac* was among the ships anchored at Norfolk when Welles ordered the yard's commandant to "defend at any hazard, repelling by force, if necessary, any and all attempts to seize . . . the vessels and stores under your charge." But when the attack came, the yard's defense was bungled, and the commandant gave orders to burn the *Merrimac* rather than lose the ship to the enemy. However, the Confederates converted the burned-out hull into the ironclad *Virginia*, one of the greatest weapons of the Confederate States Navy. Eventually, the *Virginia* fought the ironclad *Monitor* in a battle that would involve the *Decatur*'s plucked captain, Isaac Sterrett, and his former lieutenant, George Morris, who had walked the beach at Seattle draped in weapons and wrapped in a poncho—they would be enemies.[3]

In March 1863, the *Decatur* came to life again, outfitted as a floating battery with "several 68-pounders and some long 32-pounders" to defend San Francisco Harbor as the Civil War spread into the Pacific West. During the war, California experienced considerable unrest: the state was a Democratic stronghold, and nearly all its elected officials had been born in the Old South. There were rumors that thirty thousand Confederate sympathizers planned to take California out of the Union and, with other western states and territories, form a Pacific Republic. The Mare Island Navy Yard magazine was a magnificent prize of war, and the yard was rife with rumors that conspirators planned to seize or blow up the stores of ammunition. Every officer and employee at Mare Island and every officer whose ship called at the yard was required to take a loyalty oath to the Union. Throughout the war, San Franciscans were worried (or hopeful) that a Confederate privateer would intercept the gold steamers or that a Confederate warship would slip into the bay and open fire on the city.[4]

The Civil War recommissioned the *Decatur* and also offered work to the ship's former crew members. Among the *Decatur* warrant officers, Gunner Robert Stocking, who had been dismissed as a drunkard in San Francisco in late 1855, found a new life working at the Portsmouth Navy Yard during the Civil War, alongside *Decatur* sailmaker Augustus Warren. Antebellum seamen, ordinary seamen, and landsmen composed the "small but influential number of lifelong sailors" in the Civil War navy who knew the ropes and lore and set the rowdy shipboard tone. Currently, it is difficult to research enlisted sailors during the Civil War except for African American sailors and those from certain states. For instance, familiar *Decatur* men who enlisted from Massachusetts in the Civil War navy included James Daily, Augustus Furlong, Archibald Sprague, George Sargeant, and Albert Towle, whose ranks on the *Decatur* had ranged from ship's boy to boatswain's mate. Henry Nobrega, *Decatur* landsman, turned up in the crew of the flagship *Niagara*, writing an 1862 letter in Portuguese to his aunt in New York City, inquiring for any "news from Madeira." Charles Cloyd, Henry Cogswell, Adolph Duncan, William Keith, Martin Winter, and other Decaturs served in the U.S. Navy from New York. For the *Decatur* African American sailors, Civil War service diminished rather than enhanced their status: Dennis Sycamore served on the *Decatur* as a landsman; nearly ten years later, he remained a landsman on the *Fahkee*. Robert Shorter, who had sailed the squadron voyage through, left the *Decatur* classified as a seaman—an aristocrat of skill—and sailed during the first years of the Civil War on the *Brandywine* as a black petty officer, a sailmaker's mate. However, by 1865, at fifty years of age, he was rated only a laborer on board the steamer *Fahkee*. Many enlisted men, white or black, whose antebellum naval experience was in warships under sail did not advance in the ironclad, steam-driven Civil War navy; however, their officers did.[5]

Alfred Thayer Mahan observed that Southern officers before the war held stronger convictions about slavery and states' rights than their Northern colleagues. Quoting Stephen Decatur's toast to his country, right or wrong, Mahan judged it "bad morality but a powerful force" as the meaning of "country" shifted radically for military men. After Lincoln's election, many Southern officers in the U.S. Navy resigned their commissions and followed their states out of the Union and into the emerging Confederate States of America. Between November 12, 1860, and January 24, 1861, forty-seven naval officers from South Carolina, Florida, Georgia, Alabama, and Mississippi resigned. Secretary Toucey accepted their decisions and was censured by the House of Representatives for his "grave error" in "accepting without delay or inquiry the resignation of officers of the Navy who were in arms against the government." After Gideon Welles took the secretary's chair, resigning officers were regarded as deserters and their names stricken from the roles—in the end, about 350 U.S. Navy officers resigned to go South.[6]

Civil War service allowed some of the *Decatur*'s officers to reinvent themselves in the Confederate navy. The *Decatur*'s Confederate officers form an interesting group: troubled, honorable, and bitter men who gained a second chance. Cantankerous Surgeon John Ward, who had charged Lieutenant Edward Stockton with drunkenness and brought Purser Felix Senac before a court of inquiry, resigned to join the Confederate navy. So did Surgeon Richard Jeffery, who had come through the Strait of Magellan, gathered celery to combat the hands' scurvy, and whose crab shells had smashed on the *Decatur*'s deck. It was Jeffery who wrote the resignation cited at the beginning of this chapter from on board the *Saratoga* off the west coast of Africa, dated July 12, 1861. By that late date, Welles simply struck his name from the rolls.[7]

Four other *Decatur* officers joined the Confederate navy, three of whom had been disciplined in the U.S. Navy either by court-martial or by the Efficiency Board. The sickly lieutenant Van Rensselaer Morgan was invalided off the *Decatur* and then furloughed for ill health by the Plucking Board. The drunken lieutenant Edward C. Stockton was court-martialed, pled guilty to all charges, and was dropped from the navy. Felix Senac, the *Decatur*'s second purser, the accountant who spoke with a heavy accent, was always very much a foreigner and had been accused by Surgeon Ward of insolence. And Isaac Sears Sterrett, the *Decatur*'s first captain—the master seaman—was plucked from his ship in Seattle's Elliott Bay.

The Plucking Board furloughed Sterrett for debts, drinking, and perhaps his decision to take the *Decatur* on a junket through the Strait of Magellan. Reinstated to the active list as a captain, Sterrett was given no duty but remained in limbo "awaiting orders," never assigned another ship. He resigned his commission on April 23, 1861, to join the Confederate navy in a typically laconic note: "I respectfully resign my commission as captain in the U.S. Navy." Perhaps embittered, Sterrett chose to devote his life to another service, and so did his son James, known to his father and on board the *Decatur* as "Jimmie." The elder Sterrett was assigned to the Richmond station, Confederate States Navy. He commanded the artillery batteries at Camp Pickens at Manassas on July 21, 1861, during the first battle of the Civil War, and he commanded Company C, first Virginia Artillery Regiment, in the fall of that year.[8]

In March 1862, the CSS *Virginia* (the old *Merrimac*) quickly sank two U.S. Navy ships in Chesapeake Bay, routed two more, and drove a fifth aground, fighting the ironclad *Monitor* to a draw. But by May, it was a different story: the river batteries were abandoned, the Confederate infantry was ordered to fall back to Petersburg, and Norfolk was conceded to the Union. Josiah Tatnall, formerly the unhappy captain of William Mervine's Pacific Squadron flagship *Independence*, was in command of the *Virginia*, Norfolk's last Confederate naval defense. On May 9, 1862, old messmates Tatnall, Sterrett, and George Hollins (who had "leveled Greytown") met on board the *Virginia* to devise a plan against the advancing U.S. Navy force. Tatnall, after consulting with river pilots in Sterrett's hearing, planned to lighten the *Virginia* and cautiously steam up the James River. But even lightened, the ship sailed too deep, and Tatnall decided to ground and set fire to the *Virginia*, "to destroy the ship to prevent her falling into the hands of the enemy." Isaac Sterrett may have participated in the ensuing court of inquiry that condemned Tatnall or the court martial that acquitted him. However, family matters claimed Sterrett's attention that summer.[9]

Private James Sterrett had joined the Norfolk Light Artillery Blues—the Norfolk Blues. He almost certainly was still part of the unit when the Blues fought the Sewell's Point Battery at Hampton Roads, Virginia, in March and April 1862, but he died of typhoid fever in June. Sterrett was only a boy when he accompanied his father on the *Decatur* through the Strait of Magellan, to Indian war on Puget Sound, and through the Plucking Board disgrace. The death of "my dear Jimmie" haunted his father. The diary of Sterrett's last years is tinged with regret for his son and fears for his family's safety. In 1863, his wife, Julia Sterrett, was arrested in Baltimore "for disloyalty" and eventually expelled to "her friends in the South." Their older son, Samuel Sterrett, was imprisoned as a Confederate spy at Fort Warren, in Boston Harbor. Sterrett remained close with Franklin Buchanan, Josiah Tatnall, Frederick Chatard, George Hollins, Samuel Barron, William McBlair, and Richard Jeffery—all sea officers who had taken the same long voyage he had, and who surely knew that the Confederacy would lose the war. Sterrett died a commodore in the Confederate States Navy, at Charlottesville, Virginia, on August 31, 1864.[10]

Kentuckian Van Rensselaer Morgan was assigned to the *Decatur* in 1853 as first lieutenant; at Santa Cruz, he directed the marines to form up, load their weapons, and aim them at the mutineers. Morgan was sick with chronic bronchitis and left the ship at Rio de Janeiro in 1854. The Plucking Board members reviewed Morgan's frequent detachments from duty for reasons of health, and Samuel Francis Du Pont's notes summarized their discussions: "health very bad," "not only indisposed in body but in mind," "a gentleman of good character . . . and a careful navigator, but his health has broken down," and so on. The board voted unanimously to remove Morgan from the active list and place him on furlough. However, Morgan was restored by the 1857 courts of inquiry: his witnesses were Isaac Sterrett, Thomas Phelps, Francis Dallas, George Morris, and John Jones—many of the *Decatur* officers with whom he had sailed to Rio, though neither of the ship's surgeons. Restored to the active list, Morgan languished without orders, as Sterrett did. On June 28, 1861, writing from Warrenton, Virginia, he resigned his commission in an insolent, boldly scrawled note:

> To His Excellency Abraham Lincoln, President of the United States
> I hereby resign my commission as a lieutenant in the Navy of the "United States."

Suddenly, in the Confederate States Navy, Morgan was healthy and filled with energy; he became something of a hero. Morgan was given command of the privateer CSS *Winslow*, which took at least five Union merchant ships as prizes, and he commanded the Confederate receiving ship *United States* as well as the PeeDee Navy Yard in South Carolina. Captured, Morgan was paroled in 1865. Van Rensselaer Morgan, the sickly lieutenant, found his health and hit his stride as an officer in the Confederate navy.[11]

Edward Cantey Stockton was commissioned a lieutenant in 1857, just before joining the *Decatur*. Cashiered for chronic drunkenness at Panama in June 1858, he returned to South Carolina. At secession, Stockton had no naval commission to resign, but he, too, became a new man. In the South Carolina navy, Stockton commanded the gunboat *Lady Davis,* which captured the Confederacy's first prize, on March 19, 1861. Stockton's Confederate service was truly exceptional: he served successively in the South Carolina navy, Confederate States Marine Corps, 21st South Carolina Volunteers, and then in April 1862, Stockton joined the Confederate States Navy. The drunken lieutenant redeemed himself as a martial man.[12]

Purser Felix Senac never really fit in on the *Decatur*. Originally a Spanish subject, of French descent, he seemed foreign and exotic. The Senac family lived in Pensacola and Key West, as did the Mallory family. Stephen R. Mallory had married Felix Senac's cousin, and Mallory later was elected a U.S. senator from Florida, serving as longtime chairman of the Naval Affairs Committee. Mallory secured Senac his purser's warrant, and Senac's first ship was the *Decatur*, in March 1857, at Panama. When Senac decided to resign his commission in the U.S. Navy, he was stationed on the *Susquehanna*, at Naples, Italy. On April 21, 1861, he wrote his letter of resignation:

> I have the honor to request that I may be permitted to return to the United States for the purpose of settling my accounts with a view to resigning my commission as paymaster in the Navy. Should this request not be acceded to, I hereby tender my resignation to the Department and invoke its speedy action to have me relieved from duty on this ship.

After secession, Stephen Mallory became the Confederacy's secretary of the navy, and he awarded Senac a commission in the Confederate States Navy. Senac became more than just a simple ship's accountant; he served as one of three paymasters and deal makers for the Confederacy in Europe. Early in the war, in New Orleans, Senac was paymaster for construction of the Confederate ironclad *Mississippi*. When David Farragut's fleet advanced on New Orleans, the *Mississippi* was burned on April 19, 1862, to prevent it from falling into Union hands. Afterward, the Confederate navy turned to European shipbuilders, and agents were needed to finesse European neutrality and manage the intricate finances of the Confederacy abroad, applying the proceeds of blockade-run cotton, turpentine, and tobacco.[13]

In June 1863, the Senac family slipped through the Yankee blockade on a full tide and a moonless night, bound for Bermuda to board a British merchantman for Liverpool. In England, Confederate hopes for new ships were dashed time and again. The British government refused to permit the launching of a number of steamers said to be merchant ships but clearly pierced for guns. Confederate shipbuilding contracts were then let in France, and Senac was assigned to duty in Paris. The paymaster's biographer admitted "it is not clear exactly what Senac did in Paris," but Confederate Secretary of the Navy Mallory wrote of Senac: "Should you stand in need of reliable assistance in your efforts in France, you may . . . derive it from Paymaster Senac of the Navy, who has been ordered to Liverpool to pay officers, etc. He speaks French with purity and elegance, Spanish also, possesses fine business capacity and is a gentleman of ripe judgment and rare merit." It is likely that Senac managed the outfitting of Confederate ships built or repaired in France; he was clearly responsible for French contracts for beef, revolvers, and clothing. In Paris, Senac became acquainted with Henry Hotze, the Swiss-born, Alabama-bred publisher of the *Index*, the principal Confederate newspaper in Europe. In February 1865, as the Confederacy collapsed, Senac was one of those left in Europe to settle accounts. Senac paid off the crew of the CSS *Shenandoah*, which had finally steamed into Liverpool in November 1865, after wreaking havoc on American whalers in the far North Pacific. Then Hotze and Senac became involved with a group of émigré Confederate families who proposed a new settlement in Brazil or Honduras. But Senac did not live to see the fili-buster dream; he died in 1866, and his daughter Ruby Senac spurned former *Decatur* lieutenant Joseph DeHaven to marry Henry Hotze in Paris.[14]

Some officers who had served on the *Decatur* during the Pacific Squadron cruise followed their loyalties into the Confederacy; others fought for the U.S. Navy throughout the war. Only one *Decatur* officer remained in the Pacific West. The scholarly Dr. Levi Cooper Lane had tended the *Decatur* during its fevered descent, 1857–59, coping with the invalid filibusters, the heat and humidity, the fevers, syphilis, wounds, and dysentery. In 1859 Lane resigned from the navy to join his uncle Elias Cooper in fulfilling their dream of estab-lishing a medical school in California. After leaving the *Decatur*, Lane trav-eled to Europe to study vivisection and chemistry and then returned to San Francisco to found Cooper Medical College, which eventually became the Stanford University School of Medicine.[15]

The Civil War offered many *Decatur* commissioned officers the opportunity to distinguish their careers in the U.S. Navy. The *Decatur's* last command-ing officer, Henry Knox Thatcher, was still ranked a lieutenant in 1854—at forty-eight, he was the archetypal gray-haired lieutenant. However, in 1855, he was promoted to commander in the wave of Plucking Board retirements and joined the *Decatur* in 1857. Thatcher rode inland with William Carey Jones to San José, and he brought the filibuster invalids to Panama: he com-manded the ship during its troubled final commission. During the Civil War, he was given command of the steam frigate *Colorado* in the North Atlantic Blockading Squadron. Thatcher's superior, Rear Admiral David Porter, wrote of Thatcher's wartime service:

First and foremost in the list of commodores is H. K. Thatcher. Full of honest zeal and patriotism, his vessel [the *Colorado*] was always ready for action and when he did go into it, his ship was handled with admirable skill. No vessel in the squadron was as much cut up as the Colorado. . . . I believe Commodore Thatcher would have fought his ship until she went to the bottom[. He] went into the fight with full determination to conquer or die. There is no reward too great for this gallant officer; he has shown the kind of ability naval leaders should possess, a love of fighting and an invincible courage.

In 1865, Rear Admiral Thatcher was ordered to the Gulf of Mexico, succeeding David Farragut in command of the West Gulf Squadron. When Mobile surrendered to Union forces, Thatcher pursued the Confederate fleet up the Tombigbee River until their surrender. He helped coordinate the Union campaign against Texas and gained control of Galveston Harbor, manning the forts with sailors until federal troops arrived. After the war, Thatcher returned to the Pacific to command the brand-new North Pacific Squadron.[16]

Four *Decatur* lieutenants—George Morris, Joseph DeHaven, John Clitz, and Edward Middleton—achieved some measure of renown during the Civil War in their U.S. Navy service. Dubbed a "perfect brigand in appearance" by his diarist friend Philip Johnson during the siege of Seattle, Morris was appointed a lieutenant in 1855, one of the jackass promotions. Seven years later, Lieutenant Morris commanded the sloop of war *Cumberland* during the Battle of Hampton Roads, facing the ironclad steamer *Virginia* built on the *Merrimac*'s hull. Morris earned praise for his brave command when the *Virginia* rammed and sank the *Cumberland* in a fierce, hopeless engagement, "the farewell salute of the wooden navy," when naval warfare changed forever.[17]

Joseph DeHaven also gained his lieutenancy in the Plucking Board promotion wave and was assigned to the *Decatur*, joining the ship in March 1857 at Panama. Purser Felix Senac's biographer wrote that Senac and DeHaven became close friends during that awful commission, and DeHaven commanded the two-week vigil on shore in the Gulf of Fonseca, camping out with whiskey and salt pork, watching for filibuster steamers. During the Civil War, DeHaven served with modest distinction in the North Atlantic Blockading Squadron. His wife died in childbirth in March 1863, and DeHaven traveled to Europe after the war to become an unsuccessful suitor for Felix Senac's daughter during the Confederate family's exile.[18]

John M. B. Clitz was the *Decatur*'s executive officer from 1857 through the ship's decommissioning; he brought a tougher style of discipline to the troubled ship. After the *Decatur*, Clitz returned to active service during the Civil War, commanding a series of steamers in the North Atlantic Blockading Squadron. Promoted to captain in 1866 and commodore in 1872, Rear Admiral Clitz took command of the U.S. naval forces in Asia in 1880 and retired in

FIG. 55 On March 8, 1862,
the ironclad steam frigate
CSS Virginia, built on
the burned-out hull of the
Pacific Squadron flagship
Merrimac, sank the sailing
frigate USS Cumberland
in the last stand of the Old
Navy. This engraving is from
Admiral David Dixon Porter's
definitive Naval History of
the Civil War, published in
1886. Courtesy University of
Washington Libraries.

1884. Peter Karsten quotes a contemporary source that Clitz "contracted habits of intemperance and dissipation," and he died in 1897 at St. Elizabeth's Asylum, Washington, DC, a hospital for the insane in the military.[19]

Like Morgan and Clitz, Edward Middleton served on the *Decatur* as first lieutenant and executive officer. Middleton assumed command in 1856 when Guert Gansevoort was suspended by David Farragut for public drunkenness at Mare Island. Middleton left the *Decatur* in 1857, at Panama. Born in Charleston, South Carolina, Middleton was descended from a distinguished Southern family: his grandfather had signed the Declaration of Independence, and his father served as governor of South Carolina and U.S. minister to Russia. Edward Middleton was raised on Middleton Place plantation—its gardens covered sixty acres and were tended by dozens of black slaves. Middleton's brother was one of the signers of South Carolina's Ordinance of Secession, in December 1860. However, Edward Middleton chose to remain in the U.S. Navy, as he explained in his letter that heads this chapter. He cast his lot with the Union, as did fellow Southerner David Farragut; in remaining loyal, both men closed the door on their youth. During the Civil War, Middleton was assigned distant duty in the Pacific West, commanding the sloop of war

St. Mary's off the coast of Panama. Middleton Place was burned to the ground on February 22, 1865, by a detachment of the 56th New York Volunteer Regiment. After the war, Middleton was appointed commandant of Mare Island in San Francisco while the old *Decatur* was still at anchor in the bay. Promoted to commodore, Middleton took command of the Pensacola Navy Yard in 1870 and remained at that post until his retirement.[20]

And finally, there were four especially intriguing men who served together on the *Decatur* at Seattle—Guert Gansevoort, John Taylor, Francis Dallas, and Thomas Phelps—who lived through the Civil War and beyond. The *Decatur's* second commander in the Pacific Squadron, Guert Gansevoort, was born to a prominent family in Albany, New York. His mother was soon widowed and he went to sea as a boy of eleven, midshipman on the venerable frigate *Constitution*; he grew up in the navy. In 1842, Lieutenant Gansevoort was ordered to the brig *Somers* for a training cruise, one of only two commissioned officers on board. At sea, one of the young midshipmen was accused of masterminding an improbable mutiny: to corrupt the crew, kill the officers, and turn the ship to piracy. Captain Alexander Slidell Mackenzie ordered Gansevoort to convene a council of the warrant officers to determine whether a mutiny was in the making and what should be done with the ringleaders. When the ship returned to New York, the son of the secretary of war and two other crewmembers had been hung and buried at sea; nine boys lay in double-irons. James Fenimore Cooper, America's foremost writer of naval history and sea stories, published a lengthy attack on Mackenzie that also excoriated Gansevoort for complicity in "hanging three Americans without a trial." Though Gansevoort remained loyal to his captain throughout the court of inquiry and court-martial, he confessed privately that the evidence had not been persuasive and that Mackenzie had insisted the "mutineers" be convicted. The *Somers* tragedy shadowed Gansevoort throughout his life—"devastated by guilt, pride and the exhausting power of self-justification."[21]

After the *Somers*, Gansevoort was assigned to a series of commands, including the *John Adams* during the Mexican War. His first cousin Herman Melville published the autobiographical novels *Omoo* and *Typee,* which mirrored America's growing fascination with Pacific adventure, but Melville's *White-Jacket* infuriated the naval establishment with its "studied injustice to the American Navy." Meanwhile, Gansevoort was assigned to duty on the Pacific Squadron flagship *Independence* as first lieutenant. Reviewed by the Plucking Board, Gansevoort was left in place on the seniority list, poised to replace Isaac Sterrett as captain of the *Decatur.* When he took command, leading the *Decatur* against the Indian uprising in Seattle was his big chance to put the

Somers behind him for good. But Gansevoort was suspended in San Francisco for public drunkenness and left without a ship for six years.[22]

The Civil War finally brought him orders to command the brand-new war steamer *Adirondack*, one more chance for success as "the hero of a brilliant victory," as cousin Melville put it. Gansevoort had to fight for the *Adirondack;* a rival wrote to an influential friend that Gansevoort "has had his commander's command—that is the sloop-of-war *Decatur* in the Pacific until he had [it] taken away from him on account of habitual drunkenness, and his habits are not over and above steady and correct now." Nevertheless, Gansevoort was appointed to the *Adirondack* and pursued Confederate commander Raphael Semmes on a monthlong chase until the *Adirondack* struck hard on a reef in the Bahamas. The "ship bilged with her back broken," and the steam frigate was a total loss. Gansevoort blamed Lieutenant James Parker, who admitted, heartsick, to a navigational error. After a court of inquiry and a general court-martial, Gansevoort was cleared of all charges, but Secretary Welles commented unfavorably on the decision, pointing out that it sanctioned the loss of a ship-of-war by negligent navigation, "and yet the commanding officer be relieved of all responsibility." A commander expects to receive his full share of credit for a well-managed or well-fought ship, wrote Welles, and "it is therefore not unjust to hold him to account for the consequences of negligence . . . at a time and in a sea where unusual care and vigilance were imperatively demanded."[23]

After a time, Gansevoort was given command of a harbor defense ship at Hampton Roads, Virginia, but he never commanded a cruising ship again. In the last years of his life, an acquaintance called him "a sad wreck of his former self." Promoted to commodore, he died in 1868, of "congestion of the brain." Eight years later, Melville recalled Gansevoort's attack on Vera Cruz during the Mexican War in his poem "Bridegroom Dick."

> But where's Guert Gan? Still heads he the van?
> As before Vera Cruz, where he dashed splashing through,
> The blue rollers sunned, in his brave gold-and-blue
> And, ere his cutter in keel took the strand,
> Aloft waved his sword on the hostile land!

"Prey to unavailing remorse," Gansevoort's life provided the substance for Melville's *Billy Budd,* a meditation on fate, authority, guilt, and innocence.[24]

In 1855, Captain Gansevoort recalled Surgeon John Y. Taylor to the *Decatur,* withdrawing him from loan to the U.S. Army. Taylor had accompanied army lieutenant Slaughter's command up the White River near Seattle into an Indian attack and cared for the wounded and dying. Three years earlier, as a successful Philadelphia physician, Taylor was struck by unexplained wander-lust and decided to join the navy. He submitted his boilerplate application, gathered his letters of recommendation, passed the assistant surgeon's exam, and received his warrant on September 26, 1853. Less than two months later, he was ordered to join the *Decatur* in Charlestown Navy Yard, Boston. On board, Taylor documented the cruise in words and sketches, delighted to be at sea and sailing the world, curious and adventuresome. After leaving the ship at Panama, Taylor joined the *Decatur*'s sister ship *Preble* in the Brazil Squadron in 1859, and then the brig *Dolphin* for the U.S. Navy's expedition into Paraguay.[25]

During the Civil War, Taylor served on the *Oneida* in the West Gulf Block-ading Squadron and then on the *Tuscarora* in the South Atlantic Blockading Squadron. Taylor practiced the surgery of war as he had done for Slaughter's men; his wartime reports are filled with accounts of the dead and wounded. He remained in the service and eventually directed the Naval Medical Hos-pital, at Portsmouth, Virginia. In 1902, Taylor prepared the manuscript of a planned series of books based on his original journals and illustrations; the first concerned the *Decatur*'s harrowing passage through the Strait of Magel-lan, and the doctor called it "The Memorable Cruise of the *U.S.S. Decatur*." His preface acknowledged his old friend "Thomas S. Phelps, late Rear Admi-ral, U.S. Navy, whose amiable qualities and professional attainments of the highest order are not to be forgotten and to whose kind advice and assistance, I am deeply indebted."[26]

Like Taylor, Francis Gregory Dallas was detailed by Captain Sterrett to U.S. Army captain Erasmus Keyes in Washington Territory, to serve as his aide-de-camp. Dallas's early life is difficult to research: "Dallas" was an assumed name; the original family name was Brown or Browne. After joining the navy as a midshipman on the frigate *Columbia*, Dallas sailed in the Home Squad-ron, Brazil Squadron, and the Mediterranean Squadron. During the Mexican War, he contracted yellow fever and then was severely injured, suffering a skull fracture when struck by a load of coal while the steamer he served on was fueling. Afterward, Dallas suffered periods of headache and delirium, jumping overboard in confusion on at least one occasion.[27]

While recovering from his injury, he was called back as an "oldster" to attend the Naval Academy and fought a duel in 1848 with Midshipman John Gale, "owing to matters connected with a Lady." Gale was an old enemy, Dal-las wrote; they had detested one another when they were boys in the midshipmen's berth on the *Columbia*. Dallas and Gale met with pistols at Bladensburg, where Stephen Decatur had fought his own duel, a place for "final appeal from the rhetoric of words to the logic of arms." Both midshipmen were dismissed from the navy for dueling. Friends petitioned for Dallas's reinstatement without success, and at twenty-four, he joined the navy of the Germanic Confederation as a second lieutenant on a frigate, was soon promoted to first lieutenant, and then was given command of a corvette—essentially, a sloop of war. Dallas was restored to the U.S. Navy in 1853 and assigned to the *Decatur*. On board, Sterrett rewarded his experience, promoting him to acting master and then to acting lieutenant. Dallas received his commission in the wave of Plucking Board promotions, but he barely got past the board's deliberations, where he had been reviewed for "incompetency from want of mind." But after a delay, presumably to gather additional information, the board retained Dallas on the navy's active list.[28]

After leaving the *Decatur* at Panama in 1857, Dallas had a period of easy duty on the receiving ship in Philadelphia, "leading the usual life of a bachelor in a city." He fell in love again that summer, suffering greatly when "the young lady [was] willing; mother unwilling," and confessed to his journal that he was "*distrait* about the heart" when the affair ended. Assigned to the *Dale* in the Africa Squadron, Dallas was given command of the prize *Orion*, a slave ship, and sailed it to New York, docking at the Brooklyn Navy Yard in June 1859. He took rooms at the Astor House, dined out, and enjoyed the theater. Then something snapped. Dallas wrote harrowing prose in his journal about a vast conspiracy in New York, his escape to the Merchants Hotel in Philadelphia, and then his capture and imprisonment at the Pennsylvania Hospital. On September 18, 1859, he wrote that he could not bear another night of "telegraphic torture from human bodies" and that he imagined he would die by morning. Even in this extremity, he wrote that "nothing can possibly be said against my personal character as an officer," and he apologized for neglect of duty, held against his will in the asylum. He signed himself Francis Gregory Dallas, U.S. Navy. Dallas was committed to the Pennsylvania Hospital in Philadelphia, where he lived until his death in 1890—altogether a "strange and tragic career."[29]

Thomas Stowell Phelps helped to edit Dallas's personal papers for publication. Phelps was born in Maine; his father was named Stephen Decatur Phelps. The boy entered the navy at eighteen, assigned as midshipman to the brand-new sloop of war *Preble* in the Mediterranean Squadron. Phelps returned to the Naval Academy in the first class of "oldsters" and refined his hydrographic skills in the coast survey. He joined the *Independence* in the

Mediterranean Squadron and then returned to the survey: a scientific sailor, hydrography was Phelps's great interest. By then, he was a family man: he had married Margaret Riche Levy, and their son, Thomas Stowell Phelps Jr., was born in 1848. After a brief stint on the receiving ship at Norfolk, Phelps was assigned to the *Decatur* and gained his lieutenant's commission. When he was detached from the *Decatur*, he was briefly assigned to ordnance duty at Norfolk and then joined the expedition into Paraguay with his old messmate John Taylor.[30]

Talented and experienced, Phelps advanced rapidly during the Civil War; he was appointed lieutenant commander in 1862 and commander in 1865. He was chosen to chart the Potomac River after Confederate forces destroyed the navigation buoys and was then assigned to survey North Carolina inlets behind Confederate lines. In command of the *Corwin*, Phelps fought the Confederate gunboat *Curlew* in 1861 and was also involved in three engagements with the Yorktown batteries in 1862. He rejoined the coast survey, was assigned secret work in Virginia waters, commanded the *Saugus* ironclad on North American Blockade duty, and commanded the steam sloop *Juniata* at the capture of Fort Fisher. After the war, Phelps was promoted to captain and took command of the *Saranac*, by then the flagship of the North Pacific Squadron. When Phelps returned to the Mare Island Navy Yard in 1881, he had been promoted to commodore and served as yard commandant. Appointed rear admiral, Phelps retired and began to publish a series of remarkable memoirs of the Old Navy. Thomas Stowell Phelps died at the Naval Hospital, in New York City, in 1901.

After the *Decatur*'s nine-month stay in 1855–56, Phelps visited Seattle at least twice more. In 1873, in command of the *Saranac,* Phelps steamed into Elliott Bay, and Seattle's "old settlers" threw a party and commissioned a local jeweler to craft an ornate locket, suspended by an elegant chain fashioned of gold and quartz. Henry Yesler presented Thomas Phelps with this "memento of January 26, 1856," which enclosed comparative views of Seattle in 1856 and 1873. Once again, in 1892, Admiral Phelps, now retired, visited the city and reminisced to a reporter for the *Post-Intelligencer,* emphasizing the gallantry of his division at the foot of the trail from Seattle to Lake Washington: faced with "a savage charge," he remembered, "not a man in my division budged." Phelps became one of the principal shapers of the Battle of Seattle saga.[31]

At the turn of the twentieth century, Seattle was consolidating its founding legends, and settler descendants lobbied for a public park to be named in Phelps's honor. In 1904, three years after his death, Admiral Phelps Park was dedicated on the bluff overlooking Elliott Bay to commemorate the officers "who saved the people of Seattle at the time of the Indian War." His son, Thomas Stowell Phelps Jr., was at the time commander of the *Marblehead*, stationed at the Puget Sound Navy Yard in Bremerton, and he attended the ceremony to express the family's gratitude. The surviving settlers remained convinced that the *Decatur* had saved their settlement: "There wouldn't have been a grease spot left of Seattle," Dexter Horton maintained, "if it hadn't been for the old *Decatur*." At the park's dedication, historian Edmund Meany agreed that Phelps was the "savior of Seattle" and that the *Decatur* saved the town from "complete massacre at the hands of the Indians." But the heroic Battle of Seattle soon became a fading saga and then was revived as something of a joke. Once, Seattle maps included Decatur Place, Sterrett Street, Gansevoort Street, and Phelps Place; by 1967, these memorials to war were gone. In that year, debunking historian Bill Speidel joked that he for one was "not overcome with nostalgia" by accounts of the "so-called" Battle of Seattle in the "stupid Indian War." Speidel wrote that, although Indians may have wanted to "repossess their land," they were unwilling to crawl through thorny blackberry vines or muddy their moccasins to confront well-armed marines and the ship's "boom boom" guns. To the Seattle of Century 21 and Boeing 737s, the Treaty War seemed ridiculous and embarrassing. In 1977, Phelps Park was renamed to honor local arts patron Betty Bowen. The *Decatur* symbolized aggressive American expansionism in the Pacific, and the battle and siege represented American conquest of Indian people, a history that shamed many Seattleites of the late twentieth century. From saga to satire to silence, the stories of early Seattle were made and remade, fashioned into usable history for the needs of a changing city.[32]

~

The *Decatur* sailed through the 1850s: when Seattle was a village, when Indian people rebelled against the treaties, when the Old Fogies ran the navy, when the transit was a toss-up between Panama and Nicaragua, when the Vigilance Committee took over San Francisco, when private armies fought to claim new land in Central America for slavery, and when Young America hoped that war elsewhere might avert war at home. The arc of the ship's life—indeed, of warships under sail—came to an end in the Civil War. Afterward, Old Navy men concluded that the sea's secrets were known, that science had conquered romance. Steamship captains needed drudges to serve their machines, not sailors, and an old boatswain growled, "Formerly we had wooden ships and iron men; now we have iron ships and wooden men." The *Decatur* was a sailor's warship of the wooden navy: named to honor Stephen Decatur's daring passages at arms, renowned as David Farragut's first commission, and then working twenty years of hard duty in the navy's distant squadrons. Refitted as a Civil War battery in San Francisco Harbor, the *Decatur* was finally rated as a lowly fourth-class sloop of war, a quaint curiosity. By war's end, the *Decatur*'s sister ship, the *Preble*, had already become a navy training vessel where young men surrendered to old men's nostalgia, and the *Decatur* was decommissioned for good when the war ended, "condemned as being behind the age."[33]

In the end, the *Decatur* was surveyed and condemned like any sick sailor and left the navy altogether. Appraised at $10,000, the ship was auctioned off at Mare Island on August 17, 1865, at the bargain price of $6,600. The new owners were Amos Phinney and Company, a logging firm headquartered in Port Ludlow, Washington Territory, and the *Decatur* was rigged for the coastwise lumber trade. After refitting, the ship headed north to pick up a load of lumber on Puget Sound and then return to San Francisco. Phelps noted proudly that the little five-hundred-ton-burden ship "probably spread more canvas in one suit than any two-thousand ton merchantman afloat." Loaded too high and carrying too much sail for the crew of twelve men to manage, the *Decatur* capsized in a winter storm at the mouth of the Strait of Juan de Fuca, with the loss of all hands. A passing merchant captain recognized the wrecked ship, which had come to rest "bottom up," from "her depth of keel, round fore-foot, breadth of beam and dead-rise in the floor timbers" and brought the bad news south to San Francisco. The *Decatur*, Phelps wrote, "was ground to atoms in the surf that beats without cessation upon that rockbound shore" of the Pacific Ocean.[34]

Norman Graebner has argued that American westward expansion beyond Texas made sense only as a strategic initiative to gain the three great harbors of the Pacific coast. Once gained, those harbors, their ports, and their opportunities projected American expansion onto the sea itself, requiring the growing presence of the U.S. Navy. My deck-level narrative history has followed the *Decatur*'s last assignment as a navy warship: the humble ship's five-year cruise in the weak, far-flung Pacific Squadron, traveling Melville's endless sea pastures, where the same waves that washed the docks of "newbuilt California towns" curled onto the shores of Japan and Nicaragua as the great ocean became a bay to all coasts, compelling expansionist dreamers. On the *Decatur*'s deck, more than three hundred officers, marines, and sailors lived and worked, their lives touching the ship, intersecting there, and reaching out to the long shores of the antebellum Pacific West and its "kaleidoscope of all America's and half Europe's gaudy and reckless rascals." Lured by Pacific ambitions and fantasies, adventurous seamen chased the elephant

along the continuous beaches, seeking glory, freedom, gold, pleasure, or land in personal ambitions wrapped in maritime nationalism. Many hoped for fame, fortune, and good times in the mid-1850s West; few found them.[35]

American merchant steamers, brigs, and schooners traced waterways from the Pacific terminus of the Panama railroad up to San Francisco, then on to Seattle and Honolulu, and beyond to the guano islands, the whaling grounds, and the ports of Asia. Seattle's settlers planned a fantasy city of smokestacks on Puget Sound, at the meeting point of steamship lines and a transcontinental railroad from back East, and in 1856, three U.S. Navy ships anchored off the grubby little sawmill settlement to enforce that Young America vision. In the 1850s, San Francisco exploded as an American city on California's great northern bay, site of the new Mare Island Navy Yard, the Pacific Squadron's vital center. While the *Decatur*'s sailors and marines drilled for shore actions to defend the railroad terminus at Panama, the critical passages across the Central American isthmus attracted the ambition of Young America to achieve manifest destiny in the Pacific West. Pacific filibuster initiatives confronted presidents and secretaries, commodores and commanders, and diplomats and consuls with their own antebellum dilemmas of conviction and duty. Young America once hoped to redeem the United States by conquest of the Pacific West with ships like the *Decatur,* but that initiative failed; half a century later, by 1910, much of the expansionist agenda had been accomplished by a new generation, served by an imperial steel navy.

Abbreviations

Abstracts of Service Records	Abstracts of Service Records of Naval Officers, 1789–1893, RG45, M330, reels 7–9.
ARSN	*Annual Report of the Secretary of the Navy* (Washington, DC: U.S. Government Printing Office, 1853, 1856, 1857, 1858, 1860).
Commandants' Letters	Records Collection of the Office of Naval Records and Library, Letters Received from Commandants of Navy Yards and Naval Stations, RG45, NARA.
Commanders' Letters	Letters Received by the Secretary of the Navy from Commanders, RG45, M147, reels 46–60, NARA.
Confidential Letters	Confidential Letters Sent to Commanding Officers of Squadrons and Vessels from the Secretary of the Navy, 1843–86, RG45, T829, reels 361–62, NARA.

Courts Martial	Records of General Courts Martial and Courts of Inquiry of the Navy Department, RG45, M273, reels 84–88, NARA.
Dallas Journal	Gardner W. Allen, ed., *The Papers of Francis Gregory Dallas, 1837–1859* (New York: Naval Historical Society, 1917).
Department of State, Special Missions	General Records of the Department of State, List of Documents Relating to Special Agents of the Department of State, 1789–1906, Special Missions, September 11, 1852–August 31, 1886, RG59, M77, reel 154, NARA.
Despatches from Special Agents	Despatches from Special Agents of the Department of State, 1794–1906, RG59, M37, reel 10, NARA.
Du Pont Journal	Samuel Francis Du Pont Papers, Henry Francis Du Pont Winterthur Collection of Manuscripts, Hagley Museum and Library, Wilmington, DE.
Gansevoort Letterbook	Miscellaneous Records of the U.S. Navy, Naval Records and Library, Letterbook of Guert Gansevoort, 1855–57, RG45, T239, reels 223–24, NARA.
Johnson Journal	"Private Notes of Philip C. Johnson," Special Collections, Washington State Historical Society, Tacoma, WA.
Logbook	Records of the Bureau of Naval Personnel, Log Books, USS *Decatur*, RG24, NARA.
Medical Log	Records of the Bureau of Medicine and Surgery, Headquarters Records, Medical

	Journals and Reports on Patients, Abstracts of Patients, vol. 26, USS *Decatur*, RG52, NARA.
Medical Journal	Records of the Bureau of Medicine and Surgery, Headquarters Records, Medical Journals and Reports on Patients, "A Medical Journal of the U.S. Sloop of War *Decatur*," RG52, NARA.
Mervine Letterbooks	Miscellaneous Records of the U.S. Navy, Naval Records and Library, Letterbooks of William Mervine, 1855–57, RG45, T829, reels 226–29, NARA.
NARA	National Archives and Records Administration, Washington, DC, and College Park, MD.
Naval Asylum Records	Miscellaneous Records of the U.S. Navy, Naval Records and Library, Naval Asylum Records, RG45, T829, reel 428, NARA.
Register, Circulars, and General Orders	*Register of the Navy of the United States, Including Circulars and General Orders* (Washington, DC: Armstrong, 1855, 1857).
Resignations and Dismissals	Miscellaneous Records of the U.S. Navy, Naval Records and Library, 1861 Resignations and Dismissals of Officers, RG45, T829, reels 389–390, NARA.
Squadron Letters	Letters Received by the Secretary of the Navy from Commanding Officers of Squadrons, RG45, M89, reels 36–38, NARA.

Notes

PREFACE

1   Michael L. Tate, *The Frontier Army in the Settlement of the West* (Norman: University of Oklahoma Press, 1999), xiv; Robert Erwin Johnson, *Thence round Cape Horn: The Story of United States Naval Forces on Pacific Station, 1818–1923* (Annapolis, MD: U.S. Naval Institute, 1963); Robert E. May, *Manifest Destiny's Underworld: Filibustering in Antebellum America* (Chapel Hill: University of North Carolina Press, 2002); Arrell Morgan Gibson, *Yankees in Paradise: The Pacific Basin Frontier* (Albuquerque: University of New Mexico Press, 1993); and James Valle, *Rocks and Shoals: Order and Discipline in the Old Navy, 1800–1861* (Annapolis, MD: Naval Institute Press, 1980).

2   Alison Games, "Atlantic History: Definitions, Challenges and Opportunities," *American Historical Review* 111, no. 3 (2006): 741-57 (quotation on 741).

INTRODUCTION

1   For unity of ocean histories, see Games, "Atlantic History"; Matt K. Matsuda, "The Pacific," *American Historical Review* 111, no. 3 (2006): 758–80, "intermediate environments," 762. For disease as a unifying factor in the Pacific West, see Robert T. Boyd, *The Coming of the Spirit of Pestilence: Introduced Infectious Diseases and Population Decline among Northwest Coast Indians, 1774–1874* (Seattle: University of Washington Press; Vancouver: University of British Columbia Press, 1999); and David Igler, "Diseased Goods: Global Exchanges in the Eastern Pacific Basin, 1770–1850," *American Historical Review* 109, no. 3 (2004): 693–719. For development of the American Pacific West, see Arthur Power Dudden, "Prologue" and "Unfurling the Flag," in *The American Pacific: From the Old China Trade to the Present*

(New York: Oxford University Press, 1992); Norman A. Graebner, "Empire on the Pacific," in *Empire on the Pacific: A Study in American Continental Expansion* (Santa Barbara, CA: ABC Clio, 1983); Geoffrey S. Smith, "An Uncertain Passage: The Bureaus Ran the Navy, 1842–1861," in Kenneth J. Hagan, ed., *In Peace and War: Interpretations of American Naval History, 1775–1978* (Westport, CT: Greenwood Press, 1978); and John R. Eperjesi, *The Imperialist Imaginary: Visions of Asia and the Pacific in American Culture* (Hanover, NH: Dartmouth College Press, 2005). Eperjesi expressed the shifting "terrain" of Pacific expansionism: "One would need a map designed by a situationist to capture . . . the American Pacific" in the nineteenth century (14). For the westward ambitions of American imperialism, see Albert K. Weinberg, *Manifest Destiny: A Study of Nationalist Expression in American History* (Chicago: Quadrangle, 1963); Jean Heffer, "Ambition and Modesty," in *The United States and the Pacific: History of a Frontier* (Notre Dame, IN: University of Notre Dame Press, 2002), 1–7, 65–71; and Harold Sprout and Margaret Sprout, *The Rise of American Naval Power, 1776–1918* (Princeton, NJ: Princeton University Press, 1944), 135–41. For American manhood at midcentury, see E. Anthony Rotundo, *American Manhood: Transformations in Masculinity from the Revolution to the Modern Era* (New York: Basic Books, 1993), 18–20, 167–85; Amy S. Greenberg, *Manifest Manhood and the Antebellum American Empire* (Cambridge: Cambridge University Press, 2005); and Robert E. May, "Young American Males and Filibustering in the Age of Manifest Destiny: The United States Army as a Cultural Mirror," *Journal of American History* 78, no. 3 (1991): 857–86.

2   Alfred Thayer Mahan, *From Sail to Steam: Recollections of Naval Life* (New York: Harper, 1907), 3; Harold D. Langley, *Social Reform in the United States Navy, 1798–1862* (Urbana: University of Illinois Press, 1967); Valle, *Rocks and Shoals*; and Peter Karsten, *The Naval Aristocracy: The Golden Age of Annapolis and the Emergence of Modern American Navalism* (New York: Free Press, 1972).

3   Frank Shay, ed., *American Sea Songs and Chanteys* (New York: Norton, 1948); Joanna Carver Colcord, *Songs of American Sailormen* (New York: Oak Publications, 1964); and *The Oxford Book of Sea Songs* (Oxford: Oxford University Press, 1986).

4   Josiah Royce, *California, from the Conquest in 1846 to the Second Vigilance Committee in San Francisco: A Study of American Character* (Boston: Houghton Mifflin, 1886), easy gold, 231–34. For the most comprehensive understanding of the American West, see Richard White, *"It's Your Misfortune and None of My Own": A New History of the American West* (Norman: University of Oklahoma Press, 1991) (for California population, 191). Kevin Starr, "Beyond Eldorado," in *Americans and the California Dream, 1850–1915* (New York: Oxford University Press, 1973), adventuring strangers, 65. "Men of sailor and mechanic origins were the foundations of society" in Pacific beach communities, often leading a dissipated life and "going native" in country relationships (Caroline Ralston, *Grass Huts and Warehouses: Pacific Beach Communities of the Nineteenth Century* [Honolulu: University of Hawaii Press, 1978], 136). Earl Pomeroy, *The Pacific Slope: A History of California, Oregon, Washington, Idaho, Utah and Nevada* (Lincoln: University of Nebraska Press, 1992), 40–41 (the typical 49'er was young, single, and transient, "more like a soldier" than a pioneer, and created communities that resembled the places frequented by military

men on liberty); Robert E. Ficken, *Washington Territory* (Pullman: Washington State University Press, 2002), Oregon land, 9–10; May, *Manifest Destiny's Underworld*, Walker's land offer, 195–96; "Nicaragua and the Fillibusters," *DeBow's Review*, June 1856, 689; Greenberg, *Manifest Manhood*, 19 ("recently released soldiers, urban working men, southern partisans and ardent nationalists," along with eastern men unlucky in love and unsuccessful in their fortunes, manned the filibusters); Herman Melville, *Omoo: A Narrative of Adventures in the South Seas* (New York: Modern Library, 2002), roving characters, n. 120; Leland P. Lovette, *Naval Customs, Traditions and Usage* (Annapolis, MD: U.S. Naval Institute, 1939), tramps of sea, 215.

5   For Tom Pepper, see *Oxford English Dictionary* and Mark Twain's description of "the renowned Tom Pepper, who was such a preposterous liar that he couldn't get to heaven and they wouldn't have him in hell" (*Virginia City Territory Enterprise*, February 18, 1866). See filibuster lists in *New York Times*, June 29 and 30, 1857. For Liverpool Jack, see *Daily Evening Bulletin* (San Francisco), June 18, 1856; for Sam, see *Daily Evening Bulletin*, June 30, 1856; for Edwards, see *New York Herald*, September 13, 1857. For the *Decatur* sailors, see Records of the Bureau of Naval Personnel, Log Books, USS *Decatur*, RG24, NARA, hereafter cited as Logbook. See also Carey McWilliams, *California: The Great Exception* (New York: Current Books, 1949), Gold Rush ditty, 72.

6   Howard I. Chapelle, *The History of the American Sailing Navy: The Ships and Their Development* (New York: Norton, 1949); James Mooney, ed., *Dictionary of American Naval Fighting Ships* (Washington, DC: Naval Historical Center, 1991); *Decatur* ship file, Navy Department Library, Washington, DC; "Decatur," Office of Naval Records and Library, Subject Files "U.S. Navy, 1775–1910," AC Construction of U.S. Ships, New York Navy Yard, USS *Decatur*, RG45, NARA; Gail E. Farr and Brett F. Bostwick, *John Lenthall, Naval Architect* (Philadelphia: Philadelphia Maritime Museum, 1991), 7–12, 22–23.

7   Spencer C. Tucker, *Stephen Decatur: A Life Most Bold and Daring* (Annapolis, MD: Naval Institute Press, 2005), toast, 172; Robert Allison, *Stephen Decatur: American Naval Hero* (Amherst: University of Massachusetts Press, 2005); Karsten, *Naval Aristocracy*, 25–31, 194–98; Charles J. Peterson, *The American Navy: Being an Authentic History of the United States Navy* (Philadelphia: Leary and Getz, 1858), "headlong daring" quotation, 255.

8   On the launching, see the issues of the *New York Morning Herald* and *New York American* for April 10, 1839. I avoid the naval convention of gendering ships as "she," though contemporary quotations retain that usage. Also, I avoid the use of "*sic*," which would be used here to describe "shrowds."

9   For the *Decatur* at Rio, see R. C. R., "Some Reminiscences of Philip Spencer and the Brig Somers," *United Service*, July 1890, 23. Confederate paymaster James Bulloch was a young officer on board the *Decatur* in 1841; see James D. Bulloch, *The Secret Service of the Confederate States in Europe*, 2 vols. (New York: Putnam, 1884), vol. 1, 91–93. Bulloch recalled "this model man-of-war" and its "performances [which] would seem almost incredible to officers brought up in these days of steam."

10 Loyall Farragut, *The Life of David Glasgow Farragut* (New York: Appleton, 1879), 142–50. The basic narrative of the *Decatur's* 1854–59 cruise is drawn from the ship's logbooks, a watch-by-watch, day-by-day account of events on board the ship or in which the ship was involved. For the Pacific Squadron, see Johnson, *Thence round Cape Horn, 78–80*; Heffer, *The United States and the Pacific*, 318–40; Gibson, "The Military Frontier," in *Yankees in Paradise*.

1. YOUNG AMERICA ON THE PACIFIC

1   Graebner, *Empire on the Pacific*, 1–5, "precise and calculated" program, 218; Gray H. Whaley, "Oregon, *Illahee*, and the Empire Republic: A Case Study of American Colonialism, 1843–1858," *Western Historical Quarterly* 36, no. 2 (2005): 158–78; White, "The Conquest of the West," in *Misfortune*; Eperjesi, *Imperialist Imaginary*, 3–16, 32–35; Thomas R. Hietala, "'This Splendid Juggernaut': Westward a Nation and Its People," in Sam W. Haynes and Christopher Morris, eds., *Manifest Destiny and Empire: American Antebellum Expansionism* (College Station: Texas A&M University Press, 1997), ocean frontier, 59. William Seward remarked in 1852 that the Pacific Ocean would become "the chief theatre in the events of the world's great hereafter" (Howard I. Kushner, "Visions of the Northwest Coast: Gwin and Seward in the 1850s," *Western Historical Quarterly* 4, no. 3 [1973]: 306). For manifest destiny as ordained mission, see Weinberg, "Extension of Freedom," in *Manifest Destiny* (for his remark about appetite, 43). The phrase "empire of the seas" is from *DeBow's* magazine, quoted in John H. Schroeder, *Shaping a Maritime Empire: The Commercial and Diplomatic Role of the American Navy, 1829–1861* (Westport, CT: Greenwood Press, 1985), 91.

2   For the isolation of Washington, Oregon, and California, see O. H. K. Spate, *Monopolists and Freebooters* (Minneapolis: University of Minnesota Press, 1983), 332. For navy and trade in Pacific, see O. H. K. Spate, "Exploitation of the Explorations," in *The Pacific since Magellan*, vol. 3, *Paradise Found and Lost* (Minneapolis: University of Minnesota Press, 1988), "markets of opportunity" quotation, 264; Edmund Burke to Franklin Pierce, June 14, 1852 ("magnificent purse"), quoted in Merle E. Curti, "Young America," *American Historical Review* 32, no. 1 (1926): 45. For expanding naval program under Pierce to fulfill Young America agenda, see Sprout and Sprout, *Rise of American Naval Power*. Pierce's election signified the entry of Young America into the White House, with Young American cabinet; see Yonatan Eyal, *The Young America Movement and the Transformation of the Democratic Party, 1828–61* (Cambridge: Cambridge University Press, 2007), 13, 212–13.

3   Pierce, "First Annual Message" (December 5, 1853), *New York Times*, December 6, 1853.

4   For "most ambitious program" quotation, see Geoffrey S. Smith, "An Uncertain Passage: The Bureaus Ran the Navy, 1842–1861," in Hagan, *In Peace and War*, 79–80. All other quotations in this paragraph are from James Dobbin, *Annual Report of the Secretary of the Navy* (Washington, DC: U.S. Government Printing Office, 1853), hereafter cited as *ARSN*. Navy recruits applied to receiving ships

for evaluation and assignment to a warship when they were accepted into the service.

5   Schroeder, "A New Commercial Era" and "The 'Empire of Commerce' in the Pacific," in *Shaping a Maritime Empire*, 80–81, 101–16, 121; K. Jack Bauer, *A Maritime History of the United States* (Columbia: University of South Carolina Press, 1988); Heffer, *United States and the Pacific*, golden age merchant marine, 45, Navy in Pacific, 75–88; Thomas Philbrick, *James Fenimore Cooper and the Development of American Sea Fiction* (Cambridge, MA: Harvard University Press, 1961), 85–104, 260–65, 1852 remark quoted, 187. On the launching of Young America, see *New York Times*, May 2, 1853.

6   Cruising instructions, Toucey to Long, October 1, 1857, Confidential Letters Sent to Commanding Officers of Squadrons and Vessels from the Secretary of the Navy, 1843–86, RG45, T829, reels 361–62, NARA, hereafter cited as Confidential Letters; Dudden, "Unfurling the Flag," in *American Pacific*; Robert W. Johanssen, "The Meaning of Manifest Destiny," in Haynes and Morris, *Manifest Destiny and Empire*; Greenberg, *Manifest Manhood*, 261–68; Karsten, *Naval Aristocracy*, 141–45, 150–64; Geoffrey Sutton Smith, "The Navy before Darwinism: Science, Exploration and Diplomacy in Antebellum America," *American Quarterly* 28, no. 1 (1976): 41–55, Pacific consciousness, 42–45; Gibson, *Yankees in Paradise*, "advocates" quotation, 316–17.

7   Johanssen, "The Meaning of Manifest Destiny," in Haynes and Morris, *Manifest Destiny and Empire*, Emerson quoted, 12–13. For Young America, see Eyal, *Young America Movement*; Edward L. Widmer, *Young America: The Flowering of Democracy in New York City* (New York: Oxford University Press, 1999), southern and western expansionists, 15; Robert E. Riegel, *Young America, 1830–1840* (Norman: University of Oklahoma Press, 1949); and Curti, "Young America," heart of Young America in the west, 39–40, de Leon quotations, 34. For new American masculinity, see Rotundo, "Self-Made Manhood," in *American Manhood*; and Greenberg, *Manifest Manhood*. For Young America in the west, Fogydom thwarting Young America, manifest destiny, California and Pacific empire quotations, see "Progress of Democracy vs. Old Fogy Retrograder," *United States Democratic Review*, April 1852, 301–3.

8   For O'Sullivan, see Johannsen, "The Meaning of Manifest Destiny," in Haynes and Morris, *Manifest Destiny and Empire*; Brown, *Agents of Manifest Destiny*, quotations on 9, 16. For casual racism of expansionism, see Thomas R. Hietala, "'This Splendid Juggernaut,'" in Haynes and Morris, *Manifest Destiny and Empire*; Thomas R. Hietala, "American Exceptionalism, American Empire," in *Manifest Design: American Exceptionalism and Empire* (Ithaca, NY: Cornell University Press, 2003); Whaley, "Oregon, *Illahee*, and the Empire Republic," 163–65; Weinberg, "The Mission of Regeneration," in *Manifest Destiny*; and Greenberg, "Race and Manifest Destiny," in *Manifest Manhood*. May termed O'Sullivan a "filibuster accomplice" (*Manifest Destiny's Underworld*, 112). For Douglas, see his "Do Not 'Prescribe Limits' to the Area of Expansion," in Norman A. Graebner, ed., *Manifest Destiny* (Indianapolis, IN: Bobbs-Merrill, 1968), 314–15; Franklin Pierce, inaugural address (March 4, 1853), *New York Times*, March 5, 1853. For Young American expansion-

ist agenda throughout West and on to Central America, see Widmer, "Young America Redux," in *Young America*; Frederic Rosengarten Jr., *Freebooters Must Die!* (Wayne, PA: Haverford House, 1976), James DeBow quotation, 5.

9   Leonard L. Richards, *The California Gold Rush and the Coming of the Civil War* (New York: Knopf, 2007), "heroes by the dozen" quotation, 19; Curti, "Young America," "easy and cheap" quotation, 35. For an overview of the navy's Mexican War experience, see K. Jack Bauer, *Surfboats and Horse Marines: U.S. Naval Operations in the Mexican War, 1846–1848* (Annapolis, MD: U.S. Naval Institute, 1969), postwar challenge quotation, 239, Sterrett, 49–55, 89–90, 104–15; also K. Jack Bauer, *The Mexican War, 1846–1848* (Lincoln: University of Nebraska Press, 1992), naval involvement in California, 164–200, Mexican War, 232–58. The Mexican War convinced many army officers that "Anglo-Saxon institutions could redeem benighted peoples" (William B. Skelton, *An American Profession of Arms: The Army Officer Corps, 1784–1861* [Lawrence: University Press of Kansas, 1992], 330–31). Robert E. May, *The Southern Dream of a Caribbean Empire, 1854–1861* (Baton Rouge: Louisiana State University Press, 1973), postwar rationale to expand into the "awaiting paradise," 1–21, Young America vs. "Old Fogies," 20; May, "Manifest Destiny's Filibusters," in Haynes and Morris, *Manifest Destiny and Empire*, Texas and California as "quasi-official invasions," 149, legitimizing role of manifest destiny in filibusters and racism of filibusters, 163–65; May, *Manifest Destiny's Underworld*, Mexican War veterans as potential filibuster recruits, 14, association of Young America with early filibuster efforts, 112–13; William Harwar Parker, Recollections of a Naval Officer (Annapolis, MD: Naval Institute Press, 1985), stirring memories of Mexican War, 63–127.

10 Eyal, *Young America Movement*, enthusiasm for technology, 70–77, 87, 168–69; "The Pacific Railroad instead of a War," *Daily National Intelligencer* (Washington, DC), February 18, 1853.

11 Brown, *Agents of Manifest Destiny*, California exported $20 million in gold in 1852 alone, 224; May, *Manifest Destiny's Underworld*, Clayton-Bulwer Treaty, 238; James P. Delgado, *To California by Sea: A Maritime History of the California Gold Rush* (Columbia: University of South Carolina Press, 1990), in 1853, 23,957 passengers crossed the Nicaragua transit and 27,246 crossed the Panama transit, 59; "Panama Railroad," *Harper's New Monthly Magazine*, January 1859; L. Richards, *California Gold Rush*, Panama railroad cuts time, 25–26, Vanderbilt, 135–38; *Alta California*, November 19, 1856, Nicaragua transit advertisement.

12 May, *Southern Dream of a Caribbean Empire*, Marcy an Old Fogy, 41, Hollins's destruction of Greytown as an expression of Young America wishes, 88; Brown, *Agents of Manifest Destiny*, Borland, Hollins, and Nicaragua, 221–49. See Harold P. Langley's entry on Secretary of the Navy James C. Dobbin, who approved these belligerent measures, in Paolo E. Coletta, ed., *American Secretaries of the Navy, 1775–1913* (Annapolis, MD: Naval Institute Press, 1980). David F. Long, *Gold Braid and Foreign Relations: Diplomatic Activities of U.S. Naval Officers, 1798–1883* (Annapolis, MD: Naval Institute Press, 1988), treaty and Borland, 121–29, "bright star" quotation, 124.

13 "Nicaragua and the Fillibusters," *DeBow's*, June 1856, for filibuster as expression

of manifest destiny; "The Nicaraguan Question," *United States Democratic Review*, February 1858, "Americanization" spectrum, 115–16, two-thirds of U.S. territory, 121, "every sensible man" quotation, 122–23; "Progress of Democracy vs. Old Fogy Retrograder," *United States Democratic Review*, April 1852, expansion quotations, 299; Schroeder, *Shaping a Maritime Empire*, filibuster "paves the way," 128. Slotkin argues that the colonization of Texas and the seizure of California set "a measure of precedent" for the filibusters of the 1850s; Richard Slotkin, *The Fatal Environment: The Myth of the Frontier in the Age of Industrialization, 1800–1890* (New York: Atheneum, 1985), isthmian frontier, 243. Eyal, *Young America Movement*, "dreamy hope" quotation, 11. May, *Manifest Destiny's Underworld*, Walker recruited 2518 men, 49; L. Richards, *California Gold Rush*, 2,500 Walker recruits from San Francisco alone, 140.

14 "Our Mission: Diplomacy and the Navy," *Democrat's Review*, July 1852, Young America and Fogyism in navy and diplomatic corps, 5–39, "web of Fogyism" quotation, 4; "Old Fogyism in the Navy," *United States Democratic Review*, August 1852, 160–62; "The Nomination: The 'Old Fogies' and Fogy Conspiracies," *United States Democratic Review*, April 1852, 377–78; for Mervine quotations about Young America, see Mervine to Dobbin, September 30, 1856, Letters Received by the Secretary of the Navy from Commanding Officers of Squadrons, RG45, M89, reels 36–38, NARA, hereafter cited as Squadron Letters; Levi Cooper Lane, "A Reminiscence of the Nicaraguan Filibusters," *Journal of the American Medical Association* 21, no. 6 (1893): "sanction" quotation, 960; May, "Young American Males and Filibustering," 859–61, "fantasies" quotation, 879.

15 Jones claimed as Young America hero, "Progress of Democracy vs. Old Fogy Retrograder," *United States Democratic Review*, April 1852, quotations, 292–302; James Fenimore Cooper, *Lives of Distinguished American Naval Officers* (Philadelphia: Carey and Hart, 1846), Jones, 1–10, 22, 33, 36, 40–42, flag raisings and salute, 6, 11, 12, fight quotation, 25, ambiguous concordat, 18, "ends of earth" expedition to West, 38. Cooper's novel *The Pilot* (1849) is a fictionalization of Jones's biography. For another admiring biography, see "John Paul Jones," *Harper's*, July 1855, 145–55; also see review of John Henry Sherburne's contemporary biography *The Life and Character of John Paul Jones* in "Paul Jones," *United States Democratic Review*, February 1852, "sailor of fortune," "sea king," other quotations, 153–68.

16 Peter Karsten saw deeply religious and moral roots rather than political ones in the naval sense of mission (*Naval Aristocracy*, 226–29, apolitical officers, 203–10). Another recent historian found that naval officers subscribed to a "national consensus of common identity and shared values" that superseded the claims of partisan politics, in an essentially unpoliticized navy; see Christopher McKee, *A Gentlemanly and Honorable Profession: The Creation of the U.S. Naval Officer Corps, 1794–1815* (Annapolis, MD: Naval Institute Press, 1991), 104–8 (quotation on 108). However, U.S. Army historians of a somewhat later period argue that although the soldierly ideal was apolitical, the day-to-day reality was not: Skelton, "Officers, Politicians and Civilians," in *An American Profession of Arms*, 330; Durwood Ball, *Army Regulars on the Western Frontier, 1848–1861* (Norman: University of Oklahoma Press, 2001); and Edward M. Coffman, *The Old Army: A Portrait of*

the *American Army in Peacetime, 1784–1898* (New York: Oxford University Press, 1986). Ball, *Army Regulars,* for difficulty of quantifying officer politics and three-quarters estimate, 81–82; Coffman, *Old Army,* army officers not set "off from the currents of the time" and increasingly identified politically with the Democratic Party in the 1850s, 61, 88–93; May, "Young American Males and Filibustering," West Point "breeding ground" quotations, 876.

17 "Our Mission: Diplomacy and the Navy," *Democrat's Review,* July 1852, "proximate occupation" quotation, forbidden to "speak politics," 43; Schroeder, *Shaping a Maritime Empire,* Commodore Perry on Pacific empire quotation, 158; Geoffrey S. Smith, "An Uncertain Passage: The Bureaus Ran the Navy, 1842–1861," in Hagan, *In Peace and War,* Wilkes advocacy, 92–93; Eyal, *Young America Movement,* Navy officers favored the *New York Herald,* a Young American paper, 35, Stockton, 82–83, Breese, 44. Both Isaac Sears Sterrett and Levi Cooper Lane read the *Herald,* and Lane was a correspondent for the newspaper. Philip Melvin, "Stephen Russell Mallory, Southern Naval Statesman," *Journal of Southern History* 10, no. 2 (1944): Mallory expansionism, 148ff.; Charles Oscar Paullin, *History of Naval Administration, 1775–1911* (Annapolis, MD: U.S. Naval Institute, 1968), cruise quotation, 240.

18 Weinberg, *Manifest Destiny,* expansionism in Pierce and Buchanan administrations, 190; May, "Young American Males and Filibustering," Samuel Francis Du Pont praised the "immeasurable courage" of filibusters, "sectionalist imperative" quotation, 871; Charles Henry Davis, who accepted Walker's surrender, also admired the filibuster, as discussed in chapter 7, below. The antebellum military academies became hotbeds of both Young American expansionism and intense Southern sectional feeling. Like midshipmen, U.S. Army cadets were nominated from their states and identified with their sections; at West Point during the 1850s, the cadet corps was so deeply divided that the young men insisted on marching in sectional formation. At Annapolis, when war came, fully 40 percent of midshipmen resigned their commissions to follow their states into the Confederacy. Ball, *Army Regulars,* one-third of army officers go South, 78–86, cadets march in sectional formation, 79; William S. Dudley, Going South: *U.S. Navy Officer Resignations and Dismissals on the Eve of the Civil War* (Washington, DC: Naval Historical Foundation, 1981), Navy resignations, 13. Mahan recalled the strong Southern cultural and political consciousness at the Naval Academy in the 1850s (*Sail to Steam,* 85); Eyal, *Young America Movement,* Young America at Annapolis, 150–51.

19 Mahan, *Sail to Steam,* "blood" quotation, 9; *Young America on the Pacific,* March 1854; Frank Soulé, *The Annals of San Francisco* (New York: Appleton, 1855), engine company, 623; *New York Times,* January 12, 1854, muskets; *New York Times,* February 20, 1856, racehorse; *New York Times,* May 9, 1856, steamer; *New York Times,* June 16, 1856, Young America Guards; *Daily Evening Bulletin* (San Francisco), 1855–1856 passim, Young America pen name.

1   Donald Chisholm, *Waiting for Dead Men's Shoes: Origins and Development of the U.S. Navy's Officer Personnel System, 1793–1941* (Palo Alto, CA: Stanford University Press, 2001), five secretaries in seven years, 216; Langley's entry on Dobbin in Coletta, *American Secretaries of the Navy,* Dobbin's leadership, 285–86; Alfred Thayer Mahan, *Sail to Steam,* Dobbin's innovations, xv–xvi.

2   Mahan, *Sail to Steam,* "tea kettle" quotation, 39, general review of steam in navy, 26–37, affection for age of sail, 10–11, 35–39, "marling-spike" quotation, 36. "Science has robbed the sea of its secrets," mourned one observer; "it has given us the steamship, and destroyed the sailor" ("Men of the Sea," *Atlantic Monthly,* January 1859, 47).

3   Schroeder, "The 'Empire of Commerce' in the Pacific," in *Shaping a Maritime Empire; ARSN* (1853), Dobbin on steam quotation; Paullin, *History of Naval Administration,* navy fleet figures for 1843–60, 219. Of the twenty-seven steamers in the navy at the outset of the Civil War, twenty-one were built in or after 1856 (Mahan, *Sail to Steam,* 34). Johnson, *Thence round Cape Horn,* Dulany request for two steamers, 102; Mervine to Dobbin, October 5, 1855, Squadron Letters, request for steam frigate. Such calls were discussed in the press; see, e.g., "Conditions and Necessities of Our Navy," *New York Times,* August 16, 1854; and "Washington Items," in the periodical *New Era,* July 1857. Both articles argued for doubling the squadron and assigning more steamships to the Pacific. Antebellum war steamers were compromises between sail and steam, built of wood unclad with iron, with the smokestack poking up between the masts (Sprout and Sprout, *Rise of American Naval Power,* 145).

4   *ARSN* (1853), Dobbin quotations, his emphasis; Langley, *Social Reform in the United States Navy,* 1853 navy governed by 1800 Act for the Better Government of the Navy of the United States and 1818 Rules, Regulations and Instructions for the Naval Service, 137–38, 143–44, the initiation of the naval bureaus an 1842 reform, 28–29; Paullin, "The Naval Bureaux, 1842–1861," in *History of Naval Administration;* "Our Mission: Diplomacy and the Navy," *Democrat's Review,* July 1852, "worst-administered" quotation, 41, "maggots" quotation, 42, "arbiter" quotation, 36, "oligarchy" quotation, 42. A New York "humorous weekly" described an Old Fogy as a "superannuated officeholder" (Curti, "Young America," n. 36); "Old Fogyism in the Navy," *United States Democratic Review,* August 1852, "get rid of their ideas" quotation, 162.

5   Karsten, "Where They Came From: The Social Origins of the Naval Aristocracy," "The Education of the Naval Officer," and "Naval Life and Society," in *Naval Aristocracy.* For the Wilkes scandals, see Nathaniel Philbrick, "The Reckoning," in *Sea of Glory: America's Voyage of Discovery; The U.S. Exploring Expedition* (New York: Penguin, 2003). Valle, *Rocks and Shoals,* stubborn and proud officers, 2–3, 10–14; W. F. Lynch, *Naval Life, or Observations Afloat and Ashore* (New York: Scribner, 1851), midshipman's duel, 262–67; W. Parker, *Recollections of a Naval Officer,* last duel, 132. For the *Decatur* dispute and court of inquiry, see chapter 8, below.

6   Johnson, *Thence round Cape Horn*, Mervine, 82. For Elliott Bay feud, see chapter 5, below; for Mervine irascibility, see chapter 7, below.

7   McKee, *Gentlemanly and Honorable Profession*, pre-1815 selection and training of Navy officers, 40–115; Mahan, *Sail to Steam*, generational antagonism, 29–45, 1813 memory quotation, 117; "Our Mission—Diplomacy and the Navy," *Democrat's Review,* July 1852, Fogyism blocking advancement quotations, 41, suppression of political opinions, 43; Skelton, "The West Point Experience," in *An American Profession of Arms*, 167–80; Mervine to Dobbin, March 5, 1856, Squadron Letters, Mervine's contempt; Peterson, *American Navy*, contemporary perspective on Mexican War heroism, 47; Jon Swan, "William Walker's Manifest Destiny," *Military Historical Quarterly* 13, no. 4 (2001): "romp" quotation, 38.

8   For an overview of the early U.S. Naval Academy, see Charles Todorich, "Leaving Port," in *The Spirited Years: A History of the Antebellum Naval Academy* (Annapolis, MD: Naval Institute Press, 1984), passing of the Old Navy quotation, 3, academic program, 29–30, 1851 reorganization and four-year academic program, 74–87, last duel at Annapolis, 64–65. For firsthand accounts of Annapolis in this period, see W. Parker, *Recollections of a Naval Officer;* Paullin, *History of Naval Administration;* and Mahan, *Sail to Steam.* "Education in the Navy," *Southern Literary Messenger,* September 1850, "polished manners" quotation, 522. Frederick Marryat published semiautobiographical novels about the Royal Navy. His *Mr. Midshipman Easy* (1836) was the best known. William Parker mentions his familiarity with the Marryat series (*Recollections of a Naval Officer,* 5, 24) and with Cooper's sea novels (213), as does Mahan (*Sail to Steam*, 37–38, 70–71, 96, 98, 124, 162).

9   *Register* mentioned in Dobbin to Sterrett, February 24, 1854, Letters Sent by the Secretary of the Navy to Officers, 1798–1868, RG45, M149, reels 51–53, NARA. "The Navy—Report of Secretary Toucey," *United States Democratic Review,* February 1858, drones, 103; "Old Fogyism in the Navy," *United States Democratic Review,* August 1852, "decrepit," "tottering," "firm tramp" quotations, 162; William Dixon Porter's letter to the editor, November 2, 1853, *New York Times,* for no captain born in century, responding to *Times* articles advocating a retired list. Porter, born in 1808, expressed sympathy with both Young America and the Old Fogies. Herman Melville, *White-Jacket, or The World in a Man-of-War* (New York: Modern Library, 2002), "pensioners" quotation, 113.

10 For ranks, see *Register of the Navy of the United States, Including Circulars and General Orders* (Washington, DC: Armstrong, 1855), 131–36, hereafter cited as *Register, Circulars, and General Orders;* Langley, *Social Reform in the United States Navy*, 21–40; *ARSN* (1853), Dobbin quotations. For navy reform, see Kevin Weddle, "The Efficiency Board of 1855," in *Lincoln's Tragic Admiral: The Life of Samuel Francis Du Pont* (Charlottesville: University of Virginia Press, 2005); Langley's entry on Dobbin in Coletta, *American Secretaries of the Navy*, 190–94; Valle, *Rocks and Shoals,* 65–70; Paullin, *History of Naval Administration,* 239–43; Mahan, *Sail to Steam,* 14ff.; Chisholm, *Waiting for Dead Men's Shoes,* 229–40, "most radical" quotation, 242.

11 "Act to Promote the Efficiency of the Navy," *Register, Circulars, and General Orders* (1855), 128–29; Langley, *Social Reform in the United States Navy*, 203–4; Chisholm, *Waiting for Dead Men's Shoes,* Dobbin efficiency quotation, 237; Weddle, "A Strat-

egy for a Modern Navy," in *Lincoln's Tragic Admiral,* Dobbin and Du Pont.

12   Weddle, *Lincoln's Tragic Admiral,* officers furloughed and cashiered, 70–76, "mental" quotation, 68; also Valle, *Rocks and Shoals,* 69. Of ninety-seven commanders on the 1855 navy list, twenty-one were sent to the reserved list with leave pay, twelve to the reserved list with furlough pay, and six were dropped; see Chisholm, *Waiting for Dead Men's Shoes,* 241; Dobbin to Mervine, September 29, 1855, Letters Sent by the Secretary of the Navy to Officers, RG45, M149, reels 51–53. For Mervine's complaint, see Mervine to Dobbin, September 30, 1856, Squadron Letters.

13   Chisholm, *Waiting for Dead Men's Shoes,* 73 out of 201 submit memorials, 244.

14   Mahan, *Sail to Steam,* officer quotation, 12–13; Valle, *Rocks and Shoals,* 85ff.; McKee, *Gentlemanly and Honorable Profession,* 447–57. For hard-drinking officer, see Melville, *White-Jacket,* Mad Jack, 33–35, Navy "asylum for drunkards," where men's lives were prolonged by exercise and regular hours, and they could look forward to "moderate and undeviating doses" of liquor twice each day, 53–55; Todorich, *Spirited Years,* hard drinking began at Annapolis, 87–91, 111–14; Karsten, *Naval Aristocracy,* 1856 letter to *U.S. Nautical Magazine and Naval Journal* quoted, 86; Langley, *Social Reform in the United States Navy,* seven drunken offenses committed for every sober offense in the Old Navy, 237.

15   Melville, *White-Jacket,* "inducement" quotation, 53; Valle, *Rocks and Shoals,* drinking as a form of desertion, 18; December 2 and 13, 1855, Logbook, to "splice the main brace" after hard duty. The use of the phrase "splice the main brace" to mean serving an extra tot of grog was traditional in the British navy; see Peter Kemp, ed., *The Oxford Companion to Ships and the Sea* (Oxford: Oxford University Press, 1988), 824. Henry Morris to Navy Department, Corporal Punishment and the Spirit Ration, Reports of Officers, 1850, Miscellaneous Records of the U.S. Navy, rg45, t829, reel 451, NARA, cheerfulness quotation; *ARSN* (1858), petty officers to arrest drunken enlisted men, 40.

16   Sam Silk, who served throughout the *Decatur's* commission in the Pacific Squadron, was one of the ship's "best men" and was recalled by name in Phelps's reminiscences of the cruise. However, Silk was double-ironed for drunkenness on many occasions, including May 31, 1855, and July 17, 1856 (Logbook). A first-hand observer mentions that some of the best seamen were the least sober and orderly: Charles Nordhoff, *Man-of-War Life: A Boy's Experience in the United States Navy, during a Voyage around the World in a Ship-of-the-Line* (Annapolis, MD: Naval Institute Press, 1985), 229. For discipline off Seattle, see chapter 5, below; off Panama, see chapter 8, below.

17   Shaw to Navy Department, undated, seaman liquor quotation; Harris to Navy Department, undated, bane quotation; both in Corporal Punishment and the Spirit Ration, RG45, T829, reel 451. See also Langley, "The Temperance Crusade in the Navy" and "The End to Grog," in *Social Reform in the United States Navy.*

18   Langley, "The Use and Abuse of Corporal Punishment" and "The End of Flogging," in *Social Reform in the United States Navy.* For 1850s advocates of flogging reform, see Nordhoff, *Man-of-War Life,* 121–23. After seeing one flogging, Nordhoff kept his eyes closed during future punishments on board the *Columbus.*

Melville's *White-Jacket* includes chapters entitled "A Flogging," "Some of the Evil Effects of Flogging," "Flogging Not Lawful," "Flogging Not Necessary," "Old Ushant at the Gangway," and "Flogging through the Fleet," which argue for the abolition of flogging in the U.S. Navy. For there being no good alternative to flogging, see R. B. Forbes, "Ocean Disasters: An Inquiry into Their Causes and Remedy," *Monthly Nautical Magazine and Quarterly Review,* March 1855; and Paullin, *History of Naval Administration,* 233–34. Samuel Silk, January 7, 1840, Records of General Courts Martial and Courts of Inquiry of the Navy Department, RG45, M273, reels 84–88, NARA, hereafter cited as Courts Martial.

19 Isaac Sears Sterrett to Navy Department, February 2, 1850, Corporal Punishment and the Spirit Ration, RG45, T829, reel 451, Sterrett on flogging. Isaac Sterrett would serve as the *Decatur*'s commanding officer, January 1854–December 1855. For an overview of officer responses to the end of flogging, see Langley, *Social Reform in the United States Navy,* 180–85, 197. The record made of each court-martial is introduced by reference to the Act of Congress to Provide a More Efficient Discipline for the Navy (March 2, 1855) and lists the panel of officers and the particular charges and their specifications. For discussion of subjudicial and judicial punishments, see Valle, "Rocks and Shoals," in *Rocks and Shoals.*

20 "Our Sailors and Marines," *Monthly Nautical Magazine and Quarterly Review,* October 1855, "rascals" quotation, 169.

21 Melville, *White-Jacket,* foreigners' unpatriotic influence, 380; "Our Sailors and Marines," *Monthly Nautical Magazine and Quarterly Review,* October 1855, "turf-lumps" quotation, 171, foreigners and John Bull quotation, 165.

22 *ARSN* (1853), Dobbin quotations and data.

23 *ARSN* (1853 and 1855), Dobbin quotations; Langley, *Social Reform in the United States Navy,* Dobbin's plan, 38–40, 119–21

3. BOSTON

1 January 10, 1854, Logbook; Nordhoff, *Man-of-War Life,* master's duties, 55; *ARSN* (1858), officer grades and definitions, 26–31. The *Decatur*'s voyage from Boston to Honolulu is recorded in the Logbook and retold by Thomas Stowell Phelps, "Reminiscences of the Old Navy: Eighty-three Days in the Strait of Magellan, on Board the United States Ship *Decatur,* 1854–1855," *United Service,* March 1883; by Francis Gregory Dallas in his journal, published in Gardner W. Allen, ed., *The Papers of Francis Gregory Dallas, 1837–1859* (New York: Naval Historical Society, 1917), hereafter cited as Dallas Journal; and by John Y. Taylor, "Three Months in the Strait of Magellan," Off-Routine Movements of U.S. Ships, "U.S. Navy 1775–1910," rg45, box 418, NARA. This NARA collection includes Taylor's 1902 unpaginated manuscript as well as sketches made along the way, from the Atlantic to Honolulu. A separate set of Taylor sketchbooks is held by the Beinecke Library of Western Americana, Yale University Library, and covers the *Decatur* voyage from Honolulu to Puget Sound and on to Panama. Unfortunately, Tay-

lor's journals have been lost, and no manuscript accompanies his post-Honolulu drawings.

2   For *Decatur* repairs, see Office of Naval Records and Library, Subject Files "U.S. Navy, 1775–1910," AR Repairs to U.S. Ships, USS *Decatur*, rg45, NARA; Phelps, "Reminiscences of the Old Navy: Strait of Magellan," description of *Decatur* in Charlestown Navy Yard, 243.

3   For orders, see Dobbin to Sterrett and Dobbin to Dulany, December 31, 1853, Confidential Letters. Taylor wrote that the telegram was actually received by the Charlestown Navy Yard's commandant—"Send the *Decatur* to sea immediately"— and repeated "until the commandant was well-nigh distracted" ("Three Months in the Strait of Magellan," book 1). For the *San Francisco* accident and search, see also *New York Times,* January 14, 1854. Throughout the navy records, there are variations in orthography and obvious mistakes in dating that I have corrected. For instance, Sterrett's surname was variously written Steritt, Sterett, and Sterrett—the latter spelling is his own in uncopied correspondence. Some writers used the British spelling of words—"harbour" and "defence"—and I have Americanized such spellings, though I have kept misspellings. Most difficult to deal with have been the different copyist and correspondent handwriting styles. On three occasions I assembled groups of archivists to pore over a difficult reading. In some cases, we achieved consensus; in other cases, the ornate handwriting or the hasty scrawl was simply illegible.

4   James Grant Wilson and John Fiske, eds., *Appleton's Cyclopaedia of American Biography* (New York: Appleton, 1888–89), 667; Fletcher Pratt, *Preble's Boys: Commodore Preble and the Birth of American Sea Power* (New York: William Sloane, 1950), Andrew Sterrett, 150, 209–10, 248; Mahan, *Sail to Steam*, "hustling" quotation, 47.

5   Quotations in this and the following paragraphs are from Dobbin to Sterrett, December 31, 1853, Confidential Letters. On the captain's responsibilities, see Nordhoff, *Man-of-War Life,* 53; Melville, *White-Jacket*, 23; and *ARSN* (1858), 80–87. For an overview of officers' duties, see Mahan, *Sail to Steam,* 13–18.

6   Karsten, *Naval Aristocracy*, social origins of midshipmen and academy, 7–16. Analysis of the academy's Register of Candidates, 1847–60, indicates that midshipmen were disproportionately urban, attendees of private schools, and the sons of military officers, lawyers, doctors, government officials, and merchants (Todorich, *Spirited Years*, 136–38). "Naval Discipline and Corporal Punishment," by a Lieutenant of the U.S. Navy (Boston: Charles Moody, 1850), "strict and just" quotation; Nordhoff, *Man-of-War Life*, lieutenants' duties, 53–55, "terror" quotation 54; Melville, *White-Jacket*, "omnipresent" first lieutenant, 24.

7   Seth Ledyard Phelps's early career paralleled those of Thomas Stowell Phelps and Francis Gregory Dallas; he had entered the navy in 1841 and returned to Annapolis after years at sea. See Jay Slagle, *Ironclad Captain: Seth Ledyard Phelps and the U.S. Navy, 1841–1864* (Kent, OH: Kent State University Press, 1996), 8–84. The 41'ers attended during the period described in Todorich, *Spirited Years,* 35–38, 52–54; Mahan, *Sail to Steam,* 40–55; and W. Parker, *Recollections of a Naval Officer,* 129–34.

8   For the duties of the purser and the surgeon, see Nordhoff, *Man-of-War Life*, 55–56; Melville, *White-Jacket*, 204–6.

9   Quotations from regulations concerning food and hygiene, instruments, and medicines in this and the following paragraph are from *ARSN* (1858), 87–89; *Instructions for the Government of the Medical Officers of the Navy of the United States* (Washington: A. O. P. Nicholson, 1855); Nordhoff, *Man-of-War Life*, 36–40; and Melville, "The Hospital in a Man-of-War," in *White-Jacket*.

10 *Instructions for the Government of the Medical Officers*, "temperate habits" quotation, 8. Opium was effective but came with risks: Thomas Gould, a twenty-two-year-old *Decatur* marine, became "addicted to the use of opium when he can procure it," and he injured himself and exposed himself to infections to get admitted to sick bay and receive opium. Records of the Bureau of Medicine and Surgery, Headquarters Records, Medical Journals and Reports on Patients, "A Medical Journal of the U.S. Sloop of War Decatur," RG52, NARA, hereafter cited as Medical Journal.

11 Nordhoff, *Man-of-War Life*, warrant officers' duties, 57; Melville, *White-Jacket*, officer hierarchy, 24–25, "hawse holes" quotation, 25.

12 Nordhoff, *Man-of-War Life*, petty officers' duties, 58–60.

13 For an overview of nineteenth-century sailors, see Judith Fingard, "Patterns of Seafaring Life" and "Rhythms of Port Life," in *Jack in Port: Sailortowns of Eastern Canada* (Toronto: University of Toronto Press, 1982); Margaret S. Creighton, "The Private Life of Jack Tar," *New England Quarterly* 63, no. 4 (1990): 531–57; Christopher McKee, *Sober Men and True: Sailor Lives in the Royal Navy, 1900–1945* (Cambridge, MA: Harvard University Press, 2002). McKee examined first-person accounts, including oral histories, to explore the private lives of enlisted men in the first half of the twentieth century. See also E. C. Wines, *Two Years and a Half in the Navy* (London: R. Bentley, 1833), typical sailor, 229; Paullin, *History of Naval Administration*, typical sailor, 76–79; Nordhoff, *Man-of-War Life*, sailor costume, 114; "Our Sailors and Marines," *Monthly Nautical Magazine and Quarterly Review*, October 1855, "grog shop and brothel" quotation, 169–70; Richard Henry Dana Jr., *Two Years before the Mast: A Personal Narrative of Life at Sea* (New York: Modern Library, 2001), merchant sailor costume, 7; Mahan, *Sail to Steam*, tattoos, 69; Lovette, *Naval Customs*, tattoos, 268–71; Melville, *White-Jacket*, "gallows" quotation, 377, "adolescence" quotation, 383.

14 Karsten, *Naval Aristocracy*, general description of rendezvous, 74–82; Melville, *White-Jacket*, physical examination, 328–29; Nordhoff, *Man-of-War Life*, receiving ship, 25–33; *Instructions for the Government of the Medical Officers*, surgeon's rendezvous quotations, 9.

15 *ARSN* (1858), quotations, 158–59.

16 *ARSN* (1853), pay, classifications, and recruitment, 312–31; Richard Henry Dana Jr., *The Seaman's Friend: A Treatise on Practical Seamanship* (Mineola, NY: Dover Publications, 1997), "skill" quotation, 160, general skills of merchant seamen, 159–65.

17 Valle, *Rocks and Shoals*, enlistment, 15–19; "Our Sailors and Marines," *Monthly Nautical Magazine and Quarterly Review*, October 1855, advocate's quotation; "Reg-

ulation in Relation to Recruits," in *Register, Circulars, and General Orders* (1857), clothing.

18 *ARSN* (1858), quotations, 158–59; Karsten, *Naval Aristocracy*, 5 percent of Old Navy was African American, 80; James Barker Farr, *Black Odyssey: The Seafaring Traditions of Afro-Americans* (New York: Lang, 1989), 121; Nordhoff, *Man-of-War Life*, admission of boys, 20–23.

19 The brochure "Naval Discipline and Corporal Punishment," by a Lieutenant of the U.S. Navy (Boston: Charles Moody, 1850), was included in Corporal Punishment and the Spirit Ration, RG45, T829, reel 451; Thomas Stowell Phelps, "Reminiscences of the Old Navy: Our First Cruise under Canvas, the *Preble*'s and Mine," pt. 1, *United Service*, November 1882, 486.

20 January 10, 1854, Logbook; January 10, 1854–December 31, 1855, Records of the Bureau of Medicine and Surgery, Headquarters Records, Medical Journals and Reports on Patients, Abstracts of Patients, vol. 26, USS *Decatur*, RG52, NARA, hereafter cited as Medical Log; and January 10, 1854–March 30, 1859, Courts Martial. See chapter 8, below, for comparison with 1858 crew. The logs, musters, and the final 1859 list of honorable discharges offer the best sources of information on age and place of birth, though there is a considerable margin of error. For pursers' names, see Valle, *Rocks and Shoals*, 19, 127.

21 *Decatur* ship file, Navy Department Library; *ARSN* (1858), third-class sloop defined, 24; Phelps, "Reminiscences of the Old Navy: Strait of Magellan," *Decatur*'s sailing qualities, 24; Taylor, "Three Months in the Strait of Magellan," book 1, "short and stumpy" and "clumsy sailing" quotations; "Account of Work, February 1, 1854," Office of Naval Records and Library, Subject Files "U.S. Navy, 1775–1910," AR Repairs to U.S. Ships, USS *Decatur*, RG45, "good condition" quotation and *Decatur* 1853 overhaul.

22 January 10, 1854, Logbook. On the bewilderment of a new sailor, see Nordhoff, *Man-of-War Life*, 8, 42–43; and Melville, *White-Jacket*, 11–12.

23 January 11, 1854, Logbook. Six hundred men from the *San Francisco* were rescued, 150 drowned, and another 50 died of exposure. See Taylor, "Three Months in the Strait of Magellan," book 1; and January 17, 1854, Dallas Journal. Nordhoff, *Man-of-War Life*, topmen, 60–61, aristocracy of skill, 192–93, 229, petty officers and duties, 58–60. Melville described Jack Chase, captain of the foretop, as a learned gentleman: "his hand was hard, so was not his heart . . . his manners were easy and free . . . he had a polite courteous way of saluting you" (*White-Jacket*, 13–15). Melville, *White-Jacket*, daily deck care, 86, mealtimes, 29, ship's order, 9–12, waisters quotation, 10, topmen aristocracy, 47; *ARSN* (1858), commander's duty to teach, general description of berth deck, articles 1–3; January 21 and 22, 1854, Logbook, exercise quotations.

24 Nordhoff, *Man-of-War Life*, carronade gun crew, 62–63, gun drill, 70; Melville, *White-Jacket*, "sham fight" quotation, 64.

25 Nordhoff, *Man-of-War Life*, ship's police force and "messmate" toast, 63; Melville, *White-Jacket*, "standing armies" quotation, 374, "hate" quotation and marlinespike, 26–27; Karsten, *Naval Aristocracy*, police force, 82–83.

26 January 22, 1854, Logbook; articles excerpted, "Act for the Better Government of the Navy," *ARSN* (1858), 229–37.

27 Valle, *Rocks and Shoals*, "beyond endurance" quotation, 73; Melville, *White-Jacket*, ship as prison, 174–75, crowded and noisy, 35–36. Karsten (*Naval Aristocracy*, 81) quotes Marlinespike's letter to the editor of the *U.S. Nautical Magazine and Naval Journal*, 1856, mentioning reluctance "to submit to the incarceration of a man-of-war life." David F. Long, "The Board of Commissioners," in Hagan, *In Peace and War*, "low pay" quotation, 66; Dana, *Two Years before the Mast*, work of sailing and maintaining a merchant ship under sail, 18–20.

28 Karsten, *Naval Aristocracy*, wardroom discipline, 61, reading at sea, 69–73, Decatur's words as enduring wardroom toast, 195; Lovette, *Naval Customs*, gentlemanly atmosphere, 107–9. "An officers' mess should be comparable to a gentlemen's club in its efficient service, standard of behavior and tone of conversation" (Royal W. Connell and William P. Mack, *Naval Ceremonies, Customs and Traditions* [Annapolis, MD: Naval Institute Press, 2004], 89). Gambling was forbidden: *ARSN* (1858). Taylor, "Three Months in the Strait of Magellan," book 1, gentlemen's deportment quotations.

29 Quotation from Taylor, "Three Months in the Strait of Magellan," book 1.

4. EPISODE 1: THROUGH THE STRAIT OF MAGELLAN

1 The epigraphs are from three of the many variants of the song "The Banks of the Sacramento." See Frank Shay, ed., *American Sea Songs and Chanteys* (New York: Norton, 1948), "Liverpool to Frisco" lyrics, 82–83; "Leave Her, Bullies, Leave Her" lyrics, 145; James Murray, "Sailors' Songs with California Significance," *California Folklore Quarterly* 5, no. 2 (April 1946): "Blow, boys, blow" lyrics, 146. For the cholera epidemic, see January 28, 1854, Dallas Journal; January 28–29, 1854, Logbook.

2 *Register, Circulars, and General Orders* (1855), duties of ship's boys.

3 Quotations from John Downey, February 23, 1854; John Drew, February 23, 1854; John Barton, February 23, 1854; Richard Biddle, February 27, 1854; Samuel Kays, March 2, 1854; Samuel Taylor, March 3, 1854; all in Courts Martial. Van Rensselaer Morgan was under treatment for bronchitis from January 10 through January 17, 1854, from March 21 through May 22, 1854, and from July 31 through August 31, 1854, per Medical Logbook. He was diagnosed with chronic bronchitis on August 25, 1854 (Medical Journal).

4 February 14–22, 1854, Logbook, arrival at Hampton Roads and Gosport Navy Yard; February 23, 1854, Logbook, general court-martial witnesses listed.

5 Paul A. Gilje, *Liberty on the Waterfront: American Maritime Culture in the Age of Revolution* (Philadelphia: University of Pennsylvania Press, 2004), 80–81; March 3, 1854, Logbook, Barlow's sentence; March 15, 1854, Logbook, Biddle's and Hays's sentences.

6 Phelps's reminiscence did not mention the courts-martial; Taylor's merely noted them. February and March 1854, Logbook, shipyard work on the *Decatur* and

restocking. For Middleton's reluctance, see Middleton to Fisher, February 5, 1854, Middleton Family Collection, Middleton Place, Charleston, SC.

7   March 14, April 29, and May 10, 1854, Logbook, desertions. At least eight men successfully deserted at Norfolk. April 25, May 1 and 9, 1854, Logbook, John Wilson.

8   April 10 and May 6, 1854, Logbook, William Fletcher. For the reward, see Sterrett to Dobbin, April 28, 1854, Letters Received by the Secretary of the Navy from Commanders, RG45, M147, reels 46–60, NARA, hereafter cited as Commanders' Letters.

9   June 17, 1854, Dallas Journal, long delay at Norfolk. For officers denied leave, see Dobbin to Sterrett, May 15, 1854, Letters Sent by the Secretary of the Navy to Officers, 1798–1868, RG45, M149, reels 51–53. May 24 and 26, 1854, Logbook, Morris and auction.

10 Sterrett to Dobbin, May 17, 1854, Commanders' Letters, four deserters; June 9 and 13, 1854, Logbook, returned to ship; Dobbin to Sterrett, May 18, 1854, Letters Sent by the Secretary of the Navy to Officers, 1798–1868, RG45, M149, reels 51–53, Venable's resignation referred to; Sterrett to Dobbin, June 12, 1854, Commanders' Letters, Stocking quotations.

11 Taylor, "Three Months in the Strait of Magellan," book 1, Farragut's visit quotations.

12 June 15–17, 1854, Logbook.

13 June 21–July 29, 1854, Logbook, open-sea routine; Lynch, *Naval Life*, ship's rhythm, "ever-recurring exercise of the great guns, the boarders and the firemen, the periodical setting and relieving of the watch, and the perpetual making and shortening of sail" (113); Dana, *Seaman's Friend*, ship's bells, 169; W. Parker, *Recollections of a Naval Officer*, song written by a "poetical boatswain's mate," 153. The half pint of whiskey remembered here is not the gill of a sailor's ration in 1854, which was only a half cup. *ARSN* (1858), flag and tattoo, 35.

14 Taylor, "Three Months in the Strait of Magellan," book 1, rations; Nordhoff, *Man-of-War Life*, rations, 118–19; Melville, "A Salt-Junk Club," in *White-Jacket*, for the sailor's mess.

15 Lynch, *Naval Life*, putting to sea the cure for shoreside ills and physician quotation, 81.

16 Taylor, "Three Months in the Strait of Magellan," book 1, flying fish quotation and *Beagle*. Taylor specifically mentions carrying the *Beagle*'s charts on the *Decatur*, as well as books by Cuvier and Darwin. Charles Darwin, *The Voyage of the Beagle: Journal of Researches into the Natural History and Geology of the Countries Visited during the Voyage of H.M.S. Beagle round the World* (New York: Modern Library, 2001). As master, Phelps was responsible for the management of ship's stores and for daily observations, often noted in the Logbook on his watch; according to Taylor, Phelps also annotated the *Beagle* charts, adding new soundings and sailing directions.

17 Phelps, "Reminiscences of the Old Navy: Strait of Magellan," Gulf Stream, 243–44, "shock" quotation, 244–45. The accident went unnoted in medical records.

18 July 4, 1854, Logbook; Taylor, "Three Months in the Strait of Magellan," book 1, quotations.

19 July 5 and 28, 1854, Logbook.

20 Melville, *White-Jacket*, "ship enchanted on the sea," 325; Taylor, "Three Months in the Strait of Magellan," book 1, "painted ship" and "shark" quotations; July 11, 1854, Logbook, "Stormey petrel"; August 13, 1854, Logbook, whales.

21 August 8, 17, and 23, 1854, Logbook, water tanks; Taylor, "Three Months in the Strait of Magellan," book 1.

22 Taylor, "Three Months in the Strait of Magellan," book 1, equatorial high jinks quotations; Lovette, *Naval Customs*, traditions of crossing the line, including "charging" the captain with numerous offenses, 42–47; Connell and Mack, *Naval Ceremonies*, 74–81; Lynch, *Naval Life*, first-person account, 24–26; Greg Dening, *Mr. Bligh's Bad Language: Passion, Power, and Theatre on the Bounty* (New York: Cambridge University Press, 1992), power quotation, 48. See also the full description of the equatorial passage ceremony in Angus Curry, *The Officers of the CSS Shenandoah* (Gainesville: University Press of Florida, 2006), 102–3, and Curry's remark that the "crew were in command of the ship" during this ceremony (103). It is also possible that the ceremony seemed old-fashioned to Sterrett; Dana considered it out-of-date by 1840, in *Two Years before the Mast*. For such masculine workplace ceremonies and the equatorial crossing, see Rotundo, *American Manhood*, 65.

23 Taylor, "Three Months in the Strait of Magellan," book 1.

24 Taylor, "Three Months in the Strait of Magellan," book 1, butterfly quotation; August 27–30, 1854, Logbook, *Decatur* at Rio; Sterrett to Dobbin, September 2, 1854, Commanders' Letters; *ARSN* (1857), port salutes, 56. It is interesting that in his reflections on Rio, Taylor quoted Shakespeare, "The evil that men do lives after them; the good is oft interred with their bones," and promised to keep his peace about his shipmates on this "memorable cruise."

25 *ARSN* (1857), flag officer honors and salute, gangway ceremonies, 52–53, 60; August 30, 1854, Logbook, Salter's visit.

26 September 6, 1854, Logbook, brushes, clothing; September 1–18, 1854, Logbook, description of liberty at Rio; September 1, 1854, Logbook, Coon quotation; Sterrett to Dobbin, September 19, 1854, Commanders' Letters, unnamed *Decatur* sailor imprisoned in Rio; Taylor, "Three Months in the Strait of Magellan," book 1.

27 September 21–22, 1854, Logbook. Dulany, the Pacific Squadron commodore, was informed of the *Decatur*'s departure from Rio and the return of the dismasted *Massachusetts:* Dobbin to Dulany, December 27, 1854, Confidential Letters. Sterrett, on the *Decatur*, did not know of the *Massachusett*'s return to Rio.

28 September 22, 1854, Logbook, promotions; September 25 and October 2, 1854, Logbook, thermometers. Navy regulations required commanders to fill their petty officer vacancies from on board ship; *ARSN* (1858), 80.

29 October 12–15, 1854, Logbook.

30 Phelps, "Reminiscences of the Old Navy: Strait of Magellan," Sterrett's decision

quotations, 245–46. For quotation from Sterrett's orders, see Dobbin to Sterrett, December 31, 1853, Confidential Letters.

31 Taylor, "Three Months in the Strait of Magellan," Sterrett's son. For Isaac Sterrett and the *Reefer*, see W. Parker, *Recollections of a Naval Officer*, 72; and Willis J. Abbot, *The Naval History of the United States* (New York: Collier, 1886), vol. 2, 666–67.

32 Sterrett to Dulany, January 22, 1855, Squadron Letters; Benjamin Franklin Bourne, *The Captive in Patagonia, or Life among the Giants* (Boston: Gould and Lincoln, 1853), golden hopes quotation, 5, gold fever, 25, cruel husbands and submissive, comely women, 57, Scheherazade, 3–4. Bourne's narrative was republished in the periodical *The Literary World* throughout the early spring of 1853. Taylor occasionally used phrases that may have been lifted from Bourne; for instance, Taylor mentioned "gunning expeditions," a phrase that Bourne used (27), and Taylor's account of guanacos and bolas seems to echo Bourne's account (52–53, 70–71).

33 Phelps, "Reminiscences of the Old Navy: Strait of Magellan," storm quotations, 247; Taylor, "Three Months in the Strait of Magellan," book 1, "sea boat" quotation.

34 Phelps, "Reminiscences of the Old Navy: First Cruise," quotation, 639.

35 Darwin, *Voyage of the* Beagle, guanaco quotation, 148, tuco-tuco, 46; Taylor, "Three Months in the Strait of Magellan," book 1, observatory.

36 Taylor, "Three Months in the Strait of Magellan," book 1, shore and albatross quotations.

37 Ibid., book 2, Gregory Bay storm and *Beagle*, book 1, shore party quotations; Dana, *Two Years before the Mast*, rough weather at Cape Horn, 30–38.

38 Darwin found these birds annoying "for their never-ceasing, unvaried, harsh screams" (*Voyage of the* Beagle, 102). October 17, 1854, Dallas Journal, game ashore at Patagonia; Taylor, "Three Months in the Strait of Magellan," book 2, rhea egg and quotations. Jones and Taylor hunted together but Jeffery collected shells (Phelps, "Reminiscences of the Old Navy: Strait of Magellan," 251–52).

39 Phelps, "Reminiscences of the Old Navy: Strait of Magellan," steamer duck quotation, 248–49.

40 Ibid., 249.

41 Taylor, "Three Months in the Strait of Magellan," book 2, Elizabeth Island.

42 Ibid., Patagonia coal and steamers quotations; November 2, 1854, Dallas Journal, coal.

43 October 27–31, 1854, Logbook; Phelps, "Reminiscences of the Old Navy: Strait of Magellan," 250. Taylor counted about 130 residents ("Three Months in the Strait of Magellan," book 2).

44 Taylor, "Three Months in the Strait of Magellan," book 2, Chilean Settlement, Salas and Schysthe, howling wilderness; October 28, 1854, Dallas Journal, wooding and watering.

45 Taylor, "Three Months in the Strait of Magellan," book 2.

46 Ibid.

47 October 28, 1854, Logbook.

48 Taylor, "Three Months in the Strait of Magellan," book 2, quotations; *Daily*

National Intelligencer (Washington, DC), March 15, 1855, provisions.

49 Taylor, "Three Months in the Strait of Magellan," book 2; Phelps, "Reminiscences of the Old Navy: Strait of Magellan," 250–51; Darwin, *Voyage of the* Beagle, 208.

50 November 2, 1854, Logbook; Taylor, "Three Months in the Strait of Magellan," book 2, quotation.

51 Phelps, "Reminiscences of the Old Navy: Strait of Magellan," weather quotations, 250, scenery quotation and hunt, 252; Taylor, "Three Months in the Strait of Magellan," book 2, enthusiastic sportsman quotation.

52 Phelps, "Reminiscences of the Old Navy: Strait of Magellan," night storm quotations, 253. For a description of a similar gale, see Nordhoff, *Man-of-War Life*, 128–34.

53 November 12, 1854, Logbook, anchorage in Fortescue Bay quotation; Phelps, "Reminiscences of the Old Navy: Strait of Magellan," crabs and mussels quotations, 252.

54 Taylor, "Three Months in the Strait of Magellan," book 2, Fuegians quotation; Phelps, "Reminiscences of the Old Navy: Strait of Magellan," 253; Darwin, *Voyage of the* Beagle, quotation, 183; Robert FitzRoy, *A Narrative of the Voyage of HMS Beagle* (London: Folio Society, 1977), quotations, 110–12. Navy explorers were accustomed to categorizing societies from savage to civilized in a "romantic deification of the Anglo-Saxon race" (Smith, "The Navy before Darwinism," 55).

55 Darwin, *Voyage of the* Beagle, mimicry, 183, yammerschooner, 195; Taylor, "Three Months in the Strait of Magellan," book 2, Fuegian language quotation; Bourne, *Captive in Patagonia*, Yamaschoner Indians, 148.

56 Taylor, "Three Months in the Strait of Magellan," book 2.

57 Ibid., missionaries, picalilly quotations. Bourne considered Christianization of the Patagonians an impossible task (*Captive in Patagonia*, 230–31). *Beagle* captain FitzRoy recounted the failed effort to land missionary Richard Matthews among the Fuegians (*Narrative of the Voyage of HMS* Beagle, 118–19), the sad homecoming of the three Fuegians he had captured and taken to London, and FitzRoy's own "desire to benefit these degenerate, though by no means contemptible, human beings" (99).

58 Taylor, "Three Months in the Strait of Magellan," book 2.

59 Ibid. Neither Phelps nor Dallas referred to this encounter; nor did the Logbook.

60 Darwin, *Voyage of the* Beagle, Fuegian and looking glass, 185; Melville, *White-Jacket*, "quarter-deck faces" quotation, 95.

61 November 26, 1854, Logbook, squall; Phelps, "Reminiscences of the Old Navy: Strait of Magellan," 255.

62 Taylor, "Three Months in the Strait of Magellan," book 2, weather worsened east to west, squall quotation; Melville, *White-Jacket*, clothing, 101; Sterrett to Dulany, December 22, 1855, Squadron Letters, Sterrett quotations re gales and *Massachusetts*.

63 November 26 and December 20, 1854, Logbook, weather quotations; November 15–December 25, 1854, Medical Log, wounds and injuries.

64 December 2 and 13, 1854, Logbook, rations; Phelps, "Reminiscences of the Old Navy: Strait of Magellan," Sterrett's resolve, crew's determination, quotations,

256–57; Taylor, "Three Months in the Strait of Magellan," book 2, true sailors quotation. The *Decatur*'s boatswain wrote about a protracted passage through the strait, on short rations aboard a sloop of war, and although he did not mention the *Decatur*, the events he wrote about occurred during the right period (Mahan, *Sail to Steam*, 118).

65 Phelps, "Reminiscences of the Old Navy: Strait of Magellan," scurvy, 256–57; Taylor, "Three Months in the Strait of Magellan," book 2, scurvy quotations.

66 December 28, 2854, Logbook, arrival of *Massachusetts* and supplies; Taylor, "Three Months in the Strait of Magellan," book 2, quotations.

67 Taylor, "Three Months in the Strait of Magellan," book 2, festive quotations; Phelps, "Reminiscences of the Old Navy: Strait of Magellan," *Herald* article quoted and lamented, 257. The *Decatur* has met "with some accident" (*Daily National Intelligencer,* November 18, 1854). Sterrett to Dulany, December 22, 1855, Squadron Letters, Sterrett and the *Massachusetts;* December 19, 1854, Logbook, wooding the *Massachusetts* boilers.

68 Phelps, "Reminiscences of the Old Navy: Strait of Magellan," seventy cords, 257; December 20, 1854, Logbook, York Roads storm quotations, part tow, Robert Hamilton's death; Taylor, "Three Months in the Strait of Magellan," book 2, storm; Melville, *White-Jacket*, account of furling main topmast sail in a gale off Cape Horn, 106–7.

69 December 21, 1854, Logbook, Hamilton; Phelps, "Reminiscences of the Old Navy: Strait of Magellan," 257–58; Taylor, "Three Months in the Strait of Magellan," book 2; Lynch, *Naval Life*, death, 48–49, shore burial, 101–2; Dana, *Two Years before the Mast*, death at sea in these waters, 39–41.

70 December 23–26, 1854, Logbook; Phelps, "Reminiscences of the Old Navy: Strait of Magellan," quotations, 259.

71 December 27–31, 1854, January 1, 1855, Logbook. The Decaturs left a painted name board behind, nailed to a tree at Borja Bay (*New York Times,* November 17, 1907). Phelps, "Reminiscences of the Old Navy: Strait of Magellan," "elements" quotation, 247. Dallas, whose journal had been matter-of-fact, noted, "Have been *eighty three days* in the straits and *105 days* out from Rio" (his emphasis, January 4, 1854, Dallas Journal).

72 Phelps, "Reminiscences of the Old Navy: Strait of Magellan," 259. Taylor agreed that they had "shared impressions never to be effaced" but disagreed that the ship could have sailed through. Haskell Springer, ed., *America and the Sea: A Literary History* (Athens: University of Georgia Press, 1995), archetypal passage from Atlantic to Pacific, 96.

73 January 5–17, 1855, Logbook; Taylor, "Three Months in the Strait of Magellan," book 2, condors. Taylor brought or sent home his guanaco skull; a photograph of it is included in his collection of drawings at NARA.

74 Phelps, "Reminiscences of the Old Navy: Strait of Magellan," Jeffery's crabs, 262.

75 January 17–19, 1855, Logbook, Valparaiso, Dulany, salutes; Sterrett to Dulany, January 22, 1855, Squadron Letters, Strait of Magellan passage choice.

76 Taylor, "Three Months in the Strait of Magellan," book 3, Sterrett-Dulany dia-

logue; Dobbin to Dulany, January 3, June 13, and July 3, 1854, Confidential Letters, filibusters.

77   *New York Times*, February 9, 1855, distressing fears. "It is now 110 days since the *Decatur* was last heard from. . . . I fear she will never be heard from again" (*New York Times*, February 22, 1855). *New York Times*, March 7, 1855, "given up all hopes" quotation; *New York Times*, March 19, 1855, safety reported. The *Albany* was lost with all hands in the same storm (*New York Times*, March 20, 1855). *Ballou's Pictorial Drawing-Room Companion*, April 7, 1855, weather quotation. Account of *Massachusetts* surgeon B. Rush Mitchell in *The Friend: A Religious and Literary Journal*, March 24, 1855.

78   "Men of the Sea," *Atlantic Monthly*, January 1859, "fairy islands" quotation, 47. The original story was claimed in republication to have been published in the *New Orleans Picayune* on May 1, but proved to be an April Fools' Day prank, April 1, 1855. The story was reprinted in the *Baltimore Sun*, May 3, 1855; *North American and U.S. Gazette*, May 19, 1855; and *Friends Companion*, December 18, 1856.

79   Dobbin to Mervine, March 15, 1855, Confidential Letters, Phelps and Dallas appointments confirmed; Sterrett to Dobbin, January 4, 1855, Commanders' Letters, Phelps's report mentioned. Dobbin's secretary's note, dated March 14, 1855, jotted on Sterrett's letter accompanying Phelps's report, confirmed forward Phelps's report.

80   January 17–19, 1855, Logbook, stocking up at Valparaiso; January 24, 1855, Logbook, "calabosa" quotation.

81   Dulany's orders to Sterrett quoted in Sterrett to Mervine, August 10, 1855, Squadron Letters. January 24 and 27, 1855, Logbook. Dallas reports that twelve men deserted at Valparaiso (January 26, 1855, Dallas Journal).

82   Taylor, "Three Months in the Strait of Magellan," book 3; January 28–February 1 and February 17, 1855, Logbook; Sterrett to Dobbin, March 19, 1855, Commanders' Letters.

83   Here, Taylor's narrative ends with the sentence, "The last half of the cruise of the *Decatur* was not devoid of interesting incidents and accidents, especially during the Indian War in Washington territory, 1855–1856," but "that is another story." Taylor's narrative from Boston through Honolulu is held with his drawings at NARA; his drawings from Honolulu through leaving the ship at Panama in 1857 are held at the Beinecke Rare Book and Manuscript Library, Yale University; but his narrative of the second half of his cruise has yet to be found. March 8–June 22, 1855, Logbook, *Decatur* stay in Honolulu; "The Hawaiian Islands," *Putnam's Monthly Magazine*, March 1855, $15 million and sailors, 247; Boutwell to Dobbin, September 2, 1856, Commanders' Letters, whalers in Honolulu. For Honolulu as hub of the Pacific and its role in globalizing trade, see Igler, "Diseased Goods"; and Ralston, *Grass Huts and Warehouses*.

84   "The Islands of the Pacific," *DeBow's*, January 1855, description of Honolulu.

85   "Reminiscences of Honolulu," *Putnam's*, May 1853, *"American* town" quotation (their emphasis), 558–62; "The Hawaiian Islands," *Putnam's*, March 1855, "track of the coming trade" quotation, 245. "[Honolulu so much resembles an American town] that but for the tropical scenery in the distant landscapes, the stranger

would fancy himself in an American city" ("The Islands of the Pacific," *DeBow's,* January 1855, 86). Johnson, *Thence round Cape Horn,* measles epidemic, 94.

86 Andrew F. Rolle, "California Filibustering and the Hawaiian Kingdom," *Pacific Historical Review* 19, no. 3 (1950): 251–63; Greenberg, *Manifest Manhood,* fast young men, 251–52. Dulany to Dornin, September 13, 1853, Squadron Letters, filibusters in Hawaii; "The Hawaiian Islands," *Putnam's,* March 1855, dire rumors, 245–46, "settlers of a good class from the United States" encouraged to advance annexation and discourage filibuster, 242; "Reminiscences of Honolulu," *Putnam's,* May 1853, casual jokes about California filibusters invading Hawaii, 560; May, "Manifest Destiny's Filibusters," in Haynes and Morris, *Manifest Destiny and Empire,* 146–48; Gibson, *Yankees in Paradise,* 324–25; Dobbin to Mervine, September 29, 1855, Confidential Letters, "lawless" quotation.

87 March 14 and 19, 1855, Logbook.

88 April 2, 7, 17, 26, May 24, and June 6, 1855, Logbook, new crewmen; March 8 and 30, 1855, Logbook, Reed and Sanford spotted and discharged.

89 March 6, 8, 19, and 20, 1855, Logbook, setting ship to rights; May 19, 1855, Logbook, *Eurydice;* March 27, 1855, Logbook, governor, commissioners, and consul; March 28, 1855, Logbook, Prince Lot; April 24, 1855, Logbook, Ogden; Lovette, *Naval Customs,* salutes and ceremonies, 98–101; March 8, 1854, Dallas Journal, combined list of ships.

90 March 28, 1855, Logbook, *Huleina;* April 2, 1855, Logbook, whaleship *Mary* in distress; April 7, 1855, Logbook, *Rolian;* June 1–3, 1855, Logbook, *New World;* Sterrett to Mervine, August 10, 1855, Squadron Letters, Sterrett on *New World.*

91 Mervine to Meade, March 6, 1855, Squadron Letters, *Massachusetts* orders. For *Decatur* direct order, see Mervine to Sterrett, May 24, 1855, and Mervine to Bailey, May 24, 1855, Squadron Letters. On July 24, 1855, Mervine complained that he had no communication from the *Decatur;* Miscellaneous Records of the U.S. Navy, Naval Records and Library, Letterbooks of William Mervine, 1855–57, RG45, T829, reels 226–29, NARA, hereafter cited as Mervine Letterbooks. August 10, 1855, Squadron Letters, Sterrett's explanation to Mervine. For redirection, see Farragut to Bailey, undated, then copied and sent on to Dobbin, Records Collection of the Office of Naval Records and Library, Letters Received from Commandants of Navy Yards and Naval Stations, RG45, NARA, hereafter cited as Commandants' Letters. It is likely that Wheeler requested a warship when he was briefly imprisoned by General Pedro Xatruch, at which time he "threatened to bring down the wrath of the United States Navy on his captors" (Laurence Greene, *The Filibuster: The Career of William Walker* [Indianapolis: Bobbs-Merrill, 1937], 116). On the Xatruch-Wheeler incident, see also William Walker, *The War in Nicaragua* (Detroit: Blaine Ethridge, 1971), 119.

92 Dobbin to Mervine, September 5, 1854, Confidential Letters, Mervine's orders; Toucey to Long, October 1, 1857, Squadron Letters, cruising ground; letter to the editor, *New York Times,* August 16, 1854, twelve ships for "nation fast rising."

93 Mervine to Dobbin, July 24, 1855, Mervine Letterbooks, "services" quotation; Mervine to Sterrett, May 24, 1855, Squadron Letters, "absent" quotation; Mervine to Sterrett, June 20, 1855, Squadron Letters, order reiterated, "Straits" and "sav-

ages" quotations. Mervine was frustrated with Sterrett, but he was equally blunt with other commanders about delays that were neither "expedient or necessary," for instance, Commander Edward Boutwell at Honolulu and Papeete: Mervine to Toucey, [month illegible] 17, 1857, Squadron Letters.

94 Sterrett to Dobbin, June 23, 1855, Commanders' Letters, Indians and cruise quotations; Thomas Stowell Phelps, "Reminiscences of Seattle, Washington Territory, and the U.S. Sloop-of-War "Decatur" during the Indian War of 1855–56," *United Service Magazine,* December 1881, 673; June 6, June 24–July 19, and July 21, 1855, Logbook; see also Mike Vouri, "Raiders from the North: The Northern Indians and Northwest Washington in the 1850s," *Columbia* 11, no. 3 (1977): 24–35.

95 July 24, 1855, Logbook, *Active* and great guns; July 27, 1855, Logbook, Neal and desertions; July 23, 1855, Dallas Journal, arrival at Port Townsend twenty-five days after leaving Honolulu, firing quotation.

96 *Puget Sound Courier,* July 27, 1855, *Decatur*'s arrival and Northern Indian quotation; Sterrett to Dobbin, August 7, 1855, Commanders' Letters, distribution and race south.

97 Arnold S. Lott, *A Long Line of Ships: Mare Island's Century of Naval Activity in California* (Annapolis, MD: U.S. Naval Institute, 1954), 30–41; Johnson, *Thence round Cape Horn,* 104–5; Paullin, *History of Naval Administration,* 222–24; and *ARSN* (1853), Dobbin quotation.

98 August 6 and 12–29, 1855, Logbook. Sterrett reported his arrival to Mervine and to the Department of the Navy: August 7, 1855, Commanders' Letters and Mervine Letterbooks. Farragut to Dobbin, August 16, 1855, Commandants' Letters.

99 For general navy in gold rush and reference to desertion, see Johnson, "The Gold Mania," in *Thence round Cape Horn;* and Delgado, "The Navy in the Gold Rush," in *To California by Sea.* Soulé, *Annals of San Francisco,* gold and naval desertions, 164, 205, 214, 225, 252. For San Francisco, see Robert M. Senkewicz, *Vigilantes in Gold Rush San Francisco* (Stanford, CA: Stanford University Press, 1985); and L. Richards, *California Gold Rush.* Earl Pomeroy pointed out that "forty-nine was a fraud," but the fact that everyone was not successful at making money does not seem to have deterred the navy's deserting dreamers (Pomeroy, *Pacific Slope,* 47). Sterrett to Mervine, September 7, 1855, Squadron Letters, *Decatur*'s lack of full complement of men. The *Decatur* seldom sailed with a full complement—regulations allowed for a deficiency of 25 percent; *ARSN* (1858), 25. August 8, 9, 13–15, 18, 22, 29, and September 6, 1855, Logbook, discharges and desertions. "During the entire day . . . the midshipmen and others were engaged in ferreting them out of their hiding-places on shore. . . . They came in all imaginable stages of intoxication; some with blackened eyes and broken heads, some still more severely injured, having been stabbed in frays with the . . . soldiers. . . . For several days . . . the *Neversink* presented a sad scene. She was more like a mad-house than a frigate" (Melville, *White-Jacket,* 226).

100 Mervine to Dobbin, October 19, 1855, Squadron Letters, Mervine quotation; *New York Herald,* August 15, 1856, rice pudding quotation. Harking back to naval tra-

dition, Mervine drummed two deserters ashore to the "Rogue's March": Mervine to Dobbin, January 4, 1856, Squadron Letters. Lott, *Long Line of Ships, Independence* deserters, 32; "An Act to Provide a More Efficient Discipline for the Navy," *Register, Circulars, and General Orders* (1855), punishment for aiding desertion, 129–30. For daily desertions, see *Daily Evening Bulletin* (San Francisco), October 15, 18, and 19, 1855.

101 Age and place of birth information on Silk, Shorter, Lewis, and Cloyd taken from Medical Log. Shorter's race is drawn from John Ryan's court-martial; April 5, 1856, Courts Martial. Unlike another seafaring African American, Charles Benson, Shorter was not a cook or steward but a highly skilled seaman. For Benson, see Michael Sokolow, *Charles Benson: Mariner of Color in the Age of Sail* (Boston: University of Massachusetts Press, 2003), 1–5, 44–50.

102 For monthly pay rates, see *Register, Circulars, and General Orders* (1855); Langley, *Social Reform in the United States Navy*, coal heaver pay rate, 80.

103 Sterrett to Mervine, September 7, 1855, Squadron Letters, delay at San Francisco; Sterrett to Mervine, August 14, 1855, Squadron Letters, Bright quotation; Farragut to Dobbin, August 14, 1855, Commandants' Letters, Bright resignation; September 7, 1855, Logbook, Drinkhouse.

104 Sterrett to Mervine, August 10, 1855, Squadron Letters, "surprise" and "depredations" quotations, territorial threat; Mervine to Alden, November 23, 1855, Squadron Letters, extermination of whites; Sterrett to Mervine, September 7, 1855, Squadron Letters, Ebey mentioned.

105 August 30, 1855, Logbook, grounding; August 30, 1855, Dallas Journal; Sterrett to Farragut, August 30, 1855, Commandants' Letters, wormholes; August 30, 1855, Commandants' Letters, dry-dock controversy, five notes back and forth.

106 September 10, 1855, Logbook, encounter with Mervine; Mervine to Dobbin, September 11, 1855, Squadron Letters, mention of Oregon Indians; Sterrett to Dobbin, September 7, 1855, Mervine Letterbooks.

107 Sterrett to Mervine, September 7, 1855, Squadron Letters, "greatest danger" quotation; September 8–28, 1855, Logbook, gunnery, small arms, boarding practice.

108 For the Efficiency Board of 1855, see Weddle, *Lincoln's Tragic Admiral*, 59–84; and Chisholm, *Waiting for Dead Men's Shoes*, 229–40.

109 For the notes on Sterrett and quotations, see Commanders section, Du Pont Journal, Samuel Francis Du Pont Papers, Henry Francis Du Pont Winterthur Collection of Manuscripts, Hagley Museum and Library, Wilmington, DE, 256–57, hereafter cited as Du Pont Journal. See also Weddle, *Lincoln's Tragic Admiral*, 70.

110 Weddle, *Lincoln's Tragic Admiral*, officers furloughed and cashiered, 70–76; Valle, *Rocks and Shoals*, 69; *New York Times*, September 18, 1855. Of ninety-seven commanders on the 1855 navy list, twenty-one were sent to the reserved list with leave pay, twelve to the reserved list with furlough pay (as Sterrett was), and six were dropped; Chisholm, *Waiting for Dead Men's Shoes*, pay scale, 237, analysis, 241.

111 Dobbin to Mervine, September 29, 1855, Confidential Letters, Pacific Squadron outcomes; Mahan, *Sail to Steam*, jackass lieutenants, 22–23.

112 "A Review of the Proceedings of the Navy Department in Carrying into Effect the

Act Entitled, 'An Act to Promote the Efficiency of the Navy,'" by a Civilian (N.p.: Towers Printers, n.d.), reaction and "plowing the deep" quotation, 8.

5. EPISODE 2: SEATTLE

1   Kent Richards, *Isaac I. Stevens: Young Man in a Hurry* (Provo, UT: Brigham Young University Press, 1979), Young America Democrat, 95–96; Dobbin to Mervine, April 18, 1855, Confidential Letters, legislature's request. Dobbin responded directly to the legislature, informing that body of his instructions to Mervine, and his letter was published in *Pioneer and Democrat*, July 6, 1855.

2   Mervine to Sterrett, May 24, 1855, Squadron Letters, orders; *Puget Sound Courier*, June 31, 1855, "outpost" quotation; Whaley, "Oregon, *Illahee*, and the Empire Republic," settler-colonists demanding central imperial response, 158, 173; Emily Inez Denny, *Blazing the Way* (Seattle: Rainier Printing Co., 1909), landing and "reverberations" quotation, 75. For Washington Territory, in general, including Seattle and the Treaty War, see Robert E. Ficken, *Washington Territory*; Coll Thrush, "Seattle Illahee," in *Native Seattle: Histories from the Crossing-Over Place* (Seattle: University of Washington Press, 2007); Alexandra Harmon, *Indians in the Making: Ethnic Relations and Indian Identities around Puget Sound* (Berkeley and Los Angeles: University of California Press, 1998); Matthew Klingle, "All the Forces of Nature Are on Their Side," in *Emerald City: An Environmental History of Seattle* (New Haven, CT: Yale University Press, 2007); Brad Asher, *Beyond the Reservation: Indians, Settlers, and the Law in Washington Territory, 1853–1889* (Norman: University of Oklahoma Press, 1999); J. A. Eckrom, *Remembered Drums: A History of the Puget Sound Indian War* (Walla Walla, WA: Pioneer Press, 1989); and Kurt R. Nelson, *Fighting for Paradise: A Military History of the Pacific Northwest* (Yardley, PA: Westholme Publishing, 2007), 108–11. For comparative history of the Royal Navy in the far northwest, see Barry M. Gough, *The Royal Navy and the Northwest Coast of North America, 1810–1914: A Study of British Maritime Ascendancy* (Vancouver: UBC Press, 1971) and *Gunboat Frontier: British Maritime Authority and Northwest Coast Indians, 1846–90* (Vancouver: UBC Press, 1984).

3   In 1881 Phelps published the first of a number of memoirs of his naval service. The first article concerned the *Decatur*'s stay at Seattle—a "faithful account" based on his "rough notes." He later referred to "a map of the town in 1855" that he had drawn and indicated that he had made many other unpublished sketches, only one of which is known (fig. 25). The bird's-eye view and eastward-looking sketch of the settlement (figs. 28 and 30) were signed by Phelps as commodore, a rank he achieved in 1879. Likely, he reinked the drawings at the same time he reviewed his journals, preparing both for publication. For reference to many other drawings, now lost, see Phelps to Rossiter, November 20, 1891, Anthony Kimmel Itzler Papers, New-York Historical Society, New York, NY.

4   Thrush, "Seattle Illahee," in *Native Seattle*, dependence of settlers on Native people, 40–65, native geography, 220–55; *Puget Sound Courier*, July 20, 1855, Yesler's

lumber exports; Phelps, "Reminiscences of Seattle," Yesler's mill and town site described, 670.

5 Frederic James Grant, *History of Seattle, Washington* (New York: American Publishing, 1891), territorial Indian/"white" populations, 99. Phelps estimated that, within a radius of thirty miles, there were "one hundred and seventy men, women and children," combining the settler refugee population from the countryside with the settled population at Seattle ("Reminiscences of Seattle," 671). *Seattle Post-Intelligencer,* June 7, 1892, Phelps recalls a total settler population of about 150. For Yesler and Susan Suquardle relationship, see obituaries of their daughter, Julia, described as "Henry Yesler's daughter," *Seattle Post-Intelligencer,* February 11, 1907, and *Seattle Times,* February 11, 1907. On the newcomers' misjudgments of Native people, see Harmon, *Indians in the Making,* 55–57. Phelps, "Reminiscences of Seattle," "few hours" quotation, 674.

6 Descendants of Seattle's founding families participated in the Pioneer Association and the Daughters of the Pioneers of Washington State and published filiopietistic accounts of settlement, including the Battle of Seattle. These prolific writers include Roberta Frye Watt and Sophie Frye Bass, as well as writer and artist Emily Inez Denny, the daughter of David Denny and niece of Arthur Denny, both founders. Roberta Frye Watt, *The Story of Seattle* (Seattle: Lowman and Hanford, 1931), *Decatur* answer to prayer and "wings" quotation, 208. For explorations of Seattle memory and reimagining usable pasts, see Thrush, "The Haunted City," in *Native Seattle;* and Harmon, "Settlers and Indians," in *Indians in the Making.*

7 Phelps's battle plan notes that the "hills and woods [were] thronged with Indians," and local historian Thomas Prosch also identified the Indians with the woods: "the savages infesting the forests in the vicinity of Seattle." See Thomas W. Prosch, *A Chronological History of Seattle from 1850 to 1897* (Seattle, 1901), 75, 80.

8 Sterrett to Farragut, November 29, 1855, Mervine Letterbooks, "destitute" quotation; Sterrett to Dobbin, December 5, 1855, Squadron Letters, military situation and "command the town" quotation. For a description of the blockhouse and general narrative, see Emily Inez Denny, "The Founding of Seattle and Indian War," pts. 1 and 2, *Washington Historian* 1, no. 2 (1900): 65–69, and 1, no. 3 (1900): 110–14; Emily Inez Denny, *Blazing the Way,* 82. Phelps, "Reminiscences of Seattle," Fort Steilacoom, 675, organization of ship's crew, 682.

9 *Puget Sound Courier,* August 31, 1855, news and rumors, e.g., burning of barn near Steilacoom; *Puget Sound Courier,* September 28, 1855, murders of men en route to Colville gold mines; *Puget Sound Courier,* October 5, 1855, construction of fort at Seattle. Mason's note to Sterrett enclosed in Sterrett to Mervine, October 15, 1855, Squadron Letters. October 15, November 11 and 27, 1855, Logbook, supply Mason, Ebey, and Hays; Sterrett to Dobbin, December 5, 1855, Squadron Letters, arms and ammunition supply. Such arms supplies were reported in the two Puget Sound newspapers, e.g., *Pioneer and Democrat,* November 16, 1855.

10 *Puget Sound Courier,* October 19, 1855. The *Courier's* political rival agreed that

the territory was "extremely fortunate" to have the ship's protection; *Pioneer and Democrat,* October 12, 1855, November 16, 1855.

11 Sterrett to Mervine, October 15, 1855, Squadron Letters. The *Decatur* also transported unnamed Indian prisoners, for instance, taking "an Indian prisoner on board to convey to Steilacoom by request of Judge A. Chenoweth, Associate Justice and Judge of the 3rd District, Washington Territory," and transferring another prisoner to the revenue cutter *Jefferson Davis.* See October 4 and 16, 1855, Logbook.

12 Arthur A. Denny, *Pioneer Days on Puget Sound* (Seattle: Lowman and Hanford, 1908), "land sharks" quotation, 80–81; Grant, *History of Seattle,* Sterrett, Mason, and Denny, 100; White, *Misfortune,* dependence of Western settlers on the federal government for patronage, jobs, contracts, and many federal services, 57–59; and Tate, "Dining at the Government Trough," in *Frontier Army in Settlement of the West.*

13 Phelps, "Reminiscences of Seattle," White River murders, 677–78; Ezra Meeker, *The Tragedy of Leschi* (Seattle: Historical Society of Seattle and King County, 1980), 94–95; Grant, *History of Seattle,* 104–5; Clarence B. Bagley, *History of Seattle* (Chicago: S. J. Clarke, 1916), vol. 1, 57–58; Cornelius Hanford, *Seattle and Environs* (Chicago and Seattle: Pioneer Historical Publishing, 1924), vol. 1, 107–8. Dallas sets the garrisoning earlier than October 29, 1855: "Block House at Seattle garrisoned and everything on the *qui vive* to repel an Indian attack" (October 16–November 20, 1855, Dallas Journal). October 29, 1855, Logbook, marine guard garrisoned at Seattle for first time. This small guard of eight to twelve men eventually grew to include all the marines and all four divisions of armed sailors. October 30, 1855, Logbook, canoes down the Duwamish.

14 December 5, 1855, Sterrett to Dobbin, Squadron Letters.

15 "In the early afternoon, Seattle, an Indian chief, with several other Indians visited the ship. Fired two guns, one with a stand of grape, the other with a shell to show them the effect of the show" (October 31, 1855, Logbook). Indian cooperation was essential: "friendly Indians here inform me that there are one hundred Indians near Steilacoom who purpose . . . taking the place" (Gansevoort to Hewitt, January 6, 1856, Miscellaneous Records of the U.S. Navy, Naval Records and Library, Letterbook of Guert Gansevoort, 1855–57, RG45, T239, reels 223–24, NARA, hereafter cited as Gansevoort Letterbook). Glassley argued that some in every tribe decided to fight against the treaties rather than all members of a given tribe choosing to fight or not to fight; see Ray Hoard Glassley, *Indian Wars of the Pacific Northwest* (Portland, OR: Binfords and Mort, 1972), 127.

16 For instance, *Decatur* logged the purchase of 394 pounds of fresh beef at Seattle (December 11, 1855, Logbook). Phelps relates an amusing story about prices for supplies charged to the *Decatur* by Port Townsend merchants: the prices were so high that when Sterrett showed his market book to a group of California investors interested in building a whaling station at Port Townsend, they decided against that site (Phelps, "Reminiscences of Seattle," 674). For *Decatur* distributing tallow, coffee, sugar, tea, and "quantities of supplies" and his hire as carpenter, see Nicholas V. Sheffer reminiscence, *Lynden Tribune,* August 12 and 19, 1909; and Alonzo Russell reminiscence, "Statement of Alonzo Russell," at www.historylink.

org. October 8, 1855, Logbook, Jones and Sargent; October 9, 1855, Logbook, Mason and Robinson; October 20, 1855, Logbook, McKinnon, Gray, and Mason. The Logbook throughout October and November 1855 is also the source for references to wooding and watering parties and blockhouse construction.

17 Summary courts-martial instituted: "An Act to Provide a More Efficient Discipline for the Navy," *Register, Circulars, and General Orders* (1855), 129–30. October 24 and 25, 1855, Courts Martial, John Dennison, quotations. Both summary and general courts-martial list charges and then the specifications of each charge, record testimony before the court, and conclude with the court's decisions and punishments. Per the Logbook, dozens of *Decatur* crewmen were punished subjudicially in October for sneaking off from duty to get drunk in Seattle's woods.

18 October 25, 1855, Courts Martial, John Peckham.

19 January 17, 1856, Courts Martial, William Robinson, quotations; Sterrett to Dobbin, June 12, 1854, Commanders' Letters, effort to replace Stocking, who was "repeatedly drunk on duty."

20 Phelps, "Reminiscences of Seattle," "floating population" quotation, 699; Charles Prosch, *Reminiscences of Washington Territory* (Seattle, 1904), gamblers rife along "entire coast" of Pacific, 46. The *Decatur* became involved in recapturing two U.S. Army deserters "calling themselves William Brown and James Kelly," who were apprehended by "the citizens of Seattle while trying to make their escape in a clandestine way" and were returned to Fort Steilacoom (October 26–27, 1855, Logbook).

21 Sterrett to Dobbin, November 4, 1855, Squadron Letters, "several tribes" quotation; Sterrett to Mervine, November 13, 1855, Mervine Letterbooks, tribes uniting and "suffering" quotations. Sterrett also mentioned the likelihood of winter famine (Sterrett to Farragut, November 29, 1855, Mervine Letterbooks). Farragut sent this letter on to Mervine.

22 October 16–November 20, 1855, Dallas Journal, quotations; October 17, 1855, Logbook, displays of power, e.g., howitzer practice; October 27, 1855, Logbook, small-arms practice; October 30, 1855, Logbook, marines; Sterrett to Dobbin, November 4, 1855, Squadron Letters, and Sterrett to Mervine, November 13, 1855, Mervine Letterbooks, steamer needed and Seattle safe as long as *Decatur* there quotations; Johnson, *Thence round Cape Horn*, Sound's disadvantages for sail, 98.

23 Mervine to Dobbin, December 4, 1855, Squadron Letters, general Indian war quotation; Mervine to Swartwout, October 19, 1855, Squadron Letters, Walker's outrage quotation and *Massachusetts* orders; Mervine to Alden, November 23 and 29, 1855, Squadron Letters, dispatch of *Active;* Mervine to Dobbin, December 4, 1855, Squadron Letters, *Active* manning and steamer. Nearly a year later, Mervine referred to Alden's difficulty in getting his accounts passed, as the department was unwilling to meet the merchant marine pay scale: Mervine to Dobbin, September 18, 1856, Squadron Letters.

24 Bagley, *History of Seattle,* Crosbie plan, vol. 1, 62–63.

25 Sterrett to Dobbin, December 5, 1855, Squadron Letters, military situation; November 23, 1855, Dallas Journal, and November 23, 1855, Logbook, Dallas

detailed. An anonymous correspondent to the *San Francisco Herald* was on board the *Decatur,* and his articles were reprinted in the *New York Times:* e.g., "Great Alarm at Seattle; General War Apprehended," *New York Times,* November 29, 1855. The writer referred to Sterrett in the third person and does not seem to be either Taylor or Dallas since he remained on board the ship when those two officers were detailed elsewhere.

26 Sterrett to Dobbin, December 5, 1855, Squadron Letters, "troublesome" quotation; *Puget Sound Courier,* November 30, 1855, Sterrett at Steilacoom; Sterrett to Farragut, November 29, 1855, Mervine Letterbooks, encounter quotations; Phelps, "Reminiscences of Seattle," settlers' behavior, 678–79.

27 Sterrett to Farragut, November 29, 1855, Mervine Letterbooks; Erasmus D. Keyes, *Fifty Years Observations of Men and Events, Civil and Military* (New York: Scribner, 1884), situation, including "Dr. Taylor from the Navy," 251–53.

28 Sterrett to Farragut, November 29, 1855, Mervine Letterbooks.

29 *Puget Sound Courier,* November 30, 1855, Sterrett resolution; also *Pioneer and Democrat,* December 7, 1855; quoted by Sterrett's hometown paper, *Baltimore Sun,* January 19, 1856; Bagley, *History of Seattle,* vol. 1, 61–62, premature retirement and petition "to the President"; T. Prosch, *Chronological History of Seattle,* 75; C. Hanford, *Seattle and Environs,* vol. 1, 104; and Abbie Hanford, "Reminiscences of the Indian War of 1855," *Washington Historian* 2, no. 3 (1901): 118. Dobbin to Mervine, September 29, 1855, Letters Sent by the Secretary of the Navy to Officers, 1798–1868, RG45, M149, reels 51–53, formal notice of removal of Sterrett and promotion of Gansevoort; Gansevoort to Francis, November 8, 1855, and Gansevoort to Ebey, December 5, 1855, Gansevoort Letterbook, Gansevoort's November and December movements; Mervine to Gansevoort, October 30, 1855, Gansevoort Letterbook, quotation Mervine's orders; Sterrett to Dobbin, December 5, 1855, Squadron Letters; Gansevoort to Mervine, December 12, 1855, Squadron Letters, *Leonesa.*

30 November 20–December 1, 1855, Logbook, Steilacoom voyage; *Puget Sound Courier,* December 7, 1855, "gallant style" quotation; Sterrett to Dobbin, December 5, 1855, Squadron Letters; Phelps, "Reminiscences of Seattle," 679; "Notes from E. E. Riddell, Postmaster at Tracyton," vertical file 715, Special Collections, University of Washington Libraries, Seattle, WA. Riddell gathered "notes" from eyewitnesses to describe the *Decatur's* visit to Port Madison.

31 For the attack, see Phelps, "Reminiscences of Seattle," 679–80; Grant, *History of Seattle,* 103–4; C. Hanford, *Seattle and Environs,* vol. 1, 109–10; Bagley, *History of Seattle,* 61; Sterrett to Dobbin, postscript, December 5, 1855, Squadron Letters, serious war, prowess, and regiments quotations.

32 December 7–9, 1855, Logbook, *Decatur* aground; Phelps, "Reminiscences of Seattle," 680–83; Sterrett to Dobbin, December 9, 1855, Commanders' Letters.

33 Phelps, "Reminiscences of Seattle," loud report quotation, blankets, 681; December 8, 1855, Logbook, splice main brace and flowing water quotation.

34 December 8, 1855, Logbook.

35 December 9, 1855, Logbook, general damage and first survey; Sterrett to Dobbin, December 9, 1855, Commanders' Letters, *Decatur* aground quotations.

36 Sterrett to Dobbin, December 9, 1855, Commanders' Letters, orders referred to. This is a separate communication from that describing the grounding but dated the same day.

37 Petition variously mentioned, including *Evening Post,* May 17, 1856, and *Daily Scioto Gazette,* May 3, 1856; the petition itself has not been found. *New York Herald,* April 26, 1856, Davis and resolutions quotations; "Memorial to the President of the United States, Relative to Commander Isaac S. Sterrett, U.S.N.," December 21, 1855, *Territorial Laws* (Olympia, 1856), territorial resolution quotations.

38 Sterrett to Du Pont, March 11, 1856, and Du Pont to Sterrett, March 17, 1856, Correspondence, Samuel Francis Du Pont Papers, Hagley Museum and Library. "Efficiency of the Navy," *Monthly Nautical Magazine and Quarterly Review,* October 1855, black list, 165. Sterrett's hometown newspaper, the *Baltimore Sun,* published the list on September 19, 1855; *Daily National Intelligencer,* April 16, 1856, Sterrett memorial "asking to be restored to his former position."

39 For the *Somers,* see Philip James McFarland, *Sea Dangers: The Affair of the* Somers (New York: Schocken, 1985); Leonard F. Guttridge, *Mutiny: A History of Naval Insurrection* (New York: Berkeley, 1992), 87–116; and Buckner Melton, *A Hanging Offense: The Strange Affair of the Warship* Somers (New York: Free Press, 2003). For Gansevoort and the *Somers,* see Hershel Parker, *Herman Melville: A Biography,* vol. 1, *1819–1851* (Baltimore, MD: Johns Hopkins University Press, 1996), 293ff.; C. Hanford, *Seattle and Environs,* only local mention of *Somers,* vol. 1, 110–11; Lieutenants section, Du Pont Journal, Gansevoort quotations.

40 Gansevoort to Mervine, December 12, 1855, Squadron Letters, and December 16, 1855, Gansevoort to Mervine, Gansevoort Letterbook, ship quotations; December 12, 1855, Logbook, survey quotations.

41 Surveyors to Gansevoort, enclosure in Gansevoort to Dobbin, January 10, 1856, Commanders' Letters, survey and unseaworthy quotations; Records of Boards of Survey on Ships and Their Equipment, USS *Decatur,* RG19, NARA, survey and note quotations; Phelps, "Reminiscences of Seattle," 681; Gansevoort to Dobbin, February 29, 1856, Commanders' Letters, general vessel concerns.

42 See December Logbook for garrison and alarms. Thomas Prosch claimed that hostile Indians hoped to seize the *Decatur* "while she lay aground near Port Blakely . . . and secure a large quantity of arms, ammunition, clothing and provisions" (*Chronological History of Seattle,* 75). Since the ship was actually aground there for such a short period of time, it is tempting to interpret Prosch's comment as expressing the fear that Indians could attack and even capture a damaged ship, wherever it was.

43 December 11–January 29, 1856, Logbook, garrison, day-to-day repairs; March 11, 1856, Logbook, iron braces; Gansevoort to Dobbin, January 10, 1856, Commanders' Letters, unfit for purpose quotation. For the *Decatur* repairs, also see entry for December 16, 1855, in "Private Notes of Philip C. Johnson," Special Collections, Washington State Historical Society, Tacoma, WA, hereafter cited as Johnson Journal.

44 Mason to Gansevoort, December 28, 1855, Gansevoort Letterbook, relocation quotations; Gansevoort to Mason, December 28, 1855, Gansevoort Letterbook,

labor quotation; December 26 and 27, 1855, Logbook, hiring local carpenters; Asher, *Beyond the Reservation*, Yesler objection to relocation, 53.

45 For *Active*, see December 21 and 26, 1855, January 6, 9, 10, 1856, Logbook. Mervine to Dobbin, November 18, 1855, January 4 and 18, 1856, Squadron Letters, Pacific Squadron need for steam, *Hancock* and *Massachusetts;* Farragut to Dobbin, December 3, 1855, Commandants' Letters, *Hancock* quotation.

46 Phelps, "Reminiscences of Seattle," weather, 698; December 16, 18, 21 ("decks" quotation), 24, 26, 1855, Logbook.

47 December 15, 1855, Logbook, return of Taylor. See Gansevoort Letterbook for Keyes to Gansevoort, December 16, 1855, Keyes's plea to keep Dallas; December 13, 1855, Gansevoort orders to Dallas; December 14, 1855, Gansevoort orders to Drake; Drake to Gansevoort, December 13, 1855; Gansevoort to Swartwout, February 3, 1856, pilot Slater quotations. Jeffery wrote approvingly of Taylor, who "volunteered, when medical assistance was much wanted, to perform a tedious and difficult march through a hostile country. . . . and acquitted himself of his severe duties very creditably"; Jeffery to Whelan, March 31, 1857, Records of the Bureau of Medicine and Surgery, Headquarters Records, Correspondence to the Bureau from Surgeons and Assistant Surgeons, RG52, NARA. For volunteer reminiscences of this period, see Henry A. Smith, "Battle of Seattle," typescript, undated; and C. H. Hanford, "Address on the Occasion of Unveiling the Historical Tablet at the Foot of Cherry Street," November 13, 1905, Library, Museum of History & Industry, Seattle, WA.

48 The Danish boy was Nicholas Grig, and one of the two old men was Hans Carl (Medical Log). Although the evidence is inconclusive, Jepsen's account of drunken officers on the *Decatur* may include Gansevoort, whose behavior was remembered forty years later by some Native people as "ungentlemanly." See Hans Jacob Jepsen's diary, excerpted, MSS 2234-3, box 19, folder 1, Lucile McDonald Collection, Manuscripts Division, University of Washington Libraries. Testimony by Indian witnesses that referred to Gansevoort emerged in a lawsuit in which a Seattle woman sued for an inheritance, arguing that her white American father had lived in a long-term relationship with her Duwamish mother at the time of the battle. Though only the judge's summary has survived, the context suggests that Gansevoort's "ungentlemanly" behavior was sexual in nature and involved a Native woman. Hershel Parker referred to the "alcoholism and venereal infections" that destroyed Guert and Stanwix Gansevoort; Parker, *Herman Melville: A Biography*, vol. 2, *1851–1891* (Baltimore, MD: Johns Hopkins University Press, 2002), 529. For the judge's summary, see "In re Matthias" estate, *Graham vs. Matthias et al., Federal Reporter* 63 (St. Paul, MN, 1894); and for a general report of the case, see *Seattle Post-Intelligencer*, July 27, 1894.

49 Alden to Dobbin, January 7, 1856, Commanders' Letters, hostile Indians and tampering quotation; Gansevoort to Dobbin, January 10, 1856, Commanders' Letters, Leschi and Quiemuth in party; January 6, 1856, Johnson Journal. The word "spy" was used by Emily Inez Denny, a child at the time of these events, in describing such "friendly" Indians (*Blazing the Way*, 78).

50 Alden to Dobbin, January 7, 1856, Commanders' Letters, Alden's quotations re

Gansevoort. Phelps's account of this controversy is uncharacteristically muted, merely commenting that the launch and howitzer were indispensable to the protection of Seattle and "Captain Gansevoort declined to let them go out of the bay" ("Reminiscences of Seattle," 682). There is no mention of this conflict between naval officers in settler accounts, but Bancroft referred briefly to the disagreement: Hubert Howe Bancroft, *History of Washington, Idaho and Montana, 1845–1889* (San Francisco: History Co., 1890), 124–25.

51 Alden to Dobbin, January 7, 1856, Commanders' Letters.

52 Gansevoort to Dobbin, January 10, 1856, Commanders' Letters, Gansevoort explanation and quotations; see also Gansevoort to Alden, January 10, 11, 16, 1856, Gansevoort Letterbook. Gough argues that the HBC was a sincere ally of the United States during the Treaty War, Gough, *Gunboat Frontier*, 57–59.

53 Alden to Dobbin, January 12, 1856, Commanders Letters, quotations; enclosure in Alden to Dobbin, January 12, 1856, Commanders' Letters, Keyes's narrative. Keyes's autobiography does not mention the matter (*Fifty Years Observations of Men and Events*).

54 Gansevoort to Dobbin, January 10 and 18, 1856, Commanders' Letters.

55 Mervine to Gansevoort, October 30 and December 3, 1855, Commanders' Letters, Mervine's orders; Gansevoort to Dobbin, January 18, 1856, Commanders' Letters, quotations; Alden to Dobbin, December 16, 1855, Commanders' Letters, quotation.

56 Gansevoort to Alden, January 16, 1856, Gansevoort Letterbook.

57 Bagley, *History of Seattle*, ship guaranteed safety, vol. 1, 65; Grant, *History of Seattle*, 104; E. Denny, *Blazing the Way*, 82. James Albert Wirth is the "little Swiss midshipman," but there was no crewmember by that name on the *Decatur;* Sophie Frye Bass, *When Seattle Was a Village* (Portland, OR: Metropolitan Press, 1937), 85. However, Midshipman George Upham Morris gave the teenager Alice Mercer his Bible, which was donated in 2008 by descendants of the Mercer family to the University of Washington Libraries, Special Collections. Watt, *Story of Seattle*, friendly marines, 246.

58 January 18–20, 1856, Logbook, quotations on John Drew's death. Drew was ironed on December 16 and 25, 1855 (Logbook). The Logbook lists him as again released from confinement on January 10, 1856, with no notice of the initiation of this punishment—likely, it would have been on January 8. A. Hanford, "Reminiscences of the Indian War of 1855," Milton Holgate dinner party and "brave boy" quotation, 121–22. Phelps retold the Drew story in every edition of his narrative; locally, Meeker, Bancroft, and Grant mentioned it. Watt, Bass, and Hanford ignored the incident. Emily Denny briefly mentioned the death of "Jack" Drew (*Blazing the Way*, 76); Bill Speidel wrote that Drew was shot after trying "to rape a young lady" (Speidel, *Doc Maynard: The Man Who Invented Seattle* [Seattle: Nettle Creek, 1978], 206).

59 January 19, 1856, Logbook, haul ship into bay; January 19–25, 1856, Logbook, restoring ship; January 24, 1856, Logbook, Stevens; Thomas Stowell Phelps, *Reminiscences of Seattle, Washington Territory, and the U.S. Sloop-of-War "Decatur" during the Indian War of 1855–1856* (Seattle: Alice Harriman Co., 1908), San Francisco

quotation and accusation that *Decatur* officers encouraged panic, 22. This 1908 edition of Phelps's memoirs includes mention of Stevens's visit and accusation, which are not discussed in Phelps's *United Service* article. In 1905, Ezra Meeker also described the governor's visit (*Tragedy of Leschi*, 139–42, New York quotation, 141). Stevens's recent biographer reported that the governor said instead, "Do not now talk of leaving us in our hour of adversity" in an effort to revitalize settler spirits (K. Richards, *Isaac I. Stevens*, 259–61). Phelps interview, *Seattle Post-Intelligencer*, June 7, 1892, Gansevoort declined tour.

60 January 9 and 16, 1856, Logbook, supply blockhouses; *Pioneer and Democrat*, March 28, 1856, beyond Collins, next local blockhouse fifteen miles up Duwamish River; Phelps, *Reminiscences of Seattle* (1908), "worthies" and "embryo soldiers" quotations, 21. Professional soldiers viewed civilian soldiers with general contempt (Skelton, *An American Profession of Arms*, 210–11), but Phelps and Johnson make very specific accusations.

61 January 26, 1856, Dallas Journal, forty women; E. Denny, "Founding of Seattle and Indian War," Blaine family, 111; January 25, 1856, Logbook, death of Carl.

62 Gansevoort to Dobbin, January 31, 1856, Commanders' Letters, Indians cross Lake Washington quotation; Phelps, "Reminiscences of Seattle," Jim's information quotation, 683; Meeker, *Tragedy of Leschi*, "particular favorite" quotation, 144. Emily Denny described "Yoke Yakeman" as Denny Jim, who warned Gansevoort ("Founding of Seattle and Indian War," 111).

63 Gansevoort to Dobbin, January 31, 1856, Commanders' Letters, Battle of Seattle report; Phelps, *Reminiscences of Seattle* (1908), general battle, 20–21; and Phelps, "Reminiscences of Seattle," general battle and clothing quotations, 684ff.

64 January 26, 1856, Dallas Journal, "prowling" quotation; Phelps, "Reminiscences of Seattle," "sentry" quotation, 683.

65 Phelps, "Reminiscences of Seattle," Leschi, 680–81. Phelps did not revise this section in later editions as he did with other stories, like Governor Stevens's visit. In an 1892 Seattle interview, Phelps reiterated the story (*Seattle Post-Intelligencer*, June 7, 1892). Cornelius Hanford derides Phelps's Leschi story as a "romantic narrative" (*Seattle and Environs*, vol. 1, 113); Meeker does not contradict the Leschi story but generally deplores Phelps's memoir as a "wild story" (*Tragedy of Leschi*, 132) and a "grotesque account" (147).

66 Gansevoort to Dobbin, January 30, 1856, Commanders' Letters, "private source" quotation; Phelps, "Reminiscences of Seattle," general account of battle, 683, 693–97, 2000 natives, 694; Phelps, *Reminiscences of Seattle* (1908), 20ff.; and Phelps's interview, *Seattle Post-Intelligencer*, June 7, 1892. Johnson wrote that estimates of the number of attackers varied from 50 to 730 (January 27, 1856, Johnson Journal). Dallas thought that the Indian force numbered "at the least calculation . . . some 700 or 800" (January 26, 1856, Dallas Journal). The Logbook (January 25–27, 1856) provides no specific number of attackers. Bagley estimated 300 (*History of Seattle*, vol. 1, 73). Thomas Prosch estimated 800 (*Chronological History of Seattle*, 78). For Gansevoort's boots quotation, see E. Denny, "Founding of Seattle and Indian War," 111; and E. Denny, *Blazing the Way*, 79.

67 Phelps, "Reminiscences of Seattle," Ki-cu-mu-low Chinook quotation, 689. The

Klickitat were one of the eastern Washington tribes resisting the treaties with arms.

68 Phelps, "Reminiscences of Seattle," Gansevoort and Flanders quotations, cowards and delinquents, 689; January 26, 1856, Logbook, Pepper's house; Gansevoort to Dobbin, January 31, 1856, Commanders' Letters, Battle of Seattle report. For first shot, see Alonzo Russell's reminiscence: "Statement of Alonzo Russell," at www. historylink.org. The navy's "first shot" was widely reported without reproach: *New York Observer and Chronicle*, March 6, 1856; *New York Evangelist*, March 6, 1856. According to Abbie Hanford, Midshipman Morris observed by telescope "a body of Indians" robbing a house, reported this, and was ordered by Gansevoort to fire the howitzer ("Reminiscences of the Indian War of 1855," 120).

69 Phelps, "Reminiscences of Seattle," "legs" quotation, 689; E. Denny, *Blazing the Way*, babies, biscuits, 80.

70 Phelps, "Reminiscences of Seattle," cooled to work quotation, 690; January 26, 1856, Dallas Journal, battle account; C. Prosch, *Reminiscences of Washington Territory*, Taylor and Port Madison men on line, 82.

71 Demons quotations: Phelps, *Reminiscences of Seattle* (1908), 30; and Phelps, "Reminiscences of Seattle," 692. "Statement of Alonzo Russell," low shot.

72 Phelps, "Reminiscences of Seattle," 691–92; Grant, *History of Seattle*, 106; and T. Prosch, *Chronological History of Seattle*, 78. Klakum was one of the twenty-one Indian warriors tried at Seattle on May 15, 1856, "on a charge of being hostile" but found "guilty of legitimate warfare" and discharged (Phelps, "Reminiscences of Seattle," 702).

73 Gansevoort to Dobbin, January 31, 1856, Commanders' Letters, "friendly chief" quotation; Phelps, "Reminiscences of Seattle," number of Indian dead and wounded, 694; *New York Times*, February 28, 1856, an eyewitness account claimed that thirty-five Indians were killed; Grant, *History of Seattle*, claim that no Indian was hit in the battle, 111. In one unfootnoted article, the unnamed second "civilian" was said to have been eating breakfast at "Mother Damnable's" when he heard the shooting begin on January 26, stepped outside, and was shot in the head; see Bernard C. Nalty and Truman R. Strobridge, "The Defense of Seattle, 1856: 'And Down Came the Indians,'" *Pacific Northwest Quarterly* 55, no. 3 (1964): 109. The dead man was named "Robert Wilson" according to Arthur Denny (*Pioneer Days on Puget Sound*, 87), but he was called "Christian White" in a letter from William Bell to Arthur Denny published in the *Pioneer and Democrat*, February 1, 1856, and in Bagley, *History of Seattle*, vol. 1, 65. Phelps referred to "a young man (Pocock or Wilson, as he called himself)," who left the front line for a drink of water and was shot (*Reminiscences of Seattle* [1908], 29). The original fated boy was Herman Melville's Billy Budd.

74 Muskets quotation from Floyd Jones, September 1, 1854, Steilacoom Barracks, "Indian Affairs on the Pacific," 34th Cong., 1st sess., Ex. Doc. 76 (Washington, DC, 1857). Greenberg, *Manifest Manhood*, martial manhood, 12–14. Gansevoort to Dobbin, January 31, 1856, Commanders' Letters, "gallant" quotation. Leschi threatened Gansevoort man-to-man (February 1, 1856, Johnson Journal).

75 Phelps, "Reminiscences of Seattle," "braver man" quotation, 690, "die in our

tracks" and "fate of Seattle" quotations, 692, Suquardle's dance, 693; January 25, 1856, Logbook, death of Hans Carl. John Denson was noted as "hospital steward" at his discharge in San Francisco (December 3, 1856, Logbook), and he may have been the young black man who left Carl's body to fight in Seattle. One example of how Phelps "sweetened" his colorful narrative is moving Carl's death from January 25 to the following day at the height of the battle ("Reminiscences of Seattle," 690). February 6, 1856, Johnson Journal, Morris as "brigand" quotation; Phelps, *Reminiscences of Seattle* (1908), officer costume, 38–39. The filibuster costume in Nicaragua included a blue flannel shirt and a "Kossuth" slouch hat, and every filibuster soldier carried a weapon (*New York Times,* February 27, 1857). The Hungarian freedom fighter Lajos Kossuth was much admired by Young America. Starr, *Americans and the California Dream,* similar prospector costume, 61. Examining studio portraits from the California gold rush, Pomeroy noted that elite sitters wished to be photographed wearing a rough-and-ready costume, while "men of a lower class" preferred to dress up (*Pacific Slope,* 41–42); for filibuster costume and character, see also Greenberg, *Manifest Manhood,* 141–43.

76 Phelps, "Reminiscences of Seattle," 671–77; Harmon, *Indians in the Making;* Thrush, *Native Seattle;* and Asher, *Beyond the Reservation.*

77 *Puget Sound Courier,* April 25, 1856, Chief Seattle reports "Bill"; Stevens to Gansevoort, February 17 and 23, 1856, Gansevoort Letterbook, one hundred native auxiliaries quotations; Phelps, "Reminiscences of Seattle," Patkanim and the bounties quotations, 701; February 11, 1856, Johnson Journal, Patkanim; *Puget Sound Courier,* February 29, 1856, Patkanim's mission reported with four heads taken; *Pioneer and Democrat,* March 28, 1856, Patkanim took twenty heads in his last engagement. Asher suggests that the Snoqualmie fighters may have perceived the heads as "substitutes," standard in native legal culture (*Beyond the Reservation,* 23–33, 140–41). T. Prosch, *Chronological History of Seattle,* Patkanim's visit to San Francisco and "friendlies" quotation, 80; *New York Herald,* May 17, 1856, Patkanim was paid $10,000–$12,000, and his warriors were "fed for some time" for their services.

78 William W. Elmendorf, *Twana Narratives: Native Historical Accounts of a Coast Salish Culture* (Seattle: University of Washington Press, 1993), Frank Allen quotation, 154–55; Watt, *Story of Seattle,* Indians had never "engaged in such warfare before," 237.

79 Grant, *History of Seattle,* no building left in King County, 112; February 11 and 15, 1856, Johnson Journal, deserted, best citizens leaving; *Pioneer and Democrat,* February 15, 1855, "depopulated" quotation; *Pioneer and Democrat,* March 7, 1856, King County "laid in ashes." "Families, in particular have this mania to get away. . . . the population will be exceedingly small in a short time" (*Puget Sound Courier,* April 24, 1856). Watt, *Story of Seattle,* Woodin's tannery and Plummer's sawmill burned, as well as Holgate, Bell, Hanford, Collins, and Maple homes, and "everything in King County, except buildings at Alki," 239–45, birth, 245.

80 For scattered alarms, see March 22, 1856, and April 4, 1856, Logbook; February 22, 1856, Logbook, Washington's birthday; Watt, *Story of Seattle,* Catharine Blaine recalled three false alarms in one night, 229; Glassley, *Indian Wars of the Pacific*

Northwest, skirmishes on March 4 and 8, 129; January 29, 1856, Johnson Journal, "Big Indian" quotation; February 1, 1856, Johnson Journal, farcical; February 17, 1856, Johnson Journal, fearful Gansevoort.

81 February 3, 1856, Johnson Journal, tent description; February 17, 1856, Johnson Journal, whooping; February 7, 11, 12, 19, 1856, Johnson Journal, Lake Washington canoes, rat-tail files, and garrison quotations; February 8–22, 1856, Logbook, garrison, drill and onshore work.

82 The *Seattle Post-Intelligencer* reprinted an edited version of Phelps's reminiscence on January 20, 1882, omitting his indictment of settler cowardice. February 6, 1856, Logbook, second blockhouse; Phelps, "Reminiscences of Seattle," barricades and second blockhouse, 695–96, "floating population" quotation, 699, cowardly, 689, "vicious element" quotation, 698; *Pioneer and Democrat,* February 1, 1856, musters incomplete; February 6 and 12, 1856, Johnson Journal, Seattle townspeople quotations; and February 11, 1856, Johnson Journal, Gansevoort order. Swartwout reported that Olympia was "well defended by the volunteer forces" while Seattle had "very few volunteers for its protection" (Swartwout to Dobbin, March 9, 1855, Commanders' Letters).

83 Mervine to Gansevoort, January 13, 1856, Squadron Letters, Swartwout, command and Mazatlan quotations, Gansevoort's orders; May, *Manifest Destiny's Underworld, Archibald Gracie,* 236–37.

84 February 9, 1856, Gansevoort Letterbook, petition.

85 *Pioneer and Democrat,* February 29, 1856, *Massachusetts* arrival; Swartwout to Dobbin, January 20 and February 25, 1856, Commanders' Letters, Mervine ordered Swartwout to take command. Mervine noted it was essential to send to Puget Sound "all the available Naval Force which can be spared" (Mervine to Alden, November 23, 1855, Squadron Letters). Mervine to Dobbin, January 18, 1856, Squadron Letters, settlers massacred quotation; Lott, *Long Line of Ships,* outfitting *Massachusetts,* 38–39; Farragut to Gansevoort, February 14, 1856, Gansevoort Letterbook, supplies. On February 26, captain's clerk Charles Francis died of hepatitis, the third Decatur to die in Seattle. Swartwout, Gansevoort, and Alden led the funeral procession, followed by officers, marines, and crewmen and "a number of the citizens of Seattle," marching "to the place of burial where the last sad rites were paid the deceased." Francis was buried "immediately in front of the block house" (February 26, 1856, Logbook; Gansevoort to Dobbin, March 9, 1856, Commanders' Letters).

86 Swartwout to Dobbin, April 7, 1856, Commanders' Letters, pilot; Swartwout to Dobbin, April 24, 1856, Commanders' Letters, Indian hires quotations; Bagley, *History of Seattle,* Swartwout's eight-man Indian crew is named, vol. 1, 67.

87 Survey, February 29, 1856, Commanders' Letters, forwarded by Swartwout to Dobbin.

88 March 1, 1856, Logbook, General Orders; Melville, *White-Jacket,* antagonism of interests and usage quotation, 207–8; Karsten, *Naval Aristocracy,* officer pursuit of glory, 257–63.

89 March 14–22, 1856, Logbook, brush cutting; Phelps, "Reminiscences of Seattle," well-laid-out town quotation, 696, rifle whiskey and drunken brawl, vicious ele-

ment and dealers quotations, 695–98; C. Prosch, *Reminiscences of Washington Territory*, Steilacoom soldiers quotations, 47–48.

90 Mervine to Toucey, [month illegible] 17, 1857, Squadron Letters, "recklessness" quotation. References to dissolute sailors abound in Old Navy reminiscence: Lynch, *Naval Life*, 105; Nordhoff, *Man-of-War Life*, 205–11; Paullin, *History of Naval Administration*, 229; Phelps, "Reminiscences of the Old Navy: First Cruise," 632–33; and Phelps, "Reminiscences of Seattle," 695.

91 Patrick McCann, April 5, 1856, Courts Martial.

92 John Ryan, ibid.

93 On average, 5 percent of the antebellum navy was black; see Karsten, *Naval Aristocracy*, 60. For monthly pay rates, see *Register, Circulars, and General Orders* (1855). Though the emphasis is on black American seamen in the merchant marine rather than the U.S. Navy, see W. Jeffrey Bolster, "Pillar of the Community," in *Black Jacks: African American Seamen in the Age of Sail* (Cambridge, MA: Harvard University Press, 1997).

94 William Flynn, April 10, 1856, and Robert Logan, April 25, 1856, Courts Martial. On January 19, 1856—the day the *Decatur* was refloated—the Logbook noted without explanation that *Decatur* marine William McCarty "was brought on board by two Indians and confined in double irons." His offense was not noted and he was not brought before a summary court-martial. Another sailor, James Fox, was confined in double-irons for drunkenness on that day, apparently in a separate incident. Since "for drunkenness" is specified in Fox's case and not in McCarty's, it is tempting to suppose that McCarty was "molesting" Indians.

95 Peter Handerson, July 11, 1856, Courts Martial.

96 Cochrane and Dixon, May 12, 1856; White and Lenz, April 25, 1856; McCann and Smith, April 26, 1856; all in Courts Martial.

97 C. Prosch, *Reminiscences of Washington Territory*, proclivities, 47–48. According to one local popular historian, Madame Damnable operated a "whorehouse," and Sam Silk actually said, "It's Annie—I used to know her when she operated a whorehouse at Fell's Point in Baltimore" (Speidel, *Doc Maynard*, 121–31). The *Decatur*'s medical logbooks document a rate of reported venereal infection varying over the cruise from 22 to 27 percent.

98 Phelps, "Reminiscences of Seattle," Silk and Madame Damnable quotations, 696–98. I have supplied the profanity that Phelps omitted. In referring to Madame Damnable's prototype, "the famous Frenchwoman" formerly residing at Callao, and in using Silk to associate her with Baltimore's red-light district, Phelps may be suggesting her occupation as a madame.

99 Peter Lines, July 5, 1856, Courts Martial, quotations; for notions of "fairness" among sailors, see Gilje, *Liberty on the Waterfront*, 245–50.

100 July 27, 1855, Johnson Journal, hard party quotations; February 19, 1856, Johnson Journal, Gansevoort drinking quotation; February 26, 1856, Johnson Journal, demijohn.

101 March 2, 20–22 and April 4–5, 1856, Logbook. Stevens to Davis, March 21, 1856, force to Lake Washington; Stevens to Swartwout, March 15, 1856, and Swartwout to Stevens, March 16, 1856, exchange re dangers; Wool to Stevens, March

7, 1856, dismissive quotations re five companies; Casey to Wool, May 2, 1856, no depredations quotations; all letters from "Indian Hostilities in Oregon and Washington Territories," 34th Cong., 1st sess., Ex. Doc. 118 (Washington, DC: Wendell, 1856). Stevens's plan in March 1856 was similar to Crosbie's suggestion, back in October or November 1855. For anti-Wool editorials, see, e.g., *Pioneer and Democrat,* March 7, 1856, and throughout spring 1856.

102 Clarence B. Bagley, *History of King County, Washington* (Chicago: S. J. Clarke, 1929), Brannan, vol. 1, 173; Phelps, "Reminiscences of Seattle," Indian murders quotation, 704; T. Prosch, *Chronological History of Seattle,* shot on spot quotation, 81; Asher, *Beyond the Reservation,* Collins, 138–39.

103 Swartwout to Gansevoort, April 15, 1856, Gansevoort Letterbook, cruise quotations; Swartwout to Dobbin, April 7, 1856, Commanders' Letters, attack unlikely.

104 April 14–May 7, Logbook, Victoria trip; April 23, 1856, Logbook, Douglas visit.

105 Swartwout to Gansevoort, April 15, 1856, Gansevoort Letterbook, advice; Phelps, "Reminiscences of Seattle," officers at Victoria, 702; February 23, 1856, Johnson Journal; Gansevoort to Swartwout, May 10, 1856, Gansevoort Letterbook, Victoria; Gansevoort to Mervine, June 16, 1856, Squadron Letters, sea quotation; Phelps, "Reminiscences of Seattle," cruise was "twelve hours of hard beating against a strong westerly wind, with an ugly sea," 702.

106 Swartwout to Dobbin, April 7, 1855, Commanders' Letters, personnel, Swartwout's mini-squadron quotations; John Carty, October 11, 1856, Courts Martial, Swartwout armed sentries; Dallas to *Hancock,* March 29, 1856, Dallas Journal; Farragut to Gansevoort, March 13, 1856, Gansevoort Letterbook; Swartwout to Gansevoort, March 31, 1856, Gansevoort Letterbook, marines.

107 Swartwout to Dobbin, June 2, 1856, Commanders' Letters, quotations; Gansevoort to Swartwout, May 29, 1856, Gansevoort Letterbook; May 29–31, 1856, Logbook.

108 For honorable discharges, see John Cray and Henry Wade, November 14, 1855, and Robert Hicks, February 20, 1856, Logbook. July 27, 1855, Logbook, Humphrey Davis release at Port Townsend; *Puget Sound Courier,* August 24, 1855, Davis obituary quotations. For monthly pay rates, see *Register, Circulars, and General Orders* (1855); T. Prosch, *Chronological History of Seattle,* Washington Territory prices, 58–59, laborers' wages, 59. Thomas Cooper, Bartlet Maher, Charles Wilson, and Harley Burr deserted the *Decatur* in July 1855; Franklin Gray, Price, Bass, and Mason deserted during October 1855 through June 1856 (Logbook).

109 Phelps, "Reminiscences of Seattle," "rough characters" quotation, 672, cowardly volunteers, 689, 698, "cruel and senseless, treatment of Indians by whites," 675, 702. Many pioneers bristled at Phelps's judgment, never retracted in the many editions of his memoirs. Bagley asserted that settlers were not cowardly and that only the "timid and irresolute" behaved badly (*History of Seattle,* vol. 1, 75). As a staunch defender of Leschi, Ezra Meeker was a debunker of the Treaty War and admitted that there were doubtless "some poltroons" but also noted Phelps's "evident bias" caused by the lieutenant's "manifest desire to magnify the part he and his men played in repelling the attack" (*Tragedy of Leschi,* n. 145); Meeker disparaged the fight, "if it can be called fighting" (144). Alice Harriman, editor

of the posthumous 1908 publication of Phelps's *Reminiscences*, argued that Seattle had no "floating population" but that every man was a family man and there were "no cowards" when it "came to actual fighting" (*Reminiscences of Seattle,* n. 40). For Leschi's "race consciousness," see Watt, *Story of Seattle,* 202. *ARSN* (1856), Dobbin's pioneers quotation, 408. Nicholas Sheffer recalled that Susan Suquardle was present in Seattle and on board the *Decatur* at the same time as Catharine Blaine (*Lynden Tribune,* August 19, 1909).

110 C. Prosch, *Reminiscences of Washington Territory,* "lazy people" quotation, 27.

111 June 1, 1856, Logbook, passengers; Phelps, "Reminiscences of Seattle," Northern Indians quotations, 704–5; Swartwout to Gansevoort, June 3, 1856, Gansevoort Letterbook, departure. For admiration of distant Indians that explains Phelps's pride in relationship with "northern Indians," see John Lutz, "Inventing an Indian War," *Journal of the West* 38, no. 3 (1999): 7–13.

6. SAN FRANCISCO

1   Swartwout to Dobbin, June 2, 1856, Commanders' Letters, *Decatur* condition; "Report of John Lenthall, Bureau of Construction," *ARSN* (1854), 476; Gansevoort to Mervine, June 16, 1856, Squadron Letters, voyage; Gansevoort to Dobbin, June 16, 1856, Commanders' Letters; June 1–14, 1856, Logbook.

2   June 14, 1856, Logbook, *Decatur* at navy yard; Gansevoort to Mervine, June 16, 1856, Squadron Letters, report; Mervine to Dobbin, August 12, 1856, Squadron Letters, Mervine's regret; Mervine to Gansevoort, August 13, 1856, Gansevoort Letterbook, orders.

3   Dobbin to Gansevoort, March 6, 1856, Letters Sent by the Secretary of the Navy to Officers, 1798–1868, RG45, M149, reels 51–53, Dobbin and secretary of war commendations; Davis to Dobbin, March 5, 1856, Gansevoort Letterbook, Davis note; *New York Times,* February 28, 1856, praise for Gansevoort; Johnson, *Thence round Cape Horn,* army complaints against Gansevoort, 107; Mervine to Gansevoort, December 3, 1855, Gansevoort Letterbook, commissions and warrants.

4   Lott, *Long Line of Ships,* Mare Island in 1856 and *Warren* quotation, 34–35.

5   June 16–July 23, 1856, Logbook; Gansevoort to Mervine, June 16, 1856, Squadron Letters.

6   For the 1856 Vigilance Committee, see Roger W. Lotchin, "The Revolution of 1856," in *San Francisco, 1846–1856: From Hamlet to City* (Urbana: University of Illinois Press, 1997); Senkewicz, *Vigilantes in Gold Rush San Francisco;* Philip J. Ethington, *The Public City: The Political Construction of Urban Life in San Francisco, 1850–1900* (Cambridge: Cambridge University Press, 1994); L. Richards, *California Gold Rush;* and Royce, *California,* 438–65. See Ball, "Stop Them: Regulars, Filibusters and Vigilantes in San Francisco, 1851–1856," in *Army Regulars,* for army role; Lott, *Long Line of Ships,* navy yard involvement, 40–44; and Johnson, *Thence round Cape Horn,* 108–9; also Farragut to Dobbin, June 3 and 19, July 2 and 17, 1856, Commandants' Letters, quotations; July 26, 1856, Logbook, outfitting ship.

7   Terry to Boutwell, July 3, 1856, enclosure in Boutwell to Dobbin, Commanders' Letters, seizure and secession; Boutwell to Dobbin, July 3, 1856, Commanders' Letters, "batter the city" quotation; Farragut to Dobbin, July 2, 1856, Commandants' Letters; Senkewicz, *Vigilantes in Gold Rush San Francisco*, possible corruption of Ashe, 175–76.

8   Farragut, *Life of David Glasgow Farragut*, Vigilance Committee, 169, 186–87; Farragut's *Life* reprints correspondence between Farragut and Dobbin, Boutwell, and the Vigilance Committee at the time, more fully available in the Commanders' Letters. For Terry and the *John Adams*, see Commanders' Letters: Boutwell to Dobbin, August 13, 1856; Farragut to Boutwell, July 1, 1856, Vigilance Committee; Boutwell to Dobbin, July 3, 1856; Farragut to Boutwell, July 2, 1856.

9   Farragut to Dobbin, August [illegible but certainly prior to August 19] 1856, Commandants' Letters; Lott, *Long Line of Ships*, armada, 44; *Alta California*, August 30, 1856, navy attack on San Francisco like Greytown quotation; *San Francisco Daily Evening Bulletin*, July 29, 1856, satirical quotations.

10   Mervine to Dobbin, August 12, 1856, Squadron Letters.

11   August 18, 1856, Logbook, Gansevoort "suspended from duty by Captain Farragut"; Farragut to Dobbin, August 18, 1856, Commandants' Letters, Gansevoort quotations; H. Parker, *Herman Melville*, vol. 2, 429; John Almy to Wise, March 21, 1862, Harry Augustus Wise Papers, Manuscripts Division, New-York Historical Society, Gansevoort removed from command of the *Decatur* "on account of habitual drunkenness."

12   Farragut to Dobbin, August 18, 1856, Commandants' Letters; Gansevoort to Dobbin, August 19, 1856, Commanders' Letters.

13   *Journal of the Senate of the United States of America*, 34th Cong., 3rd sess., January 31, 1857, stricken paragraph, 145.

14   Mervine to Dobbin, September 18, 1856, Squadron Letters, Gansevoort's habits, officers' accountability quotations; *Decatur* officers to Dobbin, August 19, 1856, Commanders' Letters, petition, note on margin dated September 17, 1856; Gansevoort to Dobbin, September 19, 1856, Commanders' Letters, breezy note.

15   Welsh to Mervine, October 2, 1856, Confidential Letters, Gansevoort on furlough and replacement by Middleton; Gansevoort to Dobbin, October 15, 1856, Commanders' Letters, detachment; Gansevoort to Dobbin, November 12 and December 12, 1856, Commanders' Letters, awaiting orders; Gansevoort to Toucey, June 24, 1858, Commanders' Letters, job hunt quotation.

16   Farragut to Dobbin, August 29, 1856, Commandants' Letters, "drunkard" quotation; Middleton to Dobbin, August 29, 1856, Letters Received by the Secretary of the Navy from Commissioned Officers below the Rank of Commander and from Warrant Officers, RG45, M148, reels 239–40, NARA, Stocking suspension; November 5, 1856, Logbook, Stocking leaves ship.

17   Royce, *California*, prosperity of 1853 followed by depression in 1854 and 1855, 422–23, 431; *Alta California*, November 19, 1856, filibuster recruiter quotation; *Daily Evening Bulletin*, December 21, 1855, more than $44,000,000 in gold; *Alta California*, June–November 1856, auctions and failed partnerships; *Alta California*, September 13 and 14, October 23, 1856, quotations.

18 July 20, 1856, Logbook, fight; November 8, 1856, Logbook, Silk, McCarty, and Williamson.

19 James Simpson, September 30, 1856, Courts Martial, quotations; October 7, 1856, Logbook.

20 Corbin's injuries: July 21, 1856, Medical Log, and July 21, 1856, Medical Journal.

21 *Alta California,* November 10, 1856, Coon; *Daily Evening Bulletin,* November 6 and 20, 1856, Brown and desperado.

22 See *Daily Evening Bulletin,* September 23, 1856, for Kingsbury assault; October 23, 1856, trial; November 5, 1856, "notorious" quotation; November 8 and 10, 1856, sailors declared "not entitled to vote"; February 9, 1857, general description of Werth and "chivalry" quotations. See *Alta California,* November 5, 9, 11, 1856, for Werth and *Decatur* sailors; November 5, 1856, "violent and indecent" quotation. With some errors, the Werth incident was also reported in the *New York Times,* December 6, 1856.

23 Mervine to Middleton, September 29, 1856, Squadron Letters.

24 September 6 and 10, 1856, Logbook. There were a number of unsuccessful desertions in San Francisco. For example, Jackson Abbott was retaken. After a summary court-martial, he was sentenced lightly "in consideration of the previous good conduct of this prisoner and particularly while in the presence of the enemy at Seattle." Middleton disagreed and noted on the jacket of the document that the court had a "misapprehension of its authority" and that desertion was so great a crime that it "cancels all previous merits"; December 16, 1856, Courts Martial.

25 Farragut to Mervine, November 19, 1856, Squadron Letters, crewing up quotations; Mervine to Dobbin, November 19, 1856, Squadron Letters.

26 Charles H. Davis, *Life of Charles Henry Davis, Rear Admiral* (Boston: Houghton Mifflin, 1899), "reckless life" quotation, 107–8; Royce, *California,* "floating population" quotations, 50, 100; January 8, 1857, Logbook, departure; *San Francisco Herald,* January 9, 1857.

7. EPISODE 3. NICARAGUA

1 February 2, 1857, Logbook, first timed exercise; March 9, 1857, Logbook, anchor off Panama. Dallas, who rejoined the *Decatur* in San Francisco, mentions drilling the men with broadswords and at the great guns (February 2 and 4, 1857, Dallas Journal). Melville, *White-Jacket,* drill quotation, 67; Mervine to Dobbin, March 18, 1857, Squadron Letters, *Decatur* arrival Panama.

2 Dobbin, *ARSN* (1856); Davis to Toucey, December 7, 1857, Commanders' Letters, Honolulu statistics; Mervine to Dobbin, June 30, 1856, Squadron Letters, Samoa quotation.

3 For the Guano Island Act, see 43rd Cong., 1st sess., *United States Statutes at Large* 18, part 1 (1873–75): 1080; *ARSN* (1857), Davis takes possession, 575; Davis to Toucey, October 3, 1857, Commanders' Letters. Mervine gained notoriety for his insistence that "the guano enterprise is a stupendous fraud"; Mervine to Dobbin,

April 20, 1857, June 30, 1856, Squadron Letters. Mervine to Toucey, May 18, 1857, Squadron Letters, petition enclosed. After slavery was abolished in Peru, the Chincha Islands guano was dug and loaded, first by Chinese labor and later by Polynesian labor, under Peruvian license. This brutal work—an *"affraux travail,"* according to an eyewitness—led many to commit suicide; see H. E. Maude, *Slavers in Paradise: The Peruvian Slave Trade in Polynesia, 1862–1864* (Stanford, CA: Stanford University Press, 1981), 1–2, 26, quotation, 98.

4   Swartwout to Dobbin, November 23, 1856, Commanders' Letters, *Massachusetts* attack; Mervine to Swartwout, February 28, 1857, Squadron Letters, disrespect quotation; Mervine to Dobbin, June 6, 1857, Commanders Letters, arrogance; and Mervine to Swartwout, April 16, 1857, Mervine Letterbooks, arrogance quotation. Swartwout wrote directly to Dobbin on many occasions in 1857 involving decisions related to Mervine's responsibility, for instance, September 10 and 14, 1857, Commanders' Letters. Mervine to Dobbin, March 5, 1856, Squadron Letters, refusal to sign court-martial; Mervine to Dobbin, September 30, 1856, Squadron Letters, officer indiscipline and dissolution of navy (Mervine seems here to clearly be referring to Du Pont, although he may have had other politically minded officers in mind); Dobbin to Mervine, September 1, 1856, Confidential Letters, rebuke of Mervine quotation. It is very likely that abolitionist Whig/Republican Mervine and North Carolina Democrat Dobbin were in political disagreement.

5   Stevens to "Captain," Navy Yard, Benicia, California, April 17, 1857, Squadron Letters, steamer quotation; Mervine to Toucey, October 2, 1857, Squadron Letters, no officers available; Mervine to Toucey, June 18, 1857, Squadron Letters, dispatch refused quotation; Wool to Jefferson Davis, December 18, 1856, "Indian Affairs on the Pacific," 34th Cong., 1st sess., Ex. Doc. 76 (Washington, DC, 1857); Mervine to Dobbin, March 3, 1857, Squadron Letters, *Massachusetts;* Phelps, "Reminiscences of Seattle," admiration and principle quotations, 701–3. Farragut was also convinced that Ebey's beheading was retribution (Farragut to Dobbin, October 28, 1857, Commandants' Letters). According to Lutz, Ebey's beheading was "clearly retaliation" ("Inventing an Indian War," 10). Mervine to Toucey, October 20, 1857, Squadron Letters, imminent danger quotation; Mervine to Farragut, October 19, 1857, Squadron Letters, *St. Mary's* officers to *Massachusetts.*

6   It took two and a half days to cross the isthmus in 1849 (Keyes, *Fifty Years Observations of Men and Events,* 224). The ocean trip around Cape Horn by sail took five to eight months (Starr, *Americans and the California Dream,* 52–53). For general railroad trip descriptions, see "A Trip on the Panama Railroad," *Harper's,* October 1855; "The Panama Railroad," *Harper's,* January 1859; and *New York Times,* November 5, 1857.

7   Long, *Gold Braid,* 6,000 men died, 136; "A Trip on the Panama Railroad," *Harper's,* October 1855, fever quotations.

8   For the Panama riot, see *New York Times,* April 30, 1856; May, *Manifest Destiny's Underworld,* 234–35; and Long, *Gold Braid,* 136–38. Mervine to Toucey, April 5, 1857, Squadron Letters, calamity quotations. According to the *Alta California*

(November 9, 1856), the *London Times* characterized Buchanan's administration as a "filibustering government" after Corwine's report appeared. Schroeder, *Shaping a Maritime Empire*, occupying force and Corwine report quotation, 129–30. March 5–9, Dallas Journal, prepare *Decatur* quotation. Mervine took charge of the *Decatur*, for instance, ordering the divisions to beat to quarters; May 29, 1857, Logbook. *New York Herald*, May 2, 1857, "possession" quotation.

9   For Mervine's signals to the *Decatur*, see, e.g., March 9, 14, 15, 1857, Logbook. March 9, 19, 30, 1857, Mervine Letterbooks, Mervine notes. Mervine had complained that the *Decatur* was slow in arriving and that the ship had "not been heard from [on March 3] though she sailed from San Francisco on the 5th of January," implying that Middleton was dilatory; Mervine to Toucey, March 3, 1857, Mervine Letterbooks. Connell and Mack, *Naval Ceremonies*, changing command, 63–64; March 31, 1857, Logbook, Mervine visit and inspection, officers changeover; April 5, 1857, Logbook, Thatcher inspects ship; August 20, 1857, Logbook, list of second cruise officers; Middleton to Toucey, March 30, 1857, Squadron Letters, officers detached.

10 April 10, 1857, Logbook, "ship to rights" quotation; April 11, 1857, Logbook, "ataunto" quotation; March 13–15, 1857, Logbook, scrubbing clothes and hammocks, fresh provisions, wooding and watering; April 15 and May 15, 1857, Logbook, officer complement complete.

11 March 5–9, 1857, Dallas Journal, old Spanish town; "A Trip on the Panama Railroad," *Harper's*, October 1855, general description of Panama and townspeople.

12 Cockfight description and hulls quotation from "Tropical Journeyings: Panama," *Harper's*, September 1859. Greenberg notes that cockfighting was a common entertainment up the coast in San Francisco saloons as well (*Manifest Manhood*, 236).

13 March 13–14, 1857, Logbook, *Decatur* receives powder, shot, and grape; late March, April, and early May, 1857, Logbook, drills nearly daily; April 2, 1857, Logbook, fit launch for action; March 5–9, 1857, Dallas Journal, *Independence* prepared for Panama railroad attack. Thatcher asked how many coxswains he was entitled to, because the six small boats of the *Decatur* were "in constant use"; Thatcher to Dobbin, April 17, 1857, Commanders' Letters. Welsh to Mervine, September 17, 1856, and December 3, 1856, Confidential Letters, U.S. Panama policy; Mervine to Dobbin, September 2, 1856, Squadron Letters, general situation and contingencies quotation; Mervine to Bailey, December 11, 1856, Mervine Letterbooks; Mervine to Dobbin, March 18, 1857, Squadron Letters, fears that filibuster would enslave Panama's black population; Long to Sinclair, May 31, 1858, Squadron Letters, consul to navy ships re signals; Mervine to Ingraham, April 16, 1857, Mervine Letterbooks, infantry and artillery drills, Sterrett's distribution of arms, request for arms and powder; *New York Herald*, May 5 and 17, 1857, navy's marine-style drills in Panama harbor.

14 Mervine to Gansevoort, January 13, 1856, Squadron Letters, Mazatlan filibusters and "deluded Young Americans" quotation. This filibuster was not William Walker's more famous Sonora adventure.

15 For Walker filibusters, see May, *Manifest Destiny's Underworld*; May, *Southern Dream*

of a Caribbean Empire; Ralph Lee Woodward Jr., *Central America: A Nation Divided* (New York: Oxford University Press, 1999); Rosengarten, *Freebooters Must Die!* 175–457; William O. Scroggs, *Filibusters and Financiers: The Story of William Walker and His Associates* (New York: Macmillan, 1916); Brown, *Agents of Manifest Destiny;* and Walker's own account, *The War in Nicaragua* (Mobile: Goetzel, 1860). Walker impressed even those who disagreed with him (May, *Manifest Destiny's Underworld,* 79). Swan, "William Walker's Manifest Destiny," Walker Sonoran recruits quotation, 39–40; L. Richards, *California Gold Rush,* Sonora venture and backing of California senators, 139–40; Amos Aschbach Ettinger, *The Mission to Spain of Pierre Soulé, 1853–1855: A Study in the Cuban Diplomacy of the United States* (New Haven, CT: Yale University Press, 1932), Young American California senators, 165. For Walker's early biography and his Sonoran filibuster, see May, *Manifest Destiny's Underworld,* 1–44; Rosengarten, *Freebooters Must Die!* 35–56; and Walker, *The War in Nicaragua,* 16–24 (page numbers refer to the 1971 reprint). *New York Times,* February 27, 1857, physical description of Walker.

16 For the Nicaragua transit, see May, *Manifest Destiny's Underworld,* 174–77; L. Richards, *California Gold Rush,* 137–41; Scroggs, *Filibusters and Financiers,* 71–81; and Brown, "To Unite the Two Great Oceans," in *Agents of Manifest Destiny.* For contemporary articles on undeveloped riches of Nicaragua, see "Commercial and Other Characteristics of Central America," *DeBow's,* January 1855; "Nicaragua and the Fillibusters," *DeBow's,* June 1856, 2000 Americans per month and stars and stripes quotation, 673; "Fillibustering," *Putnam's,* April 1857. The indefatigable E. G. Squier published widely on the opportunities of Central America and Nicaragua, including *Travels in Central America: Particularly in Nicaragua* (New York: Appleton, 1853), *Notes on Central America* (New York: Harper and Brothers, 1855), and "Nicaragua: An Exploration from Ocean to Ocean," *Harper's,* October and November 1855, and "Reminiscences of Central America," *DeBow's,* October 1860, "so low in the scale" and "foreigners" quotations, 427. The introduction to this last article indicates that Squier was describing a visit to Nicaragua in 1856, though the date of publication was four years later.

17 Greenberg, *Manifest Manhood,* "booster narrative" quotation, 55–56. Greenberg is wonderful on the promise of Central American female sexuality, compliant to the irresistible American man in 1850s popular literature. See also Heffer, *The United States and the Pacific,* sexual promise of Central America, 104–9; May, *Manifest Destiny's Underworld,* four women for every man, 195; Brown, *Agents of Manifest Destiny,* filibuster motives, 458–59; "Nicaragua and the Fillibusters," *DeBow's,* June 1856, "misery" quotation, 673–74; "The Nicaraguan Question," *United States Democratic Review,* February 1858, 118; Squier, "Reminiscences of Central America," *DeBow's,* October 1860, race quotation, 411; "Central America—Its Institutions and Policy and Political Questions Involved," *DeBow's,* July 1856; "Filibustering," *Putnam's,* April 1857, "ignorance" quotation, 427.

18 Walker, *The War in Nicaragua,* Wool, 28. May terms Walker's version of Wool's remarks "unsubstantiated, but possibly true" (*Manifest Destiny's Underworld,* 146). Wool later published a letter in the *New York Times,* July 25, 1857, responding to Walker's claim that he had essentially sanctioned the first filibuster to Nicara-

gua. Wool wrote that Secretary Davis had chastised him for arresting the Sonora filibusters, so Wool was convinced that he "had no authority to interfere" with Walker. Wool also wrote that it was his memory that Walker's filibuster, from the start, had the intent of "conquering several states in [Central America] and forming them into an independent slave confederacy." The original group of sixty included one Hawaiian, Kanaka John (Greene, *Filibuster*, 261). *New York Times*, April 10, 1857, Walker and the financiers; Slotkin, *Fatal Environment*, manifest destiny agent and *Herald* Waterloo quotation, 252; Robert E. May, "Manifest Destiny's Filibusters," in Haynes and Morris, *Manifest Destiny and Empire*, role of press in Walker recruitment, 159–60, racism's expression and appeal, 164–65; May, *Manifest Destiny's Underworld*, role press, 66–73.

19 "Nicaragua and the Fillibusters," *DeBow's*, June 1856, Pierce and Americanization quotations, 671, *Uncle Sam* and rifles, 687–89; Slotkin, *Fatal Environment*, folktale and manifest destiny combined for Walker's nickname, 114. For the tale, also see Scroggs, *Filibusters and Financiers*, 128; May, *Manifest Destiny's Underworld*, 47–48; and Rosengarten, *Freebooters Must Die!* 100. Brown argues that the tale was "calculated fiction" (*Agents of Manifest Destiny*, 308).

20 *New York Times*, February 27, 1857, high times of Walker; "The Experience of Samuel Absalom, Filibuster," *Atlantic Monthly*, December 1859, 660. May's chapter "John Goddard's Lesson" in *Manifest Destiny's Underworld* describes the varied appeals of the Walker filibusters to recruits. May, *Manifest Destiny's Underworld*, Young Americans throng Granada, 112; Slotkin, *Fatal Environment*, Walker's propaganda apparatus, 250–51. For the appeal of heroic passages at arms for men "to embrace martial practices they might have disavowed at home," see Greenberg, "William Walker and the Regeneration of Martial Manhood," in *Manifest Manhood*, 133. L. Richards, *California Gold Rush*, 2,500 recruits from San Francisco, 140; *New York Times*, February 27, 1857, seeing the elephant in Nicaragua.

21 May, *Manifest Destiny's Underworld*, filibuster pay, 97; *Alta California*, November 19, 1856, recruiter and *Orizaba*; September 7, 1855, and February 18, 1856, Logbook, Drinkhouse; *Easton Argus*, March 3, 1859, Drinkhouse obituary. For Drinkhouse on the *Granada* and crew lists, see December 25, 1856, and April 11, 1857, folders 141 and 142, Callender I. Fayssoux Collection of William Walker Papers, 1856–60, Latin American Library, Tulane University, New Orleans, LA. *Young America on the Pacific*, March 1854, "Sailor of manifest destiny views," 3.

22 May, *Southern Dream of a Caribbean Empire*, free transportation and mingled with passengers, 98–99. For descriptions of the transit, see Squier, "Nicaragua: An Exploration from Ocean to Ocean," *Harper's*, October and November 1855; and "The Experience of Samuel Absalom, Filibuster," *Atlantic Monthly*, December 1859.

23 May, "William Walker in Nicaragua" and "William Walker and the South," in *Southern Dream of a Caribbean Empire*; Woodward, *Central America*, crash program, 144. See Walker, "The Walker Administration," in *The War in Nicaragua*, for Americanization, or "reorganization," as Walker put it, including language and slavery. For the slavery decree and Wheeler, see May, *Manifest Destiny's Underworld*, 263–67; and May, *Southern Dream of a Caribbean Empire*, 97–98. Walker, *The War in*

Nicaragua, Wheeler recognition, 141, *el ministro filibustero*, 298; Brown, *Agents of Manifest Destiny*, 307, 348. The *Raleigh Weekly Register* regularly ran articles from *Il Nicaraguense* acknowledging "Hon. John H. Wheeler, United States Minister at Granada" as their source. Randall O. Hudson, "The Filibuster Minister: The Career of John Hill Wheeler as United States Minister to Nicaragua, 1854–1856," *North Carolina Historical Review* 49, no. 3 (1972): 280–97. Priest to Marcy, September 9 and 11, 1855, Despatches from U.S. Consuls in San Juan del Sur, RG59, T152, reel 1, NARA, landing and extortion. Mervine wrote that Walker had committed "unwarrantable outrages," robbing American transit passengers, impressing some into his army, and extorting funds from Priest (Mervine to Swartwout, October 19, 1855, Squadron Letters).

24 For quotations from Walker, see Walker, *The War in Nicaragua*, irrepressible, 263, argument that the slavery decree presented opportunity for Central American empire to the slaveholding South, 264–80, avoid revolution, 265, bind, 266, slavery benefits, 271, empire, 276, beyond limits, 277, enemies, 278, naturalized Nicaraguans, 279. Slotkin, *Fatal Environment*, Walker as opportunist, nuanced by the subtle contradictions of his convictions, 246–49; May, *Southern Dream of a Caribbean Empire*, "darling" quotation, 106, independent slave republic, 134; "Nicaragua," *DeBow's*, January 1857, new acquisition quotations, 106, 108.

25 May suggests that Wheeler may have pressured Walker to reinstate slavery in Nicaragua (*Southern Dream of a Caribbean Empire*, 107). Brown, *Agents of Manifest Destiny*, Marcy reproof of Wheeler, 311–12; Rosengarten, *Freebooters Must Die!* Wheeler a white supremacist, 140–41; Joseph S. Fowler, "Memoir of the Author," in John Hill Wheeler, *Reminiscences and Memoirs of North Carolina and Eminent North Carolinians* (Columbus, OH: Columbus Printing Works, 1884), Wheeler on Walker and race quotations, iv–v. One of Wheeler's slaves described him as a conniving little office-seeker, scheming in Washington hallways and taverns: Henry Louis Gates, ed., *The Bondwoman's Narrative*, by Hannah Crafts (New York: Warner Books, 2002), 150, 157–60, 197; see Crafts's characterization of "Riggs of the Naval Department" as "almost dead," whom "Trotter" would be likely to succeed and who would then favor Wheeler's cause (160). "Trotter" is likely code for "Dobbin," as both refer to horses. Walker, *The War in Nicaragua*, Wheeler and Marcy, 166–68, 231–33, 238, 247–48, 298–99, 351–54; May, *Manifest Destiny's Underworld*, Marcy had directed Wheeler to "abstain from official dealings with Walker's government," 122. Langley argues that Pierce was mistaken in his hope that Dobbin would "balance" his cabinet against Jefferson Davis; rather, Dobbin proved to be a staunch supporter of Southern states rights (Coletta, *American Secretaries of the Navy*, 279–80n297). Chisholm agrees that Pierce overestimated Dobbin's support for the Union (*Waiting for Dead Men's Shoes*, 220). Brown, *Agents of Manifest Destiny*, Dobbin a "man with Southern rights sentiments," 110, Dobbin recommended Wheeler as minister to Nicaragua, 263; Hudson ("Filibuster Minister") argues that Wheeler's efforts to get Dobbin elected as U.S. senator from North Carolina, albeit unsuccessful, earned the future navy secretary's "undying friendship and gratitude," and Dobbin in turn secured Wheeler his appointment.

26 Willard Carl Klunder, *Lewis Cass and the Politics of Moderation* (Kent, OH: Kent

State University Press, 1996), "spread-eagle" quotation, 289; Brown, *Agents of Manifest Destiny,* meeting, 342; *New York Herald,* May 24, 1856, meeting and Cass letter quotation; May, *Southern Dream of a Caribbean Empire,* Cass as Young America stalwart, 23; Long, *Gold Braid,* "advance agent" quotation, 130; May, *Manifest Destiny's Underworld,* Pierce's growing disapproval of filibuster, 121–27, national phenomenon/Southern crusade, 252, 268–69; Eyal, *Young America Movement,* Pierce's "gradually weakening stomach" for the filibuster, 137.

27   "The Nicaraguan Question," *United States Democratic Review,* February 1858, "buccaneer war" and driven into corner quotations, 117; Mervine to Dobbin, December [day illegible], 1856, Squadron Letters, proclamation quotations; "The Experience of Samuel Absalom, Filibuster," *Atlantic Monthly,* December 1859, filibuster day quotation, 57, and failure of first filibuster; Hine to Marcy, March 10, 1857, Despatches from U.S. Consuls in San José, Costa Rica, RG59, T35, reel 1, NARA, deserters; *New York Times,* April 30, 1857, failure of Walker filibuster.

28   Orders quoted in *New York Times,* July 7, 1857; Davis to Mervine, March 4, 1857, Squadron Letters, Walker and law of nature. For political application of this "law of nature" to American expansion, see Samuel S. Cox, "The Law of Growth Demands Intervention in Mexico and Central America," in Graebner, *Manifest Destiny;* Walker, *The War in Nicaragua,* Davis meetings, 385–88; Greenberg, *Manifest Manhood,* filibuster virtues, "true men" quotation, 158; Rotundo, *American Manhood,* 18–20. Contemporary journalists also noted the "decidedly Saxon features" of Walker's men; e.g., "Nicaragua and the Fillibusters," *DeBow's,* June 1856, 687.

29   *New York Herald,* July 2, 1857, Mervine a Black Republican and Mervine distaste quotation; May, *Southern Dream of a Caribbean Empire,* Marcy an Old Fogy, 41; Walker, *The War in Nicaragua,* Davis, Mervine, and Marcy advancing British interests, 415, old friends insinuation, n. 422; May, *Manifest Destiny's Underworld,* Black Republicans support Mora against Walker, 277; *New York Times,* March 30, 1857, quotations re Davis and landing of *Sierra Nevada* ("Foreign nations will have a right to suppose the *St. Mary's* was sent there to protect the landing of filibusters, rather than to enforce the observance of the Neutrality Laws"). Secretary of War Jefferson Davis declared that the navy should not be "a constabulary force to stand at foreign ports and arrest persons suspected of a misdemeanor"; Senator Stephen R. Mallory, chairman of the Senate Committee on Naval Affairs and future secretary of the Confederate States Navy, agreed (Brown, *Agents of Manifest Destiny,* 423).

30   Davis to Mervine, May 15, 1857, Squadron Letters. For a general description of the negotiations, see Brown, *Agents of Manifest Destiny,* 395–407; Long, *Gold Braid,* 130–36; Greene, *Filibuster,* 290–95; and Walker, *War in Nicaragua,* 228–34, 386–88, 409–29. Long, *Gold Braid,* "terms" negotiated by Davis with Walker, 132; Rosengarten, *Freebooters Must Die!* Walker surrendered to navy, not to Mora, 175; Greene, *Filibuster,* 291–96; May, *Manifest Destiny's Underworld,* account of negotiation and surrender that mentions *Decatur,* 205–10. *New York Herald,* January 28, 1858, Walker surrendered "to the stars and stripes." Davis to Mervine, April 15, 1857, Squadron Letters, Davis reluctant to help "a man [Drinkhouse] who has

deserted from our fleet to abandon another in extremity."

31 For Walker's legacy of anti-American feeling in Central America, see May, epilogue and "The State Department's Albatross," in *Manifest Destiny's Underworld*.

32 Mervine to Toucey, May 18, 1857, Squadron Letters, Walker; Mervine to Calvo, May 17, 1857, Squadron Letters, "peaceful" quotation; *New York Times*, July 14, 1857, filibuster crossing.

33 Mervine to Toucey, June 2, 1857, Squadron Letters, Walker and marines; Francis X. Holbrook, "The Navy's Cross—William Walker," *Military Affairs* 39, no. 4 (1975): *Decatur* marines, 200; Veragua filibuster reported May 2, 1857, in *New York Times*; *New York Herald*, June 29, 1857, Walker boards train; May, *Manifest Destiny's Underworld*, marine guard, 235, immediate plans to return to Nicaragua, 49; Long, *Gold Braid*, "frantic enthusiasm" quotation, 132.

34 *New York Times*, August 5, 1857, McCorkle's duty described; McCorkle to Davis, May 30, 1857, and McCorkle to Mervine, June 18, 1857, Squadron Letters, trek quotation; Mervine to Toucey, July 3, 1857, Squadron Letters, condition quotation.

35 Mervine to Toucey, June 19, 1857, Squadron Letters, arrival of the *Mora* with 304 filibusters at Panama; Mervine to Totten, June 19, 1857, Mervine Letterbooks, Mervine requests Colonel G. M. Totten, superintendent of the Panama Railroad Company, to convey the filibusters, "relying for your compensation on the justice and magnanimity of the government"; Mervine to Toucey, July 3, 1857, Squadron Letters, Mervine's draft on navy for passage; *New York Times*, June 30 and July 14, 1857, accounts of arrivals.

36 Mervine to Thatcher, June 3, 1857, Squadron Letters, quotations from orders; Mervine to Toucey, June 2, 1857, Squadron Letters, impressments; Mervine to Toucey, June 18, 1857, Squadron Letters, *Decatur* to Costa Rica; "Holidays in Costa Rica," pt. 2, *Harper's*, February 1860, Young Anderson's Costa Rica home quotation, 322. Jones regarded Anderson as a "discomfited transit adventurer": Jones to Cass, November 28, 1857, General Records of the Department of State, List of Documents Relating to Special Agents of the Department of State, 1789–1906, Special Missions, September 11, 1852–August 31, 1886, RG59, M77, reel 154, NARA, hereafter cited as Department of State, Special Missions; Toucey to Mervine, May 16, 1857, Confidential Letters, "protection" quotation.

37 Cass to Jones, May 15, 1857, Department of State, Special Missions, quotations from orders; Jones to Cass, May 16, 1857, Despatches from Special Agents of the Department of State, 1794–1906, RG59, M37, reel 10, NARA, hereafter cited as Despatches from Special Agents.

38 *New York Times*, November 7, 1867, Jones obituary. Benton's will bequeathed his Washington residence to his daughter, William Carey Jones's wife, and named Jones as his "literary legatee" (*New York Times*, April 13, 1858). Benton intended Jones to be his biographer (*New York Times*, November 9, 1858). For Blair quotations, see *New York Times*, April 13 and May 26, 1858, and November 6, 1860. Jones hotly denied Benton's accusations.

39 Jones's letter was published on May 15, 1856, in the *Savannah (GA) Daily Morning News*, which cited it as reprinted from the *Washington Union*; Ettinger, *Mission to*

Spain of Pierre Soulé, Weller a Young American, 165.

40   "Official Proceedings of the National Democratic Convention, Held in Cincinnati, June 2–6, 1856. Pub. by Order of the Convention" (Cincinnati: Enquirer Co., 1856), platform quotations; Walker, *The War in Nicaragua*, Soulé, 275n. For Soulé's political convictions, his appointment in Spain, and his role in writing the Ostend Manifesto, see Ettinger, *Mission to Spain of Pierre Soulé*.

41   Cass to Jones, May 15, 1857, Department of State, Special Missions, Jones's orders; May, *Manifest Destiny's Underworld*, as a result of the U.S. Navy's intervention, one-quarter of those rescued rejoined a filibuster, 106–7, and many former filibusters later joined the Confederate forces, 282–84.

42   Enclosure, Cass to Jones, May 15, 1857, Department of State, Special Missions.

43   Jones to Cass, May 16, 1857, Despatches from Special Agents, Jones's saddle. Surgeon Lane reported that Jones was "well equipped for traveling the mountainous routes of this country" (*New York Herald*, July 29, 1857). For charges against Priest, see Cass to Jones, July 6, 1857, Department of State, Special Missions; and West to Cass, June 30, 1857, Despatches from U.S. Consuls in San Juan del Sur, RG59, T152, reel 1. West, formerly with Walker's army, wrote that Priest "acted disgracefully" and that the consul was "immoral, dissipated and not strictly honorable." Those who favored Walker's invasion of Central America disapproved of both Marquis Hine and John Priest. For Venable, see *New York Herald*, October 5, 1857. See also Hine's virulently anti-Walker article in *New York Times*, August 16, 1858.

44   Mervine to Toucey, May 1, 1857, Squadron Letters, *St. Mary's* and *Decatur*.

45   Swan, "William Walker's Manifest Destiny," three-hour meeting between Walker and Buchanan, 45; L. Richards, *California Gold Rush*, Buchanan as consummate doughface, 196; *ARSN* (1857), Toucey quotations, 574; "The Navy—Report of Secretary Toucey," *United States Democratic Review*, February 1858, Toucey on Davis, 104; *New York Evening Post*, June 17, 1857, Walker, Buchanan, Dobbin quotations; Long, *Gold Braid*, Davis exceeding his orders, Walker meeting Buchanan, conspiracy among Marcy, Mervine, and Davis, and censure quotations, 132–33; Holbrook, "The Navy's Cross—William Walker," 200; Rosengarten, *Freebooters Must Die!* Buchanan encouraging Walker, 180. Dobbin died in Fayetteville, NC, on August 4, 1857.

46   Jones to Cass, June 2 and 7, 1857, Department of State, Special Missions, filibusters and Davis, leading minds and Thatcher, expeditions, admiration for Walker quotations. For Jones's "twofold purpose"—to "get Walker and his men out of the country with their own consent" and to resolve the transit difficulties—see *New York Times*, July 15, 1857. Jones also instructed Paulding to send the *Cyane* to pick up filibusters on the Atlantic side, at Greytown. *New York Herald*, June 29, 1857, Amur River; *New York Herald*, September 4, 1857, Jones's mission "a profound mystery," he enjoys "keeping up the mystery"; *New York Herald*, October 5, 1857, "mysterious stranger" quotation.

47   Jones to Cass, June 7, 1857, Department of State, Special Missions, steamers; Jones to Buchanan, June 3 and 5, 1857, Department of State, Special Missions, Greytown and quotations. Lane was seldom identified by name in his *Herald* despatches from Central America, but the writer's location is always on board the

Decatur. In 1859, on at least one occasion, his article was signed L.C.L. (*New York Herald,* March 31, 1859). Additionally, the *Decatur* correspondent referred to personal experiences at the New York Emigrant Hospital, where Lane had worked, and often described medical matters. His reports appeared about twice monthly, beginning June 20, 1857. Occasional articles by Lane also appeared in the *New York Times,* for instance, March 13 and 30 and April 14, 1859.

48 Mervine to Toucey, July 18, 1857, Mervine Letterbooks, *Decatur;* June 29–July 2, 1857, Logbook; *New York Herald,* July 28, 1857, *Decatur* voyage to Punta Arenas; *New York Herald,* September 13, 1857, Canas incident; *New York Times,* March 27, 1858, Punta Arenas quotation; *New York Herald,* July 29, 1857, Punta Arenas quotation.

49 July 4, 1857, Logbook, celebration; June 28–July 27, 1857, Logbook, at Punta Arenas; "bride" quotation, *New York Herald,* July 29, 1857; account of *Decatur* marine and "spare change" quotations, *New York Herald,* September 18, 1857. Lane's mention here of Young America does not likely refer to the Democratic Party expansionist wing but to the youthful nation itself.

50 For the quotations about Costa Rica, see "Nicaragua and the Fillibusters," *DeBow's,* June 1856; and *New York Times,* March 27, 1858. Jones to Cass, marked "Private and Confidential," June 7, 1857, Department of State, Special Missions, quotation.

51 Thatcher described this journey in "Memorandum of Journey from Punta Arenas to San José," a loose sheet of paper inserted in the journal he kept while on the *Brandywine,* 1839–41; his journals for the 1857–59 command of the *Decatur* have not been located. For all quotations in this paragraph, see Henry Knox Thatcher Papers, Special Collections, Hay Library, Brown University Libraries, Providence, RI. *New York Herald,* July 28, 1857, Amur River; *New York Herald,* September 13, 1857, Thatcher and Scott's trip.

52 Thatcher, "Memorandum of Journey from Punta Arenas to San José."

53 Thatcher to Mervine, August 4, 1857, Commanders' Letters, Mora quotation, meeting of Thatcher, Mora, and Hine. For Hine, see *New York Times,* March 27, 1858.

54 The *Decatur's* role is mentioned in *ARSN* (1857), 574. Mervine to Toucey, June 18, 1857, Squadron Letters, Thatcher to spend "a few days" awaiting Jones. Royston was the former chief of Walker's military hospital at Rivas, which one filibuster called "that wretched hole whence few ever came out" ("The Experience of Samuel Absalom, Filibuster," *Atlantic Monthly,* December 1859, 665). Royston's note to Thatcher included with Hoff to Toucey, August 18, 1857, Commanders' Letters. In Mervine's absence, Hoff, captain of the *Independence,* was the senior naval officer at Panama and reported the *Decatur* rescue to Toucey. Thatcher to Mervine, August 4, 1857, "misery" quotation, included with Hoff to Toucey, August 18, 1857, Squadron Letters.

55 Thatcher to Canas, July 17, 1857, and Canas to Thatcher, July 19, 1857, included with Hoff to Toucey, August 18, 1857, Commanders' Letters. July 27, 1857, Logbook, filibusters board *Decatur;* Royston's note to Thatcher, included with Hoff to Toucey, August 18, 1857, Commanders' Letters, list of filibusters. Thatcher indicated that he had brought twenty-six "distressed Americans of the late Army

of Gen'l Walker" to Panama (Thatcher to Hoff, August 5, 1857, Commanders' Letters). The spelling of these surnames is highly variable throughout the correspondence and Logbook; for instance, it seems clear that Donoha is Donoghue and Firrell is Frizzell. The *Decatur* filibusters were reported in the *New York Times*, September 4, 1857, with place of birth and injury: Major Dolan, Louisiana, disabling wounds on left thigh and right shoulder; Captain Rayburn, Wisconsin, left thigh; Captain West, Louisiana, right leg; Private Cole, New York, hospital attendant; Private Boyle, New York, left leg; Private Clark, New York, right leg; Private Kipp, New York, ulcer on right foot; Private Burns, Ireland, right hand; Private Donoghue, Ireland, ulcers on left leg; Private Frizzell, Ireland, wounds on right leg, ulcers on right foot; Private Dewitt, Germany, left leg; Private Graham, Massachusetts, both shoulders; Private Ides, Massachusetts, general debility and partial loss of sight; Private Green, Germany, hospital attendant; Private Langerman, Germany, hospital attendant; Private Sigamund, Germany, general debility; Private McCall, Illinois, right leg amputated; Private Cason, Arkansas, both thighs and right leg; Private Madison, Sweden, left hand and thigh; Private Goss, England, general debility; Private Anauski, Poland, sore feet; Private Davis, Tennessee, right leg; Private Ingraham, New York, chronic disease; Private Forbes, Massachusetts, severe cut, left breast.

56 For Punta Arenas filibusters and deserters, see *New York Herald*, July 29, 1857, and *New York Times*, September 4, 1857; Lane, "Reminiscence of the Nicaraguan Filibusters," 960–61. Lane also described the filibusters' "general predisposition to ulceration . . . in persons who have been the subjects of exposure, hunger and overwork, through which the blood had been impoverished and the strength of the body greatly reduced" (*Surgery of the Head and Neck* [Philadelphia: P. Blakiston, 1898], 34–35). *New York Times*, October 5 and 17, 1857, description of invalid filibusters on board and *Decatur* a hospital ship.

57 *New York Herald*, July 28, 1857, description of forty or fifty former filibusters at Punta Arenas as "poor, sickly set of whom many have died," lame from "jiggers in their feet," living on charity; *New York Herald*, September 4, 1857, thirty or forty left behind at Punta Arenas; *New York Herald*, September 13, 1857, daily rial allowance suspended. The number of filibusters on board the *Decatur* is a vexed question because their very presence, let alone their food and doctoring and their arrivals and departures, was not noted in the daily ship's record.

58 For the surgeons' examination, see Mervine to surgeons, November 2, 1857, Squadron Letters; Surgeons Potter, War, and Turner to Mervine, November 1, 1857, Squadron Letters, quotations; also Mervine to Toucey, November 16, 1857, Squadron Letters. August 16, 1857, Logbook, filibusters identified as Ananski, Cole, Langeman, Boyle, and Dolan sent to San Francisco.

59 Thatcher to Toucey, November 17, 1857, Commanders' Letters, filibuster conditions and Toucey's clerk's note on Thatcher note; *New York Times*, October 5, 1857, *Decatur* officers and crew raise money to send some invalids home; and *New York Times*, October 17, 1857, filibusters on the *Decatur* "are living on the bounty of the ward room officers and men." In September and October 1857, six filibusters left the *Decatur*: Royston, West, Kipp, Rayburn, Bouton, and Clark, but the

John Adams sent back to the *Decatur* McCall, Frizzell, Cason, Ide, and Madison. McCall is probably the "Call" described with leg amputation. Mervine to Toucey, October 20, 1857, Squadron Letters, Mervine's approval quotations.

60 *New York Times,* August 15, 1857, September 4, 1857, Jones robbed; *New York Times,* November 5, 1857, Edwards as Jones's traveling companion, libel, cheating at cards, and blabbing quotations; *New York Herald,* September 4, 1857, Edwards incident; *New York Herald,* September 13, 1857, uncertain morals and slippery identity quotations, Edwards; *New York Herald,* September 18, 1857, Edwards fled Vigilance Committee. The *Times* reported $600 stolen; the *Herald* $700. The *Times* Costa Rican correspondent reported that Edwards turned Jones's documents over to the Vanderbilt interests (*New York Times,* September 4, 1857); Jones to Cass, August 3, 1857, Department of State, Special Missions, trip quotation.

61 The *Times* San José correspondent reported that Jones was "daily expected" in the Costa Rican capital (*New York Times,* July 29, 1857). Jones to Cass, June 7, 1857, Despatches from Special Agents, voyage and Costa Rica mission reassessed. Lane attributed the "exceedingly long voyage" to "tropical calms" (*New York Herald,* July 29, 1857).

62 *New York Times,* March 27, 1858, general description of San José; Thomas Meagher, "Holidays in Costa Rica II: San José," *Harper's,* January 1860, general description, 146–52, infantry barracks exhibition quotation, 158.

63 Jones to Cass, September 2, 1857, Department of State, Special Missions, Jones and Mora quotations; *New York Times,* August 15, 1857, "friendly" quotation; *New York Times,* November 5, 1857, Mora/Jones contretemps quotations.

64 *New York Times:* July 1, 1857, "UNO" dispatch; July 4, 1857, "whatever power" quotation; July 18, 1857, Jones to negotiate with Walker; August 15, 1857, "UNO" to editor, Jones incommunicado; September 4, 1857, Jones a spy who "appears to enjoy keeping up the mystery"; August 10, 1858, satirical note. Brown, *Agents of Manifest Destiny,* Jones "blundering, bibulous character," 420–21; *New York Herald,* March 27, 1858, Jones's drinking; *New York Herald,* June 29, 1857, Jones's mission "secret and mysterious."

65 *New York Times,* October 5, 1857, "bust-up" quotation; Jones to Cass, September 2, 1857, Department of State, Special Missions, Stroebel and the unnamed baker quotations. The *New York Times* correspondent referred to 350 filibusters in San José, "all kindly treated by our government" (*New York Times,* July 29, 1857). *New York Herald,* October 5, 1857, Stroebel and wife came to Punta Arenas with the Royston party and declined passage on the *Decatur.*

66 Stroebel to Jones, August 27, 1857, enclosure with Jones to Cass, September 2, 1857, Despatches from Special Agents, quotations; Jones to Calvo, August 21, 1857, Calvo to Jones, August 21 and 27, 1857, enclosures with Jones to Cass, September 2, 1857, Despatches from Special Agents.

67 *New York Times,* September 4, 1857, Republican appointees; *New York Times,* October 5, 1857, Stroebel as dodgy character quotations (the article refers to Stroebel as a "drunken Jew").

68 Jones to Cass, September 5, 1857, Despatches from Special Agents, decree; Hine

to Cass, September 4, 1857, Despatches from U.S. Consuls in San José, RG59, T35, reel 1, "imbroglio" quotation.

69 Enclosure, Jones to Cass, September 14, 1857, Despatches from Special Agents, Punta Arenas filibusters, petition, and quotations.

70 Mervine to Toucey, July 18, 1857, Squadron Letters, hundreds of Walker's men remain but mostly deserters; May, *Manifest Destiny's Underworld*, survivors and deserters, 203–5, Henningsen claimed that 2,518 men joined Walker's first fili-buster, quoted, 49; Hine to Marcy, June 9 and July 25, 1857, Despatches from U.S. Consuls in San José, RG59, T35, reel 1, San José filibuster quotations. Filibusters were hospitalized in San José as late as 1859: one was from New York and was "fearfully emaciated," another was from Louisville, Kentucky, and the third was from Chicago, and at seventeen, "he took it into his head to join the Filibusters" and gain "lots of the richest land." Desperately ill and homesick, he burst into tears while talking with an American journalist (Meagher, "Holidays in Costa Rica," *Harper's*, January 1860, 162).

71 Jones to Young, September 5, 1857, reiterated, Jones to Buchanan, October 2, 1857, Letters of Application and Recommendation during the Administra-tions of Franklin Pierce and James Buchanan, 1853–1861, RG59, M967, reel 24, NARA; Cass to Jones, July 30, 1857, Department of State, Special Missions, Cass postsurrender orders to Jones quotations; Cass to Jones, October 8, 1857, Depart-ment of State, Special Missions, Nicaragua/Costa Rica treaty quotation.

72 *New York Herald*, October 5, 1857, Jones on mail steamer *Columbus*, San Juan del Sur quotations; *New York Herald*, December 29, 1857, local feeling against John Priest; Jones to Cass, and enclosures re Priest, September 28, 1857, Department of State, Special Missions; also Priest to Cass, January 26, 1858, Despatches from U.S. Consuls in San Juan del Sur, RG59, T152, reel 1; Jones to Cass, November 28, 1857, January 1, 1858, Despatches from Special Agents, "insolence" quotation; Rosengarten, *Freebooters Must Die!* "highway" quotation, 127.

73 *New York Times*, June 8, 1857, Walker touring South; "Fillibustering," *Putnam's*, April 1857, Richmond's letter, 431–32, slave republic in Central America and extreme slave states quotation, 430, *New Orleans Delta* quoted, 432; Brown, "The Later History of Filibusterism," in *Agents of Manifest Destiny*; May, "Manifest Des-tiny's Filibusters," in Haynes and Morris, *Manifest Destiny and Empire*, decline in Northern support for filibuster, 161; May, *Manifest Destiny's Underworld*, Southern argument that Central American slave republic might make secession unneces-sary, 274ff.; Eyal, *Young America Movement*, eclipse of Young America by section-alism, 6–12, 79, 115, 137–39; David M. Potter, *The Impending Crisis, 1848–1861* (New York: Harper and Row, 1976), expansionist/nationalist quotation, 197.

74 *New York Times*, December 23, 1857, *Fashion*; Rosengarten, *Freebooters Must Die!* *Fashion* and second filibuster, 182–95, Chatard "chagrined" by his failure, 184; Holbrook, "The Navy's Cross—William Walker," genuinely mortified to find that the *Fashion* carried filibusters, 200; Long, *Gold Braid*, Chatard "befuddled," 133; Brown, *Agents of Manifest Destiny*, Chatard's "fumbling bellicosity," 416; May, *Manifest Destiny's Underworld*, Chatard "ineffective," 160. Walker, once landed, was on sovereign soil and untouchable; it is tempting to see Chatard as acting on a

Southern naval officer's sympathies for the filibuster. May identified numerous examples of Southern army officers' support for the filibuster, especially among those who later served in the Confederate States Army (Chatard served in the Confederate States Navy) ("Young American Males and Filibustering," 857–86). For Chatard's service in the Confederate States Navy, see *Officers in the Confederate States Navy, 1861–1865* (Washington, DC: U.S. Government Printing Office, 1898). Most members of the *Fashion* filibuster were Southern (*New York Times,* June 30, 1857). "The Nicaraguan Question," *United States Democratic Review,* February 1858, "thousands of young southerners" quotation, 118.

75 May, *Manifest Destiny's Underworld,* Paulding and the *Fashion,* 160–61; May, *Southern Dream of a Caribbean Empire,* 113–18; Holbrook, "The Navy's Cross—William Walker"; Scroggs, *Filibusters and Financiers;* Long, *Gold Braid,* 133–36; Brown, *Agents of Manifest Destiny,* 414–20; *New York Times,* January 29, 1858, Central American joy at failure of second filibuster; Greenberg, *Manifest Manhood,* Paulding as a "personification of restrained manhood" in contrast to Walker's undisciplined violence, 157–58; Paulding to Toucey, quoted in *National Era,* January 7, 1858; Greene, *Filibuster,* Paulding to wife, 308–9; *New York Times,* December 28, 1857, Cass quotation re Paulding; *New York Times,* January 8, 1858, Buchanan to Congress; *The Independent,* December 31, 1857, Walker "rejoicing" quotation; Coletta, *American Secretaries of the Navy,* Toucey's treatment of Paulding, 312. "Should [a naval officer] take Walker, he will be rebuked; should he—a la Chatard—permit him to land, he will be removed from his command. A pleasant dilemma" (letter to the editor, *New York Times,* December 30, 1857); Long, *Gold Braid,* Buchanan's report to Senate, 135.

76 Coletta, *American Secretaries of the Navy,* biography of Toucey; Brown, *Agents of Manifest Destiny,* Toucey's orders vague, 415, orders quoted, 433; Greene, *Filibuster,* Toucey's "vague suggestions" quotation, 305; Long, *Gold Braid,* orders "ambiguous" quotation, 134, Paulding praised or condemned sectionally, 134; Chisholm, *Waiting for Dead Men's Shoes,* Toucey a Northerner with Southern leanings, 258; Sprout and Sprout, *Rise of American Naval Power,* 146; Holbrook, "The Navy's Cross—William Walker," vacillation quotation, 201, lack of direction, 197.

77 *New York Times,* January 11, 1858, quotation, Toucey to Almy; Holbrook, "The Navy's Cross—William Walker," chance joke quotation, 200; Toucey to Paulding, December 18, 1858, Confidential Letters, Toucey's nearly identically worded orders to Paulding; *New York Times,* October 29, 1858, suggestion that naval officers use red tape to justify inaction; May, *Manifest Destiny's Underworld,* Pierce and Buchanan administration officials sincere in antifilibuster policies, quotations, 123–27; Klunder, *Lewis Cass and the Politics of Moderation,* halfhearted enforcement quotation, 293. The *New York Times* Panama correspondent observed that "half a dozen United States ships-of-war have been loafing about the ports of Nicaragua for the past four months, for what reason it would be hard to guess, as President Buchanan is proverbially indisposed to take any responsibility on his shoulders, and our naval commanders in general are very fond of red tape and circumlocution" (*New York Times,* October 29, 1858). In 1860 and early 1861, Toucey did not move to protect navy bases in the South and gracefully accepted

the resignations of U.S. Navy officers as they headed South; he was later rebuked by the Senate for his inaction, with clear suggestion of culpability.

78 *New York Times,* December 23, 1857, legitimate as Buchanan quotation; Holbrook, "The Navy's Cross—William Walker," Walker letter to Buchanan, 201. The Lake Nicaragua meeting and Jones's loss of temper were reported by the *New York Times,* March 1, 1858, and the *New York Herald,* March 27, 1858, quotations from both articles.

79 *New York Herald,* November 7, 1857, lost his baggage quotation; *New York Herald,* November 6, 1857, wedding ring; *New York Herald,* January 1, 1858, "seldom sober"; *New York Herald,* May 31, 1858, "quarreled with everybody." A lonely voice in defense of Jones's sobriety claimed that he feigned drunkenness "as a ruse" to elicit information (*New York Herald,* June 28, 1858). Jones to Cass, September 28, 1857, Despatches from Special Agents, sinister influences; Jones to Cass, November 2, 1857, Despatches from Special Agents, treachery.

80 Jones to Cass, January 30, 1858, Despatches from Special Agents, Fields quotation and Jones's suggestion that Nicaragua could not resist a five-hundred-man filibuster.

81 *New York Herald:* January 28, 1858, quotations re Jones's lamentable conduct in Rivas, including Brother Jonathan; December 29, 1857, January 28, March 30, and March 31, 1858, drunken Jones; March 6, 1858, Jones leaving on bad terms. *New York Times,* January 29, 1858, general optimism re Lamar; Brown, *Agents of Manifest Destiny,* Jones's "bumbling," 434. Lamar visited "his old friend Col. Kinney," who—though no friend of Walker's—was a filibuster in his own right (*New York Herald,* January 28, 1858).

82 *New York Herald,* January 30, 1858, Cass "out of all patience" for Jones to return to states; *New York Herald,* November 7, 1857, Cass should advertise for Jones in the Lost and Found column; Cass to Lamar, April 15, 1858, Diplomatic Instructions of the Secretary of State, 1801–1906, Central American States, May 29, 1833–July 25, 1858, RG59, M77, reel 27, NARA, Lamar's instructions; Cass to Jones, October 8 and December 29, 1857, Department of State, Special Missions, Lamar; Cass to Jones, June 28, 1858, Department of State, Special Missions, chilly dismissal; Jones to Cass, September 28, 1857, January 1 and 30 and April 7, 1858, Department of State, Special Missions, Jones's disappointments.

83 Slotkin, *Fatal Environment,* recapture myth quotation, 255, discussion of *War in Nicaragua,* 255–61; headline from January 1858 *Memphis Evening Ledger* quoted in May, *Manifest Destiny's Underworld,* 266; Walker, *The War in Nicaragua,* quotations, 279–80, 405, 431; *National Era,* January 7, 1858, reinstitution of slavery; "Late Southern Convention at Montgomery," *DeBow's,* June 1858, Southern Commercial Convention and resolution quotations, 603–4.

84 May, "Manifest Destiny's Filibusters," in Haynes and Morris, *Manifest Destiny and Empire,* pan–Central American resistance, 167–68; Greeley, *The Independent,* August 30, 1860, quotation; Lane, "Reminiscence of the Nicaraguan Filibusters," navy support of filibusters quotations, 960; Slagle, *Ironclad Captain,* Walker and pirates quotations, 93–94; *New York Times,* July 7, 1857, Davis's actions perceived as rescue; Hine to Cass, May 18, 1859, Despatches from U.S. Consuls in San José,

RG59, T35, reel 1, Mora furious; May, *Manifest Destiny's Underworld*, "riddled" quotation, 127, rescue quotation, 206.

85 Scroggs, *Filibusters and Financiers*, Mora/Martinez May 1, 1858, resolution, 361; *New York Times*, February 9, 1859, quotation; Jones to Cass, May 26 and June 22, 1859, Despatches from Special Agents; *New York Herald*, March 30, 1858, "Rum" Carey Jones only "won laurels with sugar cane distillers," Monroe Doctrine. A judicious observer concluded, "I do not believe [Jones] has been particularly successful in his diplomacy in these countries" (*New York Times*, March 27, 1858). *New York Herald*, November 30, 1858, hopes for Lamar; May, *Manifest Destiny's Underworld*, Lamar and failed Nicaraguan treaties, 243–44; Brown, *Agents of Manifest Destiny*, 215, Lamar, 433–39; *New York Times*, May 31 and June 28, 1858, Greytown rumor and Lamar's despair.

86 J. Rea, "Seeing the Elephant," *Western Folklore* 28, no. 1 (1969): 21–26; *New York Times*, February 27, 1857, "proportions" quotation; May, *Southern Dream of a Caribbean Empire*, fourth filibuster, 130–31; *Easton Argus*, March 3, 1859, Drinkhouse obituary.

8. EPISODE 4. PANAMA

1 The chapter subtitle is taken from Herman Melville, *Moby Dick, or The Whale* (New York: Penguin, 2001), 200 (originally published 1851).

2 Paullin, *History of Naval Administration, Merrimac*, 221-22; *New Era*, July 30, 1857, Long, the *Merrimac*, and two Pacific Ocean squadrons recommended; Long to Kelley, December 14, 1857, Squadron Letters, *Saranac* frugality.

3 Long to Kelley, December 14, 1857, Squadron Letters, *Saranac* cruising; Johnson, *Thence round Cape Horn*, weary round, 109. The *Decatur* returned to Panama on August 4, 1857, and remained at anchor in the harbor until June 12, 1858. Hoff to Toucey, September 3, 1857, Commanders' Letters, readiness; Mervine to Ingraham, April 16, 1857, Squadron Letters, enervated; Mervine to Dobbin, December 3, 1856, Squadron Letters, exhalations; Melville, *White-Jacket*, idleness, 383. Melville referred to idleness on a sailing frigate at sea; the *Decatur*'s situation in port was far worse. Even visitors who passed through quickly wrote that no "whites can escape deterioration upon the Isthmus" ("A Trip on the Panama Railroad," *Harper's*, October 1855, 621). *New York Herald*, December 1, 1857, Lane's first reference to debilitation, 10 percent on sick list; *New York Herald*, December 19, 1857, "debilitated by protracted sojourn in this depressing climate." For contemporary medical understanding of "noxious vapors" and "bad air," see "What Kind of Ships Generate Disease?" *U.S. Nautical Magazine*, October 1856, 8-12.

4 Lynch, *Naval Life*, "filthy girdle" around a ship, 23; Melville, "Wash-Day and House-Cleaning in a Man-of-War," in *White-Jacket;* Paullin, *History of Naval Administration*, "dogs" quotation, 229.

5 Ruschenberger to Whelan, April 14, 1857, Records of the Bureau of Medicine and Surgery, Headquarters Records, Correspondence to the Bureau from Surgeons and Assistant Surgeons, RG52, dysentery on *Independence*.

6   The *Decatur's* Medical Log was chronological; I have resorted it alphabetically to be used as a biographical source and have also analyzed the sickness reports over the course of the voyage. The Medical Journal, more detailed and discursive, exists only for the first half of the Pacific Squadron cruise. Deborah Hayden, *Pox: Genius, Madness and the Mystery of Syphilis* (New York: Basic Books, 2003), is an excellent overview of the course of venereal infection prior to the introduction of antibiotics; she refers to the frequent illusion that the disease had been "cured" because of a remission of symptoms. See also Harold D. Langley, *A History of Medicine in the Early U.S. Navy* (Baltimore, MD: Johns Hopkins University Press, 1995). I am deeply grateful to Dr. Langley for his help in understanding the *Decatur's* Medical Journal and Log.

7   Examples of men condemned from the ship: Nicholas Andrews, seaman, age twenty-three, born in Greece, last treated April 12, 1857, for chronic fever, condemned and sent home; William Henderson Gray, age twenty-two, born in Ireland, last treated January 19, 1855, for chronic venereal infection, condemned and discharged. For the process of survey, condemnation, and pension, see General Order, July 17, 1855, *Register, Circulars, and General Orders* (1855). Ward to Thatcher and Thatcher to Toucey, January 29, 1858, Commanders' Letters, Wright survey; Thatcher to Mervine and surgeons to Mervine, May 18, 1857, Squadron Letters, Raymond survey.

8   October 25, 1857, Logbook, five filibusters from *John Adams*, Cason; December 18, 1857, Logbook, Lane with filibuster. Surgeons assigned to ships on both the Atlantic and Pacific coasts of Central America wrote to the Navy Bureau of Medicine and Surgery about epidemics of Panama fever after Walker's filibusters came aboard: Addison to Whelan, August 12, 1857, and Horner to Whelan, October 2, 1857, Panama fever, and Duvall to Whelan, January 26, 1859, yellow fever on *Jamestown*, Records of the Bureau of Medicine and Surgery, Headquarters Records, Correspondence to the Bureau from Surgeons and Assistant Surgeons, RG52; *New York Herald*, October 17, 1857, filibusters on board the *Decatur*, "for whom no provision is made by the Navy Department, and who are living on the bounty of the ward room officers and men"; *New York Herald*, October 5, 1857, cholera brought "into the country by filibusters who returned from Nicaragua"; *New York Herald*, December 1, 1857, two filibusters leave *Decatur* for Panama jobs.

9   For scraping and painting, see, e.g., September 21 and November 5 and 18, 1857, Logbook. December 29, 1857, work halted because of sun; August 25, 1857, American consul visit; August 27, 1857, Paulding; September 9, 1867, English consul; December 9, 1857, Governor of Panama; February 22, 1858, Washington's birthday in Panama; all in Logbook.

10   "An Act to Amend an Act Entitled 'An Act to Promote the Efficiency of the Navy,'" in *Register of the Commissioned and Warrant Officers of the Navy of the United States* (Washington, DC: Nicholson, 1857), quotation; Weddle, *Lincoln's Tragic Admiral*, one-third of the original 201 disciplined officers were restored, 82. Sterrett's hometown newspaper considered the original board actions "precipitate and ill-advised" (*Baltimore Sun*, September 13, 1859).

11   *ARSN* (1855), 11-12.

12 Phelps, "Reminiscences of Seattle," Sterrett quotation, 681. For Sterrett's witnesses, see Sterrett to Toucey, April 22, 1857, Office of Naval Records and Library, Subject Files "U.S. Navy, 1775-1910," NI Miscellaneous re Officers Removed from the Active List in 1855, box 271, RG45, NARA. It is striking how many of Sterrett's witnesses resigned their commissions to join the Confederate States Navy: Isaac Mayo, Thomas ap Catesby Jones, Josiah Tattnall, Franklin Buchanan, Richard Jeffery, and Van Rensselaer Morgan. *New York Herald,* July 14, 1857, Sterrett dissipation; *New York Herald,* June 8 and December 22, 1857, Sterrett and Morgan reinstated.

13 *New York Herald,* July 10, 1847, Perry's testimony; *New York Herald,* July 14, 1857, Jones's testimony; Dobbin to Sterrett, February 11, 1856, Letters Sent by the Secretary of the Navy to Officers, 1798-1868, RG45, M149, reels 51-53, Dobbin commendation of Sterrett; *Olympia Pioneer and Democrat,* March 19, 1858, quotations; Phelps, "Reminiscences of Seattle," Sterrett quotations, 681. Phelps published this wholehearted approval of Sterrett's exoneration two decades after Sterrett resigned his commission to join the Confederacy, when the two men had become enemies.

14 Mahan, *Sail to Steam,* quotation, 20, pay reduced for jackass lieutenants, 22-23, general sense of approval of Plucking Board, 17-24; Paullin, *History of Naval Administration,* "pruning knife" quotation, 243; Chisholm, *Waiting for Dead Men's Shoes,* a contemporary stated that two-thirds of the furlough list ought to have been dropped, 239; Thatcher to Dupont, March 31, 1856, Samuel Francis Du Pont Papers, Hagley Museum and Library, Thatcher's support for Du Pont's "severe struggle" and resistance to courts of review. Thatcher himself was promoted to commander in the wave of Plucking Board promotions; Thatcher to Dobbin, September 2, 1856, Commanders' Letters. James Valle pointed out the tripling of naval judicial activity during the 1850s due to the twin sources of newly introduced summary courts-martial to deal with the postflogging breakdown in discipline and the appeals of officers removed from their positions by the Plucking Board (*Rocks and Shoals,* 4). Kevin Weddle contends that the officer corps was better qualified for both Civil War navies because of the Retiring Board (*Lincoln's Tragic Admiral,* 83), and board actions were the fourth most significant policy initiative in the navy between 1839 and the Civil War, joining steam propulsion, the creation of navy bureaus, and the institution of the U.S. Naval Academy (65).

15 *New York Herald,* December 29, 1857, "unchanging summer" and monotony quotations and general description of health of *Decatur* officers and men; Thatcher to Toucey, November 17, 1857, Squadron Letters, four injured filibusters remained on board the *Decatur* throughout winter 1857. Labey, September 15, 1857; Jarvis, December 18, 1857; Conlan, August 29, 1858; Dubrow, October 14, 1858; all in Medical Log. See also Melville, "Killing Time in Harbor," in *White-Jacket.*

16 Valle, *Rocks and Shoals,* desertion, 106ff. Logbook: October 27, 1857, empty dinghy; November 3, 1857, cutter crew; e.g., September 8, 9, and 30 and October 2, 1857, other desertions; e.g., November 3, 1857, and January 9, 1858, search for deserters; e.g., December 6 and 13, 1857, onshore arrests. Thatcher to Toucey, October 30, 1857, Commanders' Letters, sailmaker quotation. Thatcher was for-

tunate in getting Ware Branson, the sailmaker sent to take Chevalier's place; Branson later published a richly illustrated manual, *The Art of Sailmaking* (Boston: Butts, 1864), intended to teach "the most approved methods of cutting and making sails of every description" (1).

17 Thatcher to Toucey, August 19, 1857, Commanders' Letters, survey quotation.

18 Karsten, *Naval Aristocracy*, tricing, 85. When the Logbook qualifies "confinement," it is most often "tricing" and sometimes "in brig" or "below forecastle."

19 George Charles, October 2, 1857, Courts Martial.

20 Henry Williams, January 20, 1858, Courts Martial.

21 James Wilson, April 29, 1858, Courts Martial.

22 James Daily, January 20, 1858, Courts Martial.

23 Karsten, *Naval Aristocracy*, n. 116, "his lordship" quotation; Melville, *White-Jacket*, stew-pans and tropical heat, 80.

24 Melville, "Smuggling in a Man-of-War," in *White-Jacket*, nothing and nowhere quotation, 176.

25 For these medical histories, see Medical Log; *Brooklyn Daily Standard Union*, February 15, 1889, Coghlan obituary.

26 Joseph McDonald, Robert Watson, Charles Boland, George Harris, Hendrik Guy, and Augustus Furlong, February 24, 1858, Courts Martial.

27 John Coulyer and Edward Murphy, April 29, 1858, Courts Martial.

28 *New York Herald*, March 1, 1858, increase in fever, crew debilitated. See Logbook entries for March 25, 1858, dry rot; July 17, 1857, water condemned; November 10, 1857, spoiled beef; November 18, 1857, water use. Comparison of the Logbook entries for May 1856 with those for May 1858 shows not only the dramatic increase in the number of subjudicial punishments but the increasing gravity of the infractions and a dramatic decline in the frequency of practice and drills: for instance, the small arms drill held on June 7, 1858, was the first in more than a month.

29 Boutwell to Dobbin, March 30, 1856, Commanders' Letters, hard service quotations. Commissions in "all remote seas" were shortened from three years to two in 1857; *ARSN* (1857), 584. *New York Herald*, May 31, 1858, prolonged stay quotation; Ward to Thatcher, December 13, 1857, enclosure in Thatcher to Toucey, December 24, 1857, Commanders' Letters, Jarvis survey. For Bradley, Adams, and Stockton illnesses, see Medical Log entries for July 14-18, 1857, and February 21 and May 9, 1858.

30 September 30 and October 20, 1857, and April 19, 1858, Logbook, Stockton leave; January 14, 1858, Logbook, his return mentioned; *New York Herald*, November 5 and 6, 1857, Stockton arrived in New York City.

31 Thomas Berry, May 28, 1858, and William Martin, May 31, 1858, Courts Martial.

32 "Act for Better Government of the Navy," *ARSN* (1858), 229-37.

33 Ward to Thatcher, June 9, 1858, Squadron Letters, quotations here and in next paragraph.

34 *New York Times*, June 28, 1858, exhilarated quotation; *New York Times*, June 30, 1858, sponge incident and quotations, apology quotation.

35 Thatcher to Long, June 9, 1858, Squadron Letters, suspension and Stockton quotations.

36 Edward Stockton, June 11, 1858, Courts Martial; Stockton to Toucey, June 28, 1858, Letters Received by the Secretary of the Navy from Commissioned Officers below the Rank of Commander and from Warrant Officers, RG45, M148, reels 239-40, Stockton resignation; Long to Toucey, June 12, 1858, Squadron Letters, Stockton court-martial, debilitated quotation.

37 Long to Thatcher, May 31, 1858, Squadron Letters, Long's orders; Long to Sinclair, May 31, 1858, Squadron Letters, *Vandalia* takes over Panama duty; *New York Times,* May 29, 1857, petition for navy protection in the Chincha Islands; at the time of the petition, there were more than sixty American ships there.

38 Long to Toucey, July 26, 1858, Squadron Letters, state of squadron; Toucey to Long, November 30, 1857, and June 30 and August 19, 1858, Confidential Letters, various orders to Long.

39 Long to Toucey, August 11, 1858, Squadron Letters, *Decatur* leaky, decayed port bends; Long to Toucey, December 30, 1858, Squadron Letters, *Decatur* unseaworthy quotation; *ARSN* (1860), ships such as the *Decatur* "not worth repairing," 3-6, 305-6, quotation on 306. Naval constructor John Lenthall, who designed the *Decatur,* had long maintained that this class of sloops of war should not be kept in active service.

40 Thatcher to Long, May 8, 1858, Squadron Letters, medical survey request; surgeons to Long, May 11, 1858, Squadron Letters, medical survey quotations; Thatcher to Toucey, May 29, 1858, Commanders' Letters. Frizzell was profiled in a description of the storeship *Relief*'s cruise but was mistakenly reported to have been eight months on board the *St. Mary's* (*New York Times,* July 14, 1858). Frizzell was the last filibuster on the *Decatur* (May, *Manifest Destiny's Underworld,* 209). Twenty-five chronic invalids who were taken to New York in July 1858 were drawn from the *Merrimac, Saranac, Vandalia,* and *Decatur* and included but were not limited to filibusters (*New York Times,* July 14, 1858). Twenty-six men crossed the isthmus to Aspinwall, including two invalid crewmen and John "Laselle" from the *Decatur* (*New York Herald,* June 14, 1858).

41 Long to Toucey, July 19, 1858, Squadron Letters, Long to Callao with *Decatur;* W. Parker, *Recollections of a Naval Officer, Decatur* speedy and *Merrimac* sluggish, 188; *New York Herald,* August 16, 1858, Lane on reduction of sick list during cruise. Lane specifically noted the improvement in health of two unnamed officers, who he had feared would need to return stateside to recuperate; June 13-September 30, 1858, Medical Log, sample *Decatur* injuries at sea.

42 July 18, 1858, Logbook, Hombra; July 19, 1858, Logbook, burial; Thatcher to Toucey, August 26, 1858, Commanders' Letters, death certificate forwarded. See Lane, *Surgery,* 1016, for a possible reference to Hombra; in that massive textbook, Lane reviewed a lifetime of surgical experience and often referred to cases that might have taken place on the *Decatur,* for instance, syphilitic tumors (149) and the effects of arsenic (881-82). Connell and Mack, *Naval Ceremonies,* burial at sea, 72-73; Melville, "The Last Stitch" and "How They Bury a Man-of-War's Man at Sea," in *White-Jacket.*

43 July 7, 1858, Logbook, Payta; July 8-10, 1858, Logbook, visits; Long to Toucey, July 25, 1858, Squadron Letters, debilitated quotation.

44 For salutes and visits, see Logbook entries for August 2, 10, 16, 24, 26, 29, and 31 and September 1, 1858. The man termed "General Castillo" in the *Decatur's* Logbook is likely Peruvian president Ramón Castilla y Marquesado.

45 Ward to Thatcher, July 9, 1858, Squadron Letters, Senac complaint, quotations.

46 August 26, 1858, Logbook, court of inquiry; Felix Senac, Court of Inquiry, August 26, 1858, Courts Martial, quotations; *ARSN* (1858), forbidden to duel, appropriate to accept apology quotation, 39.

47 Long to Toucey, August 30, 1858, Squadron Letters; Toucey to Long, May 2, 1859, Confidential Letters, Ward to *Saranac.*

48 Ecuador crisis quotations from White's note, enclosure in Long to Toucey, November 26, 1858, Squadron Letters; *New York Times,* December 22, 1858, general situation; Scroggs, *Filibusters and Financiers,* rumored expeditions from California against Nicaragua at this time, 378; *Decatur* orders, August 19, 1858, referred to in Long to Toucey, December 30, 1858, Squadron Letters; Thatcher to Toucey, September 25, 1858, Commanders' Letters, quality quotation; Thatcher to Toucey, October 15, 1858, Commanders' Letters, cannon powder; Long to Toucey, January 5, 1859, Squadron Letters, cannon powder; also noted as "receipted to the Peruvian government for 1000 lbs of cannon powder, which was procured on loan" (September 29, 1858, Logbook).

49 September 29-October 3, 1858, Logbook, cruise quotation; *New York Herald,* November 30, 1858, exercise carronades quotation; Thatcher to Toucey, October 15, 1858, Commanders' Letters, Lamar.

50 Thatcher to Toucey, October 23, 1858, Commanders' Letters.

51 *New York Herald,* November 30, 1858, attempted murder and treatment quotations.

52 Thomas Murray, December 20, 1858, Courts Martial; December 30, 1858, Logbook, sentence.

53 October 21, 1858, Logbook, Weckell; November 27, 1858, Logbook, Lamar visit; December 18, 1858, Logbook, Martinez visit; Long to Toucey, December 30, 1858, Squadron Letters, Lamar and Realejo.

54 Long to Toucey, December 30, 1858, Squadron Letters, military operations quotation. Long injured his leg at Honolulu, falling down a hatchway in the *Merrimac* (W. Parker, *Recollections of a Naval Officer,* 212). Edwards to Whelan, January 4, 1859, Records of the Bureau of Medicine and Surgery, Headquarters Records, Correspondence to the Bureau from Surgeons and Assistant Surgeons, RG52, Long's leg and influenza quotations; Edwards to Whelan, June 12, 1859, Records of the Bureau of Medicine and Surgery, Headquarters Records, Correspondence to the Bureau from Surgeons and Assistant Surgeons, RG52, Cape Horn.

55 Lane, *Surgery,* compassionate surgery quotation, 842-43. Lane referred to other civilian cases seen in Panama and Nicaragua (e.g., 832), making it likely that the Chinandega surgery was not an isolated case for the naval surgeon. Lane to Whelan, December 20, 1858, Records of the Bureau of Medicine and Surgery, Headquarters Records, Correspondence to the Bureau from Surgeons and Assis-

tant Surgeons, RG52, Lane request. Lane's eager curiosity leaps from his decades of publications.

56 November 22, 1858, Logbook, Lilleston; December 6, 1858, Logbook, Senac.

57 Analysis of 1858 muster from Logbook, Medical Log, and punishment records.

58 August 12, 1858, Logbook, first sailor ironed to a stanchion; Thatcher to Toucey, December 31, 1858, Commanders' Letters, bimensal Return of Punishments, enclosure.

59 Quotations from Statement of Thomas Murray, enclosure, and from Long's note, enclosure, January 3, 1859, with Murray general court-martial, December 20, 1858, Courts Martial.

60 May, *Manifest Destiny's Underworld*, third Walker filibuster on *Susan*, 50-51; *New York Times*, December 30, 1858, Costa Rican Congress quotation; *New York Times*, January 1, 1859, filibuster army rumored to land in Honduras on the Atlantic side and cross the isthmus to the Bay of Fonseca; *New York Times*, March 14 and 30, 1859, *Hermann* and Fonseca rumors. The *Hermann* was believed to have already landed five hundred filibusters on the Pacific coast in November, eluding "American armed vessels" (*New York Times*, December 2, 1858). "The Treaty with Nicaragua," *United States Democratic Review*, June 1858, California sponsorship of third filibuster and scolding, 425.

61 Long to Thatcher, May 5, 1859, Squadron Letters, orders; Long to Toucey, January 28, 1859, Squadron Letters, Long seeks to clarify authority and mentions making inquiries of Lamar on December 22, 1858, on the same topic, quotations.

62 Long to Commanding Officer, *St. Mary's*, May 5, 1859, Squadron Letters, proclamation excerpted; *New York Times*, November 1, 1858, proclamation reported; Long to Thatcher, January 24, 1859, Squadron Letters, Lamar quotation, *Decatur* ordered to Gulf of Fonseca to intercept expedition; Long to Toucey, January 28, 1859, Squadron Letters, Fonseca expedition.

63 January 20, 1859, Logbook, flagstaff; January 23, 1859, Logbook, "distressed Americans" quotation.

64 Thatcher to Long, January 27, 1859, Squadron Letters.

65 January 27, 1859, Logbook, DeHaven and seventeen men to shore; February 2, 1859, Logbook, more supplies.

66 DeHaven to Thatcher, February 14, 1859, enclosure in Thatcher's report on Gulf of Fonseca observations, Thatcher to Long, February 16, 1859, Squadron Letters; *New York Times*, March 3, 1859, DeHaven expedition reported.

67 Casares to Thatcher and Thatcher to Casares, February 13, 1859, Squadron Letters, diplomatic notes; *New York Times*, March 30, 1859, Yankee arms, breakfast, and Thatcher quotations; February 12-16, Logbook, *Decatur* at La Union; Thatcher to Long, February 16, 1859, Squadron Letters.

68 Long to Thatcher, January 24 and February 26, 1859, Squadron Letters, orders to *Decatur;* Long to Toucey, February 28, 1859, Squadron Letters; *New York Times*, July 29, 1858, *Filibustero* quotation.

69 *National Era*, April 7, 1859, *Decatur* mistaken for filibuster ship; *Daily National Intelligencer*, April 2, 4, and 6, 1859, bridges burned; *Ohio Statesman*, April 3, 1859, "annihilated" quotation; *New York Herald*, March 31 and April 16 and 19, 1859;

New York Times, March 3, 1859; *Baltimore Sun,* April 1, 1859.

70 Thatcher to Long, March 16, 1859, Squadron Letters, no sign of *Hermann;* Long to Thatcher, February 26, 1859, Squadron Letters, orders; March 23, 1859, Logbook, "minutiae" quotation; *New York Times,* June 30, 1858, *Decatur* to be decommissioned; *New York Times,* June 3, 1858, "old-fashioned" quotation.

71 Long to Thatcher, March 23, 1859, Squadron Letters, quotations; Long to Toucey, March 31, 1859, Squadron Letters.

72 April 1-May 24, 1859, Logbook; Melville, *White-Jacket,* 311.

73 May 24, 1859, Logbook, Mare Island; May 28-June 1, 1859, Logbook, stripping ship, splice main brace.

74 Toucey to Long, February 16, 1859, Confidential Letters, Thatcher directed to give honorable discharges where appropriate; May 28, 1859, Logbook, Murray; May 25, 1859, Logbook, fifty men; June 2, 1859, Logbook, liberty. See also "Descriptive List of the Men of the U.S.S. *Decatur* who were shipped on the Pacific Coast and Discharged at San Francisco . . . Designating those who are entitled to the 'Honorable Discharge,'" March 25, 1859, Miscellaneous Records of the U.S. Navy, Muster Rolls, USS *Decatur,* RG45, T829, reel 3, NARA.

75 Edwards's death was not noted in the Medical Log; his death was reported on March 26, 1859 (Thatcher to Toucey, Commanders' Letters). *New York Herald,* March 31, 1859, Lane on Edwards.

76 Melville, *White-Jacket,* 9. Silk's discharge described him as dark, short, and a "professional seaman" (Thatcher to Toucey, February 23, 1859, Commanders' Letters). *ARSN* (1855), asylum quotation, 93; Silk, 1860 U.S. Federal Census, Philadelphia Ward 1, Marine Asylum, 678; Silk, 1870 U.S. Federal Census, Philadelphia Ward 26, District 87, 460.

77 June 20, 1859, Logbook, *Decatur* out of commission; *San Francisco Times,* June 25, 1859, "venerable" quotation; *New York Times,* August 7, 1861, receiving ship; *New York Herald,* October 20, 1859, *Decatur* in ordinary and *Saginaw.*

78 Mahan, *Sail to Steam,* Buchanan last president, 87; R. D. Gholson to J. Black, February 14, 1861, Washington Territorial Papers, Washington State Archives, Olympia, WA, resignation quotation.

9. THE CIVIL WAR AND BEYOND

1 Paullin, *History of Naval Administration,* ranks, 300–301, grog quotation, 235, statistics, 249–51; Mahan, *Sail to Steam,* "scarecrows" quotation, 34; Spencer C. Tucker, *Blue and Gray Navies: The Civil War Afloat* (Annapolis, MD: Naval Institute Press, 2006), 1861 and 1865 figures for ships, officers, and expenditures, 1; *New York Herald,* November 8, 1861, Young America takes control.

2 Paullin, *History of Naval Administration,* "posture of defense" quotation, 269.

3 Ibid., Welles's Norfolk Navy Yard quotation, 273.

4 ZC Ship History file, Navy Department Library, *Decatur* refitted as harbor battery; Lott, *Long Line of Ships,* effect of Civil War on Mare Island, 71–88. Lott claims that the *Decatur* was stripped of the battery and suggests that was the final disposi-

tion (80), but the ship's Civil War outfitting is described in *Daily Evening Bulletin* (San Francisco), March 12, 1863, and in ZC Ship History file, Navy Department Library.

5   Michael J. Bennett, "Any Man Can Become a Soldier: The Making of Union Sailors," in *Union Jacks: Yankee Sailors in the Civil War* (Chapel Hill: University of North Carolina Press, 2004), "lifelong sailors" quotation, 26. Although Bolster is concerned with the merchant marine, see his "Toward Jim Crow at Sea," in *Black Jacks*. For Massachusetts sailors, see www.massachusettscivilwar.com. For New York sailors, see Abstracts of Muster Rolls for Men Who Served in the United States Navy during the Civil War, series B0803–85, New York State Archives, Albany, NY. For Nobrega, see Nobrega to DaSilva, May 20, 1862, copy in possession of author, courtesy David Degrella. For Robert Shorter and Dennis Sycamore, see their name entries in "African American Sailors in the Union Navy," www.itd.nps.gov.

6   Mahan, *Sail to Steam*, 85–90, 149–55, toast quotation, 86; Curry, *Officers of the CSS Shenandoah*, 26–35; Paullin, *History of Naval Administration*, 216ff.; and Dudley, *Going South*, "grave error" quotation, 13.

7   Every *Decatur* line officer who resigned his commission had been disciplined, including Isaac Sterrett, Van Rensselaer Morgan, and Edward Stockton; of the warrant officers, Senac was "foreign" and Ward was a difficult man, whom Long had reprimanded. Of those who joined the Confederate States Navy, only Surgeon Richard Jeffery seems to have been a wholly ordinary naval officer. In his *The Road to Secession: A New Perspective on the Old South* (New York: Praeger, 1972), William L. Barney argued that secessionists had generally been antebellum "outsiders." Robert E. May rebuts this position in "Psychobiography and Secession: The Southern Radical as Maladjusted Outsider," *Civil War History* 34, no. 1 (1988): 46–69. Jeffery to Welles, July 12, 1861, Miscellaneous Records of the U.S. Navy, Naval Records and Library, 1861 Resignations and Dismissals of Officers, RG45, T829, reels 389–390, N;ARA, hereafter cited as Resignations and Dismissals.

8   Sterrett's resignation, April 23, 1861, Resignations and Dismissals; U.S. War Department, *War of the Rebellion: A Compilation of the Official Records of the Union and Confederate Armies*, (Washington, DC: Government Printing Office, 1880–1901), cdl.library.cornell.edu/moa, Sterrett at Manassas, series 1, vol. 2, Beauregard to Cooper, April 2, 1862, 501; *Baltimore Sun*, September 17, 1864, brief Sterrett obituary.

9   For *Monitor* and *Merrimac*, see Tucker, "The First Clash of Ironclads," in *Blue and Gray Navies;* and J. Thomas Scharf, "Hampton Roads," in *History of the Confederate States Navy* (New York: Rogers and Sherwood, 1887). Tatnall's court-martial and acquittal reported in the *New York Times,* July 29, 1862; for Sterrett's involvement "as a member of the [Tatnall] court," see Wilson and Fiske, *Appleton's Cyclopaedia of American Biography*, 667.

10 For James Sterrett, see October 15 and December 5, 1862, April 10 and June 5, 1863, Isaac Sears Sterrett Diary, Manuscripts Division, Virginia Historical Society, Richmond, VA; Kenneth Wiley, *Norfolk Blues: The Civil War Diary of the Norfolk*

Light Artillery Blues (Shippensburg, PA: Burd Street Press, 1997), James Sterrett mentioned, 23, 46, 231, 241, 297; *Baltimore Sun,* June 25, 1862, James Sterrett's death; *Baltimore Sun,* September 5, 1863, Samuel Sterrett imprisoned; *New York Herald,* July 2, 1863, Julia and Samuel Sterrett. For brief mentions of Isaac Sterrett's Confederate Navy career, see U.S. War Department, *War of the Rebellion,* series 1, vol. 5, Cooper to Johnston, November 16, 1861, 960, and series 1, vol. 2, Beauregard to Cooper, August 26, 1861, 501. Tatnall's report to Mallory was published in the *New York Times* on May 28, 1862. The report mentions Sterrett on the *Virginia,* as does U.S. Naval War Records Office, *Official War Records of the Union and Confederate Navies in the War of the Rebellion* (Washington, DC: Government Printing Office, 1894–1922), cdl.library.cornell.edu/moa, "Report of Flag Officer Tatnall, C.S. Navy," series 1, vol. 7, 336. See also Wilson and Fiske, *Appleton's Cyclopaedia,* 667.

11 Morgan, Lieutenants section, Du Pont Journal; Morgan resignation, June 28, 1861, Resignations and Dismissals; Scharf, *History of the Confederate States Navy,* Morgan Civil War career, n. 669.

12 Terry Foenander's excellent website http://home.ozconnect.net/tfoen/csnindex3.htm provided initial information concerning Stockton's Civil War service, and Foenander emailed me scans of Florida Confederate Pension File no. A 04178. For Stockton's Confederate States Navy service, also see Florida Confederate Card File in U.S. Naval War Records Office, *Official Records of the Union and Confederate Navies in the War of the Rebellion,* series 1, vol. 5, "Testimony of Lieutenant Edward C. Stockton," 654; and Ralph W. Donnelly, *The Confederate States Marine Corps: The Rebel Leathernecks* (Shippensburg, PA: White Mane, 1989), 258–59.

13 Regina Rapier, *Felix Senac: The Saga of Felix Senac; Being the Legend and Biography of a Confederate Agent in Europe* (n.p.: Bulletin of Art and History, 1970); Senac's resignation, April 21, 1861, Resignations and Dismissals.

14 Rapier, *Felix Senac,* quotation and Mallory letter, 141. Bulloch did not mention Senac by name, although there are occasional references to "Confederate agents acting in France" (Bulloch, *Secret Service of the Confederate States in Europe,* vol. 2, 63). Mallory to Bulloch, May 26, 1863, *Official Records of the Union and Confederate Navies in the War of the Rebellion,* judgment and merit quotation, series 2, vol. 2, 429; May, *Southern Dream of a Caribbean Empire,* postwar Confederate exiles as colonists in Central or South America, 255–58.

15 For Lane, see chapter 8 above; and John L. Wilson, *Stanford University School of Medicine and the Predecessor Schools: An Historical Perspective,* http://elane.stanford.edu/wilson/.

16 George Henry Preble, *Henry Knox Thatcher, Rear Admiral U.S. Navy* (Boston: printed for private distribution, 1882), quotation; "Rear Admiral Henry K. Thatcher," biography, Thatcher Papers, Hay Library, Brown University Libraries; William B. Cogar, *Dictionary of Admirals of the U.S. Navy,* vol. 1, *1862–1900* (Annapolis, MD: Naval Institute Press, 1989), 192–93; Abstracts of Service Records of Naval Officers, 1789–1893, RG45, M330, reels 7–9, NARA, hereafter cited as Abstracts of Service Records.

17 C. Hanford, *Seattle and Environs,* vol. 1, "wooden navy" quotation, 117; Abstracts of Service Records.

18 Rapier, *Felix Senac,* DeHaven widowed and a suitor for Senac's daughter, 193–98; Abstracts of Service Records.

19 Abstracts of Service Records; Karsten, *Naval Aristocracy,* Clitz quotation, 58.

20 Middleton to his sister Eliza, March 28, 1861, Edward Middleton Papers, Southern Historical Collection, Manuscripts Department, Wilson Library, University of North Carolina at Chapel Hill; Abstracts of Service Records; ZB Files, Navy Department Library; for family history, see www.middletonplace.org.

21 Guert Gansevoort's older brother, Peter, had failed admission to West Point, was then appointed a midshipman in the navy, and was lost at sea; his younger brother, Stanwix, also entered the navy, but service proved "too much for his health and his character," and he resigned to live a long, reclusive, besotted life, an embarrassment to the family. For general Guert Gansevoort biography, see H. Parker, *Herman Melville,* vol. 1, 61, 141–42, 241–43, 293–98, 494–95, 602; and vol. 2, 475, 529, 598; also see Alice P. Kenney, *The Gansevoorts of Albany: Dutch Patricians in the Upper Hudson Valley* (Syracuse, NY: Syracuse University Press, 1969). James Fenimore Cooper, "Proceedings of the Naval Court Martial in the Case of Alexander Slidell Mackenzie . . . to Which Is Appended an Elaborate Review" (New York: Langley, 1844), 289, 336–43; *New York Herald,* January 19, 1843. H. Parker notes Gansevoort's drinking problems and his fall from "family success" (*Herman Melville,* vol. 1, 141) to "poor tormented Guert" (495, 602, guilt quotation, 475). Gansevoort confided in cousin Hunn Gansevoort, who in turn told Thurlow Weed; Thurlow Weed, *Life of Thurlow Weed* (New York: Da Capo Press, 1970), 516–18.

22 Melville and Gansevoort were so physically alike that they were mistaken for brothers (H. Parker, *Herman Melville,* vol. 1, 294). Michael Paul Rogin, "Guert Gansevoort: Masters and Slaves," in *Subversive Genealogy: The Politics and Art of Herman Melville* (New York: Knopf, 1983). Samuel Francis Du Pont, whose patronage was significant to Guert Gansevoort's career, deplored Melville's *White-Jacket* (H. Parker, *Herman Melville,* vol. 1, "injustice" quotation, 721).

23 ZB files, Navy Department Library; Abstracts of Service Records; Almy to Wise, March 21, 1862, Henry Augustus Wise Papers, Manuscripts Division, New-York Historical Society, Gansevoort 1862 habits; H. Parker, *Herman Melville,* vol. 2, Gansevoort "continued to drink," 475, *Adirondack,* 513–15; Gansevoort to Welles, July 28, 1862, and August 4, 1862, Gansevoort Letterbook, Gansevoort chasing Semmes; *New York Times,* November 12, 1862, Gansevoort court-martial; *New York Times,* September 5 and 21 and November 16, 1862, Welles comment. Parker strongly suggests that Du Pont and other "old Navy associations" stood between Gansevoort and conviction at his 1862 court-martial (H. Parker, *Herman Melville,* vol. 1, 297; vol. 2, 519).

24 *New York Times,* July 17, 1868, obituary; Weed, *Life of Thurlow Weed,* "wreck" and "remorse" quotations, 758; Melville, "Bridegroom Dick," in Robert Penn Warren, ed., *Selected Poems of Herman Melville* (Boston: Godine, 2004), "Guert Gan" quotation, 287–88.

25 Taylor application, ZB files, Navy Department Library.

26 Abstracts of Service Records; Taylor, "Three Months in the Strait of Magellan," Phelps quotation.

27 Allen, introduction to Dallas Journal; Dallas to Conner, September 16, 1846, and Barrington to Dallas, May 8, 1848, Dallas Journal; ZB Files, Navy Department Library.

28 Dallas to Thomson, August 9, 1850, "Lady" quotation. Dallas to Mason, June 21, 1848, school and duel; Dallas to Harrison, May 24, 1848; Dallas to Dibble, May 24, 1848; Statement of Francis Henderson, May 28, 1848; Gale to Dallas, June 6, 1848; Sterrett to Dallas, January 13, 1854; all in Dallas Journal. Todorich, *Spirited Years*, Annapolis during this period, 54–55; W. Parker, *Recollections of a Naval Officer*, duel, 132; "The Bladensburg Dueling Ground," *Harper's,* March 1858, logic quotation; Du Pont Journal, Passed Midshipmen section, Dallas evaluation.

29 July 3 and September 23, 1857, Dallas Journal, quotations; June 14–September 18, 1859, Dallas Journal, breakdown. This section of Dallas's personal journal was not included in the published *Papers of Francis Gregory Dallas* and is held at the New-York Historical Society. Todorich, *Spirited Years*, strange career quotation, 64. Under the Pennsylvania Health Insurance Portability and Accountability Act, Dallas's thirty years of files at the Pennsylvania Hospital are unavailable to researchers.

30 Cogar, *Dictionary of Admirals of the U.S. Navy;* ZB Files, Navy Department Library; Abstracts of Service Records.

31 *Puget Sound Dispatch,* September 11, 1873, first visit; *Seattle Post-Intelligencer,* June 7, 1892, second visit and quotations.

32 Sophie Frye Bass, *Pigtail Days in Old Seattle* (Portland: Metropolitan Press, 1937), "saved" quotation, 151, *Decatur*-themed streets, 151, 174–76; *Seattle Post-Intelligencer,* July 30, 1904, Meany's remarks; minutes, July 28, 1904, Board of Park Commissioners, Seattle Municipal Archives, Horton quotation and park; William C. Speidel, *Sons of the Profits* (Seattle: Nettle Creek, 1967), quotations, 66–67, 220–22; Speidel, *Doc Maynard,* quotations 127, 205–11.

33 W. Parker, *Recollections of a Naval Officer,* "wooden men" quotation, 24; *Daily Evening Bulletin,* August 18, 1865, "behind the age" quotation.

34 *Daily Evening Bulletin,* August 18, 1865, sale; *Daily Evening Bulletin,* October 18, 1865, *Decatur* as lumber ship; *Daily Evening Bulletin,* December 13, 1865, and May 5, 1866, quotations; Phelps, "Reminiscences of the Old Navy: Eighty-three Days," "canvas" and "atoms" quotations, 264–65. Phelps believed that the *Decatur* had wrecked off the Oregon coast but he was in error; for an account of the wreck washing ashore, see *Washington Standard,* January 13, 1866.

35 Graebner, *Empire on the Pacific,* harbors, 218; Melville, *Moby Dick,* Pacific Ocean quotation, 525; Achmed Abdullah, *Dreamers of Empire* (New York: Stokes, 1929), "kaleidoscope" quotation, 245.

Bibliography

PUBLISHED SOURCES

Abbot, Willis J. *The Naval History of the United States.* Vol. 2. New York: Collier, 1886.

Abdullah, Achmed. *Dreamers of Empire.* New York: Stokes, 1929.

Allen, Gardner W., ed. *The Papers of Francis Gregory Dallas, 1837–1859.* New York: Naval Historical Society, 1917.

Allison, Robert. *Stephen Decatur: American Naval Hero.* Amherst: University of Massachusetts Press, 2005.

Annual Report of the Secretary of the Navy. Washington, DC: U.S. Government Printing Office, 1853, 1856, 1857, 1858, 1860.

Asher, Brad. *Beyond the Reservation: Indians, Settlers, and the Law in Washington Territory, 1853–1889.* Norman: University of Oklahoma Press, 1999.

Bagley, Clarence B. *History of King County, Washington.* Vol. 1. Chicago: S. J. Clarke, 1929.

———. *History of Seattle.* Vol. I. Chicago: S. J. Clarke, 1916.

Bancroft, Hubert Howe. *History of Washington, Idaho and Montana, 1845–1889.* San Francisco: History Co., 1890.

Ball, Durwood. *Army Regulars on the Western Frontier, 1848–1861.* Norman: University of Oklahoma Press, 2001.

Barney, William L. *The Road to Secession: A New Perspective on the Old South.* New York: Praeger, 1972.

Barnhart, Jacqueline Baker. *The Fair but Frail: Prostitution in San Francisco, 1849–1900.* Reno: University of Nevada Press, 1986.

Bass, Sophie Frye. *Pigtail Days in Old Seattle.* Portland, OR: Metropolitan Press, 1937.

———. *When Seattle Was a Village.* Seattle: Lowman and Hanford, 1947.

Bauer, K. Jack. *A Maritime History of the United States.* Columbia: University of South Carolina Press, 1988.

————. *The Mexican War, 1846–1848*. Lincoln: University of Nebraska Press, 1992.

————. *Surfboats and Horse Marines: U.S. Naval Operations in the Mexican War, 1846–1848*. Annapolis, MD: U.S. Naval Institute, 1969.

Bennett, Michael J. *Union Jacks: Yankee Sailors in the Civil War*. Chapel Hill: University of North Carolina Press, 2004.

Bolster, W. Jeffrey. *Black Jacks: African American Seamen in the Age of Sail*. Cambridge, MA: Harvard University Press, 1997.

Bourne, Benjamin Franklin. *The Captive in Patagonia, or Life among the Giants*. Boston: Gould and Lincoln, 1853.

Boyd, Robert T. *The Coming of the Spirit of Pestilence: Introduced Infectious Diseases and Population Decline among Northwest Coast Indians, 1774–1874*. Seattle: University of Washington Press; Vancouver: University of British Columbia Press, 1999.

Branson, Ware. *The Art of Sailmaking*. Boston: Butts, 1864.

Brown, Charles H. *Agents of Manifest Destiny: The Lives and Times of the Filibusters*. Chapel Hill: University of North Carolina Press, 1980.

Bulloch, James D. *The Secret Service of the Confederate States in Europe*. 2 vols. New York: Putnam, 1884.

Chapelle, Howard I. *The History of the American Sailing Navy: The Ships and Their Development*. New York: Norton, 1949.

Chisholm, Donald. *Waiting for Dead Men's Shoes: Origins and Development of the U.S. Navy's Officer Personnel System, 1793–1941*. Palo Alto, CA: Stanford University Press, 2001.

Coffman, Edward M. *The Old Army: A Portrait of the American Army in Peacetime, 1784–1898*. New York: Oxford University Press, 1986.

Cogar, William B. *Dictionary of Admirals of the U.S. Navy*. Vol. 1, *1862–1900*. Annapolis, MD: Naval Institute Press, 1989.

Colcord, Joanna Carver. *Songs of American Sailormen*. New York: Oak Publications, 1964.

Coletta, Paolo E., ed. *American Secretaries of the Navy, 1775–1913*. Annapolis, MD: Naval Institute Press, 1980.

Connell, Commander Royal W., and Vice Admiral William P. Mack. *Naval Ceremonies, Customs and Traditions*. Annapolis, MD: Naval Institute Press, 2004.

Cooper, James Fenimore. *Afloat and Ashore*. New York: Dodd, Mead, 1844.

————. *Lives of Distinguished American Naval Officers*. Philadelphia: Carey and Hart, 1846.

————. "Proceedings of the Naval Court Martial in the Case of Alexander Slidell Mackenzie . . . to Which Is Appended an Elaborate Review." New York: Langley, 1844.

Creighton, Margaret S. "The Private Life of Jack Tar." *New England Quarterly* 63, no. 4 (1990): 531–57.

Curry, Angus. *The Officers of the CSS Shenandoah*. Gainesville: University Press of Florida, 2006.

Curti, Merle E. "Young America." *American Historical Review* 32, no. 1 (1926): 34–55.

Dana, Richard Henry, Jr. *The Seaman's Friend: A Treatise on Practical Seamanship*. Mineola, NY: Dover Publications, 1997. Originally published in 1879.

————. *Two Years before the Mast: A Personal Narrative of Life at Sea.* New York: Modern Library, 2001. Originally published in 1840.

Darwin, Charles. *The Voyage of the* Beagle: *Journal of Researches into the Natural History and Geology of the Countries Visited during the Voyage of H.M.S.* Beagle *round the World.* New York: Modern Library, 2001. Originally published in 1839.

Davis, Charles H. *Life of Charles Henry Davis, Rear Admiral.* Boston: Houghton Mifflin, 1899.

Delgado, James P. *To California by Sea: A Maritime History of the California Gold Rush.* Columbia: University of South Carolina Press, 1990.

Dening, Greg. *Mr. Bligh's Bad Language: Passion, Power, and Theatre on the Bounty.* New York: Cambridge University Press, 1992.

Denny, Arthur A. *Pioneer Days on Puget Sound.* Seattle: Lowman and Hanford, 1908.

Denny, Emily Inez. *Blazing the Way.* Seattle: Rainier Printing Co., 1909.

————. "The Founding of Seattle and Indian War." Pts. 1 and 2. *Washington Historian* 1, no. 2 (1900): 56–69; no. 3 (1900): 110–14.

Donnelly, Ralph W. *The Confederate States Marine Corps: The Rebel Leathernecks.* Shippensburg, PA: White Mane, 1989.

Dudden, Arthur Power. *The American Pacific: From the Old China Trade to the Present.* New York: Oxford University Press, 1992.

Dudley, William S. *Going South: U.S. Navy Officer Resignations and Dismissals on the Eve of the Civil War.* Washington, DC: Naval Historical Foundation, 1981.

Eckrom, J. A. *Remembered Drums: A History of the Puget Sound Indian War.* Walla Walla, WA: Pioneer Press, 1989.

Elmendorf, William W. *Twana Narratives: Native Historical Accounts of a Coast Salish Culture.* Seattle: University of Washington Press, 1993.

Eperjesi, John R. *The Imperialist Imaginary: Visions of Asia and the Pacific in American Culture.* Hanover, NH: Dartmouth College Press, 2005.

Ethington, Philip J. *The Public City: The Political Construction of Urban Life in San Francisco, 1850–1900.* Cambridge: Cambridge University Press, 1994.

Ettinger, Amos Aschbach. *The Mission to Spain of Pierre Soulé, 1853–1855: A Study in the Cuban Diplomacy of the United States.* New Haven, CT: Yale University Press, 1932.

Eyal, Yonatan. "Trade and Improvements: Young America and the Transformation of the Democratic Party." *Civil War History* 51, no. 1 (2005): 245–68.

————. *The Young America Movement and the Transformation of the Democratic Party, 1828–61.* Cambridge: Cambridge University Press, 2007.

Farr, Gail E., and Brett F. Bostwick. *John Lenthall, Naval Architect.* Philadelphia: Philadelphia Maritime Museum, 1991.

Farr, James Barker. *Black Odyssey: The Seafaring Traditions of Afro-Americans.* New York: Lang, 1989.

Farragut, Loyall. *The Life of David Glasgow Farragut.* New York: Appleton, 1879.

Ficken, Robert E. *Washington Territory.* Pullman: Washington State University Press, 2002.

Fingard, Judith. *Jack in Port: Sailortowns of Eastern Canada.* Toronto: University of Toronto Press, 1982.

FitzRoy, Robert. *A Narrative of the Voyage of HMS* Beagle. London: Folio Society, 1977. Originally published in 1839.

Games, Alison. "Atlantic History: Definitions, Challenges and Opportunities." *American Historical* Review 111, no. 3 (2006): 741–57.

Gates, Henry Louis, ed. *The Bondwoman's Narrative*, by Hannah Crafts. New York: Warner Books, 2002.

Gibson, Arrell Morgan. *Yankees in Paradise: The Pacific Basin Frontier*. Albuquerque: University of New Mexico Press, 1993.

Gilje, Paul A. *Liberty on the Waterfront: American Maritime Culture in the Age of Revolution*. Philadelphia: University of Pennsylvania Press, 2004.

Glassley, Ray Hoard. *Indian Wars of the Pacific Northwest*. Portland, OR: Binfords and Mort, 1972.

Graebner, Norman A. *Empire on the Pacific: A Study in American Continental Expansion*. Santa Barbara, CA: ABC-Clio, 1983.

———, ed. *Manifest Destiny*. Indianapolis, IN: Bobbs-Merrill, 1968.

Grant, Frederic James. *History of Seattle, Washington*. New York: American Publishing, 1891.

Greenberg, Amy S. "A Gray-Eyed Man: Character, Appearance and Filibustering,. *Journal of the Early Republic* 20, no. 4 (2000): 673–99.

———. *Manifest Manhood and the Antebellum American Empire*. Cambridge: Cambridge University Press, 2005.

Greene, Laurence. *The Filibuster: The Career of William Walker*. Indianapolis: Bobbs-Merrill, 1937.

Guttridge, Leonard F. *Mutiny: A History of Naval Insurrection*. New York: Berkley, 1992.

Gough, Barry M. *Gunboat Frontier: British Maritime Authority and Northwest Coast Indians, 1846–90*. Vancouver: UBC Press, 1984.

———. *The Royal Navy and the Northwest Coast of North America, 1810–1914: A Study of British Maritime Ascendancy*. Vancouver: UBC Press, 1971.

Hagan, Kenneth J., ed. *In Peace and War: Interpretations of American Naval History, 1775–1978*. Westport, CT: Greenwood Press, 1978.

Hamersly, Lewis R. *The Records of Living Officers of the U.S. Navy and Marine Corps*. Philadelphia: Lippincott, 1870.

Hanford, Abbie. "Reminiscences of the Indian War of 1855." *Washington Historian* 2, no. 3 (1901): 113–22.

Hanford, Cornelius. *Seattle and Environs*. Vol. 1. Chicago and Seattle: Pioneer Historical Publishing, 1924.

Harmon, Alexandra. *Indians in the Making: Ethnic Relations and Indian Identities around Puget Sound*. Berkeley and Los Angeles: University of California Press, 1998.

Hayden, Deborah. *Pox: Genius, Madness and the Mystery of Syphilis*. New York: Basic Books, 2003.

Haynes, Sam W., and Christopher Morris, eds. *Manifest Destiny and Empire: American Antebellum Expanionism*. College Station: Texas A&M University Press, 1997.

Heck, J. G., and Spencer Fullerton Baird. *Pictorial Archive*. New York: Rudolph Garrigue, 1851.

Heffer, Jean. *The United States and the Pacific: History of a Frontier.* Notre Dame, IN: University of Notre Dame Press, 2002.

Hietala, Thomas R. *Manifest Design: American Exceptionalism and Empire.* Ithaca, NY: Cornell University Press, 2003.

Holbrook, Francis X. "The Navy's Cross--William Walker." *Military Affairs* 39, no. 4 (1975): 197–203.

Hudson, Randall O. "The Filibuster Minister: The Career of John Hill Wheeler as United States Minister to Nicaragua, 1854–1856." *North Carolina Historical Review* 49, no. 3 (1972): 280–97.

Igler, David. "Diseased Goods: Global Exchanges in the Eastern Pacific Basin, 1770–1850." *American Historical Review* 109, no. 3 (2004): 693–719.

"Indian Affairs on the Pacific." 34th Cong., 1st sess., Ex. Doc. 76. Washington, DC, 1857.

"Indian Hostilities in Oregon and Washington Territories." 34th Cong., 1st sess., Ex. Doc. 118. Washington, DC: Wendell, 1856.

Instructions for the Government of the Medical Officers of the Navy of the United States. Washington: A. O. P. Nicholson, 1855.

Johnson, Robert Erwin. *Thence round Cape Horn: The Story of United States Naval Forces on Pacific Station, 1818–1923.* Annapolis, MD: U.S. Naval Institute, 1963.

Karsten, Peter. *The Naval Aristocracy: The Golden Age of Annapolis and the Emergence of Modern American Navalism.* New York: Free Press, 1972.

Kemp, Peter, ed. *The Oxford Companion to Ships and the Sea.* Oxford: Oxford University Press, 1988.

Kenney, Alice P. *The Gansevoorts of Albany: Dutch Patricians in the Upper Hudson Valley.* Syracuse, NY: Syracuse University Press, 1969.

Keyes, Erasmus D. *Fifty Years Observations of Men and Events, Civil and Military.* New York: Scribner, 1884.

Klingle, Matthew. *Emerald City: An Environmental History of Seattle.* New Haven, CT: Yale University Press, 2007.

Klunder, Willard Carl. *Lewis Cass and the Politics of Moderation.* Kent, OH: Kent State University Press, 1996.

Kushner, Howard I. "Visions of the Northwest Coast: Gwin and Seward in the 1850s." *Western Historical Quarterly* 4, no. 3 (1973): 295–306.

Lane, Levi Cooper. "A Reminiscence of the Nicaraguan Filibusters." *Journal of the American Medical Association* 21, no. 6 (1893): 960–61.

———. *Surgery of the Head and Neck.* Philadelphia: P. Blakiston, 1898.

Langley, Harold D. *A History of Medicine in the Early U.S. Navy.* Baltimore, MD: Johns Hopkins University Press, 1995.

———. *Social Reform in the United States Navy, 1798–1862.* Urbana: University of Illinois Press, 1967.

Letts, J. M. *California Illustrated: Including a Description of the Panama and Nicaragua Routes.* New York: R. T. Young, 1853.

Lewis, Oscar. *Sea Routes to the Gold Fields: The Migration by Water to California, 1849–1852.* New York: Alfred A. Knopf, 1949.

Long, David F. *Gold Braid and Foreign Relations: Diplomatic Activities of U.S. Naval Officers, 1798–1883*. Annapolis, MD: Naval Institute Press, 1988.

Lotchin, Roger W. *San Francisco, 1846–1856: From Hamlet to City*. Urbana: University of Illinois Press, 1997.

Lott, Arnold S. *A Long Line of Ships: Mare Island's Century of Naval Activity in California*. Annapolis, MD: U.S. Naval Institute, 1954.

Lovette, Leland P. *Naval Customs, Traditions and Usage*. Annapolis, MD: U.S. Naval Institute, 1939.

Lutz, John. "Inventing an Indian War." *Journal of the West* 38, no. 3 (1999): 7–13.

Lynch, W. F. *Naval Life, or Observations Afloat and Ashore*. New York: Scribner, 1851.

Mahan, Alfred Thayer. *From Sail to Steam: Recollections of Naval Life*. New York: Harper, 1907.

Marryat, Captain Frederick. *Frank Mildmay, or The Naval Officer*. Ithaca, NY: McBooks Press, 1998. Originally published in 1829.

———. *Mr. Midshipman Easy*. Ithaca, NY: McBooks Press, 1998. Originally published in 1836.

Matsuda, Matt K. "The Pacific." *American Historical Review* 111, no. 3 (2006): 758–80.

Maude, H. E. *Slavers in Paradise: The Peruvian Slave Trade in Polynesia, 1862–1864*. Stanford, CA: Stanford University Press, 1981.

May, Robert E. *Manifest Destiny's Underworld: Filibustering in Antebellum America*. Chapel Hill: University of North Carolina Press, 2002.

———. "Psychobiography and Secession: The Southern Radical as Maladjusted Outsider." *Civil War History* 34, no. 1 (1988): 46–69.

——— *The Southern Dream of a Caribbean Empire, 1854–1861*. Baton Rouge: Louisiana State University Press, 1973.

———. "Young American Males and Filibustering in the Age of Manifest Destiny: The United States Army as a Cultural Mirror." *Journal of American History* 78, no. 3 (1991): 857–86.

McFarland, Philip James. *Sea Dangers: The Affair of the* Somers. New York: Schocken, 1985.

McKee, Christopher. *A Gentlemanly and Honorable Profession: The Creation of the U.S. Naval Officer Corps, 1794–1815*. Annapolis, MD: Naval Institute Press, 1991.

———. *Sober Men and True: Sailor Lives in the Royal Navy, 1900–1945*. Cambridge, MA: Harvard University Press, 2002.

McWilliams, Carey. *California: The Great Exception*. New York: Current Books, 1949.

Meeker, Ezra. *The Tragedy of Leschi*. Seattle: Historical Society of Seattle and King County, 1980. Originally published in 1905.

Melton, Buckner F. *A Hanging Offense: The Strange Affair of the Warship* Somers. New York: Free Press, 2003.

Melville, Herman. *Billy Budd, Sailor, and Selected Tales*. Oxford: Oxford University Press, 1998. Begun in the 1880s; published posthumously in 1924.

———. *Moby Dick, or The Whale*. New York: Penguin, 2001. Originally published in 1851.

———. *Omoo: A Narrative of Adventures in the South Seas*. New York: Modern Library, 2002. Originally published in 1847.

————. *Typee: A Peep at Polynesian Life.* New York: Modern Library, 2001. Originally published in 1846.

————. *White-Jacket, or The World in a Man-of-War.* New York: Modern Library, 2002. Originally published in 1850.

Melvin, Philip. "Stephen Russell Mallory, Southern Naval Statesman." *Journal of Southern History* 10, no. 2 (1944): 137–60.

Mooney, James, ed. *Dictionary of American Naval Fighting Ships.* Washington, DC: Naval Historical Center, 1991.

Murray, James, "Sailors' Songs with California Significance." *California Folklore Quarterly* 5, no. 2 (1946): 143–52.

Nalty, Bernard C., and Truman R. Strobridge. "The Defense of Seattle, 1856: 'And Down Came the Indians.'" *Pacific Northwest Quarterly* 55, no. 3 (1964): 105–10.

Nelson, Kurt R. *Fighting for Paradise: A Military History of the Pacific Northwest.* Yardley, PA: Westholme Publishing, 2007.

Nordhoff, Charles. *Man-of-War Life: A Boy's Experience in the United States Navy, during a Voyage around the World in a Ship-of-the-Line.* Annapolis, MD: Naval Institute Press, 1985. Originally published in 1855.

Officers in the Confederate States Navy, 1861–1865. Washington, DC: U.S. Government Printing Office, 1898.

Official Records of the Union and Confederate Navies in the War of the Rebellion. Washington, DC: U.S. Government Printing Office, 1921.

Parker, Hershel. *Herman Melville: A Biography.* Vol. 1, *1819–1851.* Baltimore, MD: Johns Hopkins University Press, 1996.

————. *Herman Melville: A Biography.* Vol. 2, *1851–1891.* Baltimore, MD: Johns Hopkins University Press, 2002.

Parker, William Harwar. *Recollections of a Naval Officer.* Annapolis, MD: Naval Institute Press, 1985. Originally published in 1883.

Paullin, Charles Oscar. *History of Naval Administration, 1775–1911.* Annapolis, MD: U.S. Naval Institute, 1968.

Peterson, Charles J. *The American Navy: Being an Authentic History of the United States Navy.* Philadelphia: Leary and Getz, 1858.

Phelps, Thomas Stowell. *Reminiscences of Seattle, Washington Territory, and the U.S. Sloop-of-War "Decatur" during the Indian War of 1855–1856.* Philadelphia: Hamersly, 1881.

————. "Reminiscences of Seattle, Washington Territory, and the U.S. Sloop-of-War "Decatur" during the Indian War of 1855–56." *United Service,* December 1881, 669–706.

————. *Reminiscences of Seattle, Washington Territory, and the U.S. Sloop-of-War "Decatur" during the Indian War of 1855–1856.* Seattle: Alice Harriman Co., 1902 and 1908.

————. *Reminiscences of Seattle, Washington Territory, and the U.S. Sloop-of-War Decatur during the Indian War of 1855–1856.* Seattle: Farwest Lithograph, 1932.

————. "Reminiscences of the Old Navy: Eighty-three Days in the Strait of Magellan, on Board the United States Ship *Decatur,* 1854–1855." *United Service,* March 1883.

————. "Reminiscences of the Old Navy: Our First Cruise under Canvas, the *Preble*'s and Mine." Parts 1 and 2. *United Service,* November and December 1882.

Philbrick, Nathaniel. *Sea of Glory: America's Voyage of Discovery; The U.S. Exploring Expedition*. New York: Penguin, 2003.

Philbrick, Thomas. *James Fenimore Cooper and the Development of American Sea Fiction*. Cambridge, MA: Harvard University Press, 1961.

Pim, Bedford. *The Gate of the Pacific*. London: L. Reeve and Co., 1863.

Pomeroy, Earl. *The Pacific Slope: A History of California, Oregon, Washington, Idaho, Utah and Nevada*. Lincoln: University of Nebraska Press, 1992.

Porter, David D. *The Naval History of the Civil War*. New York: Sherman Publishing Co., 1886.

Potter, David M. *The Impending Crisis, 1848–1861*. New York: Harper and Row, 1976.

Pratt, Fletcher. *Preble's Boys: Commodore Preble and the Birth of American Sea Power*. New York: William Sloane, 1950.

Preble, George Henry. *Henry Knox Thatcher, Rear Admiral U.S. Navy*. Boston: printed for private distribution, 1882.

Prosch, Charles. *Reminiscences of Washington Territory*. Seattle, 1904.

Prosch, Thomas W. *A Chronological History of Seattle from 1850 to 1897*. Seattle, 1901.

Ralston, Caroline. *Grass Huts and Warehouses: Pacific Beach Communities of the Nineteenth Century*. Honolulu: University of Hawaii Press, 1978.

Rapier, Regina. *Felix Senac: The Saga of Felix Senac; Being the Legend and Biography of a Confederate Agent in Europe*. N.p.: Bulletin of Art and History, 1970.

Rea, J. "Seeing the Elephant." *Western Folklore* 28, no. 1 (1969): 21–26.

Register of the Navy of the United States, Including Circulars and General Orders. Washington, DC: Armstrong, 1855, 1857.

"A Review of the Proceedings of the Navy Department in Carrying into Effect the Act Entitled, 'An Act to Promote the Efficiency of the Navy,'" by a Civilian. N.p.: Towers Printers, n.d. Held by New-York Historical Society.

Richards, Kent. *Isaac I. Stevens: Young Man in a Hurry*. Provo, UT: Brigham Young University Press, 1979.

Richards, Leonard L. *The California Gold Rush and the Coming of the Civil War*. New York: Knopf, 2007.

Riegel, Robert E. *Young America, 1830–1840*. Norman: University of Oklahoma Press, 1949.

Rogin, Michael Paul. *Subversive Genealogy: The Politics and Art of Herman Melville*. New York: Knopf, 1983.

Rolle, Andrew F. "California Filibustering and the Hawaiian Kingdom." *Pacific Historical Review* 19, no. 3 (1950): 251–63.

Rosengarten, Frederic, Jr. *Freebooters Must Die!* Wayne, PA: Haverford House, 1976.

Rotundo, E. Anthony. *American Manhood: Transformations in Masculinity from the Revolution to the Modern Era*. New York: Basic Books, 1993.

Royce, Josiah. *California, from the Conquest in 1846 to the Second Vigilance Committee in San Francisco: A Study of American Character*. Boston: Houghton Mifflin, 1886.

Scharf, J. Thomas. *History of the Confederate States Navy*. New York: Rogers and Sherwood, 1887.

Schroeder, John H. *Shaping a Maritime Empire: The Commercial and Diplomatic Role of the American Navy, 1829–1861*. Westport, CT: Greenwood Press, 1985.

Scroggs, William O. *Filibusters and Financiers: The Story of William Walker and His Associates.* New York: Macmillan, 1916.

Senkewicz, Robert M. *Vigilantes in Gold Rush San Francisco.* Stanford, CA: Stanford University Press, 1985.

Shay, Frank, ed. *American Sea Songs and Chanteys.* New York: Norton, 1948.

Skelton, William B. *An American Profession of Arms: The Army Officer Corps, 1784–1861.* Lawrence: University Press of Kansas, 1992.

Slagle, Jay. *Ironclad Captain: Seth Ledyard Phelps and the U.S. Navy, 1841–1864.* Kent, OH: Kent State University Press, 1996.

Slotkin, Richard. *The Fatal Environment: The Myth of the Frontier in the Age of Industrialization, 1800–1890.* New York: Atheneum, 1985.

Smith, Geoffrey Sutton. "The Navy before Darwinism: Science, Exploration and Diplomacy in Antebellum America." *American Quarterly* 28, no. 1 (1976): 41–55.

Sokolow, Michael. *Charles Benson: Mariner of Color in the Age of Sail.* Boston: University of Massachusetts Press, 2003.

Soulé, Frank. *The Annals of San Francisco.* New York: Appleton, 1855.

Soulé, Frank, John H. Gihon, and James Nisbet. *The Annals of San Francisco.* New York: D. Appleton, 1855.

Spate, O. H. K. *Monopolists and Freebooters.* Minneapolis: University of Minnesota Press, 1983.

———. *The Pacific since Magellan.* Vol. 3, *Paradise Found and Lost.* Minneapolis: University of Minnesota Press, 1988.

Speidel, William C. [Bill]. *Doc Maynard: The Man Who Invented Seattle.* Seattle: Nettle Creek, 1978.

———. *Sons of the Profits.* Seattle: Nettle Creek, 1967.

Springer, Haskell, ed. *America and the Sea: A Literary History.* Athens: University of Georgia Press, 1995.

Sprout, Harold, and Margaret Sprout. *The Rise of American Naval Power, 1776–1918.* Princeton, NJ: Princeton University Press, 1944.

Squier, E. G. *Nicaragua: Its People, Scenery, Monuments, and the Proposed Interoceanic Canal.* London: Longman, Brown, Green and Longmans, 1852.

———. *Notes on Central America.* New York: Harper and Brothers, 1855.

———. *Travels in Central America: Particularly in Nicaragua.* New York: Appleton, 1853.

Starr, Kevin. *Americans and the California Dream, 1850–1915.* New York: Oxford University Press, 1973.

Swan, Jon. "William Walker's Manifest Destiny." *Military Historical Quarterly* 13, no. 4 (2001): 38–47.

Tate, Michael L. *The Frontier Army in the Settlement of the West.* Norman: University of Oklahoma Press, 1999.

Thrush, Coll. *Native Seattle: Histories from the Crossing-Over Place.* Seattle: University of Washington Press, 2007.

Todorich, Charles. *The Spirited Years: A History of the Antebellum Naval Academy.* Annapolis, MD: Naval Institute Press, 1984.

Tucker, Spencer C. *Blue and Gray Navies: The Civil War Afloat.* Annapolis, MD: Naval Institute Press, 2006.

————. *Stephen Decatur: A Life Most Bold and Daring*. Annapolis, MD: Naval Institute Press, 2005.

U.S. Naval War Records Office. *Official War Records of the Union and Confederate Navies in the War of the Rebellion*. Washington, DC: Government Printing Office, 1894–1922. cdl.library.cornell.edu/moa.

U.S. War Department. *War of the Rebellion: A Compilation of the Official Records of the Union and Confederate Armies*. Washington, DC: Government Printing Office, 1880–1901. cdl.library.cornell.edu/moa.

Valle, James. *Rocks and Shoals: Order and Discipline in the Old Navy, 1800–1861*. Annapolis, MD: Naval Institute Press, 1980.

Vouri, Mike. "Raiders from the North: The Northern Indians and Northwest Washington in the 1850s." *Columbia* 11, no. 3 (1977): 24–35.

Walker, William. *The War in Nicaragua*. Detroit: Blaine Ethridge, 1971. Originally published in 1860.

Warren, Robert Penn, ed. *Selected Poems of Herman Melville*. Boston: Godine, 2004.

Watt, Roberta Frye. *Four Wagons West*. Portland, OR: Metropolitan Press, 1931.

————. *The Story of Seattle*. Seattle: Lowman and Hanford, 1931.

Weddle, Kevin. *Lincoln's Tragic Admiral: The Life of Samuel Francis Du Pont*. Charlottesville: University of Virginia Press, 2005.

Weed, Thurlow. *Life of Thurlow Weed*. New York: Da Capo Press, 1970. Originally published in 1884.

Weinberg, Albert K. *Manifest Destiny: A Study of Nationalist Expression in American History*. Chicago: Quadrangle, 1963.

Whaley, Gray H. "Oregon, *Illahee,* and the Empire Republic: A Case Study of American Colonialism, 1843–1858." *Western Historical Quarterly* 36, no. 2 (2005): 158–78.

"What Kind of Ships Generate Disease?" *U.S. Nautical Magazine* 5, no. 1 (1856): 8–12.

Wheeler, John Hill. *Reminiscences and Memoirs of North Carolina and Eminent North Carolinians*. Columbus, OH: Columbus Printing Works, 1884.

White, Richard. *"It's Your Misfortune and None of My Own": A New History of the American West*. Norman: University of Oklahoma Press, 1991.

Widmer, Edward L. *Young America: The Flowering of Democracy in New York City*. New York: Oxford University Press, 1999.

Wiley, Kenneth. *Norfolk Blues: The Civil War Diary of the Norfolk Light Artillery Blues*. Shippensburg, PA: Burd Street Press, 1997.

Wilson, James Grant, and John Fiske, eds. *Appleton's Cyclopaedia of American Biography*. New York: Appleton, 1888–89.

Wilson, John L. *Stanford University School of Medicine and the Predecessor Schools: An Historical Perspective*. Available online at http://elane.stanford.edu/wilson/.

Wines, E. C. *Two Years and a Half in the Navy*. London: R. Bentley, 1833.

Woodward, Ralph Lee, Jr. *Central America: A Nation Divided*. New York: Oxford University Press, 1999.

ARCHIVAL COLLECTIONS

Beinecke Rare Book and Manuscript Library, Yale University, New Haven, CT. Collection of Western Americana. John Y. Taylor Collection.

Hagley Museum and Library, Wilmington, DE. Samuel Francis Du Pont Papers, Henry Francis Du Pont Winterthur Collection of Manuscripts.

Hay Library, Brown University Libraries, Providence, RI. Special Collections. Henry Knox Thatcher Papers.

Latin American Library, Tulane University, New Orleans, LA. Callender I. Fayssoux Collection of William Walker Papers, 1856–60.

Middleton Place, Charleston, SC. Middleton Family Collection.

Museum of History and Industry, Seattle, WA. Special Collections.

National Archives and Records Administration, Washington, DC, and College Park, MD. Old Navy Records.

Navy Department Library, Washington, DC. Special Collections.

New-York Historical Society, New York, NY. Francis Gregory Dallas Papers, Anthony Kimmel Itzler Papers, and Henry Augustus Wise Papers, Manuscripts Division.

New York State Archives, Albany, NY. Abstracts of Muster Rolls for Men Who Served in the United States Navy during the Civil War, series B0803–85.

Seattle Municipal Archives, Seattle, WA.

University of Washington Libraries, Seattle, WA. Special Collections.

Virginia Historical Society, Richmond, VA. Manuscripts Division. Isaac Sears Sterrett Diary.

Washington State Archives, Olympia, WA. Washington Territorial Papers.

Washington State Historical Society, Tacoma, WA. Special Collections.

Wilson Library, University of North Carolina at Chapel Hill. Edward Middleton Papers, Southern Historical Collection, Manuscripts Department.</btx>

NATIONAL ARCHIVES AND RECORDS ADMINISTRATION

RG19, RG24, RG45, and RG52 records held at NARA, Washington, DC. RG59 records held at NARA, College Park, MD.

Microfilm

RG45, M89, reels 36–38, Letters Received by the Secretary of the Navy from Commanding Officers of Squadrons.

RG45, M125, reel 354, Letters Received by the Secretary of the Navy from Captains.

RG45, M147, reels 46–60, Letters Received by the Secretary of the Navy from Commanders.

RG45, M148, reels 239–40, Letters Received by the Secretary of the Navy from Commissioned Officers below the Rank of Commander and from Warrant Officers.

RG45, M149, reels 51–53, Letters Sent by the Secretary of the Navy to Officers, 1798–1868.

RG45, M260, reels 7, 16, Records Relating to Confederate Naval and Marine Personnel.

RG45, M273, reels 84–88, Records of General Courts Martial and Courts of Inquiry of the Navy Department.

RG45, M330, reels 7–9, Abstracts of Service Records of Naval Officers, 1789–1893.

RG45, T239, reels 223–24, Miscellaneous Records of the U.S. Navy, Naval Records and Library, Letterbook of Guert Gansevoort, 1855–57.

RG45, T829, reel 3, Miscellaneous Records of the U.S. Navy, Muster Rolls, USS *Decatur*.

RG45, T829, reels 226–29, Miscellaneous Records of the U.S. Navy, Naval Records and Library, Letterbooks of William Mervine, 1855–57.

RG45, T829, reels 361–62, Confidential Letters Sent to Commanding Officers of Squadrons and Vessels from the Secretary of the Navy, 1843–86.

RG45, T829, reels 389–390, Miscellaneous Records of the U.S. Navy, Naval Records and Library, 1861 Resignations and Dismissals of Officers.

RG45, T829, reel 428, Miscellaneous Records of the U.S. Navy, Naval Records and Library, Naval Asylum Records.

RG45, T829, reel 451, Corporal Punishment and the Spirit Ration, Reports of Officers, 1850, Miscellaneous Records of the U.S. Navy.

RG59, M37, reel 10, Despatches from Special Agents of the Department of State, 1794–1906.

RG59, M77, reel 27, Diplomatic Instructions of the Secretary of State, 1801–1906, Central American States, May 29, 1833–July 25, 1858.

RG59, M77, reel 154, General Records of the Department of State, List of Documents Relating to Special Agents of the Department of State, 1789–1906, Special Missions, September 11, 1852–August 31, 1886.

RG59, M967, reel 24, Letters of Application and Recommendation during the Administrations of Franklin Pierce and James Buchanan, 1853–1861.

RG59, T35, reel 1, Despatches from U.S. Consuls in San José, Costa Rica.

RG59, T152, reel 1, Despatches from U.S. Consuls in San Juan del Sur.

Hard Copy

RG19, Records of Boards of Survey on Ships and Their Equipment, USS *Decatur*.

RG24, Records of the Bureau of Naval Personnel, Log Books, USS *Decatur*.

RG45, John Y. Taylor, "Three Months in the Strait of Magellan." Off-Routine Movements of U.S. Navy Ships, "U.S. Navy, 1775–1910," box 418.

RG45, Office of Naval Records and Library, Subject Files "U.S. Navy, 1775–1910," AC Construction of U.S. Ships, New York Navy Yard, USS *Decatur*.

RG45, Office of Naval Records and Library, Subject Files "U.S. Navy, 1775–1910," AR Repairs to U.S. Ships, USS *Decatur*.

RG45, Office of Naval Records and Library, Subject Files "U.S. Navy, 1775–1910," MH Health Conditions--General Hygiene and Sanitation.

RG45, Office of Naval Records and Library, Subject Files "U.S. Navy, 1775–1910," NI Miscellaneous re Officers Removed from the Active List in 1855.

RG45, Office of Naval Records and Library, Subject Files "U.S. Navy, 1775–1910," OJ Joint Military and Naval Operations.

RG45, Records Collection of the Office of Naval Records and Library, Letterbooks of U.S. Naval Officers.

RG45, Records Collection of the Office of Naval Records and Library, Letters Received from Commandants of Navy Yards and Naval Stations.

RG52, Records of the Bureau of Medicine and Surgery, Headquarters Records, Correspondence to the Bureau from Surgeons and Assistant Surgeons.

RG52, Records of the Bureau of Medicine and Surgery, Headquarters Records, Medical Journals and Reports on Patients, Abstracts of Patients, vol. 26, USS *Decatur.*

RG52, Records of the Bureau of Medicine and Surgery, Headquarters Records, Medical Journals and Reports on Patients, "A Medical Journal of the U.S. Sloop of War Decatur."

Index

Page numbers in italic indicate illustrations.

Marcy, William, 194–95; and alleged Marcy-Mervine-Davis conspiracy, 198, 207

Mare Island Navy Yard, 62, 101–5, 147–48, 161–74, 179–80, 266–71, 274, 281–82, 288–89

Marines on the *Decatur*, 45, 50

Martin, William, 245–47

Martinez, Tomas, 219, 222, 225, 258, 265

Mason, Charles (acting governor), 114, 130

Mason, Charles (seaman), 48, 103, 231

Mason, John, 98, 118, 158

Massachusetts, 69, 88–94, 101, 121, 130, 147–52, 180

Maury, Matthew, 63

May, Robert E., viii, 25, 26, 196, 221, 225

McBlair, William, 276

McCann, Patrick, 150–51

McCarty, Dennis, 58, 169

McCorkle, David, 3–4, 26, 200

McDonald, Joseph, 239–43

McKinnon, Daniel, 56, 52, 118

Melville, Herman, 32, 38, 40, 53, 266, 269–70, 282–83, 288

Merchantman, 163

Merrimac, 29, *191*, 225, 227–28, 250–58, 266, 273; as the *CSS Virginia*, 273, 276, 280, *281*

Mervine, William 20, 31; and Charles Henry Davis, 197; as commodore of the Pacific Squadron, 101, 104, 108, 120–21, 130, 147–48, 178–80, 213, 317n100; and David Farragut, 96, 101, 166, 173, 179–80; and Edward Middleton, 170, 182–83; and feuds, 179; and filibusters, 147, 198–202, 213–14, 218; as fogy, 23, 33, 198; and Guert Gansevoort, 128, 133–34, 147, 162, 166, 234; and Henry Knox Thatcher, 186–87, 201–2, 210–11; and Isaac Ster-

rett, 101–2, 104–7, 113, 115–16, 119–20, 127; and Isaac Stevens, 179–80; and Isaac Toucey, 201–2, 213–14, 218; and James Alden, 121, 132–34, 147; and James Dobbin, 106–7, 120–21, 166, 179, 207; and Panama, 180–88, 199–201; political convictions of, 6, 147, 197–98; and reforms, 29, 33, 179; and Samuel Swartwout, 179; and William Marcy, 198, 207; on William Walker, 121, 197–98

Mexican War, 15–16, 20–21, 31, 72, 189, 282–84

Middleton, Edward, 60, 139, 165, 184, 281–82

Miller, James, 45, 66, 98, 118–19, 126, 139, 162, 184

Mora, Joaquin, 196, 199, 210

Mora, Juan Rafael, 196, 210, 215–16, 225

More, Thomas, 243, 268

Morgan, Van Rensselaer, 42, 57–60, 69, 234–35, 277

Morris, George, 43, 137, 142, 184, 234, 280

Murphy, Edward, 243, 261

Murphy, John, 262

Murray, Thomas, 256–57, 267

Native people, *86, 96, 99, 123, 143*; in Hawaii, *100;* in Nicaragua, *188;* in Strait of Magellan, 77, 84–87, *86*, 94–95; in and near Seattle, 109–11, 120–22, 130, *143*, 143–45, 151–52, 155, *156*, 159–60

Naval Asylum, 41, 107, 234, 270

Navy, U.S., 5–14, 28–39, 42–48. See also *Decatur;* Pacific Squadron

Neal, George, 102–3, 230

New World, 100–101

Nicaragua, 175–226, *260, 264;* and American annexation, 22, 205, 223; 258; and American booster narrative, 189–90; resolutions by

and concerning, 224, 225–26, and transit, *11*, 21–22, 189–90, *193*, 194, *198*, 265. See Walker, William; Walker filibusters

Nobrega, Henry, 274

Norris, Edward, 62, 103

Owhi, 139

Pacific Squadron, 5, 17, 25, 29, 93–94, 148, 162; and California, 4, 8–10, 15–25, 56, 101, 104–6, 161–67, 262; and communication, 101–2, 106, 255; cruising ground and duties of, 18–19, 178–79, 227–28, 250; and desertion, 8–10, 95, 104–5, 118–19, 158–59, 172–74, 193–94, 236–38, 270, 294n4, 308n1; and Ecuador, 255; and feuds, 30–31, 179; and guano, 121, 147, 178–79, 206, *250*, 250–51; and Hawaii, 4, 25, 94, 96–98, 178, 250; and Mare Island Navy Yard, 62, 101–5, 147–48, 161–74, 179–80, 266–71, 274, 281–82, 288–89; medical history of, 228–31; and Pacific expansionism, 17–19, 22–27, 180–87, 225; and Panama, 179–87, 199–200, 213, 227–49; and Peru, 252–53, 255; and reforms, 120, 178, 244, 280, 286; shipyard work of depicted, 171; and Vigilance Committee, 163–64, 170; and wages, 105, 172; and Walker's filibusters, 188, 192, 197–202, 211–14, 220, 225, 231–32, 251, 262–65; and Washington Territory, 4–5, 15–17, 102–8, 120–25, 162, 180, 234; and William Carey Jones, 202, 205, 207–8

Pacific West, 3–12, 15–27, 160, 288–89; and commerce, 9, 16–18, *18*, 96, 100–101, 110, 167, 189, 280; contemporary depictions of,

LORRAINE McCONAGHY *is the public historian at the Museum of History and Industry in Seattle.*